Bolivia

the Bradt Travel Guide

David Atkinson

www.bradtguides.com

Bradt Travel Guides Ltd, UK
The Globe Pequot Press Inc, USA

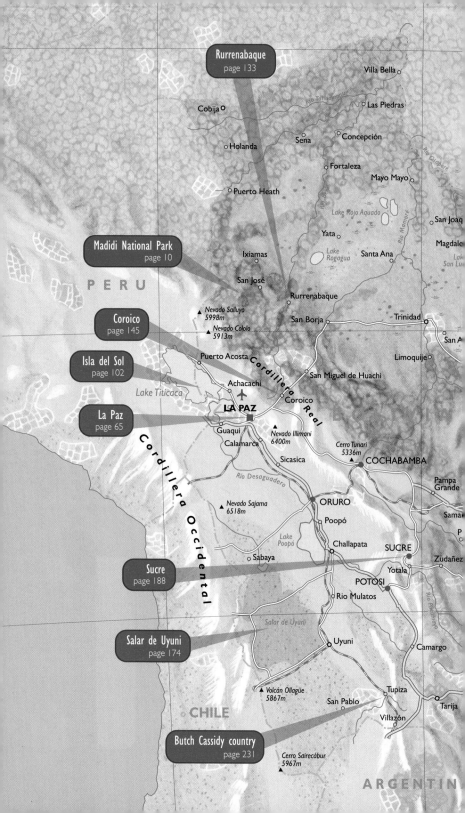

Rurrenabaque
page 133

Villa Bella

Cobija

Las Piedras

Holanda

Sena

Concepción

Fortaleza

Mayo Mayo

Puerto Heath

Río Tahuamanu

Río Guaporé

Lake Rojo Aquado

San Joaq

Madidi National Park
page 10

PERU

Ixiamas

Yata

Lake
Rogagua

Santa Ana

San José

Magdale

Lake
San Lu

Rurrenabaque

Nevado Salluyo
5998m

San Borja

Trinidad

Coroico
page 145

Nevado Cololo
5913m

San A

Isla del Sol
page 102

Puerto Acosta

Cordillera Real

San Miguel de Huachi

Limoquije

Achacachi

Lake Titicaca

LA PAZ

Coroico

La Paz
page 65

Guaqui

Nevado Illimani
6400m

Cerro Tunari
5336m

COCHABAMBA

Calamarca

Sicasica

Pampa
Grande

Cordillera Occidental

Río Desaguadero

Nevado Sajama
6518m

ORURO

Sama

Poopó

P

Lake
Poopó

Challapata

SUCRE

Sucre
page 188

Sabaya

Zudañez

Yotala

POTOSI

Río Pilcomayo

Río Mulatos

Salar de Uyuni

Salar de Uyuni
page 174

Uyuni

Camargo

Volcán Ollagüe
5867m

Tupiza

CHILE

San Pablo

Tarija

Villazón

Butch Cassidy country
page 231

Cerro Sairecábur
5967m

ARGENTIN

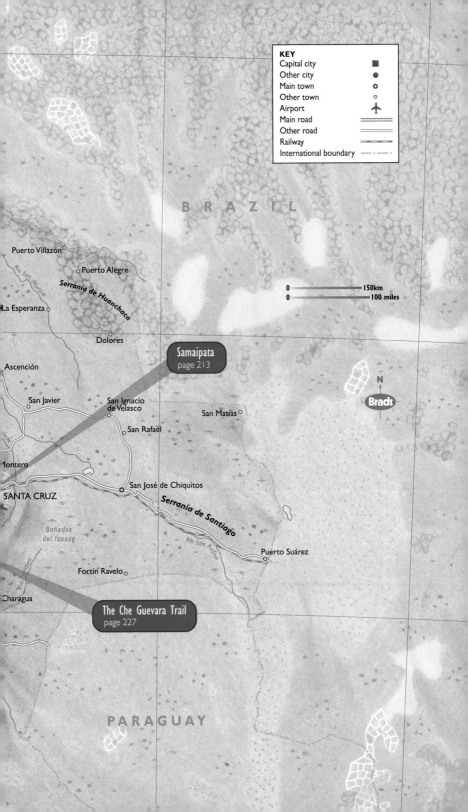

KEY
Capital city ■
Other city ●
Main town ○
Other town ○
Airport ✈
Main road
Other road
Railway
International boundary

B R A Z I L

Puerto Villazón
Puerto Alegre
Serranía de Huanchaca
La Esperanza
Dolores

Río San Martín

0 ————————— 150km
0 ————————— 100 miles

Samaipata
page 213

N
Bradt

Ascención
San Javier
San Ignacio
de Velasco
San Matías
San Rafael
Montero
San José de Chiquitos
SANTA CRUZ
Serranía de Santiago
Bañados
del Izozog
Río San Rafael
Puerto Suárez
Fortín Ravelo
Charagua

The Che Guevara Trail
page 227

P A R A G U A Y

Bolivia
Don't
miss…

The world's most dangerous road
Mountain biker and bus on
La Paz–Coroico road
(JB) page 148

Shopping in La Paz
Wool stall in the Mercado Negro,
La Paz
(RC) page 84

Wine tasting in Tarija
La Concepción winery
(DA) page 243

Trekking and wildlife
Campsite at the foot of the Sarani Pass in the Cordillera Real
(RC) page 121

Ecolodges
Chalalan guest cabin, Madidi National Park
(DA) page 140

top Looking back on the Cordillera Real from the Chulumani Trail (HB)
above left Laguna Jurikhota, with the glacier of Cerro Condoriri beyond (RC)
above right Ice climber on Mount Huayna Potosí, Cordillera Real (JB)
below left Hikers on the Choro Trail (DA) page 122
below right Cairn trail marker, Cordillera Real (RC)

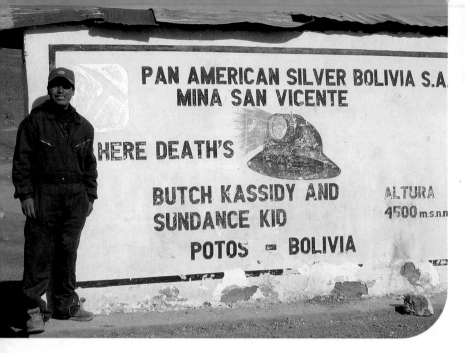

top · San Vicente, site of the last stand of Butch Cassidy and the Sundance Kid (DA) page 234
below left · Indigenous supporters at Evo Morales's inauguration parade, La Paz (JB)
below right · Shaman blessing newly married couple, La Cumbre (JB)

Author

David Atkinson (*www.atkinsondavid.co.uk*) came to Bolivia as a volunteer and went home a father. He first arrived in La Paz in 2004 to help out at the *Llama Express*, a local English-language magazine. After discovering what a rich vein of stories is to be found in Latin America's poorest country, he returned as a correspondent for the UK media and to research this guide.

During this time he retraced the final footsteps of Che Guevara, went in search of the graves of Butch Cassidy and the Sundance Kid and ended up co-presenting a community radio show (in Spanish) with Bolivia's leading troupe of drag queens, La Familia Galan.

David's stories about Bolivia have appeared in UK publications such as *Wanderlust* and *Geographical* magazines, the *Weekend FT* and the *Daily Telegraph*.

He is a member of the British Guild of Travel Writers and a contributor to BBC travel programmes.

These days David lives in the UK with his Bolivian wife and baby daughter.

FEEDBACK REQUEST

Every effort has been made to ensure that the details contained within this book are as accurate and up to date as possible. Inevitably, however, things change, especially in a country like Bolivia that spends every minute of the day in a state of quasi flux. Any information regarding changes to infrastructure, tours, transport routes and facilities for travellers, or simply relating to your experiences of travelling in Bolivia - good or bad - would be very gratefully received. Such feedback is priceless when compiling further editions, and in ensuring pleasant stays for future visitors. Bradt Travel Guides Ltd, 23 High St, Chalfont St Peter, Bucks SL9 9QE; ℡ 01753 893444; e info@bradtguides.com; www.bradtguides.com.

PUBLISHER'S FOREWORD *Hilary Bradt*

The first Bradt travel guide was written in 1974 by George and Hilary Bradt on a river barge floating down a tributary of the Amazon. In the 1980s and '90s the focus shifted away from hiking to broader-based guides covering new destinations – usually the first to be published about these places. In the 21st century Bradt continues to publish such ground-breaking guides, as well as others to established holiday destinations, incorporating in-depth information on culture and natural history with the nuts and bolts of where to stay and what to see.

Bradt authors support responsible travel, and provide advice not only on minimum impact but also on how to give something back through local charities. In this way a true synergy is achieved between the traveller and local communities.

* * *

With this book Bradt Travel Guides comes full circle. We started in Bolivia, so it is fitting and proper that, 32 years later, we should publish a guide solely on Bolivia. David Atkinson knows the country better than I could ever hope to. It remains one of my favourite countries and David loves it too. Knowledge and passion – that's what makes a perfect Bradt author.

First published January 2007

Bradt Travel Guides Ltd, 23 High Street, Chalfont St Peter, Bucks SL9 9QE, England.
www.bradtguides.com
Published in the USA by The Globe Pequot Press Inc, 246 Goose Lane,
PO Box 480, Guilford, Connecticut 06475-0480

British Library Cataloguing in Publication Data
A catalogue record for this book is available from the British Library
ISBN-10: 1 84162 165 X   ISBN-13: 978 1 84162 165 4

Photographs David Atkinson (DA), Hilary Bradt (HB), James Brunker (JB), Ruth Croome (RC), Ian Middleton (IM), Laurence Mitchell (LM)
Front cover Diablada dance, Oruro festival (Tony Morrison/South American Pictures)
Back cover Spectators in traditional cholita garb, tinku festival, Macha (DA), Sailing boat, Lake Titicaca (JB)
Title page Pokotia monolith, Tiahuanaco (JB), Kantu flowers, *Cantua buxifolia*, by Lake Titicaca (HB), Colonial street lamp on town hall, Potosí (JB)
Illustrations Carole Vincer   **Maps** Alan Whitaker, Dave Priestley

Typeset from the author's disc by Wakewing
Printed and bound in Italy by Legoprint SpA, Trento

Acknowledgements

A book of this kind is, inevitably, a labour of love. Especially when it comes down to one man covering a country of 1.1 million square kilometres with limited resources but a keen desire to spread the word. It involves the assistance of a raft of people too numerous to mention, plus the interference of an array of others, notably in Santa Cruz, to make a difficult journey even harder.

Overall I remain indebted to the volunteer staff of the *Llama Express* and to Alix Shand of the Speakeasy Institute, both in La Paz, plus to Caroline Calvert, Jo Wright and Rob Conway for their highly valuable yet unpaid contributions to the text. Thanks also to the staff of Gravity Assisted Mountain Biking and America Tours, both in La Paz, for their practical assistance in the face of strikes, cancellations and social upheaval. And special thanks to Patricia and Neil for making sense of things back in the cold light of the British winter.

Finally, thanks to Maya for making it all worthwhile. I hope that one day this book will inspire her own odyssey through life in some small way.

Contents

LIST OF MAPS

1 Nobody ever has change for anything, so keep a ready supply of coins and small denomination notes, especially for buses and taxis.

2 Take a cheap flask with you in your luggage. Fill it up with hot water at breakfast each day and keep a small supply of coffee sachets and tea-bags. This will prove a life-saver when you find yourself on a cold, overnight Andean bus journey.

3 Take along a small head torch in your luggage and keep it in your daypack. This will prove essential in places where the street lighting is poor or even non-existent.

4 Keep a photocopy of your passport and the green entry card with arrival date with you at all times. You can be asked frequently for your passport (sometimes just to enter museums), but this is best left behind in the hotel – ideally in the safe.

5 Don't overpack. Remember you can buy just about anything, notably warm clothes, at markets across Bolivia for a fraction of the price you're paying for that fleece back home.

6 Learn some basic Spanish before you go as very little English is spoken, especially outside of the bigger cities.

THE AUTHOR'S PICKS

BEST TOURIST INFORMATION OFFICE Ranking Bolivia, Uyuni (page 171)
BEST HOTEL Hostal de Su Merced, Sucre (page 193)
BEST ECOLODGE Albergue Ecologico La Estancia, Isla del Sol (page 103)
BEST COMMUNITY PROJECT Chalalan, Madidi National Park (page 137)
BEST WILDLIFE SPOTTING Madidi National Park (page 136)
BEST FESTIVAL Carnival in Oruro (page 165)
BEST SET LUNCH La Posada, Sucre (page 194)
BEST BAR Joy Ride Café, Sucre & Moskkito Bar, Rurrenabaque (pages 194 and 141)
BEST BARGAIN Fruit juice carts around major cities
BEST SHOPPING Tailor's shops around major cities
BEST ADRENALIN RUSH Gravity Assisted Mountain Biking, La Paz to Coroico (page 148)
BEST TOUR OPERATOR America Tours, La Paz (page 72)
BEST FOR NATURE Madidi National Park (page 139)

Introduction

Bolivia is a really strange country. Culturally diverse, geographically exceptional and striking in so many other ways, there's really nowhere else quite like it. The country where McDonald's failed, where the Spanish left the living legacy of their colonial conquest and where ancient cultures still exist shoulder to shoulder with the trappings of modernity, it's the ideal destination for tourists looking for something new.

And that's the key attraction: Bolivia offers a more authentic experience of Latin America. Neighbouring countries have the cultural heavyweight attractions and wider range of options for traveller-friendly facilities, but Bolivia has the innocence that comes with a country where tourism is still in its fledgling stages and the hordes and cash-in prices that are mainstays of other Latin American destinations are still not even on the agenda.

Bolivia also stands apart with its unique blend of cultures and climates due in part to its long-standing isolation from the rest of the world. As such, Bolivia's indigenous religions, dialects, clothes, music and medicines all remain intact, untouched by the passing of time and an integral part of daily life. Nowhere else in the Americas is the life on the street so vibrant with the mix of big-city living and the ancient traditions of the indigenous culture that permeate every aspect of daily life.

What's more, the country's topography sets it apart, with only Nepal able to match the diversity of its landscapes. Indeed, in many ways Bolivia is two countries in one: the high-altitude Altiplano and the lowland, tropical Oriente. The contrast between these two extremes couldn't be more marked and is apparent across the board – from the local psyche of the people to the lifestyles they lead.

But it's the people, ultimately, that make Bolivia so unique. Over 60% of the country is derived from indigenous stock and they fight hard to maintain their culture with its folkloric traditions and ancient beliefs. The other side of the coin, however, is a country with a modernising infrastructure. Only in Bolivia can you sit in an international-style café with executives hunched over their wi-fi laptops, while women in traditional garb hawk lemons on the street outside.

It's this clash of cultures that makes Bolivia so vibrant – an organic, evolving destination.

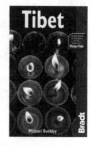

Part One

GENERAL INFORMATION

Location Landlocked at the heart of Andean South America

Neighbouring countries Brazil, Peru, Chile, Argentina and Paraguay

Size/area 1.1 million km²

Climate Varies with altitude; humid and tropical to cold and semi-arid

Status Democratic republic

Population 9 million

Capital Sucre (official), La Paz (administrative)

Other main towns Santa Cruz de la Sierra, Cochabamba, Potosí, Oruro, Uyuni, Rurrenabaque

Life expectancy 62.5 years male; 67.8 years female

Economy Bolivia remains highly dependent on foreign aid until it can develop its substantial natural resources.

GDP Purchasing power parity – US$20.88 billion; GNI per capita: US$1,010 (World Bank, 2006)

Languages Spanish, plus a variety of indigenous tongues, notably Quechua, Aymara and Guarani

Religion 92% of the country is officially Catholic, plus indigenous faiths

Currency 1 Boliviano (Bs) = 100 centavos

Exchange rate (as of December 2006) US$1=8.00Bs, £1=15.44Bs, €1=10.46Bs

National airline AeoSur and Lloyd Aéreo Boliviano

International telephone code +591

Time GMT –4 hours

Electrical voltage 110 and 220 volts, AC50Hz; US-style, flat two-pin plugs

Weights and measures Metric

Flag La Tricolor

National anthem No official name, known as the *hymno nacional*

National flower La Kantuta

National animal Condor

National sport Football

Public holidays 1 January; Monday, Tuesday and Wednesday of Carnival Week; Thursday, Friday and Saturday of Easter Week; 1 May; 16 July; 6 August; 12 October; 2 November; 25 December

Background Information

GEOGRAPHY AND CLIMATE with James Brunker (www.magicalandes.com)

Landlocked in the heart of South America, Bolivia covers 1,098,580km², the fifth-largest country in South America. It borders Peru to the west and northwest, Brazil to the north and east, Paraguay to the southeast, Argentina to the south and Chile to the west. The country gained its independence on 6 August 1825 but subsequently became involved in several wars with neighbouring countries, losing about half of its original territory in the process. Today its location means its wide diversity of climates and eco-regions is one of the main attractions for tourists visiting the country.

Bolivia, sometimes called the Tibet of South America, also has numerous claims to fame based around its high altitude: the world's highest navigable lake (page 95), the highest commercial airport (page 69), the highest capital city (page 65) and the highest ski-run, although the long-term potential of the last is currently being seriously undermined by the effects of global warming (page 88).

NATIONAL PARKS AND PROTECTED AREAS Bolivia is one of the most bio-diverse countries in the world, being ranked in the top ten and containing 66 of the 112 ecosystems found globally. Much of this diversity and its wildlife is protected within 22 national parks and over 60 other protected areas, covering approximately 18 million hectares or 15% of the country's total area (the second- highest percentage of any country in the western hemisphere). The Bolivian national parks authority, SERNAP (Servicio Nacional de Areas Protegidas), estimates that 150,000 people live within the boundaries of these state-protected areas, the large majority of indigenous extraction from Aymara, Quechua and Guarani tribes. The first national park to be founded was Sajama (in Oruro Department), on 2 August 1939, though most have been established in the last 20 years. The diversity of the parks is huge, spanning climatic zones from the high-altitude Altiplano (high plateau) and glaciers of Sajama National Park to Otuquis National Park in Bolivia's tropical, lowland Pantanal region. Amboro National Park, located near Santa Cruz, has more than 800 species of birds alone, while Madidi National Park, north of La Paz, contains some 11% of the world's species of flora and fauna and was described by National Geographic as being the most bio-diverse national park on the planet. These two parks are also the most visited by tourists, with 80,000 visitors per year between them.

The National Day of Protected Areas, held annually on 4 September since 2005, aims to raise awareness of Bolivia's natural riches. 'There's little knowledge amongst Bolivians about what is a protected area and how it can actually benefit the country,' says Viviane van Owen of WWF Bolivia, which is supporting the event and manages environmental programmes in Bolivia's Pantanal and Amazon regions. 'There is an overall lack of scientific investigation into our natural diversity due to a lack of funding. Hence it's quite possible that whole new species exist in the parks that we don't know about yet.'

3

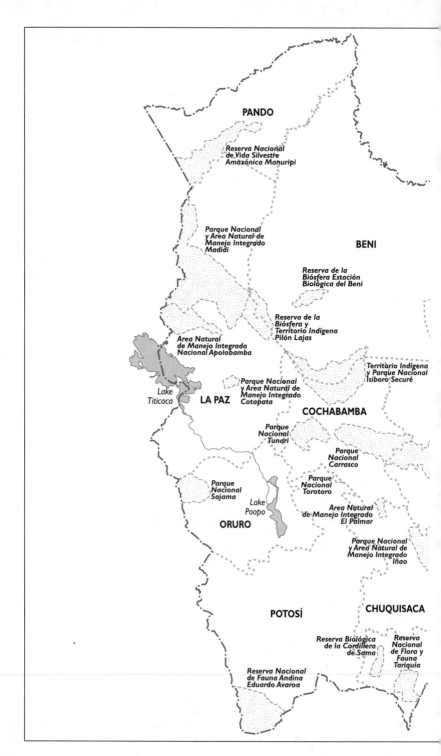

PANDO

Reserva Nacional
de Vida Silvestre
Amazónica Manuripi

BENI

Parque Nacional
y Área Natural de
Manejo Integrado
Madidi

Reserva de la
Biósfera Estación
Biológica del Beni

Reserva de la
Biósfera y
Territorio Indígena
Pilón Lajas

Area Natural
de Manejo Integrado
Nacional Apolobamba

Territorio Indígena
y Parque Nacional
Isiboro Securé

Parque Nacional
y Área Natural de
Manejo Integrado
Cotapata

Lake
Titicaca   LA PAZ

COCHABAMBA

Parque
Nacional
Tunari

Parque
Nacional
Carrasco

Parque
Nacional
Sajama

Lake
Poopo

Parque
Nacional
Torotoro

ORURO

Area Natural
de Manejo Integrado
El Palmar

Parque Nacional
y Área Natural de
Manejo Integrado
Iñao

POTOSÍ

CHUQUISACA

Reserva Biológica
de la Cordillera
de Sama

Reserva
Nacional
de Flora y
Fauna
Tariquía

Reserva Nacional
de Fauna Andina
Eduardo Avaroa

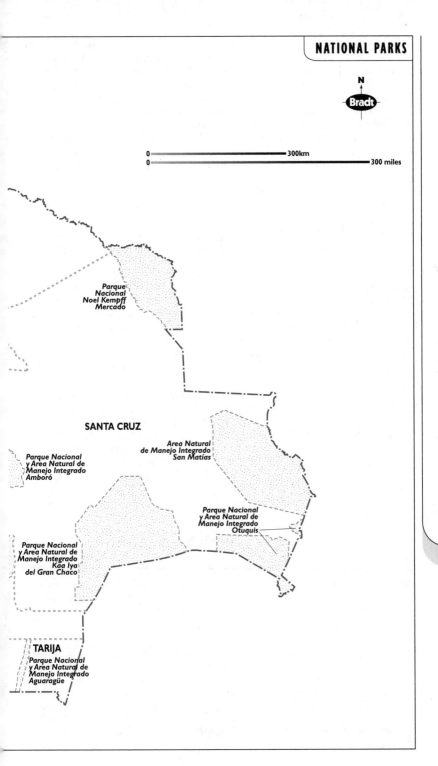

N

Bradt

0 |—————————————| 300km
0 |—————————————| 300 miles

Parque
Nacional
Noel Kempff
Mercado

SANTA CRUZ

Area Natural
de Manejo Integrado
San Matías

Parque Nacional
y Area Natural de
Manejo Integrado
Amboró

Parque Nacional
y Area Natural de
Manejo Integrado
Otuquis

Parque Nacional
y Area Natural de
Manejo Integrado
Kaa Iya
del Gran Chaco

TARIJA

Parque Nacional
y Area Natural de
Manejo Integrado
Aguaragüe

Background Information GEOGRAPHY AND CLIMATE

It costs from US$250,000 annually to run a park at a basic level, but the Bolivian government – plagued by social unrest and stretched to deal with the country's crushing rural poverty – has a budget of just US$500,000 per year for its entire national park network. Currently, over 90% of vital funding comes from private sources. To the Bolivian authorities, boosting tourism to the country's protected areas is seen as the solution to the funding crisis and crucial to moving Bolivia's fledgling tourism industry onto the next level. 'Tourism and communities have to develop hand in hand but we are concerned that, in parks such as Madidi, all the tourism is currently concentrated into a small percentage of the park's 1.9m hectares,' says Oscar Loayza, head of planning for SERNAP. 'Bolivia has huge potential for national park tourism given its enormous natural capital, but we are taking a cautious approach. Tourism is the means but not the end,' adds Loayza.

Bolivia's 22 national parks are as follows.

1 Parque Nacional Sajama The park covers 81,000ha in the northwestern corner of Oruro Department next to the Chilean border and the main road between La Paz and Arica (Chile). It was established to protect the unique altiplano flora, fauna and spectacular scenery, including Bolivia's highest peak, the extinct 6,542m Sajama volcano, popular with mountaineers. Due to its high altitude (above 4,200m) the park's climate is cold, dry and windy, though clear blue skies are common throughout the winter. The park boasts 108 species of fauna (including Andean cat, puma, armadillo, vicuña and condor), and 154 species of flora; among which the rare Queñua tree (*Polylepis tarapacana*) grows up to altitudes of 5,100 and constitutes the world's highest forest. Around 2,000 inhabitants of Aymara origin live in the park; the villages in the region are notable for their small, rustic adobe churches.

2 Parque Nacional Tunari Located to the west of Cochabamba, this park covers 300,000ha, including the highest summit in the region, Cerro Tunari (5,035m). It also contains forested valleys around Cochabamba and many lakes (these providing much of Cochabamba's water supply). The park enjoys a temperate and moderate climate in the valleys, giving way to colder conditions in the mountains. So far 13 species of mammals (including Andean cat and viscacha) and many bird species (including torrent duck) have been recorded, along with numerous tree and plant species in the forested areas. Around 75,000 to 90,000 people of Quechua descent live in the park; this is increasing as Cochabamba expands into the Park's fringes.

3 Parque Nacional y Territorio Indígena Isiboro-Sécure Covers 1.2 million hectares between the departments of Beni (Moxos district) and Cochabamba in the northwest part of the Chaparé region. Part of the so-called Vilcabamba-Amboro corridor, the park contains a wide range of habitats between 180m and 3,000m above sea level including tropical forest, savannah and mountains, with a corresponding variation in climate. More than 600 species of birds (some endemic) have been recorded, and mammal species include spectacled bear, black caiman and jaguar. The variety of plants species is equally impressive, with 402 species so far registered, a total that is estimated to rise to around 3,000.

The park was originally populated by indigenous communities, including the Yuracaré, Trinitario and Chimán groups. Many settlers and squatters have invaded the area however, not helped by political disputes over which department should administer the park, and its closeness to the coca-producing areas of the Chaparé.

4 Parque Nacional Noel Kempff Mercado This is one of the world's most spectacular parks covering over 1.5 million hectares in the northeast of Santa

Cruz Department on the Brazilian border. It contains seven distinct ecosystems and is best known for its Amazonian forest, spectacular waterfalls and the unique mountain and rock formations of the Huanchaca plateau, said by some to have inspired Sir Arthur Conan Doyle's *The Lost World*. It was declared a UNESCO World Heritage site in 2000. The climate is generally tropical.

So far 2,700 plant species have been recorded (some estimate this could rise to 4,000), as well as 139 mammal species (including jaguar, tapir, river dolphin, giant anteater, giant armadillo and river otter) and over 600 bird species, 74 reptile species, 62 amphibian species and 250 fish species.

A few small indigenous Guarayo communities live in the region, and people of Chiquitano origin moved into the area in the 19th century. Today's population does not exceed 1,500.

5 Parque Nacional Toro Toro The park covers 16,570ha in the north of Potosí Department (Charcas province), though it is best accessed from Cochabamba. The altitude ranges from 1,900m to 3,600m above sea level and the climate is temperate, typical of the dry inter-Andean valleys.

It boasts 329 species of flora and 600 species of plant life, plus 49 species of animals including Andean deer, Andean cat and occasionally puma. The park is best known though for its numerous palaeontological remains (including dinosaur footprints and fossils), rock paintings, waterfalls and limestone canyons and caves (including the famous Huma Jalanta cave system, thought to be Bolivia's largest).

Quechua-speaking indigenous communities live in the Toro Toro Valley.

6 Parque Nacional Carrasco Easily accessed from Cochabamba or Santa Cruz as it lies between the new and old roads linking the two towns, the park covers 622,600ha and is bordered by Amboró National Park to the east. The park's altitude varies between 300m to 4,700m above sea level and it preserves a wide range of forest habitats, from tropical lowland to high-altitude cloud forest. The climate is similarly varied depending on the altitude and is noted for its high rainfall (up to 5,000mm per year in places).

It is estimated the park contains over 3,000 species of plants, of which only 614 are so far officially registered, including more than 300 species of orchids. Fifty-one mammal species have been recorded (including spectacled bear, jaguar and Andean cat) and the park contains an estimated 700 species of birds, of which just 247 are officially registered. Of these the most notable is the rare and unusual oilbird; a large colony can easily be visited from Villa Tunari, the main base for exploring the park.

Assessing the park's human population is problematic; the park has suffered problems similar to neighbouring Amboró with many coca farmers and *campesinos* having moved into the region to escape DEA (Drug Enforcement Administration) activity in the nearby Chaparé region.

7 Reserva Nacional de Fauna Andina Eduardo Avaroa (REA) The park covers 817,455ha in the extreme south of Potosí Department in the province of Sud Lípez. It is renowned for the spectacular high-altitude desert and volcanic scenery of the Cordillera Occidental, including geysers, salt and mineral lakes. Of these lakes, Lagunas Colorada and Verde are the most famous and an integral part of the popular jeep tours through the area. The climate is cold, dry and windy; tempartures vary between 25°C during the day to -30°C at night and annual rainfall is on average less than 100mm.

Around 190 species of flora (including the queñua tree, thola and the very slow growing yareta plant) and 23 mammal species (including vicuña, viscacha and

Andean fox) can be found in the park. It is best known for its bird life; 80 species have been recorded, including the three flamingo species (Chilean, Andean and James's). Laguna Colorada is one of the most important breeding grounds in the world for the latter, and as a result enjoys further protection as the Laguna Colorada Wildlife Sanctuary within the park.

Only 2,412 people inhabit Sud Lipez province (mainly of Aymara origin), of which around 600 live within the reserve boundaries (the reserve covers 40% of the province's area). It is one of the most visited parks in the country, with over 30,000 visitors per year.

8 Reserva Nacional de Vida Silvestre Amazónica Manuripi-Heath The reserve covers 747,000ha in the southeast of Pando Department, between the important Manuripi and Madre de Dios rivers. As the name suggests, the reserve protects tropical Amazonian forest and the climate is hot and wet.

Flora and fauna found in the reserve are typical of the Amazon region, including jaguar, puma, giant river otter, caiman, several species of monkey and a large number of palm species.

A population of roughly 1,600 lives in the reserve in various communities, though this figure varies seasonally as many inhabitants travel for the Brazil nut harvest.

9 Reserva Nacional de Flora y Fauna Tariquía The reserve covers around 245,000ha in the southeast of Tarija Department. It is noted for its mountain scenery (the altitude varies between 900m and 3,400m above sea level), well-preserved forests and the remains of some Jesuit and Dominican missions. The climate is temperate to warm, depending on altitude.

Currently 808 species of flora have been registered (this includes 112 species of tree) but estimates suggest this could increase to 1,500. So far, 406 species of fauna have also been registered.

Around 3,400 people live in the reserve, most of whom have migrated from the Tarija valleys and to a lesser extent from the Chaco.

10 Reserva Biológica de la Cordillera de Sama Covering 108,000ha in the west of Tarija Department, the reserve protects the Cordillera de Sama and is noted for its mountain scenery (up to 4,700m above sea level) and high-altitude lakes. The latter are important as the main water supply for Tarija. The climate is temperate to cold, with annual rainfall between 300mm and 800mm per year.

Wildlife is typical of high-Andean ecosystems with vicuña, puma, Andean cat, viscacha, Andean condor and three species of flamingo all present.

Some 4,000 people live in 12 communities in the higher regions of the reserve, mostly of Aymara and Quechua origin.

11 Área Natural de Manejo Integrado Nacional Apolobamba Situated in the far west of La Paz Department and bordering Peru, the park covers over 480,000ha. It includes the spectacular scenery of the Cordillera Apolobamba (with many peaks over 5,000m; the highest, Chaupi Orko, reaches 6,044m) and the cloud and subtropical Yungas forest on its eastern slopes, where it borders Madidi National Park. The climate varies greatly with altitude with severe conditions possible at high altitudes and on the peaks. The park was formed in 1972, declared a UNESCO Biosphere Reserve in 1977 and known as the Reserva Nacional de Fauna de Ulla Ulla from 1983 until assuming its current name in 1999.

There are 807 species of flora registered but estimates put the actual figure at around 1,500. In terms of fauna, 275 species have been identified, including puma, vicuña, spectacled bear and bird species such as Andean condor and torrent duck.

Many traditional Quechua and Aymara villages can be found in the region (some 3,500 families in 76 communities), the best known being Charazani, Curva and Pelechuco. This is the region where the Kallawaya live; travelling medicine men who are known throughout South America for their healing powers based on a wide range of traditional techniques. The communities are famous for their fiestas and intricate brightly coloured weavings.

12 **Reserva de la Biosfera Estación Biológica del Beni** Set up by Conservation International in 1982, the reserve covers some 334,000ha along the Maniqui River in southwest Beni Department. The climate is tropical with high rainfall.

Around 480 bird species, including the harpy eagle, have been recorded, as well as over 200 mammal species (including jaguar, giant river otter and several monkey species) and an estimated 1,500 plant species. The world's largest black caiman population can be found in Laguna Normandia.

The Chimané group lives in the region and there are also people of the small Movima group in the northern part of the reserve. There have been conflicts between the Chimané people and loggers.

13 **Reserva de la Biosfera y Tierra Comunitaria de Origen Pilón Lajas** The reserve covers 400,000ha in the southwest of Beni Department, borders Madidi National Park and was declared a unique habitat by the UN in 1997. Some of South America's most intact Amazonian forest systems are found here. The climate is generally hot and humid, though cooler in higher regions which reach 3,000m above sea level.

There are 624 registered species of flora but estimates put the actual figure at over 2,500. Mahogany trees are common, which has led to logging in many areas and considerable pressure to allow legal deforestation. To date, 748 species of fauna have been identified, including jaguar and caiman.

Various indigenous communities live within the reserve, mainly Chimáne, Tacana and Mosetén groups. The Mapajo Indigenous Ecotourism Project works with several of these communities.

14 **Área Natural de Manejo Integrado El Palmar** Covers nearly 60,000ha of the Cordillera Oriental in Chuquisaca Department. The scenery is mountainous with deep canyons (altitude in the park ranges between 1,000m and 3,200m above sea level) and the climate is temperate and dry, with annual rainfall a little over 300mm.

There are 270 species of plants of which four are endemic, plus 24 species of mammals and 112 species of birds, including the Andean condor, five species of woodpecker and eight species of parrot.

There are scattered communities within the ÁNMI, mainly of people of Quechua origin living in the valleys.

15 **Área Natural de Manejo Integrado San Matias** This is the second-largest protected area in Bolivia, covering over 2.9 million hectares in the eastern Santa Cruz Department bordering Brazil. It protects some of the world's best-preserved wetlands, the headwaters of the River Paraguay, and in many ways resembles Brazil's famous Pantanal region. The climate is sub-tropical.

Some 874 species of flora have been recorded including many types of palm. Fauna so far recorded includes jaguar, ocelot, turtle, harpy eagle and many species of amphibian.

Around 6,000 people who are mainly of Chiquitano and Ayoreo descent live within the ÁNMI.

16 Parque Nacional y Área Natural de Manejo Integrado Amboró One of Bolivia's best-known national parks, Amboró covers 430,000ha in the west of Santa Cruz Department adjoining the Carrasco National Park. It is easily accessed from the main Santa Cruz – Cochabamba road or for the higher regions from the village of Samaipata. Ranging from 300m to 3,300m it covers a unique area where the Andean foothills, Amazon basin, Chaco scrubland and eastern plains meet, making it one of the most bio-diverse regions of the planet. The climate is temperate at higher altitudes, tropical at lower ones and annual rainfall varies between 1,400mm and 4,000mm.

So far 2,659 species of flora have been identified but estimates put the actual figure closer to 3,500. Fauna figures are equally impressive with over 130 mammal species recorded so far, including spectacled bear, jaguar, tapir, ocelot and giant river otter. Among the bird species are quetzal, cock of the rock and hoatzin; the park is also one of the last refuges of the endangered horned curassow.

The park has seen many conflicts between authorities, conservationists and settlers since its formation in 1973, with many coca growers displaced from the nearby Chaparé region by DEA activity. This came to a head in 1995 when, with regional elections looming, 200,000ha was re-designated as a multiple use area and effectively opened to settlement and cultivation. Conservationists fear this could set a dangerous precedent.

17 Parque Nacional y Área Natural Madidi One of the most significant national parks in the world, Madidi covers nearly 1.9 million hectares in the northeast of La Paz Department, and is usually visited from the small town of Rurrenabaque. Ranging from altitudes of 200m to 6,000m above sea level, it includes a wide range of ecosystems and was described by National Geographic and Conservation International as the most bio-diverse area of the planet.

Statistics concerning the park's flora and fauna are staggering. It is estimated to contain up to 6,000 species of flora and so far 620 bird species have been identified, though it is estimated this could rise to over 1,000. This represents 90% of species found in Bolivia and around 10% of the world total. In addition around 44% of New World mammal species and 38% of tropical amphibian species can be found here. Notable residents include Andean condor, harpy eagle, jaguar, puma, tapir, giant anteater and many species of monkey.

Various Quechua communities live in the highlands and there are Tacana, Esse, Eja and Mosetén communities in the lowlands. The community of San José de Uchupiamonas operates the Chalalan Ecolodge, possibly Bolivia's most successful community-based ecotourism project. However, illegal logging is a problem in many areas. Plans for a major hydroelectric project on the Beni River near Rurrenabaque have been shelved and there is talk about building a road between the villages of Apolo and Ixiamas which would split the park in two if it went ahead.

18 Parque Nacional y Área Natural de Manejo Integrado Cotapata Covers 40,000ha to the northeast of La Paz, and is easily accessible from La Cumbre on the main La Paz–Yungas road. Parts of the Cordillera Real and the Yungas valleys and forests are found on its eastern slopes; the altitude varies from 1,000m to 5,900m above sea level and the climate correspondingly. The popular pre-Colombian 'El Choro' Trail runs through the park.

Around 1,800 plant species and 204 species of fauna have been recorded, including a range of mountain and sub-tropical species.

Various Aymara communities inhabit the highlands, and some have migrated down in to the valleys which they share with mestizos; it is estimated some 1,600 people in total live in the park.

19 **Parque Nacional y Área Natural de Manejo Integrado Kaa-Iya del Gran Chaco** Located in the south of Santa Cruz Department and covering over 3.4 million hectares, this is the largest national park in Latin America. It includes a large section of the Gran Chaco plains, the unusual and extensive Bañados de Izozog wetlands and a unique desert forest habitat; the climate is generally hot and arid.

So far around 880 species of flora and 514 fauna species have been recorded. The latter includes 59 large mammals and 301 birds, many of which are unusual desert-dwelling species.

The park was founded in 1996 by the various Guaraní, Chiquitano and Ayoreo indigenous communities that live in the area, in conjunction with various environmental groups. It is unusual in being one of very few parks worldwide where the administration is entrusted to its indigenous inhabitants.

20 **Parque Nacional y Área Natural de Manejo Integrado Otuquis** Covers just over 1 million hectares in the extreme southeast of Santa Cruz Department. It protects sections of the Chaco plains which are often suspect to flooding and interrupted by low-lying hills, and resembles Brazil's nearby Pantanal region. The climate is sub-tropical with annual rainfall of around 1,100mm.

Little research has been done in the area so far, but 59 species of mammals have been registered and 50 fish species that concentrate during the flooding season. The Park is also notable for a wide variety of unusual forest ecosystems. There are 18 small settlements in the park with a total population of around 400.

21 **Parque Nacional y Área Natural de Manejo Integrado Serrania del Aguaragüe** A small park covering 108,000ha in a strip 10km by 111km in the east of Tarija Department (Gran Chaco province). The Aguaragüe range separates the Chaco plains from the hills of Tarija Department and contains a wide variety of forest habitats. The climate is temperate and wet.

There are many bird and animal species including jaguar, fox, anteater, armadillo and various parrot species.

There are 30 indigenous communities in the park with a total of over 10,000 inhabitants.

22 **Parque Nacional y Área Natural de Manejo Integrado Serrania del Iñao** The most recent area to be accorded national park status (2004), it is located in Chuquisaca. Ongoing research has identified a large variety of native flora and fauna typical of the forest ecosystem.

A handful of indigenous Guarani communities live here.

For more information check the SERNAP website (*www.serenap.gov.bo*).

NATURAL HISTORY
with *Joe Tobias (www.neomorphus.com) & James Brunker (www.magicalandes.com)*

Bolivia is one of the ten most biodiverse countries in the world, and it also supports more extensive wilderness and intact habitat than most of its neighbours. The country can be divided into 12 eco-regions, including the humid Amazon, the Cerrado savannas, the flooded Pantanal, the dry Chaco and the Andean Yungas forests. Many of these regions are hugely important, both in terms of research into biological diversity and the conservation of biological resources. Research and conservation are especially significant, as Bolivian habitats are under threat from deforestation, burning, contamination, illegal hunting and the replacement of local varieties with foreign species.

According to the US Department of State's Bureau for International Narcotics and Law Enforcement Affairs (INL) Bolivia remains the world's third-largest producer of cocaine, the drug derived from the leaf of the coca plant (*Erytheoxyelum coca*) that has been cultivated in the Andes for millenia.

The coca leaf has long been chewed by Quechua and Aymara Indians to stave off hunger and fatigue. In Bolivia and the rest of the Andean region, coca is legally used as an infusion to make tea, for medicinal purposes (one effect of chewing coca is to aid digestion), and for rituals. It is an essential part of daily life in rural areas and revered by the indigenous peoples as a sacred plant. A complex chemical process is required to isolate and concentrate certain alkaloids in the leaf and make cocaine, a substance with completely different properties to the leaf. However, because it provides the base ingredients, the coca plant is classified as a controlled substance. As a result medicines, teas, soft drinks and other products based on coca cannot be legally exported. (For more information on the coca plant and cocaine visit www.cocamuseum.com.)

After a five-year slump, South America's cocaine output rose by 2% in 2004. Bolivia produced around 118 tonnes of cocaine that year, up 35% from 2003, according to the UN World Drug Report.

The UN gathered its data from satellite images of production areas, taken from helicopters and planes, as well as from collaborative work with local authorities, who conducted field studies and interviewed local farmers. Estimates of the cultivated area in Bolivia's Yungas region, the only one where growing coca is legal, differ widely, but the UN indicates something in the region of 18,000ha.

Despite exceeding its international commitment to eradicate 8,000ha of coca in 2004, Bolivia's coca cultivation increased 6% overall, mainly as a result of increased illegal cultivation in the Chaparé region. What's more, the INL claims, the Bolivian government failed to give political support to programmes advocating drug prevention and to undertake an effective social communication programme to explain the dangers that excess coca production, drug production and consumption pose to Bolivian society. Cocaine usage is

Inventories of Bolivia's flora and fauna are still incomplete but, to date, researchers have identified around 14,000 species of native plants (not including ferns, moss and algae). The real figure is probably much closer to 20,000 species. With regards to fauna, 356 species of mammals have been recorded, along with over 1,400 species of birds, 203 species of amphibians, 266 species of reptiles and around 600 species of fish. Plant and animal endemism is concentrated in a few eco-regions related to the Andes: Yungas forests, foothill forests, and the Inter-Andean dry forests .

Bolivia is known as a 'mega-diverse' country. It ranks fourth in the world in terms of the number of butterfly species it supports; among the top ten countries in terms of bird and mammal diversity; and among the top fifteen for fresh water fish, amphibians and tiger beetles.

The Amazon Basin extends into the north-east quadrant of Bolivia. It is particularly high in species richness, but low in endemism (in other words, there are lots of species, but they almost all occur in neighbouring Peru and Brazil). Amazonian habitats remain fairly extensive, but difficult to reach – not many people visit the rainforests of Pando, for instance. Some important parks and reserves protect Amazon forests, at least in theory. The most important are Madidi National Park and the Manuripi-Heath reserve.

Outside Amazonia, Bolivian parks embrace large areas of natural habitat. Noel Kempff Mercado National Park, in easternmost Santa Cruz, includes large areas of spectacular forest and savanna near a remote *meseta* (the Serranía de Huanchaca).

still relatively low in Bolivia. Many Bolivians are unaware of the social problems it causes and generally see them as a foreign problem rather than a Bolivian one. The perceived emphasis in the past on eradication (depriving the *campesinos* who grow coca of their main source of income) rather than concentrating on developing alternatives has led many to feel that they are being made scapegoats for someone else's problem. This feeling has been enhanced by political conditions attaching the availability of foreign aid (on which Bolivia heavily depends) to coca eradication programmes. In addition, Bolivia remains a transit country for a significant amount of Peruvian cocaine and increasing amounts of Colombian cocaine destined for Europe and other South American countries.

Nevertheless, in 2004 special counter-narcotics police units destroyed 2,254 cocaine base labs and made 4,138 arrests in 5,836 operations. Cocaine seizures rose 11.8% over the previous year.

In September 2004, President Mesa approved a new National Drug Strategy for the next four years that included a plan of action for the Yungas. The plan focused on combining eradication of coca, alternative development efforts to encourage coca growers to engage in legal and economically viable alternatives, and vigorous law enforcement. However, in speeches leading up to his accession as the new president of Bolivia in January 2006, Evo Morales threatened to scrap the counter-narcotics and law enforcement programme in Bolivia.

The coca leaf will now seek a new future under the country's first indigenous president, the leader of the coca growers. Evo Morales. According to sources, Morales wants to change the anti-drug policy embodied in Law 1008, decriminalise the production of coca, but without completely liberalising it, and get coca removed from the United Nations list of controlled substances. While this would make it easier to develop and market alternative products based on the coca plant, many feel it will also lead to an increase in the cultivation of coca destined for cocaine production.

The future of Bolivian coca production and the US government's efforts to eradicate the coca leaf remained in a state of flux as the new president took office.

Some of the best examples of extensive dry Chaco forests fall within the Gran Chaco National Park. Yungas forests fall within several important parks and reserves, including Cotopata, Carrasco, Amboró and, in the far south, Tariquia. The parks of Sajama and Eduardo Avaroa protect the stark landscapes, flamingo lakes and snowy peaks of the high Andes bordering Chile.

There are numerous issues facing Bolivia while, under-funded and wracked by social conflict, it attempts to conserve its massive natural wealth. The main challenges include stemming the tide of deforestation by logging corporations, illegal syndicates and small-scale farmers, especially within parks and reserves. Other key issues involve the rescue and conservation of traditional knowledge, the management of natural resources, the improvement of agricultural technologies and the alleviation of poverty in local populations. As well as being a grave humanitarian issue in its own right, the latter results in severe pressure on natural resources simply to satisfy basic needs.

For more information, see the website of the Fundación Amigos de la Naturaleza (FAN), an environmental organisation based in Santa Cruz, Bolivia (*www.fan-bo.org*).

FLORA AND FAUNA Bolivia's diverse natural features ensure that its plant life and vegetation are correspondingly diverse. The range of wildlife also varies closely with the landscape. In the Andes, for example, llamas and alpacas are the norm, while

Andean condors and flamingos can also be found. Lake Titicaca, meanwhile, is home to trout, pejerrey or kingfish, other native fish species such as ispi and guarachi, a unique giant frog discovered by Jacques Cousteau, and a large number of birds. These latter include the Titicaca flightless grebe, a globally threatened species.

The tropical zones of the country are especially diverse, although rapid development means habitats are coming increasingly under threat. Nevertheless, common animal sightings include monkeys, toucans, parrots, peccaries and piranha. Closer to the ground, amateur botanists can spot a cornucopia of shrubs, vines, ferns and grasses while mahogany trees, though declining in number, can still be found in some of the country's naturally forested areas.

Types of vegetation Bolivia's flora divides into three categories: macro-thermic, meso-thermic and micro-thermic.

The first is found in areas with an altitude of 100–2,000m with a climate ranging from tropical to subtropical. This accounts for roughly 40% of the total land mass, taking in the forests and savanna of the south and the Oriente, as well as pre-montane forests in the foothills of the Andes. Many thousands of species are found in this region, including such iconic and economically important varieties as the Brazil nut tree (*Bertholettia excelsa*) and cacao (*Theobroma cacao*).

The second category equates to the foothill and mid-montane zone, which cuts a vast swathe across the country, following the slope of the Andes from the border with Peru in the north to the Argentine border in the south. The predominant habitat varies according to fluctuations in topography and rainfall, generally comprising evergreen cloud-forests or deciduous forests with columnar cacti in the drier Valles region of Chuquisaca and Santa Cruz. In the wetter Yungas region, the agricultural specialities include coca and coffee.

The third and final category covers the west of the country and divides into three areas, namely the Cordillera Occidental between 5,000 and 6,500m, the Cordillera Central with its trademark Andean lagunas, and the Altiplano, which covers much of the departments of La Paz, Oruro and Potosí. This region is floristically simple, the most notable species being various species of *Polylepis* tree (usually called queñua), thola shrub species, ichu grass, yareta (or llareta), khota, lampaya and a variety of high Andean flowering plants. Around Lake Titicaca there are large beds of a species of reed called totora.

Around 50 species of native plants are commonly domesticated worldwide, and around 3,000 medicinal species are used at a local or regional level. Several of Bolivia's native species are also commercially important on an international level, such as chilli peppers, rocoto peppers, sweet peppers, potatoes, peanuts, beans, manioc and a variety of palms.

Types of mammal Bolivian fauna can also be divided into three categories, following the floristic sections above. The macro-thermic region, incorporating the tropical lowlands, the humid northeast of and the tropical and subtropical savannas of the southeast, supports a dazzling array of wildlife. Of the many species found in this region, some of the most celebrated include jaguar, ocelot, tapir, capybara, peccary, sloth and giant otter.

The second category is concerned with fauna living to the east of the Cordillera Central and the zone to the south of the Cordillera Real as well as the lowland valleys approaching the border with Peru. The fauna in this region is dependent on the available grazing land and, at times, at the mercy of available grazing land. Spectacled bears are found in this region.

The last category focuses on the higher-altitude areas of the Cordilleras Occidental and Central and, as such, comprises a more typically Andean range of fauna. At similarly high altitude the vast expanse of Lake Titicaca, despite its high altitude, also supports a variety of animal life. The main species to be found in this region include three cameloid species (vicuña, the domesticated llama and alpaca), viscacha, Andean fox, Andean deer, puma (rare) and Andean cat (rare).

Birdlife In terms of birds, lower elevations are highly diverse. The Pantanal is a wonderland of waterbirds, including storks, herons, kingfishers, terns, raptors and parrots. By contrast, the splendours of the Amazon forests are often concealed, but here it is possible to find, with a little patience, curassows, guans, trumpeters, macaws, toucans, cotingas, manakins and motmots. Out in the Santa Cruz savannas large birds include rheas and seriemas. Upslope, in the Andean rivers and forests, look for torrent duck, dippers, cock-of-the-rock, oilbirds, woodpeckers, jays, and a multitude of hummingbirds.

At the highest altitudes, the avifauna is different again. There are few species, but many are easily identifiable or spectacular. Here the Andean condor soars, and other familiar birds include the mountain caracara, lesser rhea (or suri), flamingoes of three species in alkaline lakes (Chilean, Andean and James), Andean goose, Andean gull, Andean lapwing, puna ibis, crested duck, puna teal, Andean and giant coot, Andean flicker, Andean hillstar (the world's highest living hummingbird)and sierra finches.

BIODIVERSITY TODAY The biggest event for years in Bolivian conservation happened in February 2005 when a team of researchers from the New York-based Wildlife Conservation Society, led by British-born conservationist Robert Wallace, discovered a new species of titi monkey in Madidi National Park.

The 29 known species of titi monkeys are all found in the tropical forests of South America. They weigh in at less than 1.2 kilos and can reach 60cm in height. Unlike many primates, the monogamous titis live in small groups of about six. Although difficult to spot from the ground, their distinctive territorial cries help give them away. Dr Wallace and his team spent nearly three years observing the previously undiscovered population, taking audio and video footage, and making comparisons with other primate species.

The team subsequently auctioned the right to name the monkey via the website www.charityfolks.com, raising US$650,000 for Madidi to be channelled through Fundesnap, a private foundation created to raise sustainable sources for funding protected areas. A Canadian casino bought the name and the monkey was subsequently christened *Callicebus avrei palatti* (Golden Palace). The real value of the auction was the publicity, with the sale finally putting the national park well and truly on the tourist map.

This is one success story for Bolivian biology and conservation, and also serves to illustrate the mysteries that await any traveller to remote parts of the country. Unfortunately, biodiversity conservation remains low on the agenda in Bolivia, but the tourist can make a little difference. One of the best ways to support parks and small-scale conservation projects is to visit them, to pay a little into the local economy via tour fees, accommodation fees and to guides and guards. It all helps to make conservation economically sustainable, and to drive home the commercial value of protecting important areas of biodiversity and natural beauty. It's a lot of fun too.

Forestry In 2005, Bolivia certified more than two million hectares of its forests, making the country the world leader in tropical forest certification.

Bolivia was one of the first countries to initiate efforts promoting the conservation of its forests through sustainable management and Forest Stewardship

David Ricalde

The International Ecotourism Society defines the term 'ecotourism' as 'responsible travel to natural areas that conserves the environment and promotes the well-being of local people.' But what exactly does ecotourism mean to Bolivia?

By the mid-1980s, when the first serious large-scale nature protection projects were implemented in Bolivia, ecotourism was just an attractive concept for the conservation movement and scientific community. The idea of implementing ecotourism in remote locations was better established in the unpopulated Manu and Tambopata rainforests of southeast Peru, where a group of young Peruvian conservationists under the guidance of Charles Munn, a zoologist from the Wildlife Conservation Society, had implemented a ground-breaking initiative.

In this case the conservationists targeted high-spending tourists interested in visiting remote sites equipped with basic but comfortable lodges and surrounded by well-preserved rainforest with healthy populations of animals. This area, like many in the Amazon, was at the time home to an abundance of wildlife seriously threatened by human activities, such as the white-lipped peccary, the Brazilian tapir, the black Caiman, the harpy eagle and six species of wild macaws. In addition, the rainforest was home to indigenous communities, low-scale agriculturalists and Brazil nut-gatherers, living in poverty amid a biologically spectacular landscape.

These conservationists realised that, in the long term, southeast Peru and northwest Bolivia could become the best-preserved track of rainforest in the Amazon. They also realised that neither conventional conservation schemes, nor science, would be able to mitigate poverty, or encourage economic alternatives to provide local employment. Hence they chose enthusiastic local entrepreneurs and implemented an innovative model for nature tourism based around the attraction of local animals for birders and nature lovers.

This model was tested and successfully applied in the Manu River and Tambopata River, giving to birth to nature tourism in the Peruvian Amazon. It was subsequently used by ecotourism consultants working on a new project in the northwest of Bolivian Amazonia: the Chalalan Ecolodge (see page 140). This lodge was to be managed by the San José de Uchupiamonas community, a small Quechua-Tacana indigenous group living inside Madidi National Park.

Chalalan opened in 1998 and trumped other attempts at lodges in the Beni Biological Reserve. and in Noel Kempff Mercado National Park as a successful application of the Peruvian model. Today Chalalan is the only ecolodge from Ecuador to Bolivia to be fully

Council (FSC) forest certification. This was a trend that began early in the 1990s and grew stronger following the passing of the country's forestry law in 1995.

The certified forest sector in Bolivia currently generates about US$16 million annually from exports. This includes such certified products as doors, furniture, floorboards, parquets, chairs, veneers, handicrafts and sawn timber. These products are mainly exported to the United States and the United Kingdom.

Since 2002, Bolivia has been acknowledged internationally as working towards the sustainable harvesting of forest resources and received, that same year, the 'Gift to the Earth', a recognition awarded by WWF for the first one million certified hectares.

In the following three years, Bolivia duplicated its certified extension, which to date covers over 2.2 million hectares of tropical forest certified under the FSC logo. Of the 16 certified forest operations, 13 are forest concessions, two are private properties, and one is an indigenous communal land.

owned and operated by local people, who traditionally depended on low-yielding subsistence economies due to their lack of technology and isolation from markets. Currently, a small group of people from the community of San José de Uchupiamonas, now well-trained in tourism management, is producing more gross income in a single month than the whole agricultural production of the entire community in a year.

As in the case of Manu and Tambopata in Peru, nature tourism in northwest Bolivia has become a strong economic factor to complement other long-term efforts in saving large areas of well-preserved rainforests threatened by selective logging, illegal hunting, destructive cattle ranching and low-yield slash and burn agriculture. Sadly, short-sighted politicians and developers still see the appeal of these destructive schemes despite the threat to the area's biodiversity.

In Madidi National Park indigenous people and other settlers are still fighting to defend their traditional territories, but nature-oriented tourism is able to secure more direct employment and generate income for the community, while maintaining the unparalleled biodiversity of the region. With such tourism showing a sustained growth of over 15–20% worldwide each year, the development of sustainable tourism to remote locations in the Amazon will directly benefit locals more than traditional industries such as agriculture, forestry and ranching, which have often been promoted by rich and resourceful national corporations with a keen eye for profits.

Some experts claim there is not yet sufficient technology to maximize the development of the Amazon region. Peru recently initiated a project to build an ambitious road network, connecting Brazil with the ports of the Pacific Ocean. Little consideration seems to have been taken as to how this project will impact on the Bahuaja Sonene National Park, one of the richest rainforests in this country. Indeed, such a project could irreversibly affect the ecologically complex plant–animal relationships, or even worse, lead to the cultural extinction and fragmentation of several indigenous groups in the Amazon.

As a conservationist I sincerely hope that ecotourism or responsible tourism can give rise to more opportunities for local people to benefit directly from the economic input that international visitors bring to remote locations in the Amazon, and foster a better understanding of the invaluable biodiversity and living cultures that still exist in such areas. After all, these places are still home to indigenous communities and, as such, they deserve the opportunity to be part of the new development trends in Bolivian ecotourism.

David Ricalde has over 25 years' experience as a field scientist and conservation biologist in the Amazon and Andes. He has worked as a consultant to the Manu, Tambopata and Madidi ecotourism projects. He works at America Tours in La Paz.

The WWF Bolivia office in Santa Cruz is located at Avenida Beni, Calle Los Pitones #2070 (☏ *(03) 343 0609;* f *(03) 343 0406;* e *wwfbolivia@wwfbolivia.org; www.panda.org*).

HISTORY

The history of Bolivia is one of conflict and turmoil. Named after Simón Bolívar, the Venezuelan-born liberator of northern South America, Bolivia traces a zigzag historical path from ancient civilisation to the poorest country in the continent today. The country may have shaken off Spanish rule to form the independent republic of Bolivia in 1825, but its road to independence was marred by successive and continuing military coups (nearly 200 at the last count), social revolts and crushing poverty. Ironically, Bolivia was one of the first countries in South America to start agitating for independence, but was one of the last to gain it.

1538	The Spanish conquer Bolivia, which then becomes part of the vice-royalty of Peru.
1545	*Cerro Rico*, aka Silver Mountain, is discovered close to the city of Potosí and Spain starts to ransack the immense wealth, using indigenous slaves as workers.
1824	The Venezuelan freedom fighter, Simón Bolívar, after whom Bolivia is named, liberates the country from Spanish rule.
1825	Bolivia gains its independence with Simón Bolívar as its first-ever president.
1879–84	Bolivia loses its mineral-rich, coastal territory to Chile in the bitter War of the Pacific.
1903	Bolivia loses more territory to Brazil in another dispute.
1932–35	Bolivia loses yet more territory to Paraguay after it is defeated in the Chaco War.
1952	Following the overthrow of a military regime, Victor Paz Estenssoro returns from exile to become president and introduces social and economic reforms.
1967	A peasant uprising led by Ernesto Che Guevara is squashed and Che is executed by the Bolivian military after being betrayed by local peasants.
1971	Colonel Hugo Banzer Suarez comes to power after staging a military coup, postponing elections and crushing trade union activity.
1982	The military junta hands over power to a civilian administration led by Siles Zuazo, leading to a resumption of aid by US and European countries

Bolivians celebrate Independence Day on 6 August. Actually, the event is celebrated over several days, most of them featuring parades of various civic groups. The 4th sees the parade of students, the 6th government officials and ministers and the 7th the seemingly obligatory display of military muscle. It's 5 August, however, the night of the *verbena*, an open-air festival, when Bolivians take to the streets to party throughout the night.

HISTORICAL OVERVIEW The founding fathers of Bolivia are traditionally identified as the ancient Tiahuanaco civilisation dating from AD600, although historians have traced signs of civilisation as far back as 7000BC. The people of Tiahuanaco were Aymara Indians and skilled craftsmen with both a grasp of textiles and carving. They constructed impressive temples and had highly organised agricultural systems. Many of their artefacts are on display today at the Tiahuanaco site, one of Bolivia's most visited tourist attractions (see page 104).

Despite their early prowess, however, the civilisation appears to have mysteriously died out and, by the time the foot soldiers of the Quechua-speaking Inca army conquered the region around AD1200, they found little resistance from a civilisation on its last legs.

The Incas went on to control much of Bolivia until the Spanish conquest. The well-organised social structure of the Inca civilisation was crushed by the conquest and its people displaced. The Spanish, and the *criollos*, people of Spanish descent born in the region, took over the best farming land and built regal haciendas while the indigenous community was sold into slavery.

It was the discovery of the silver reserves in Potosí's Cerro Rico, however, that really put Bolivia on the map. While the conquered Indians were put to work in the silver mines, the Spanish established the royal mint in Potosí to convert the silver into coins. As a result, Potosí grew in stature to become a major world city

1989	The leftist Jaime Paz Zamora becomes president and enters a power-sharing pact with former dictator Hugo Banzer.
1999	Encouraged by moves to prosecute former Chilean dictator Augusto Pinochet, pressure builds to launch an inquiry into Banzer's role during the repression of the 1970s.
2000	Vice-President Jorge Quiroga, later to lose to Evo Morales in the 2005 election race, is sworn in as president, replacing Hugo Banzer who is suffering from cancer.
2002	Gonzalo Sanchez de Lozada wins a clear victory and becomes president for a second time.
2003	Around 80 people are killed and hundreds injured in protests fuelled by government plans to export natural gas via Chile. President Sanchez de Lozada resigns under pressure of protests and is succeeded by his deputy, Carlos Mesa.
2005	Protests over energy resources bring La Paz, and the national government, to a standstill. As angry street protests continue, President Mesa resigns. Supreme Court head Eduardo Rodriguez is sworn in as the caretaker president.
2005	Socialist leader of MAS Evo Morales is confirmed the winner of presidential elections.
2006	The first indigenous Bolivian president takes office on 22 January promising a radical programme to turn Bolivia around.

while, ironically, its natural resources were siphoned off by llama caravans taking the silver across the Altiplano to the Pacific coast for shipment to Spain.

The initial talk of revolution and independence from the Spanish can be traced back to 1809 but the first key event came in 1825 when Simón Bolívar, better known as 'the Liberator', pushed forward with a campaign for independence across the Andes. But despite his success, Bolivia was subsequently passed from pillar to post, first as part of a Peruvian–Bolivian federation and then as a republic that failed to achieve nation status.

The next phase of Bolivia's development was characterised by weak governments and disputes over boundaries – issues that persist to the current day. Chile defeated Bolivia and Peru in the War of the Pacific (1879–83) and subsequently made a grab for its small stretch of coastline, leaving it a landlocked country without access to the trading advantage offered by the sea. Argentina followed suit with a grab for land in the Chaco region while Brazil annexed the Arce region in 1903. The final crushing blow came during the Chaco war with Paraguay (1932–35) when Bolivia again surrendered a large area of land. These conflicts had together reduced the total area of the country by over a quarter. Today the excellent Museo del Litoral Boliviano (see page 88) has exhibits that testify to the devastation wrought by these conflicts on the Bolivian land mass.

The period following the Chaco war was one of introspection for Bolivia with politicians and intellectuals alike pondering how to recover from such stinging defeats and rebuild national confidence. This process led to the formation of the National Revolutionary Movement (MNR), which would go on to dominate Bolivian politics for the next generation.

PRE-COLUMBIAN HISTORY Little remains by way of clues to the presence of early humans in Bolivia due to the harsh climate of the Altiplano region, the flat, upper plateau sandwiched between the Cordillera Occidental and the Cordillera Oriental. Historians believe the first human inhabitants arrived around 7000BC and hunted the indigenous llamas with rough stone tools shaped to points. The archaeologist Dick Edgar Ibarro Grasso recorded many such items at the site of Viscachani, one of the earliest Altiplano settlements.

Early humans followed the seasons, allocating periods of hunting and gathering across the Altiplano and up to the edges of Lake Titicaca. Evidence dating from around 4000BC indicates that agricultural production had also started in earnest with arable and pastoral farming, combined with the domestication of indigenous llamas and alpacas, leading to the successful basis for a fledgling civilisation.

In fact, the presence of the llamas was a major boon to the early settlers, with their dung used for fertiliser and their wool woven to form textile clothing.

Around 1000BC a new early culture developed on the southern fringes of Lake Titicaca, the Chiripa. The archaeological remains indicate a more civilised race with complex subterranean structures and highly artistic stone carvings with effigies of snakes, llamas and humans. Further evidence suggests that the Chiripa also traded metals and semi-precious stones with textiles found at sites in Chile and Peru.

Away from the Altiplano, the Cochabamba Valley also yields evidence of early humans with ceramics discovered at the site of Chullpa-Pampa, located just outside Cochabamba, that have effigies of snakes and llamas similar to those discovered at Chiripa sites, leading to speculation that these ancient races traded and shared influences among themselves.

The most important of the ancient civilisations, however, remains the Tiahuanaco, who made their home on the Altiplano to the south of Lake Titicaca from around 1000BC. This race, with their elaborate stone sculptures and large stone monoliths, were the most potent force in the civilisation of the Andes and, in their heyday, boasted an empire that stretched throughout Bolivia into Chile and Peru.

Ceramics found at Tiahuanaco bear the first representations of puma and jaguar, a motif that will come to symbolise the Tiahuanaco style during subsequent stages of the civilisation, which divides from early through to classical Tiahuanaco styles. As the civilisation matured, Tiahuanaco consolidated its control of the Bolivian Altiplano around AD200 and pushed its boundaries outwards, while other smaller settlements were growing up in the lowland areas and in the tropical regions, leaving evidence of their culture in the form of Mojocoya and Tupuraya ceramics in their wake.

When Tiahuanaco started to fall around AD11, the collapse of a unifying civilisation left the Altiplano split into disparate, tribal groups with their own cultures, religious practices and craft traditions. These chiefdoms, however, were deeply suspicious of each other and were characterised by high, hilltop fortifications, known as pucaras, that reflected the prevailing social unrest and rivalry that filled the void left by Tiahuanaco. In the Lake Titicaca basin, unity also gave way to rivalry with the land divided between two opposing Aymara fiefdoms known as Alasaa and Maasaa.

These groups traded, developed agriculture and measured their wealth in their ownership of llamas and alpacas, but remained fundamentally divided. As in-fighting between the Aymara kings and lords intensified, the way was clear for the Quechua-speaking footsoldiers of the Inca Empire to stroll in and take control of the region.

Ironically, their reign was to be severely short lived: in 1542 the area was annexed by the Spanish Viceroyalty of Peru and Bolivia's prehistory gave way to the epic tale of the Spanish conquest.

DAYS OF REVOLUTION The foundation stones of Bolivia's current social revolution were laid by miners, farmers and peasants in the 1940s. In the aftermath of the Chaco War, when much of Bolivia was wiped out, local union groups came together to push for reforms – a move often met by fierce resistance by the government. Events came to a head in 1952 when a social revolution saw private mines nationalised, universal suffrage introduced and massive land reform to shift power away from the traditional landowners and more into the hands of ordinary workers. Around this time the Bolivian Workers Central (COB) also rose to become a force in national politics.

The MNR, however, would not tolerate such insurrection and in subsequent years numerous union leaders, political opponents and journalists were exiled or sent to internment camps. Political instability continued with the 1971 coup by General Hugo Banzer Suarez, which brought economic growth to the country, but also severe human rights abuses during his seven-year period in power.

The 1970s and 1980s brought chaos, military coups and widespread corruption with the COB and the newly founded Revolutionary Movement of the Left (MIR) opposing a succession of military and puppet governments. In five years of democracy between 1978 and 1982 no fewer than ten governments came and went, while Bolivia's first and only (so far) female president, Lydia Gueiler Tejada, had a brief flirtation with office in 1980 before the return of civilian rule in 1982 to a country left devastated economically and disgraced internationally, with many of the deposed military junta implicated in massive drug-trafficking corruption scandals. By the end of the 1980s, inflation had peaked at 24,000%, the Central Bank was devoid of reserves and the peso devalued by 95%.

The presidential election in May 1989 brought political newcomer Gonzalo Sanchez de Lozada to power for the MNR party and ushered in a new era of political turmoil that would, via bloody street protests and accusations of staggering corruption, culminate in the election of Bolivia's first-ever indigenous president, Evo Morales, in December 2005. Is this a new era of Bolivia after centuries of turmoil? The next section picks up the story.

GOVERNMENT AND POLITICS

Bolivia has been rocked in recent years by political instability; two presidents (Gonzalo Sanchez de Lozada and Carlos Mesa) have been obliged to resign faced with riots, demonstrations and the blocking of key highways. Political protest reflects deep social, regional and ethnic rifts in this, one of Latin America's poorest and most unequal countries.

The political landscape in Bolivia went through a paradigm shift in December 2005, however, when Evo Morales, an activist for indigenous rights and a former coca farmer turned leftist politician, became the nation's fifth leader since 2002. More crucially, he became the country's first-ever indigenous leader. With a clear majority, Morales was the first Bolivian president to win an election outright since the country returned to democracy in 1982. An Aymara Indian, who claimed to be 'America's worst nightmare' in his campaign rhetoric, Morales won around 54% of the vote with a turnout of about 85%, much higher than in previous Bolivian elections. The National Electoral Court website (*www.cne.org.bo*) confirmed Morales as the clear winner.

Morales was inaugurated on 22 January 2006, promising to help the poor and seize control of the nation's energy reserves from multinational companies. The international press was less interested in his election pledges, however, and more intrigued by the casual dress sense of the president-elect. On a world tour before

Peter Good

Bolivia's recent instability is not just a result of political struggles but also of a clash of cultures which originated in the first days of the Spanish Conquest: the individual versus the collective. The Spanish were only concerned with the fastest way to self-enrichment, at whatever the cost to the indigenous population: a mentality that has endured to this day. The indigenous cultures were forced on the permanent defensive, unable to resist the superior weaponry that was used to massacre them. The survivors and their families were kept subjugated by feudal social, economic and political relations until the social revolution of 1952.

In the 1990s, the white elite increased the country's dependence on the US and international institutions by handing over 40% of all Bolivian production to 50 or so foreign companies. Only when the negative effects of the neoliberal reforms came to be more keenly felt by the indigenous people did the tide begin to turn. By picking up the discarded banner of economic nationalism, they realised that only by defending and controlling the country's natural resources could they hope to overcome the barriers of poverty, exclusion and injustice. They key event in this latest round of struggles was another local battle, the 'water war', where the collective action of a city and a department in defence of natural resources was able to defeat the government and a multinational company.

The political right, no longer able to hold the national stage, has retreated to a regional posture in the lowlands, unable to promote a national vision. The right has gradually been ceding ground, postponing what appears to be inevitable – the greater democratisation of the political and economic systems. The only factor that might rescue them would be US intervention, a possibility backed by the history of the US in the region over the last century.

Since World War II, the US have sent troops into Panama, Nicaragua, Haiti, Cuba, the Dominican Republic, Grenada, El Salvador, Guatemala and Colombia, some of them more than once. With South American countries being less accessible to American troops and having far greater populations and armies, the US has relied more on promoting coups against governments that don't toe the line, however legitimate they are; Guyana, Brazil and Chile suffered this, to name a few. US troops are now active in Colombia, there is a base just across the border in Ecuador, two in Peru and one in Paraguay. This

taking office, Morales met a series of world leaders, sporting a cosy-looking red, white and blue alpaca sweater. A La Paz-based online shop, BoliviaMall.com, subsequently sold more than 200 of the sweaters at £27 a pop with a rush on the item in Spain.

Upon taking office, Morales called for a minute of silence in memory of Inca rulers, rebels against Spanish rule, Argentine guerrilla Che Guevara and coca farmers who died in protests. He then vowed to seize unproductive land and to ask a constitutional assembly to be elected in July to study a plan to take control of the nation's natural resources. For a fuller profile of Evo Morales, check the web link: www.progress.org/2005/evo01.htm.

Bolivia's ex-president, Gonzalo Sanchez de Lozada, better known as Goni, fled to the US after the protests brought down his government in October 2003. In 2005, he and his ousted cabinet, who have been living in exile in Washington DC since the coup, have been formally charged with genocide. The indictment followed moves in the Bolivian Congress which voted to put the former president on trial on charges related to the deaths of at least 60 people in protests at government plans to export natural gas.

pattern of military domination is evident around the globe – there are 725 known US military bases and the country's 'defence' spending is greater than that of the rest of the world put together.

In October 2005, there was an Iberoamerican Summit in Spain, a country that in 1998 invested more in Latin America than the US, the first time in over 80 years that it has been displaced. The following month saw the Summit of the Americas in Argentina in which President Bush took part. The *New York Times* called the results 'disastrous'. The US delegation was pushing for the signing of the ALCA free trade treaty but the countries of Mercosur, which account for 75% of the region's GDP, rejected it out of hand.

In April 2005, the US Secretary of State, Condoleezza Rice, visited Costa Rica, Chile, Brazil, Colombia and El Salvador, but all the governments refused to sign any statement that criticised the rule of President Hugo Chavez of Venezuela. He is seen by many in the region as its main leader against the US, the successor to Castro.

Chavez's main support on the continent has been the 'Atlantic Block', Lula in Brazil and Kirchner in Argentina, and they have now been joined by Uruguay, which elected a left-wing government for the first time in its history. Efforts for regional integration led to the first Summit of the South American Community of Nations in September 2005, the first step on the long road to a European-style union.

Central to the summit was the question of energy, Chavez and other leaders wanting to control the continent's energy reserves to the benefit of the continent and not foreign companies. The region contains 11.5% of the world's oil and 5.2% of gas and the provision of cheap energy will be the key to the region's economic development in the future. Evo Morales in Bolivia will attempt to nationalise the gas. He will then face the might of the oil companies, the IMF, the US and the conservative elite of the lowlands around Santa Cruz. However, the size of his victory is going to make it difficult to stop him.

Given that at the 2002 election few would have predicted that there would be four presidents in three and a half years, it is unwise to forecast how it will turn out. The task facing the new government is massive and Bolivia still finds itself between a rock and a hard place, but for once there is a genuine prospect of developing a more independent economy.

Peter Good is the author of Bolivia: Between a Rock and a Hard Place, Plural Editores, 2006.

If the case gets to court, Sánchez de Lozada will become Bolivia's second former head of state to face trial since the country's return to democracy in 1982. If found guilty, he faces up to 30 years in prison.

ECONOMY

Bolivia remains one of South America's poorest countries, despite having US$70 billion worth of natural gas reserves, the second-largest in South America after Venezuela. Outside the major cities, indigenous communities still rely on subsistence agriculture, with 14.4% of Bolivia's 8.8 million-strong population living on US$1 or less per day. The tin- and silver-mining industries have long since collapsed and the US-backed coca-eradication programme has fuelled outbreaks of social unrest, which have brought the country to a violent halt several times in recent years. Today, Bolivia remains highly dependent on foreign aid, receiving over US$400 million annually.

In the western hemisphere only Nicaragua, Guatemala, Honduras and Haiti have worse poverty than Bolivia. United Nations (UN) figures also show that

John Crabtree

The landslide election victory of Evo Morales in December 2005 marks a turning point in modern Bolivian politics. Morales is the first indigenous leader to become president of this largely indigenous country. With 53.7% of the vote, he should enjoy the legitimacy that his several immediate predecessors lacked. His party, the Movimiento al Socialismo (MAS) has a majority in congress, and is committed to pushing ahead with economic and constitutional reforms.

The scale of his victory makes it easier for Morales to fend off his opponents, both domestically and abroad. The most potent source of opposition at home comes from Santa Cruz, where a powerful economic elite wishes to assert its autonomy from the government in La Paz. Internationally, Morales is distrusted in Washington, both for his origins as a coca farmers' leader and for his ties with Venezuela's President Hugo Chavez.

His victory notwithstanding, Morales will come under pressure both from these sources of opposition, as well as from erstwhile allies in Bolivia's powerful social movements. The MAS is not a structured party, rather a coalition of such movements. Expectations among the poor for a better future in this, South America's poorest country, were very high as Morales took office at the beginning of 2006, and rivals on the left were poised to take advantage of any signs of backsliding. Political stability therefore cannot be taken for granted.

For several years previously, Bolivia had been rocked by political turbulence. Two presidents (Gonzalo Sanchez de Lozada in October 2003 and Carlos Mesa in June 2005) had been forced to resign, faced with riots, demonstrations and the blocking of key highways. By the end of 2005, the country had had five presidents in as many years.

The politics of the street have long vied with those of more formal constitutional institutions. The 1952 revolution brought with it the nationalisation of the country's tin mines, while the 1970 Popular Assembly proclaimed 'co-government' with the workers. However in the 1980s a more representative system of political parties was consolidated, displacing the once-powerful union movement. Morales's election represented a victory for the country's social movements.

The return to the politics of mobilisation began in 1999 with the so-called Cochabamba 'water wars', when street protests in Bolivia's third-largest city thwarted the plans of the then Banzer administration to privatise water and sewerage services. In 2003, supported by an increasingly assertive indigenous movement and dissatisfied residents in El Alto, the first 'gas war' – prompted by plans to sell Bolivian natural gas to the United States via a pipeline through Chile – led to the ousting of Sánchez de Lozada, and his replacement by the vice-president Carlos Mesa. Then, in May and June 2005, the second 'gas war', triggered by the government's attempts to regulate oil and gas exploitation by foreign companies, delivered Mesa's resignation, and the calling of fresh presidential elections.

As the names of these 'wars' suggest, protest has often arisen because of disputes over how natural resources should be used and to the benefit of whom. As well as water and gas, there have also been protests over the eradication of coca (the leaf which provides the raw material for cocaine but which also has deep cultural significance in Bolivia) and

Bolivia has the greatest degree of economic inequality of any country in South America, with economic exploitation and poverty fuelling instability and conflict: Bolivia has suffered over 200 *coups d'état* in 180 years of independence.

Two-thirds of the nation's population now lives in poverty (compared with a Latin American average of 43%), and United Nations reports conclude that 'it will be impossible for the Bolivian state to accomplish plans for the reduction of the usage of land. Morales promises to defend the interests of coca farmers and landless peasants. Many Bolivians believe that foreign interests have systematically sought to profit from the country's riches, while they themselves remain mired in poverty.

Indigenous groups have become important political players in Bolivia, partly in defence of what are defined as customary rights (known as *usos y costumbres*). Aymaran 'nationalists', led by Felipe Quispe (aka El Mallku), want an extension of and greater respect for indigenous rights. They are concentrated on the western Altiplano highlands, but there are also influential indigenous groups in lowland Santa Cruz which see their identity and economic well-being threatened by the expansion of cash-crop agriculture (especially soya) and timber extraction on their ancestral lands.

Morales's victory also responds to a strong anti-US vein in Bolivian politics, particularly Washington's attempts to eliminate coca production. The main thrust of eradication has been aimed at the Chapare district in the Cochabamba tropics, from which Morales first emerged as leader. Before his election as president in 2005, Morales did much to help weld together opposition to coca eradication policies, with hostility to US plans for a free trade agreement of the Americas and the liberal economic policies associated with the Washington consensus.

Developing a new, more inclusive political system that represents the interests of indigenous and poor communities has so far proved an elusive quest. The need for a constituent assembly to refashion the country's constitution was voiced at the time of both gas 'wars', but little was done to meet these demands. One of Morales's main objectives is to push ahead with constitutional reform.

However, extending the rights of indigenous communities does not find favour with the economic elite of Santa Cruz, Bolivia's most prosperous department and the main hub of its economic development over recent decades. Nor do the government's plans for land reform or the extension of state ownership over potentially enormous gas deposits, located in Santa Cruz, Chuquisaca and Tarija. There have long been threats of secession in Santa Cruz, but these have gained currency in the last few years. Santa Cruz is pushing for greater local powers (*autonomías*) that will free it from the rules made in La Paz. The elite of Santa Cruz thus stands up for the interests of what is called the *media luna*, the lowland crescent stretching from Tarija in the southeast to Pando in the extreme north. Santa Cruz is also home to the most extreme right-wing groups in Bolivia: the Camba Nation and the Cruceñista Youth.

In spite of its majority, the new government therefore faces tough choices. It will be pulled in different directions by a variety of domestic power groups, but will also face strong external pressures (both from Washington and the international financial community) whose demands often conflict with the preferences of influential domestic actors. Even a strongly constituted government would find it difficult to navigate in such waters, but the MAS lacks structure, discipline and experience, as well as an accurate chart for the voyage ahead.

John Crabtree is a research associate at the Centre for Latin American Studies, Oxford. He is author of the book Patterns of Protest: Politics and Social Movements in Bolivia, published by the Latin America Bureau (www.lab.org.uk).

extreme poverty by 2015'. Malnutrition runs at 23% in Bolivia compared with 2% in Argentina. The Potosí region, notably the north of Potosí department, is the poorest.

One result has been a massive flight to the cities. Once a largely rural country, it is now over 60% urban. El Alto, the poor suburbs towering over La Paz, in particular has witnessed a huge immigration in recent years. With an annual growth rate of 5.1%, El Alto is set to double its current population from its current level of 768,587 by the year 2019 and will overtake La Paz as Bolivia's second-most populous city by 2007, second only to the fast-growing economic hub of Santa Cruz de la Sierra. In El Alto, the fertility rate is 4.2 children per woman but the infant mortality rate stands at 64 for every 1,000 babies born.

Since the year 2000, when economic problems reached crisis stage, the country's leaders have imposed structural adjustments at the insistence of the International Monetary Fund (IMF) and the World Bank. Yet economic stagnation, cuts in social expenditures and external debt payments (which absorb up to 55% of the entire gross national product) have all hit (mainly indigenous) poor and rural people the hardest.

Nevertheless, the country's economy is improving, with 2005 gross domestic product growth of 3.9%. The IMF believes the Bolivian economy has strengthened significantly, with inflation remaining in single digits, according to the statement.

Since the privatisation of Bolivia's oil and gas industries in the late 1990s, multinational energy corporations such as British Petroleum, Repsol (Spain), Total (France) and Petrobras (Brazil) have invested a total of US$3.5 billion in oil and gas extraction programmes. These companies signed contracts with consecutive Bolivian presidents, agreeing to pay an 18% royalty fee for all oil and gas extracted, though these contracts failed to obtain congressional validation as required by the constitution. However, after an initial surge of investment that reached US$600 million in 1998, the companies drastically reduced the pace of their financial inputs to US$200 million in 2004. Successive rounds of political instability have hit foreign investment hard and, since the accession of Evo Morales as the country's first-ever indigenous politician in 2006, it is too soon yet to predict how his leftist policies and plans for nationalisation of major industries will impact on inward investment.

What remains certain is that, in terms of exports, natural gas is by far Bolivia's largest revenue source with a value of US$620.5 million in 2004, or 43.81% of all exports. Bolivia has 1,529 billion cubic metres of proven reserves of natural gas, the second-largest reserves in the continent and second only to Venezuela.

QUALITY OF LIVING AND CORRUPTION According to the Worldwide Quality of Life Survey, published by Mercer Human Resource Consulting in 2005, Bolivia ranks fairly low, even in comparison with other South American countries. Mercer's study is based on detailed assessments and evaluations of 39 key quality-of-life determinants, grouped into categories such as political and social environment, socio-cultural environment, public services and transportation, and natural environment.

Overall, Buenos Aires in Argentina and Santiago in Chile rank highest at 78th and 81st respectively, while São Paulo and Rio de Janeiro in Brazil claim the 107th and 116th positions. La Paz actually comes in at 135th, just ahead of Caracas and Bogotá in Colombia, while Santa Cruz takes 143rd place, joint equal with Medellín in Colombia.

The latest edition of the annual Global Corruption Report, produced by Transparency International, ranked Bolivia at 122 out of 146 countries with a Corruption Perceptions Index score of 2.2. A presidential anti-corruption delegation (DPA) was created in Bolivia in October 2003 with the main task of ensuring compliance with the Inter-American Convention against Corruption and co-ordinating anti-corruption efforts of the judiciary, the auditor general, the public prosecutor and the bank regulator. The report indicates, however, that its effectiveness has been limited by its lack of investigative and prosecutorial powers and its success at a regional level has been mixed.

As the world trade talks in Hong Kong approached, Christian Aid was looking for the most appropriate place to take the actor Damian Lewis. Where were the issues of trade, particularly enforced liberalisation and privatisation on which they campaign, best illustrated? The answer was Bolivia. Christian Aid works on eight projects in the country, covering the rainforests in Beni to the Andean highlands.

'I was originally going to travel with Christian Aid to Africa, but the stories about the privatisation of the gas and water sectors were strongly associated with what would be discussed in Hong Kong,' says Lewis.

Since the turn of the millennium, Bolivia has seen huge riots around the issues of water and gas. The gas riots in 2003 and 2005 occurred because ordinary Bolivians felt disenfranchised by the deal, which allowed foreign companies to pay a very low rate of tax after the country's gas reserves had been privatised in 1996. Foreign companies now control the rights to Bolivian gas, paying tax into the local economy at a fraction of what similar companies would pay in many other countries. This means that Bolivia was denied much-needed revenue and remains the poorest country in South America.

During the trip, Lewis met Maxima Cari, a mother of three who had to dig a well 8m deep to find water. Even then, the water is still filthy. Her story is typical of the many who have been denied access to clean water since the privatisation of water services in 1997. To get connected to the supply, people have to pay charges that can amount to nearly half their annual salary.

'Meeting Maxima Cari was remarkable,' says Lewis. 'The poverty itself was not shocking to me, as I'd seen poverty before, but it was the reasons for her poverty which appalled me. I support Christian Aid's view that privatisation of basic services should not be forced on developing countries like Bolivia.'

British actor Damian Lewis visited Christian Aid partners Fundación Solón and CEDLA in La Paz in the spring of 2006 to see the effects of trade liberalisation on poor Bolivians. To find out more about Christian Aid's work in Bolivia, see www.christianaid.org.uk.

The Congress agreed in March 2004 on a bicameral constitutional commission which would investigate a series of high-profile cases involving corruption. They include allegations against former president Gonzalo Sánchez de Lozada. For more information, check the websites www.globalcorruptionreport.org and www.transparency.org.

NET FLOWS Research by the Inter-American Development Bank (IDB) in 2005 found that remittances (money transfers) sent to Bolivia by immigrant workers in North America, Europe and other Latin American nations totalled an estimated US$860m. The IDB report found that 650,000 Bolivians, 11% of the adult Bolivian population, now receives remittances. The average remittance to Bolivia is US$165 and is sent eight times a year. The IDB said the remittances equal 8.8% of Bolivia's gross domestic product, and 33% of its annual exports. The estimate for remittances to Bolivia was based on the results of a survey for the IDB's Multilateral Investment Fund.

Meanwhile, research by the Bolivian newspaper *La Razón* found that 61% of Bolivians expressed a desire to leave the country and make a new life elsewhere. Spain was the favoured destination, with a 24% majority in 2005, followed by 18% preferring the United States and Argentina 11%. The UK was the ideal destination for 5% of those who expressed a preference to emigrate. The main reason cited for this desire to relocate was a combination of high unemployment and a lack of potential to increase economic prosperity.

CHILD LABOUR A 2005 report on core labour standards in Bolivia by the International Confederation of Free Trade Unions (ICFTU) showed serious shortcomings in the application and enforcement of core labour standards, particularly with regard to restrictions on trade union rights, discrimination and child labour. It claims child labour is a serious problem in Bolivia, with an estimated 800,000 children engaged in some type of work. Most children work in rural areas, in agriculture, livestock and construction. Children in urban areas are engaged in commerce, manufacturing and family businesses.

For more about the plight of Bolivia's child workers, see pages 182–3, *Bolivia's child miners*.

TOURISM The latest figures (2003) from the Bolivian Vice Ministry of Tourism indicate 352,575 annual foreign tourist arrivals into Bolivia. This compares with 1.4m in Chile, 2.8m in Argentina and 3.8m in Brazil according to the World Tourism Organisation's 2003 figures (*www.world-tourism.org*).

The main reason for low arrivals in recent years has been the ongoing social instability, which reached a peak in June 2005 with the ousting of President Carlos Mesa.

The Bolivian Camara Nacional de Comercio reported the tourism sector lost US$20m during the 20-day conflict period, while inbound agents in La Paz reported up to 80% cancellations in the immediate aftermath. The longer-term damage to Bolivia's reputation is likely to take some time to address, although tourism initiatives such as the Jesuit Missions Trail (page 224) are intended to raise awareness of new attractions on a global stage.

PEOPLE

With the largest proportion of indigenous people in South America, at around two-thirds of the population, Bolivia's ethnic diversity is both its greatest cultural asset and its biggest source of social conflict.

According to a report published by the World Bank in 2005, *Indigenous Peoples, Poverty and Human Development in Latin America: 1994-2004*, indigenous people account for around 10% of the population of Latin America overall. The report, which focuses on the five countries in the region with the largest indigenous populations – Bolivia, Ecuador, Guatemala, Mexico and Peru – states that the political influence of indigenous communities, in terms of indigenous political parties and elected representatives, constitutional provisions for indigenous people or health and education policies specifically tailored to the indigenous population, 'has grown remarkably in the last 15 years'.

Since 1994, indigenous movements have brought down governments in Bolivia and Ecuador, and the poorly armed indigenous Zapatista National Liberation Army (EZLN) has gained a strong foothold in the impoverished southern Mexican state of Chiapas. Indigenous people have also had a strong influence as legislators, mayors, ministers, governors and even vice-presidents, as in the case of Aymara Indian Víctor Hugo Cárdenas, vice-president of Bolivia from 1993 to 1997.

According to studies by the Economic Commission for Latin America and the Caribbean (ECLAC), there are between 33 million and 40 million indigenous people in Latin America, belonging to around 400 different ethnic groups, each of which has its own language, social organisation and economic system.

INDIGENOUS CULTURE According to Bolivia's latest census, 63% of the country's nine million inhabitants identify themselves as members of indigenous ethnic groups. Almost one-third of the population identifies itself as Quechua, and one-quarter as Aymara, the two ethnic groups descended from the peoples of the Inca Empire, while another 6% claims other indigenous origin. However, indigenous Bolivians were not even granted citizenship until 1952, and de facto ethnic and linguistic inequality remains a daily fact of life in Bolivia.

The two-thirds indigenous majority in Bolivia are descendants of the pre-Columbian native culture that include, and even pre-date, the Incas, South America's most famous race. The other third is comprised of the white descendants of Europeans and *mestizos*, the product of mixed marriages. The legacy of the Spanish conquest lives on with much of the Spanish colonial culture adopted into society as part of dress, music and festivals.

Amongst the indigenous community there are over 30 different ethnic groups, of which the Aymara of the Altiplano and the Quechua of the lowlands are the most widely represented. In the Oriente, the diversity is split between a large number of smaller tribes, with the Guarani the largest group. The number of ethnic languages is also large with Tacana, Mojeño and Ayoreo among the 13 language groups spoken across Bolivia, of which Aymara and Quechua are the most widely spoken.

Bolivia's indigenous population is also growing, particularly in the Altiplano region, where the number of people of indigenous extraction had risen to 1.93 million in 2004 from 1.63 million in 1992, according to research for La Razon. The Amazon region has seen its indigenous population grow from 100,000 in 1992 to 133,000 by 2004 with 24 identified ethnic groups, ranging from the Araona to the Yuki.

INDIGENOUS FESTIVALS AND MUSIC One of the things that sets Bolivia apart from other Latin American destinations is the huge number and enormous vibrancy of the village festivals that seem to take place across the country on an almost constant basis. These can range from the pomp and ceremony of Gran Poder in downtown La Paz to a simple, rural ceremony in a remote village outpost involving dancing, the sacrifice of a llama and the downing of enough moonshine to keep your hangover stoked for several days to follow. Some are strictly pagan affairs while others blend indigenous beliefs and practices with a twist of Catholicism. Either way, the best Bolivian fiestas usually involve lots of drinking and dancing, so come with a spirit of willingness to join in.

Festivals are a crucial element of community life, with festival patrons climbing the strict social hierarchy that dominates community life. On the surface they are joyful affairs but, dig beneath the frivolity of dancing, drinking and consuming coca leaves, and you will find that many fiestas are underscored with a deep religious significance that harks back to ancient rites and rituals. Indeed, many originated as a means to give thanks to Pachamama, the mother earth, for the quality of the harvest, the fertility of livestock and the protection of the community in the previous year.

Whatever the event or festival, one constant factor will be the presence of Bolivian folk music, an integral element of the indigenous culture. Indeed, stone carvings at Tiahuanaco even depict ancient musicians playing *pinkillo*, a flute-like instrument, and *zampoña*, the pan pipes.

An early musical tradition in Bolivia was based on the church mass, with Jesuit missionaries bringing baroque and chamber music to the country and training the indigenous tribes as skilled musicians. This music can still be heard along the route of the Missions Trail around Santa Cruz (page 224). A UNESCO project collected more than 1,800 scores of masses, requiems and concerts composed between 1560

29

The *charango* is Bolivia's answer to the ukulele and similar to the mandolin. A ten-stringed traditional folk instrument, it comprises tough llama-gut strings arranged in five pairs across a sound box. Traditionally armadillo shell was used for the latter but, since the armadillo has been declared an endangered species in Bolivia, wood has become the more popular option.

The charango is a mainstay of Bolivia's folk music heritage, but just how the hell do you actually get a tune out of it?

'It's quite simple,' says charango master Ernesto Cavour, Bolivia's most famous folk music virtuoso, who has played concerts across the globe from Japan to Iraq. 'You need years of practice, a deep-rooted passion and an ability to focus your mind entirely on the music.

'In my classes, we spend the first few hours learning just how to hold the instrument properly and training the ear to tune it,' he adds. 'Tuning is a time-consuming process with the two B strings designed to resonate one octave apart.'

The International Charango Association is based in La Paz at the Museo de Instrumentos Musicales de Bolivia. Lessons cost from 150Bs for two classes per week spread over a month; more information from www.ernestocavour.com

and 1811 and the manuscripts are now kept in the national archive in Sucre.

The most popular form of music today, and the one with the longest tradition as both a soundtrack to celebration and a rousing call to arms in the face of adversity, is Bolivian folk music. Marching bands are popular in the Altiplano region and hark back to the first military bands. In Tarija, meanwhile, the music draws more heavily on poetry and reflects the more tropical landscape.

The most vibrant music, however, draws on Spanish and indigenous influences to form a classic folk combo of stringed instruments and drums. The *charango*, a ukulele-style instrument usually formed from an armadillo shell and using llama-gut strings, is the main instrument in the combo and La Paz-based musician Ernesto Cavour, its master. The *charango* is ubiquitous in the Bolivian folk tradition and is styled on the Spanish *viguela,* an early form of guitar.

Before the Spanish introduced the guitar, harp, organ and flute, and prior to the widespread adoption of piano, trumpet and accordion in the 19th century, pre-Columbian and indigenous wind instruments of the Andes were making sweet music. Of these, the *quena*, a reed flute; the *siku*, the Aymara name for the pan pipes; *phututos*, a pre-Hispanic trumpet fashioned from a bull's horn; *pinkillos*, reed flutes with a small mouthpiece; and *mukululos*, deeply resonating flutes shaped from wood, are still found today in traditional folk ensembles.

The first philharmonic society was formed in Bolivia in 1835 and today the country boasts a national symphony orchestra and a municipal chamber music orchestra, both based in La Paz, plus numerous church-affiliated choirs.

INDIGENOUS BELIEFS Bolivia lives and breathes the indigenous rituals and beliefs that have underscored its society since prehistoric times. From the *challa* (a ritual blessing) to fortune telling with coca leaves, ancient beliefs permeate every aspect of modern society. The starting point for anyone wishing to explore Bolivia's mystic side should be La Paz's Witches' Market (page 87), which is rammed with cures, offerings and the odd charred skeleton of a baby llama to be buried in your new home or office to ensure good luck.

The most powerful tradition that survives today, however, is that of the *kallawayas*, itinerant medicine men who wander the Altiplano for months on end.

They search for vital herbs and plants for their remedies and heal the sick, disturbed and infirmed en route. One of their favourite methods is to pass a guinea pig, often used as food in rural areas, over the entire body. By then cutting open the guinea pig and examining its organs, they claim they can determine where the sickness lies within a person's body.

The kallawayas hail from the Bautista Saavedra region of La Paz Department with the pueblo of Charazani as their main village. They have their own language, Machak Willay, which is used only in ceremonies, and base their craft around the use of natural remedies, such as garlic, camomile and cinnamon.

The kallawaya ceremony is a highly ritualised affair whereby the faith healer first calls to the spirits of the mountains to focus his mind, then incites the power of Pachamama, the mother earth, to give him strength. True kallawayas don't read your fortune, however. Their role is more like an Andean psychiatrist, aiming to help patients feel better by exploring how they can live better.

GAY BOLIVIA One of the least-known aspects of Bolivian society is the human face of the gay scene. The first official case of AIDS was recognised by the Bolivian Ministry of Health in 1985 and, by 1992, 83 cases had been reported, of which 66% were identified within the bi- and homosexual communities.

Law 810: Sexual and Reproductive Rights was approved by the Bolivian parliament on 30 April 2004, but the then-president Carlos Mesa subsequently

THE LEGEND OF THE LAKE

Lake Titicaca, the highest navigable lake on earth, is a haunted region. Ancient cultures believed the lake was an inland sea connected to the mother of all water sources. The name itself, Titicaca, means Rock of the Mountain Cat – *titi* being the Aymara name for a species of wildcat that is believed to have swum from the mainland to Isla del Sol; and *caca* being the Quechua word for rock. There is a Sacred Rock at Chincana on Isla del Sol, where legend claims that worshippers once saw the mountain cat's eyes gleaming within the sacred rock.

According to legend, in the year AD1200 the sun's twin offspring, Manco Kapac and Mama Ocilo, essentially the Inca Adam and Eve, first brought a golden rod to earth, using the Isla del Sol in Lake Titicaca as their base. They founded the Inca Empire, which flourished until 1532 when the Spanish conquered the Incas. At its height, the Inca Empire stretched from Colombia to Chile and many of the Inca trails, including, of course, the famous trail to Machu Pichu in Peru, still exist today.

Incan mythology blesses the lake as the focal point for all worship to Pachamama, the mother earth, and the mystic spirituality of the area is still apparent today in the countless ruins and traditional communities that occupy the islands. Myths tell of a submerged city between the islands of Koa and Pallala, just north of Isla del Sol. The story says there was no lake in those times, only dry land, and a temple forbidden to all except the holy virgins. One day, two men followed the priestesses to the spring by the sacred rock, where they drew water. Surprised, one of the virgins dropped her vessel, breaking the jar. The angry gods commanded the spilled water to flow until it drowned the city and became Lake Titicaca.

Although many divers, including Jacques Cousteau, have searched for the drowned city, it has never been discovered, although artefacts have been found on an underwater ridge between Koa and Pallala, including stone boxes that could have been used for ritual sacrifices. Even today, fishermen setting nets will not cross that passage, for fear of angering the spirits and provoking one of the deadly lake storms that kill on average four fishermen a year.

1

Saturday night in La Paz. I'm invited to a dinner party hosted by a fellow journalist and the guest list includes doctors, lawyers and writers. The invite says 20.00.

At 20.15 I'm at the front door with a bottle of Bolivian red for the hostess. She peers round the door looking slightly shocked and ushers me into the living room. I'm the first to arrive. By 21.00, I'm still the first. At 21.15 another guest arrives followed by a third around 21.30. At 23.30 the last guest arrives without so much as an apology and we finally sit down to eat.

By this time, however, I'm not only practically gnawing off the table leg with hunger, but I'm also assured a night of severe indigestion as, at an altitude of 3,577m above sea level, everyone in La Paz knows to eat at lunchtime and snack in the evening as the body can't metabolise heavy meals quickly before bedtime.

To the European mind, arriving three and a half hours late would be enough to end a friendship permanently. To the Bolivian guests, however, it seemed perfectly acceptable.

From my experience, some – not all, but many – Bolivians would be late for their own funeral and not even bat an eyelid. But this is more than just the *mañana* lifestyle of southern Spain or Mexico, which we dismiss as a quirk of the local culture. In the primary business cities of La Paz and Santa Cruz, this inherent tardiness, it appears, is a major facet of the national psyche with the whole country set to an automatic two-hour snooze timer. For foreigners arriving to do business in Bolivia, this casual disregard for time-keeping can be hugely frustrating.

A spokesperson for the British Embassy in La Paz puts it delicately: 'It is the experience of the British Embassy's commercial team that British businessmen visiting Bolivia will have briefed themselves, before coming to the market, that punctuality in Bolivia, and in Latin America in general, is not that which they might be used to in Britain.'

But what would be the impact on the country's economy if everyone just woke up one morning and started running on time? 'Just get over it,' says Alix Shand, an expat Brit who runs La Paz's most successful language school, the Speakeasy Institute (*www.speakeasyinstitute.com*). 'It's only uptight Brits and Germans who get stressed out by this. I've worked here for over ten years now and have just learned to adapt to the local time-keeping practices,' she says. 'Rather than fighting the relaxed nature of the Latin lifestyle, you have to learn to adapt to it and use it to your advantage.'

refused to sign it into law. The law's eight articles constitute basic human rights, such as legal access to abortion, the right to sexual education and allowing homosexual couples to marry and foster children. To this day the legislation is frozen.

'To be Bolivian and gay is easier in La Paz than elsewhere in Bolivia,' says David Aruquipa, a gay rights activist who is also the front person for La Familia Galan, Bolivia's most celebrated troupe of drag queens. 'People here are more aware of sexual rights. In Santa Cruz, for example, there are more cases of HIV and transvestites working in the sex industry, yet more discrimination. It's a very macho society.'

La Familia Galan came together in 2001 and now comprises 30 people, with new members joining from cities outside La Paz. Bolivia's first gay pride march was in Santa Cruz in 2001 and the Galans now help to organize a regular gay pride march in La Paz each June. In 1995, when they made their own first public parade, they were all arrested.

'The whole idea of the Galans is to challenge the notion of the traditional nuclear family,' says Aruquipa. 'We are a family with love, fights, disagreements and tender moments like any family, bonded together by a philosophy that diversity is essential to family life.'

According to Tim Wright, author of *Gay Organisations, NGOs and the Globalisation of Sexual Diversity: The Case of Bolivia*, most of the gay bars (and they are few and far between) don't last long, so finding gay life in Bolivia should not be organised around the concept of finding a bar. Instead, tapping into the local gay network via events and meetings is probably is a better approach.

For further reading check the websites www.boliviagay.com and www.globalgayz.com/g-bolivia.html.

LANGUAGE

In South America today there are over 7 million people who speak Quechua, the language used by the Incas. It is the most widely spoken indigenous language in the continent, with the majority of speakers located in Peru (5 million), Bolivia (1.5 million) and Ecuador (500,000). In Bolivia alone, Quechua speakers represent 30% of the population.

When the Spanish arrived, they conquered all the inhabitants of the Inca Empire. Using some of the same tactics as the Inca, the Spanish used military might and religious conditioning to subjugate the locals. They imposed a new way of life and a new belief system, banning all previous religions, but they allowed the native Indians to retain their Quechua and Aymara languages.

Indeed, The Catholic Church held services in the local language and scholars even studied Quechua, and missionaries learnt it. While this incorporated Catholicism and European ways into the culture, it didn't diminish the importance of the Quechua way of life. Even today you can see a strange mix of religions within Quechua society. Festival days and Catholic events coincide, and are celebrated with dances and songs blending the two cultures.

In modern Bolivia the diversity of ethnic groups and the differences between Aymara and Quechua cultures explain why there is not much inter-marriage within villages. Aymara and Quechua speakers even today have difficulty in understanding each other – even though the two languages actually share some words.

RELIGION

Today over 90% of Bolivians claim to be Catholics, but this wasn't always the case. At the beginning of the 16th century, the Inca Empire was at its peak, and the people worshipped Inca gods. The Spaniards arrived in 1531, led by Francisco Pizarro, and conquered the Inca Empire, bringing a whole new religion with them: Catholicism.

One of the principal justifications for the conquest of South America was the conversion of pagan people to Catholicism, an aim pursued by the monarchy with great seriousness. The Spaniards had been told by the Crown that they could conquer on the grounds of a 'just war' if any of the natives rejected Catholicism.

The Incas appeared eager to acquire Christianity, something that may have been born of their admiration for the Spaniard's military successes, as if this proved their god was stronger than the Incas'. A class of Inca nobles was left in place to act as intermediaries between the Spaniards and the natives. These people were allowed to retain control of their land, under the condition they embraced the new religion, something they did eagerly in the hope it would reduce the Europeans' severity towards them.

For many natives, it was easy to exchange the Inca religion for Catholicism as the two religions had many similarities – religious figureheads, convents and places of worship. Both had religious holidays, festivals and celebrations, something the Spanish used to their advantage, by replacing festivals, or explaining the similarities when evangelising. Inca religious ceremonies, pilgrimages and public rituals were soon banned, and a great number of ceremonial sites and idols destroyed in a violent campaign of destruction. In some cases the natives were overawed by the splendour and opulence of this new religious architecture, music and art, something that helped in their conversion.

But how did the Spanish manage to evangelise so many people? The Spanish missionaries realised upon coming to South America that they would have to incorporate the new religion into the native cultures if they ever wanted to be successful in converting the people to Catholicism. Thus the missionaries studied the languages of the Indians and the history of the native cultures, customs and traditions, to enable them to better understand the Indians' way of life. This aided them in learning how to teach the works of the Bible in the best possible way.

Despite the very best efforts of the Spanish, in some Andean areas pagan cultures survived virtually intact for many years. The official religion proved easy to supplant, but simpler and more fundamental superstitions could not be so quickly uprooted, and even today traditional beliefs survive alongside Catholic ones.

The Catholic Church's involvement in South America has been a long one, and often contentious. Faith is a natural part of any society, and not one which is easily taken away. The history of Catholicism in South America is, hence, seen by some as an evolution, rather than a repression, of this faith.

EDUCATION

While levels of literacy are comparatively low (around 87% of the population over the age of 15 can read and write), high-quality education is readily available – to those who can pay for it. To chart your child's progress through the private education system, you have to start paying from when they reach the age of three or four with a private kindergarten. From there, progress through primary and secondary schools is accompanied by increasing hikes in fees, typically around US$300 per month, plus a hefty, but returnable, deposit when the child first enters school. These private schools, owned by independent associations, often teach in both Spanish and another language, hence training students specifically for scholarships to continue their studies abroad, typically in the United States, Germany or France. At university level, 30-odd institutions across Bolivia are available to students, of which the most respected typically incur fees of around US$250 per month, more if you plan to study a large number of subjects. Given that the minimum term of study is five years (seven for a doctor), the costs add up dramatically over time. The biggest problem now facing Bolivia's student population, however, is that of over-qualification. While job prospects remain poor, students may enjoy their years of higher education at high costs to their parents but they subsequently leave college with little hope of a decent job. Hence the number of young people seeking work overseas continues to spiral upwards.

CULTURE

To talk about culture in Bolivia is, inevitably, to talk about the country's indigenous culture, which far outdates the colonial legacy of the Spanish. The Bolivian folklore is rich with traditions and legends based around the natural world. The

Hilary Bradt

In Bolivia, people of all classes make the traditional Pago a Pachamama, or sacrifice to Mother Earth, to ensure good luck (or rather to prevent bad luck) when building a new house. A Bolivian friend described an elaborate affair which she attended to inaugurate a glass factory. One llama was sacrificed for the sales department and one for the plant itself. First a pit was dug, oriented east to west, and prepared with coca leaves, herbs and incense. Bottles of beer and sweet wine were placed at each corner of the pit, which was then blessed by the priest. A *brujo* (sorcerer) was called in to 'read' the coca leaves to see what colour the sacrificial llama should be.

The beast arrived, washed and groomed and wearing a silk coat decorated with gold and silver 'coins' and paper money. It was made to drink three bottles of beer and one of *aguardiente* (apparently it offered no resistance throughout the ceremony), then to kneel first towards the sun and then towards Illimani before its throat was cut. Even then it did not struggle; it did not even blink.

The blood was sprinkled around the perimeter of the factory and in the pit, which then became the llama's grave.

On a less lavish scale, but still symbolising an offering to Mother Earth, is the *mesa con sullo*. This is what the dried llama foetuses and strange herbs and objects that are sold at the witches' market near Calle Sagárnaga in La Paz are for. If Pachamama can't have a live llama, she'll settle for a dried foetus, rubbed with fat to simulate the real thing. This must be laid on a bed of wool (white for purity), along with sweets in the shapes of different animals and devils, nuts and seeds, and gold and silver trinkets. All this is by way of returning to Mother Earth what has been taken from her. The foetus may be dressed in a coat, like a real sacrificial llama, and little bottles of sweets may take the place of the beer in the full sacrifice. The whole thing may be topped with a piece of cat's skin to represent the untameable, which still succumbs to the power of Pachamama.

When complete, the objects will be blessed, then parcelled up and buried, to the accompaniment of incantations and sprinkles of alcohol, either under the foundations of a new house, or in the countryside in view of the major snow peaks and their *achachilas* (mountain spirits).

most central tenet to this is Pachamama, the mother earth, the most powerful being after the sun in Indian mythology.

Bolivia's culture of folklore is still vibrant today and permeates every aspect of society through festivals, such as Alisitas (page 38), Carnival in Oruro (page 65) and the Aymara new year celebrations (page 107).

Background Information CULTURE

2

Practical Information

WHEN TO VISIT

The rainy season runs from November to March and is best avoided, as roads can simply wash away during this time, bringing chaos to travel itineraries. The high season is June to September when it is summer in Europe but, in fact, the heart of the Bolivian winter. Night temperatures can be savagely cold at high altitude during this time, so come prepared with warm clothes, or funds to go shopping locally. Prices are hiked across the board during Carnival (typically mid–late Feb) and during times of local fiestas. Before travelling to Bolivia, you should always check with the Foreign & Commonwealth Office (*www.fco.gov.uk*).

It is recommended that you keep copies of relevant pages of your passport and obtain comprehensive travel and medical insurance before travelling. You should check any exclusions, and that your policy covers you for the activities you want to undertake (see *Travel insurance*, page 47). Some activities, such as mountain biking, are classified as hazardous and may be excluded from personal policies.

The US State Department (*www.state.gov*) publishes an updated Consular Information Sheet about Bolivia (*http://travel.state.gov/travel/cis_pa_tw/cis/cis_1069.html*).

PUBLIC HOLIDAYS AND FESTIVALS Fiestas are big business in Bolivia. Bring your dancing shoes, your drinking boots and expect crowd participation. Saints' days, in particular, are major events in remote village communities, providing both a colourful backdrop to a visit and a chance to interact with community life. The main cultural festivals and celebrations in Bolivia are as follows. Some dates may vary slightly from year to year.

Alasitas A La Paz tradition, held in Parque Central and around Plaza Sucre in late January, it celebrates artisan crafts in miniature.

Festival of the Virgin of Candelaria One of the most important religious festivals, with major events staged in Copacabana, Cochabamba and Oruro on 2 February.

Carnival Celebrated in Oruro with a folkloric show of dancing, La Entrada, and in Santa Cruz with a more Brazilian-style street party.

Phujillay A festival celebrating a historic event in the indigenous community of Tarabuco, near Sucre; it is held each year in March.

Festival of San José The patron saint of carpenters is celebrated with events in Cochabamba and Potosí.

Easter Week Communities across Bolivia celebrate Easter with masses and prayers.

Bolivians love a good party and they don't come much better than Alasitas, the Bolivian festival of abundance. The festival, which originally dates from Inca times, is dedicated to Ekeko, the household deity of plenty and good fortune, a chubby, avuncular little chap with a penchant for good grub and the occasional hearty smoke.

The fiesta is celebrated across Bolivia at different times of the year but is relished with particular verve in La Paz, starting in January and running until Carnival in late February.

It's one of the most colourful, and unusual, festivals in Latin America, not to mention a cultural cornerstone in the calendar of the local indigenous Aymara population that makes up over half of La Paz's rich ethnic population.

Historically Alasitas marked the September harvest festival but, after the Spanish conquistadors forced a change of date upon the Aymara people, they responded by turning the whole event into a parody of the original meaning to reflect pure material greed.

The idea being that, if you take your Ekeko to be blessed by a Yatiri (an Aymara folk healer) by noon on the first day of Alasitas, the miniature items displayed on your personal shrine will become your actual possessions within the year. The offerings are becoming increasingly elaborate: from miniature US$100 bills to scale models of sports cars and airline tickets to Miami.

The Spanish colonialists may not have got the joke but little Ekeko is smiling on through.

Festival of the Cross Celebrated in rural Andean communities around 3 May, this is one of the oldest rituals still marked and signals the start of the *tinku* season (see page 186).

Gran Poder Celebrated in La Paz, parades and dancers in colourful costumes line the Prado each year in June.

Santísima Trinidad The most important festivals of saints in the Beni region, marked around the start of June.

Aymara New Year The Bolivian winter solstice, 21 June, is celebrated with firework displays and bonfires, with the ruins of Tiahuanaco providing the focus.

Festival of San Juan Bolivia's answer to Bonfire Night (except on 24 June), this saint's festival accompanies the harvest season with fields and belongings traditionally burnt for a new start.

Festival of the Virgin of Carmen Celebrations in La Paz, Cochabamba and Oruro on 16 July.

Festival of the Apostle Santiago Celebrated in Tarija on 25 July; Tarija has Santiago as its patron saint.

Festival of San Ignacio de Moxos A major saint's festival in the Beni on 31 July.

Independence Day Each year 6 August is marked by a loud gun salute and parades throughout cities across Bolivia.

Festival of the Virgin of Urkupiña This is the biggest religious festival in Cochabamba, with celebrations across the country on 15 August.

Festival of the Virgin of Guadalupe Held in Santa Cruz and Sucre on 8 September.

Festival of the Virgin of Rosario Sacred processions across the country in early October.

All Saints' Day Celebrations for All Saints and the Day of the Dead focus on cemeteries across the Andes.

Annual public holidays
1 January	New Year's Day
Monday, Tuesday and Wednesday of Carnival Week	
Thursday, Friday and Saturday of Easter Week	
1 May	Labour Day
16 July	La Paz Municipal Holiday
6 August	Independence Day
12 October	Colombus Day
2 November	Day of the Dead
25 December	Christmas Day

SUGGESTED ITINERARIES

The classic itinerary offered by most tour operators starts and ends in La Paz, taking in Lake Titicaca and the Altiplano, Sucre and Potosí, the Salar de Uyuni and, possibly, the Amazon. You can also fly into Santa Cruz, however, and make your way up towards La Paz via Sucre, a route that is a better option for those concerned about the possible effects of altitude sickness.

Aside from the obvious cultural attractions of the major cities, or of following the tourist trails that radiate out from them, such as the Jesuit Missions Trail, Bolivia has lots to offer for adventure travel fans, with hiking, trekking, biking and rafting all on the agenda. The industry for these activities is still in its relatively early stages, but a few leading operators, notably Gravity Assisted Mountain Biking in La Paz (page 72), are blazing the trail.

If you are travelling more independently, then a few days based in La Paz or Santa Cruz will prove very useful to arrange tickets, tours and itineraries before heading onwards – as will allowing some degree of flexibility to allow for transport delays and problems.

TOUR OPERATORS

Start researching any trip with a free copy of the Latin America Travel Association (LATA) Guide, available in the UK from **LATA** (✆ *020 8715 2913; www.lata.org*).

Many operators offer Bolivia as part of a wider itinerary, often taking in Peru as well, but some do specialise in purely Bolivia, with a small number of operators offering specialist trekking, climbing and nature study trips.

Otherwise, the main tour operators are as follows:

Abercrombie & Kent ✆ 0845 0700614; e info@ abercrombiekent.co.uk; www.abercrombiekent.co.uk

Andean Trails ✆ 0131 467 7086; e info@ andeantrails.co.uk; www.andeantrails.co.uk

Audley Latin America ☎ 01869 276210; e latina@
audleytravel.com; www.audleytravel.com
Bales Worldwide ☎ 0845 057 1819; e enquiries@
balesworldwide.com; www.balesworldwide.com
Cazenove & Loyd ☎ 020 7384 2332; e info@
cazloyd.com; www.cazloyd.com
Condor Journeys & Adventures ☎ 01700 841318;
e dany@explore.co.uk; www.condorjourneys-
adventures.com
Dragoman Overseas Travel ☎ 01728 861133;
e lata@dragoman.co.uk; www.dragoman.com
Exodus ☎ 0870 2405550; e sales@exodus.co.uk;
www.exodus.co.uk
Explore Worldwide ☎ 0870 333 4001; e res@
explore.co.uk; www.exploreworldwide.com
Guerba World Travel Limited ☎ 01373 858956;
e info@guerba.co.uk; www.guerba.co.uk
Journey Latin America ☎ 0208 747 8315;
e tours@journeylatinamerica.co.uk;
www.journeylatinamerica.co.uk
KE Adventure Travel ☎ 017687 73966; e info@
keadventure.co.uk; www.keadventure.com
Last Frontiers ☎ 01296 653000; e info@
lastfrontiers.com; www.lastfrontiers.com
Magic of Bolivia ☎ 020 8378 9194; e zoe@
bolivia.co.uk; www.bolivia.co.uk

Naturetrek ☎ 01962 733 051; e info@
naturetrek.co.uk; www.naturetrek.co.uk
Peregrine Adventures ☎ 0844 736 0170;
www.peregrineadventures.co.uk
Select Latin America ☎ 020 7407 1478;
e info@selectlatinamerica.co.uk;
www.selectlatinamerica.co.uk
Scott Dunn Latin America ☎ 0208 682 5030;
e latin@scottdunn.com; www.scottdunn.com
South American Experience ☎ 0870 499 0683;
e info@southamericanexperience.co.uk;
www.southamericanexperience.co.uk
Steppes Travel ☎ 01285 885333; e latinamerica@
steppestravel.co.uk; www.steppestravel.co.uk
Tim Best Travel ☎ 0207 591 0300; e info@
timbesttravel.com; www.timbesttravel.co.uk
Travel 2 Travel 4 ☎ 0870 020 2777; e enquiries@
travel2.com; www.travel2.com
Trips Worldwide ☎ 0117 311 4400; e info@
tripsworldwide.co.uk; www.tripsworldwide.co.uk
Tucan Travel ☎ 0208 896 1600; e uksales@
tucantravel.com; www.tucantravel.com
World Expeditions ☎ 0208 870 2600;
e enquiries@worldexpeditions.co.uk;
www.worldexpeditions.co.uk

RED TAPE

Currently, citizens of Argentina, Australia, Chile, Colombia, Ecuador, Israel, Paraguay, Switzerland, Uruguay, the Scandinavian countries (including Finland and Iceland), the UK, Germany, France, Belgium, the Netherlands, Luxembourg, Italy, Portugal, Spain and USA (except residents from Puerto Rico) do not require visas for stays of up to 90 days in Bolivia.

UK nationals should receive a 90-day entry stamp upon arrival at international air hubs. If you enter overland, immigration officials are likely to give you only 30 days. Ask for 90 but don't push it and always refuse to hand over any money. Extensions to your stay are easily arranged at the immigration office in La Paz (page 85).

Note: keep a photocopy of your passport in your daypack at all times for ID purposes.

GETTING THERE AND AWAY

Flights to (and within) Bolivia are on the pricey side, but remain the principal way for international tour groups to arrive into the country. Independent travellers, however, often arrive overland by bus, many coming from Peru via Lake Titicaca.

FROM THE UK, IRELAND AND EUROPE There aren't direct flights from the UK. Those who are travelling from Europe to Bolivia will need to go via Lima (Peru), Rio de Janeiro (Brazil), Sao Paulo (Brazil), Buenos Aires (Argentina) or Miami (USA), for connections to La Paz and Santa Cruz. Flight costs can differ a lot from

BORDER CROSSINGS

Crossing	Border town	Opening hours
1 TO PERU	Copacabana	08.30–19.30

The main gringo crossing as facilities are far superior, but immigration queues are longer.

2 TO PERU	Desaguadero	08.30–12.30 and 14.00–20.30

A typical snakepit border town with few facilities, but a faster crossing.

Note Peru time is one hour ahead.

Top tip Change dollars at a casa de cambia in La Paz (see page 86) before leaving for the border as rates will be far better.

3 TO CHILE	via the Salar de Uyuni	08.00–12.30 and 14.30–18.00

The Bolivian border exit from the Salar de Uyuni, heading for the Chilean town of San Pedro de Atacama, is a notoriously slow affair and often entails a mandatory but totally unnecessary 10Bs 'service charge'. Get your departure stamp in Uyuni before you leave.

Note there are also bus connections from Uyuni to the Chilean border town of Calama with onward bus connections.

4 TO CHILE	Tambo Quemado	08.00–20.00

Crossing into Chile with Arica as your final destination is relatively painless, making this a favourite visa-run option for those seeking an alternative to Peru. Just take lots of warm clothes for the six- to eight-hour journey and try to arrange a ticket with Chilebus (*in La Paz's Bus Terminal;* ✆ *228 2168, see page 69*), which has daily runs, including lunch and help with border formalities. To check out options for an overnight in Arica, see the website: www.infoarica.blogspot.com; there's a 100 Chilean pesos tax payable when leaving Arica.

Note From October to March Chilean time is one hour ahead for daylight saving.

5 TO ARGENTINA	Villazón	08.00–20.00

A quick, if poorly signposted, and pretty efficient border control with considerably less foot traffic than other Bolivian border controls.

Top tip avoid the queues for inspectors dealing with goods being transported across the border and make sure to join the queue for tourists only.

6 TO ARGENTINA	Yacuiba	08.00–20.00

A little-used crossing at Bolivia's easternmost frontier town.

one airline to another, destination to destination and according to the season of the year. Lloyd Aereo Boliviano (LAB) operate two services a week between Santa Cruz and Madrid, with connections to London on British Midland into Heathrow.

FROM NORTH AMERICA American Airlines and Lloyd Aereo Boliviano fly from Miami and Washington to Santa Cruz with connection for La Paz.

FROM AUSTRALIA AND NEW ZEALAND There are no direct flights from down under, hence you'll need to get an onward flight from London or the USA. Aerolineas Argentinas do offer flights from London to Sydney via Buenos Aires (Argentina) and from Buenos Aires to Auckland and Sydney.

Practical Information GETTING THERE AND AWAY

2

FROM WITHIN SOUTH AMERICA There are flight to Bolivia from the capitals of all South American countries, as well as Rio de Janeiro and São Paulo (Brazil). The latest innovation in the area is new flights from GOL Linhas Aereas Inteligentes, Brazil's low-cost airline, which flies from Campo Grande, in the Brazilian state of Mato Grosso do Sul, to Santa Cruz de la Sierra; more at www.voegol.com.br.

AIR PASSES Lloyd Aereo Boliviano (LAB) offer two air passes:

Vibolpass This allows you to plan your own flight route, visiting up to four different Bolivian cities at any time of the year, at reduced prices.

The programme offers four stopovers with a maximum period of 45 days, visiting each city only once (connecting flights are not classed as a stopover). Vibolpass tickets must be purchased outside Bolivia and can be purchased either in conjunction with a LAB international flight, or flights on other airlines to Bolivia. Fares: three coupons US$155; four coupons US$200; five coupons US$250. Children pay 67% of the adult fare; fares exclude all taxes and surcharges.

South American Pass This is similar to the Vibolpass, but with international flights within South America. Eight possible stopovers are permitted, visiting each city only once, within a period of 90 days. Fares start at US$530 for one to four coupons, up to US$1,070 for nine coupons. It is not possible to start this programme in Brazil.

Flight Directors (✆ 0870 2407670; e labairlines@flightdirectors.com; www.labairlines.co.uk) is the general sales agent for LAB in the UK and have relations with local agents to arrange flights and packages within Bolivia.

✚ HEALTH *with Dr Felicity Nicholson*

Healthy travel is happy travel. Here a few essential guidelines to keep you safe on the road.

IMMUNISATIONS Overall medical facilities are more basic than most travellers are used to back home, so come prepared and make sure to get your immunisations before you travel. It is advised that you visit your local GP or a travel clinic at least six weeks before your departure to gain advice from constantly updated health briefs on the area that you are travelling to. Basic vaccinations include tetanus and diphtheria (which these days come with polio vaccination – though this is not actually needed for South America), typhoid and hepatitis A. You would be advised to get a yellow fever vaccination if you are going to jungle areas of Bolivia, or if you are planning to cross into other South American countries – some will require a certificate to be shown so make sure you carry it with you. Not everyone will be able to take yellow fever vaccine in which case you may be advised to avoid certain areas, or you may require an exemption certificate in place of the formal certificate. For trips of four weeks or more, or where you are going to be more than 24 hours from medical help, rabies vaccines would be advised. The course ideally comprises three jabs that can be given over a minimum of 21 days. Hepatitis B vaccine should also be considered for longer trips or if you are working in a medical setting or with children. Again the three-dose course can be given over 21 days if time is short.

MALARIA Few areas within Bolivia are known to have active malaria problems as so much of the country is too high or coastal. However, there is a risk, mostly from the benign forms of malaria, in areas below 2,500m in the southern regions of

Beni, Pando, Santa Cruz, Tarija, Lacareja and north/south Yungas in the La Paz Department. The malaria occurs all the year round and you would be advised to take prophylactic tablets such as chloroquine and Paludrine. Higher-risk malaria in the form of *Plasmodium falciparum* exists in the Amazon Basin to the northeast of the Andes. Here stronger malaria tablets are advised, such as Lariam, doxycycline or Malarone. These drugs are obtainable only on prescription and you should discuss with your doctor which one suits you best.

At higher altitudes, there is little risk of mosquitoes that carry the parasite, but it is always worthwhile to cover up to avoid getting bitten. This particularly applies when in lower-lying parts of the country, and indeed, avoiding getting bitten is your best protection against getting malaria. Impregnating clothes with permethrin, wearing long sleeves and trousers at dusk and using a permethrin-impregnated mosquito net also reduce the risk of infection. If likely to be away from medical facilities for longer periods, then it would be worth enquiring about a malaria standby treatment.

TRAVEL CLINICS AND HEALTH INFORMATION A full list of current travel clinic websites worldwide is available from the International Society of Travel Medicine (*www.istm.org*). For other journey preparation information, consult www.tripprep.com. Information about various medications may be found on www.emedicine.com. For information on malaria prevention, see www.preventingmalaria.com.

UK

Berkeley Travel Clinic 32 Berkeley St, London W1J 8EL (near Green Park tube station); 020 7629 6233.

Cambridge Travel Clinic 48a Mill Rd, Cambridge CB1 2AS; 01223 367362; e enquiries@ cambridgetravelclinic.co.uk; www.cambridgetravelclinic.co.uk. Open Tue–Fri 12.00–19.00, Sat 10.00–16.00.

Edinburgh Travel Clinic Regional Infectious Diseases Unit, Ward 41 OPD, Western General Hospital, Crewe Rd South, Edinburgh EH4 2UX; 0131 537 2822; www.link.med.ed.ac.uk/ridu. Travel helpline (0906 589 0380) open weekdays 09.00–12.00. Provides inoculations & antimalarial prophylaxis & advises on travel-related health risks.

Fleet Street Travel Clinic 29 Fleet St, London EC4Y 1AA; 020 7353 5678; www.fleetstreetclinic.com. Vaccinations, travel products & latest advice.

Hospital for Tropical Diseases Travel Clinic Mortimer Market Building, Capper St (off Tottenham Ct Rd), London WC1E 6AU; 020 7388 9600; www.thehtd.org. Offers consultations & advice, & is able to provide all necessary drugs & vaccines for travellers. Runs a healthline (0906 133 7733) for country-specific information & health hazards. Also stocks nets, water purification equipment & personal protection measures.

Interhealth Worldwide Partnership House, 157 Waterloo Rd, London SE1 8US; 020 7902 9000;

www.interhealth.org.uk. Competitively priced, one-stop travel health service. All profits go to their affiliated company, InterHealth, which provides health care for overseas workers on Christian projects.

MASTA (Medical Advisory Service for Travellers Abroad) Moorfield Rd, Yeadon LS19 7BN; 0870 606 2782; www.masta-travel-health.com. Provides travel health advice, anti-malarials & vaccinations. There are over 25 MASTA pre-travel clinics in Britain; call or check online for the nearest. Clinics also sell mosquito nets, medical kits, insect protection & travel hygiene products.

NHS travel website www.fitfortravel.scot.nhs.uk. Provides country-by-country advice on immunisation & malaria, plus details of recent developments, & a list of relevant health organisations.

Nomad Travel Store/Clinic 3–4 Wellington Terrace, Turnpike Lane, London N8 0PX; 020 8889 7014; travel-health line (office hours only): 0906 863 3414; e sales@nomadtravel.co.uk; www.nomadtravel.co.uk. Also at 40 Bernard St, London WC1N 1LJ; 020 7833 4114; 52 Grosvenor Gardens, London SW1W 0AG; 020 7823 5823; & 43 Queens Rd, Bristol BS8 1QH; 0117 922 6567. For health advice, equipment such as mosquito nets & other anti-bug devices, & an excellent range of adventure travel gear.

Trailfinders Travel Clinic 194 Kensington High St, London W8 7RG; 020 7938 3999; www.trailfinders.com/clinic.htm

LONG-HAUL FLIGHTS, CLOTS AND DVT

Dr Jane Wilson-Howarth

Long-haul air travel increases the risk of deep vein thrombosis (DVT). Although recent research has suggested that many of us develop clots when immobilised, most resolve without us ever having been aware of them. In certain susceptible individuals, though, large clots form and these can break away and lodge in the lungs. This is dangerous but happens in a tiny minority of passengers.

Studies have shown that flights of over five and a half hours are significant, and that people who take lots of shorter flights over a short space of time form clots. People at highest risk are:

- Those who have had a clot before – unless they are now taking warfarin
- People over 80 years of age
- Anyone who has recently undergone a major operation or surgery for varicose veins
- Someone who has had a hip or knee replacement in the last three months
- Cancer sufferers
- Those who have ever had a stroke
- People with heart disease
- Those with a close blood relative who has had a clot

Those with a slightly increased risk:

- People over 40
- Women who are pregnant or have had a baby in the last couple of weeks
- People taking female hormones or other oestrogen therapy
- Heavy smokers
- Those who have very severe varicose veins
- The very obese
- People who are very tall (over 6ft/1.8m) or short (under 5ft/1.5m)

Travelpharm The Travelpharm website, www.travelpharm.com, offers up-to-date guidance on travel-related health & has a range of medications available through their online mini-pharmacy.

Irish Republic

Tropical Medical Bureau Grafton Street Medical Centre, Grafton Buildings, 34 Grafton St, Dublin 2; ☏ 1 671 9200; www.tmb.ie. A useful website specific to tropical destinations. Also check website for other bureaux locations throughout Ireland.

USA

Centers for Disease Control 1600 Clifton Rd, Atlanta, GA 30333; ☏ 800 311 3435; travellers' health hotline: 888 232 3299; www.cdc.gov/travel. The central source of travel information in the USA. The invaluable *Health Information for International Travel*, published annually, is available from the Division of Quarantine at this address.
Connaught Laboratories PO Box 187, Swiftwater, PA 18370; ☏ 800 822 2463. They will send a free list

of specialist tropical-medicine physicians in your state.
IAMAT (International Association for Medical Assistance to Travelers) 1623 Military Rd, 279, Niagara Falls, NY14304-1745; ☏ 716 754 4883; e info@iamat.org; www.iamat.org. A non-profit organisation that provides lists of English-speaking doctors abroad.
International Medicine Center 920 Frostwood Dr, Suite 670, Houston, TX 77024; ☏ 713 550 2000; www.traveldoc.com

Canada

IAMAT Suite 1, 1287 St Clair Av W, Toronto, Ontario M6E 1B8; ☏ 416 652 0137; www.iamat.org
TMVC Suite 314, 1030 W Georgia St, Vancouver BC V6E 2Y3; ☏ 1 888 288 8682; www.tmvc.com

Australia, New Zealand, Singapore

TMVC ☏ 1300 65 88 44; www.tmvc.com/au. 31 clinics in Australia, New Zealand & Singapore, including:

A deep vein thrombosis (DVT) is a blood clot that forms in the deep leg veins. This is very different from irritating but harmless superficial phlebitis. DVT causes swelling and redness of one leg, usually with heat and pain in one calf and sometimes the thigh. A DVT is only dangerous if a clot breaks away and travels to the lungs (pulmonary embolus). Symptoms of a pulmonary embolus (PE) include chest pain that is worse on breathing in deeply, shortness of breath, and sometimes coughing up small amounts of blood. The symptoms commonly start three to ten days after a long flight. Anyone who thinks that they might have a DVT needs to see a doctor immediately who will arrange a scan. Warfarin tablets (to thin the blood) are then taken for at least six months.

PREVENTION OF DVT Several conditions make the problem more likely. Immobility is the key, and factors like reduced oxygen in cabin air and dehydration may also contribute. To reduce the risk of thrombosis on a long journey:

- Exercise before and after the flight
- Keep mobile before and during the flight; move around every couple of hours
- During the flight drink plenty of water or juices
- Avoid taking sleeping pills and excessive tea, coffee and alcohol
- Perform exercises that mimic walking and tense the calf muscles
- Consider wearing flight socks or support stockings (see www.legshealth.com)
- Taking a meal of oily fish (mackerel, trout, salmon, sardines, etc) in the 24 hours before departure reduces blood clotability and thus DVT risk
- The jury is still out on whether it is worth taking an aspirin before flying, but this can be discussed with your GP.

If you think you are at increased risk of a clot, ask your doctor if it is safe to travel.

Auckland Canterbury Arcade, 170 Queen St, Auckland; ↘ 9 373 3531
Brisbane 6th floor, 247 Adelaide St, Brisbane, QLD 4000; ↘ 7 3221 9066
Melbourne 393 Little Bourke St, 2nd floor, Melbourne, VIC 3000; ↘ 3 9602 5788
Sydney Dymocks Bldg, 7th floor, 428 George St, Sydney, NSW 2000; ↘ 2 9221 7133
IAMAT PO Box 5049, Christchurch 5, New Zealand; www.iamat.org

South Africa and Namibia
SAA-Netcare Travel Clinics P Bag X34, Benmore 2010; www.travelclinic.co.za. Clinics throughout South Africa.
TMVC 113 D F Malan Dr, Roosevelt Pk, Johannesburg; ↘ 011 888 7488; www.tmvc.com.au. Consult website for details of other clinics in South Africa & Namibia.

Switzerland
IAMAT 57 Chemin des Voirets, 1212 Grand Lancy, Geneva; www.iamat.org

ALTITUDE SICKNESS The main problem in the Altiplano is altitude sickness, a condition that occurs due to a recent gain in altitude. Symptoms include dizziness, headache, fatigue, nausea, vomiting, anorexia and difficulty sleeping, although all need not be present. Men and women are affected equally. Acclimatisation is the process by which the body adapts to the lower oxygen. In order to acclimatise there should a slow ascent to altitude. The general rule of thumb is not to sleep more than 300m above sea level the previous night, although you may climb higher during that day. In this way altitude sickness should be prevented. There are a number of prophylactic medications that can also be taken to reduce the likelihood of altitude sickness. The most common prophylactic drug used is acetazolamide

(Diamox). Seek advice from your local GP or travel clinic on the use of this medication to reduce the likelihood of altitude sickness. When you first arrive, you will need to drink plenty of fluids as your body adapts to the higher altitude.

There are a number of other medications that are available for altitude sickness, but there is little or no evidence to support any of them. These include nifedipine and ginkgo biloba. Interestingly, the local population drinks a tea or chews a leaf from the coca plant, and there is currently little knowledge on why this may work (see box, *The coca leaf and altitude sickness*, opposite). If you do choose to drink the tea, make sure that it is made with water that has been boiled, and drink in moderation.

Two other conditions that occur at altitude are high-altitude cerebral oedema (HACE) and high-altitude pulmonary oedema (HAPE). HACE is a very severe form of altitude sickness, can be fatal and is characterised by symptoms of altitude sickness plus ataxia, or difficulty in walking in a straight line (you can do heel-to-toe walking to check for this). The cure is descent, oxygen and medical intervention. HAPE is also a potentially fatal disease that causes fluid to get onto your lungs. It is characterised by shortness of breath and blood brought up from the lungs. Again treatment is descent, oxygen and medical intervention.

SUNBURN Sunburn can be a major issue, especially at high altitude. Indeed, according to the Ministerio de Salud y Deportes, the ultraviolet radiation index peaks between November and February (Bolivian summer) at an average of 16, which equates to a maximum exposure time of eight minutes. That means bring a hat, sunglasses, sun block of SPF25 or above and avoid the sun between noon and 14.00 if possible.

WATER To be safe it's probably best not to drink the water in Bolivia. Besides, bottled water is widely available and not expensive to buy – go for brands like Naturagua or Vital for the best taste. Remember: *con gas* is bubbly, *sin gas* is still. If you do want to purify your own, then boiling water kills all the microbes that are likely to make you ill, although it should be noted that water will boil below 100° at altitude and so may not kill all of the bugs. Chemical methods such as iodine or chlorine do not render water as safe to drink as boiling, but are effective. The most effective is iodine, and you can also pick up neutralisers to remove the taste of the chemical. Don't forget to avoid ice and watch out for inadequately cooked or prepared food such as ice cream and salads.

STREET FOOD Street and market food can be tempting as it's so crazily cheap and readily available, but beware of places where you can't tell how hygienic they are in terms of both preparation and serving. As a rule of thumb, stick to places that look crowded with locals and a mix of people from different backgrounds and try to eat the sizzling hot food.

DIARRHOEA Diarrohea is very common in Bolivia so remember the mantra: peel it, boil it, cook it or forget it. Another common way of becoming infected is through washing your hands with dirty water. It may be worth investing in some alcohol hand rub that you can wash your hands with after using the bathroom and before meals. This has been shown to be effective in reducing the spread of infection. If you do get ill, then drinks containing sugar and salt are most easily absorbed. Sachets of rehydration mixtures, such as Diorylate or Electrolade, are particularly good, or mixing a teaspoon of salt and two of sugar in a glass of bottled or boiled water will also do the trick. Remember that travellers' diarrhoea is more often than not self-limiting, and should disappear in a few days. If it does not, then

THE COCA LEAF AND ALTITUDE SICKNESS

Rob Conway (www.blueventures.org)

Many South American nationals and Western tourists drink, chew or suck the leaf from the coca shrub (*Erythroxlyon coca*) to abate the symptoms of mountain sickness, locally known as *sorojche*. It is known that 75% of the Bolivian population living at and above 4,000m chew coca leaves, whilst only 20% are habitual chewers at 2,400m and only 3% at sea level. In a recent study it was found that within the travelling population, over 90% of those asked took coca.

The coca leaf has been used throughout the ages, was a currency and has been implicated in local magic. The coca leaf was damned by the Roman Catholics in 1569, and the Spanish, on colonising South America, used to give the local lower classes coca leaves as they felt it made them work harder and increased concentration. It became an active part of the Inquisition.

More recently mining communities declared the coca as a basic article, and its sale mandatory in mining and railroad communities. Today the leaf is an intricate part of society, where it is exchanged both as a social interchange and also in marriage. Much like the Roman Catholic Church centuries earlier, a large proportion of the Bolivian national economic budget is supported by the USA, who wish to eradicate coca from the country to reduce the widespread use of one of its constitutes, cocaine, from American soil.

So does coca work to stop altitude sickness? Initial research suggests that it may. Although only observational, recent data indicates that it works both as a treatment and a prophylaxis, thereby stopping it happening before you even get it.

If this is the case, then why does it work? Coca's most controversial and possibly most significant ingredient is cocaine. This may act to make you breathe faster, by increasing your oxygen intake and therefore counteracting the lack of oxygen in the surrounding atmosphere, although this cannot fully explain the mechanism. It could also be the centrally acting stimulating effects of the cocaine that make you feel euphoric and so reduce the symptoms of altitude sickness while you acclimatise.

The leaf has also been shown to reduce the coagulative properties of your blood, to contain high levels of both antioxidants and vitamin B12 that could have a limiting effect on altitude sickness, though none of this has been scientifically proven.

If you'd like to find out more on this or would like to help the research into whether coca is effective in stopping altitude sickness, please go to the website www.altitudesickness.org and fill out the online questionnaire.

seek medical advice. Also note that at altitude you may experience higher amounts of wind. This can be painful and rather embarrassing, but it is perfectly normal due to the reduced atmospheric pressure.

Again the Bolivians will tell you to drink coca tea in order to relieve the symptoms. In general, try to avoid very hot drinks and drink clear fluids that are either warm or tepid.

TRAVEL INSURANCE Make sure you have insurance covering the cost of repatriation if need be and remember that much of Bolivia is above 3,000m, which means that your insurance may not even cover you. Check before you leave that it will cover you at altitude, as well as declaring any predisposing conditions that you may have. And if you plan to do any climbing, then this again may not be covered. To check, the British Mountaineering Council (*www.bmc.com*) offers a range of different insurance policies that may suit your needs.

THE SIX MAIN SCAMS PLAYED ON TOURISTS IN BOLIVIA

THE FRIENDLY SOUTH AMERICAN TOURIST AND THE PLAIN-CLOTHES POLICE OFFICER A person comes up to you with some friendly comments and asks for directions. Moments later, someone else approaches waving an ID, saying he's a police officer. He asks to see your passport, along with a copy of your entry stamp to Bolivia, and your new 'friend' says that this is not unusual and shows his, encouraging you to do the same. The imposter ('plain clothes') police officer then asks to inspect your money for counterfeit bills and/or your bag for drugs. During the process the two cohorts will steal your money and/or the contents of your bag. There are some variations, including asking you to get in a taxi with them so they can go to the police station. During the taxi ride they'll search through your wallet and bag while deftly removing items. This scam is particularly common in Oruro and La Paz.

Best defence: assume that anybody claiming to be a plain-clothes police officer in a non-official location is a con artist. Ask to walk to a police officer in uniform or to the tourist police office for confirmation of their status. Carry a photocopy of your passport (a colour, laminated copy works well) and entry stamp separate from your wallet, and if pressed on the street or in a taxi, only ever show this. Don't let anyone except a uniformed police officer go through your wallet or bags and even then insist on doing it in a police station or similar official location. And never get into a taxi with a stranger.

IT'S RAINING MONEY (OR CREDIT CARDS, OR PACKETS OF WHITE POWDER, ETC) Some scams involve dropped money or other potentially valuable items. If you bend over and pick up the item, you risk falling victim to the scam. You may be accused of having stolen it – and then asked to pay to avoid arrest. You may be asked to share your find with another while having your own money taken in a deft sleight of hand. Or you may simply be pickpocketed or have your bag snatched during the whole bending-over process.

Best defence: ignore items dropped 'accidentally' in front of you. How likely is it that someone with a big wad of money would drop it while hurrying along a street – without noticing? Just keep walking, minding your own business. If anybody approaches you with 'dropped' money, a phone card or a credit card, become instantly suspicious, watch your bags and, rudely if necessary, get away from the situation.

HELPFUL CLEANERS You're walking down the street and all of a sudden some helpful person is pointing out spit, vomit, mustard or mayonnaise on your bag or the shoulder of your jacket. That person or someone else then offers to clean it off for you, and during this helpful cleaning process either of these two or a third person cleans out your pockets and bag, or runs off with the jacket or bag you have taken off to clean.

Best defence: ignore said mess that needs cleaning and keep walking. Wait until you get back to your hotel or a safe restaurant bathroom to clean up. Do not necessarily go to the nearest convenient spot as it could be a set-up to rob you in there.

SAFETY

Bolivia is generally a very safe country to travel through. Just be sensible and street smart and you should be fine. Take caution in crowded areas and after dark, making sure that your money is well concealed in inner pockets, plus keep a photocopy of your passport with you at all times. The following tips will make you more streetwise, but remember: something always happens when you least expect it.

Violent crime is rare in Bolivia and violence is rarely directed towards tourists. In more remote areas, however, there have been reports of occasional violent assaults, most recently in the autumn of 2005 when news agencies in New Zealand

THE TRAVELLER IN DISTRESS This one is a fairly common scam used in different ways by different people all over La Paz. Specifically, there's a bald or shaved-headed, wild-eyed Peruvian who claims to be from New York who's got a number of stories ranging from 'I just got out of prison' to 'I just got robbed last night' who then will ask you for money. A middle-aged woman claiming to be Canadian also tries it on sometimes.

Best defence: don't give these people anything other than a lecture about the immorality of what they're doing. They've been in La Paz for years living off kind-hearted tourists and locals, thereby ruining things for those travellers who genuinely have been stricken with misfortune. In general, be sure to verify the validity of any request for assistance, especially financial, from other travellers. If in doubt, offer non-financial assistance, like helping to go to the police or using the phone office, etc. If you sense any reluctance to take this kind of assistance the story is probably a scam.

SLASHERS OF BAGS AND PICKERS OF POCKETS These two types of scammers usually hang out in bustling markets or busy train or bus stations. Beware of anyone who bumps against you or casually brushes against your back.

Best defence: never carry large amounts of cash in your pockets or bags. It's always wise to keep valuables in a money belt underneath your clothing. And likewise, you probably shouldn't carry anything of value in the outside pockets of your backpack. In markets and bus stations it's worth carrying your small backpack in front of you to reduce the chances of anything being slashed or otherwise opened. It's also not a bad idea to distribute copies of your passport, tickets, travellers' cheques numbers, etc, to your travelling companions.

BE VIGILANT AT BUS AND TRAIN STATIONS Thieves converge in bus and train stations, waiting to prey on dazed and disorientated travellers. A favourite tactic is for this ilk to come up and ask you for directions, and while you and your friends are momentarily distracted, another of them comes over and snatches your bags and runs.

Best defence: see the above defences against bag-slashers and pickpockets. In addition, be vigilant, and don't take your eye off your packs for a millisecond. It's also a good idea to watch while things are being loaded and unloaded on your bus or train. Ideally, travel in twos and have one person watch belongings while the other deals with tickets and distractions. Even better, make a habit of hooking your leg through the loops on your backpack when sitting at restaurants, cafés, and in bus and train stations.

Note: if you do get robbed, go to the tourist police office where officials will painstakingly fill out a theft form with you that you can use for possible reimbursement of funds through your travel insurance.

Advice provided by Gravity Assisted Mountain Biking in La Paz (www.gravitybolivia.com).

reported that Vanessa Claire Johnson, 31, and her Swedish partner were shot while out walking in the Ulla Ulla National Reserve, an area popular with nature enthusiasts. The motive is likely to have been robbery.

FEMALE TRAVELLERS Take radio taxis after dark, not ordinary taxis. They may be a few Bolivianos more expensive but are a safer option. Rather than hailing a taxi on the street, head for one of the main hotels on the Prado, such as the Radisson or the Plaza, and take one of the radio taxis queuing out the front.

Likewise, avoid staying in the lowest-price lodgings and head instead for the budget hostels in busy traveller areas. For the sake of a few dollars, it's better to have the security of other travellers around you.

WHAT TO TAKE AND ELECTRICITY

Shopping in Bolivia tends to be done in markets rather than supermarkets, hence haggling is the norm and familiar items at home can be hard to find. The secret, therefore, is to come prepared without over-packing. A Thermos flask and a head-mounted torch will prove invaluable during your trip. It's also useful to bring a small supply of pencils, key rings and colouring books for visits to rural communities. It's far more responsible to offer these as gifts rather than sweets or money. On the other hand, you can buy just about everything you'll need, such as fleeces, waterproof jackets and daypacks, at local markets – and for a fraction of the price back home. A few things harder to find around the markets include contact lens solution, condoms and tampons, plus electrical adapters. The local electricity supply is primarily 110 volts in La Paz, 220 elsewhere. American (flat) two-pin plugs are the most commonly accepted.

$ MONEY AND BANKING

The official currency is the Boliviano (Bs), with around 15Bs to £1 and 8Bs to US$1 according to current rates. The US dollar is also widely accepted, so it's best to keep a mix of dollars and Bolivianos on you at all times. Try also to avoid accepting large denomination bills as nobody ever, ever, has any loose change. You can see what Bolivian banknotes look like by checking the website www.banknotes.com/bo.htm.

ATMs are widely available in larger cities but travellers' cheques are less widely accepted outside of La Paz and Santa Cruz as these have to be changed at a recognised *casa de cambio*. As a rule of thumb, changing money on the street is not recommended.

It's useful to know that Magri Turismo, a tour operator with national coverage, acts as the local American Express agent across Bolivia. Citibank also has a presence in Bolivia but refuses to handle enquiries from international customers – even if you are an account holder.

BUDGETING You can live pretty cheaply in Bolivia compared with other South American countries, getting by on US$20 per day if you stay in hostels, eat a set menu lunch and take buses everywhere. If you want to travel in a bit of style you can still keep costs down with an average double room in a three- or four-star hotel around US$40 and a slap-up meal at an international restaurant for two around US$12 with wine.

The one thing that will push the budget is internal flights, which are universally pricey in Bolivia, notably between La Paz and Santa Cruz. The cost of a return ticket is a flat-rate US$200 but, believe me, it's worth it – the alternative is a bone-shaking 20-hour bus ride along the spine of the country.

GETTING AROUND

Getting around the country is pretty cheap if you stick to the bus network and are prepared for some sleepless nights and lengthy journeys – take your iPod and a blanket.

✈ BY PLANE AeroSur (*www.aerosur.com*) is the better regarded of the two main domestic carriers with an extensive domestic network and some flights within Latin America.

AeroSur will change your flight tickets for a fee of 50Bs. You can also pay a US$15 fee to upgrade from economy to business class (so long as there is spare capacity). To do this, simply arrive at check-in one hour before departure and ask the assistant. AeroSur also offer the *Club AeroSur* loyalty scheme, whereby you earn one free flight for every five flights taken (travelling on a full-fare ticket).

Lloyd Aereo Boliviano (LAB; *www.labairlines.com*) also runs a large domestic network and has a select few international connections, including flights between La Paz and Miami.

Amazonas (*www.amaszonas.com*) has cornered the market in popular flights from La Paz to Rurrenabaque, with onward connections throughout the Amazon region. It's a small but expanding company with a widening network but, so far, still plagued by schedule problems and prone to cancelling flights at very short notice, sometimes leaving passengers stranded.

During rainy season internal flights can be subject to some major delays.

BY TRAIN Bolivia has 4,370km of railway network with Oruro the country's rail hub. There are two trains heading south from Oruro to Uyuni, Tupiza and then on to the Argentinian border at Villazon: the more comfortable **Expresso del Sur** (Tue and Fri, 15.30) and the cheaper but rougher **Wara Wara del Sur** (Sun and Wed, 19.00).

For full details of train schedules and prices, check the website www.fca.com.bo/fca1/itinerarios_tarifas_1.htm.

BY BUS The bus network is the main means of communication in Bolivia, with a huge number of bus companies based at bus terminals across the country. See separate destination chapters for more information. One company with national coverage and a well-developed network of international services is **Litoral**, based in La Paz (*Caseta #29;* ⤷ *228 1920;* e *info@litoralmiramar.com; www.litoralmiramar.com*). This border-spanning bus company has connections from La Paz to Peru and Chile, including border crossings at Arica (Chile) and Puno (Peru).

DRIVING Some would suggest that driving in Bolivia is for the brave. Others would say it's plain stupid. In a country where paved roads account for only 7% of total roads, driving is generally a skill best reserved for Bolivia's army of minibus drivers, who are well versed in negotiating the lethal combination of steep mountain roads and poor road surfaces. Worse still, 80% of roads are affected by flooding during the rainy season (Dec to Mar). If you do drive, keep to the right and make sure you have good insurance.

For more details about road conditions, contact the Servicio Nacional de Caminos in La Paz (⤷ *235 7212; www.snc.gov.bo*).

Car hire To hire a car you will need to be over 25, have your home driving licence and passport, and an international credit card. Costs are generally high and you should expect to pay a deposit of up to US$1,000. Always check very carefully what is included in the hire company's insurance and consider getting your own personal documentation translated into Spanish before arrival.

Bicycle and scooter hire To rent two-wheel transport, head for the expat-run biking specialist, Gravity Assisted Mountain Biking in La Paz (⤷ *231 3849; www.gravitybolivia.com*), located just off the Prado.

ACCOMMODATION

Standards of accommodation vary widely from cheap but dingy crash pads through to swanky international hotels with the best of the choice, obviously, available in larger cities, such as La Paz and Santa Cruz.

Kory Kramer

Bolivia offers a wide variety of mountain-biking destinations, from the wide-open, flat Altiplano with its challengingly high elevation, to the sweltering heat of the Amazon region, plus everything in between. Mountain biking as a sport is relatively new to Bolivia and, as such, many of the most spectacular possibilities are still waiting to be explored by bikers.

For one-day rides, the most developed options are all based around La Paz and, for those with little riding experience, the downhill ride from La Cumbre (just outside La Paz) to Coroico on what is sometimes called the world's most dangerous road, is the most popular route. It descends vertically 3,600m over 64km from high-altitude flora, nestled amongst snow-capped mountains, through lush rainforest before arriving amid the heat and dripping humidity of the jungle.

Alternative options from La Paz include the less trafficked, but not so scenic, Zongo Valley and Chacaltaya descents.

Hard-core, experienced, fit and acclimatised riders, however, have a much wider range of possibilities, from world-class single tracks just outside La Paz, to longer, multiple-day tours across the mysterious high plains to Sorata, with the option of continuing on to Copacabana on the shores of Lake Titicaca.

Bolivia also shares with Chile the claim to one of the longest downhill rides in the world, starting in Sajama National Park at an altitude of over 5,000m before descending westwards to the Chilean city of Arica on the Pacific coast. For those who are extremely fit (and possibly a touch insane), this ride can also be done in the opposite direction.

If you plan on bringing your own bike to Bolivia, you will need to keep in mind that the rough Bolivian terrain is very tough on bikes. The dry, dusty and rocky trails tend to eat through hubs and suspension, while wet, muddy conditions will quickly wear down the drive train – not to mention make for miserable riding conditions. The wet season in Bolivia lasts from December to February, during which time the dirt roads become mired in mud and heavy rains reduce visibility, making roads that many already consider dangerous at the best of times even worse.

You should also consider that quality name-brand parts and qualified mechanics are hard to come by in most parts of the country. If you're riding around La Paz, you can get parts from the Gravity Assisted Mountain Biking office in La Paz (page 72) and consult with their mechanics. In other areas of the country, however, you will need to be your own mechanic, equipped with spare parts and the proper tools to make your own repairs.

Most of all, make safety your priority. Numerous tour agencies in La Paz's Calle Sagarnaga offer biking trips, but many fail to adhere to basic safety standards, such as providing reflective jackets, helmets and regularly checking break cables. There have been fatalities on biking trails, including French and Israeli nationals in recent years, so be sure to ask carefully about safety and equipment before booking your trip.

Typically you can find a decent double with private bathroom for about US$25 per night; bookings are not generally necessary outside of festival periods. Homestays with Bolivian families are also an increasingly popular option with the going rate around US$8 per night for a private bedroom, a decent lunch and snack breakfast. Homestays are better arranged once on the ground and targeted more at the backpacker market.

If you are a member of the **Youth Hostel Association** (*www.hostellingbolivia.org*), your card will be welcome at selected member properties across the country; more information from www.hostellingbolivia.org.

It's also worth having a look at the **Bolivia Hostels** website (*www.boliviahostels.com*) which is run by a friendly hostel owner based in Sucre.

Finally, **Ranking Bolivia** (*rankingbolivia@hotmail.com*), a new, independent tourist information service with a growing network of offices, is also worth checking with as they keep updated records of feedback from other travellers about standards at various guesthouses in the region. They don't have a website (as yet) but will answer queries by email: *rankingbolivia@hotmail.com*.

✗ EATING AND DRINKING

Corn, potatoes and quinoa, a high-protein grain, are native to the Bolivian Andes and form a staple of the local diet, especially in the Altiplano. Lunch is the main meal of the day in this region and always starts with a hearty bowl of soup. In the more tropical south, the proximity to the Argentinian border ensures that steak is a mainstay of any meal.

To wash down your meal, Bolivia is also home to a small but respectable wine industry and a brewing industry that produces some very quaffable beers, notably the Inca, a black beer that will appeal to Guinness fans. For the more adventurous, any major Bolivian fiesta will doubtless be accompanied by lashings of *singani*, Bolivia's answer to Peruvian *pisco*.

SHOPPING

You can pick up some bargains on a Bolivian shopping spree with alpaca goods the best value and quality to be found locally. Be prepared, however, to train your eye before making a purchase, as there are plenty of fakes out there for the unsuspecting shopper.

Generally shopping hours are Monday to Friday 09.00–12.30 and 14.30–19.00, Saturday 09.00–12.30.

ARTS AND ENTERTAINMENT

Bolivia is not exactly known as a hotbed of the arts. There are few galleries and cinemas cater more for fans of Hollywood blockbusters and sub-Benny Hill local slapstick features than arthouse films. Indeed, the long-awaited cinematheque in La Paz remains a mere building site today after years of arguments, wasted opportunity and corruption. Music is, however, better represented with orchestras, concerts and live music venues, especially in the larger cities.

Culture vultures should seek out the Casa de la Cultura in major cities and consult notices about cultural presentations often located in, or close to, local tourist information offices. Another good source is the likes of the Alliance Française and Goethe Institute, which do organise exhibitions, photography events and recitals as part of their cultural exchange programme.

The key, therefore, is a little investigative work. You never know: you might unearth a cultural gem.

PHOTOGRAPHY

Keen snappers are relatively well catered for in Bolivia with developing facilities easily located in larger cities – indeed, Agfa and Kodak both have a major presence. Slide film is developed cheaply but it does tend to be more expensive to buy, hence it's best to bring a ready supply. Likewise black and white film can prove a bit tricky. On the plus side, however, you can burn your slides to a CD-Rom at

I like a few drinks at the end of a hard week the same as the next man. And I liked to think that I could take my drink, too. That is until I came to Bolivia and my whole concept of alcohol usage was turned inside out. When it comes to boozing in Bolivia there is but one rule: Bolivians may not drink for weeks on end but, when they finally do, they drink to fall down. It's a question of either complete abstinence or going all out for a three-day bender.

Worse still, the preferred tipple among Bolivians is known locally as a *chuflay*. This lethal concoction is a mix of Sprite and *singani*, a brandy-like spirit derived from the white Muscatel de Alejandria grape. It is, let me assure you, guaranteed to inspire the kind of temple-splitting hangover that leaves you curled up in the foetal position and begging for mercy.

After my first Bolivian fiesta, I swore blind I'd never touch alcohol again in my entire life. Talk about binge drinking. Beer, wine, whisky and the infamous *chuflay* were all wheeled out in quick succession. As the night progressed it became clear to me that there was no escape. Bolivian friends insisted I joined them in endless toasts to our respective health. Complete strangers insisted the token gringo of the night joined them in a hands-across-the-ocean shot of something lethal. And my Bolivian host family, with whom I was lodging and who had witnessed my previous attempts at dancing, insisted that I needed to be very, very well oiled before attempting to throw some Latino shapes on the makeshift dancefloor.

This friend-making and toast-sharing would have been all well and good if I'd had the rest of the weekend to sleep it off. The problem was, however, that I had a 07.00 bus to Peru the next day to complete a tedious but vital visa run to renew my right to remain in the country.

I have rather hazy memories of the next day on the bus to the Bolivian border town of Desaguadero. I do remember forcing open the window with all my remaining strength to gasp for fresh air in a desperate hope to avoid using the paper bag tucked into the seat in front of me.

But, most of all, as the border guard stamped my passport with three months more in Bolivia, I remember swearing that I would never, never try to drink like a Bolivian again.

photo shops around La Paz and Santa Cruz, while many places now offer facilities to download digital images from your camera to CD-Rom. And if you're still shooting on an old-style SLR, then fear not, equipment, lenses and repairs can all be found in La Paz.

ℓ MEDIA AND COMMUNICATIONS

According to the Inter Press Service news agency (*www.ipsnews.net*), Bolivia's information highway is being blocked by rural poverty.

There are barely 62,000 internet connections today in Bolivia, a country with a population of around nine million, as well as an illiteracy rate of 25.7% in the countryside and 6.44% in the cities, according to the most recent census.

The Telecommunications Superintendency reports that 40 telephone service providers offer access to the internet, of which the largest is the national telephone company, Entel, which was privatised in 1996.

Future growth of connectivity will be slow, however, according to the availability of basic telephone and electricity services, which are the main obstacles to the introduction of the new technology in remote areas.

In the few remote areas where internet service is available, rates can run as high as US$2.50 per hour, compared with US$0.25 per hour in La Paz. As a result, these services tend to be used exclusively by tourists or occasional visitors.

In urban areas, however, the network is far more developed with direct dial widely available, chips for mobile phones easily purchased and even wi-fi internet now installed at selected airports, major hotels and in some cafes. Moreover, Entel call centres and makeshift internet cafés can be found on every street corner in major towns.

PAYING A FAIR PRICE FOR YOUR SOUVENIRS

Vania Rivero (www.boliviahandicrafts.com)

Bolivia offers a wealth of artisan goods but they vary in quality. Some indigenous groups produce textiles and ceramics using traditional methods, while studios in larger cities take traditional crafts and give them a contemporary spin. As much of the best produce is exported, there are few places around La Paz where you can buy good-quality goods and be sure that a percentage of your money is going directly back into the hands of artisans (see the list below for suggestions).

The streets around the market area, notably Sagarnaga, Linares and Illampu, are full of small vendors offering goods at lower prices. But beware: these are often cheaper, Peruvian-made crafts and, while it's often possible, even encouraged, to negotiate the price down, the quality can be variable at best. For assured quality, then, stick to the better-known shops with a good reputation. The prices will be higher – a basic 100% alpaca sweater starts from US$30 – but the quality will be far superior. And besides, at this price it's still far cheaper than buying in Peru or Ecuador.

Originals of the most typical Bolivian textiles, made from llama and alpaca wool and dyed with natural inks to form designs typical of local communities, can only be found in fair trade shops in La Paz and Sucre. These designs have often been passed down through the generations in the Andes. Similarly, traditional ceramics, based on designs adapted from the culture of Tiahuanacuo, are best sourced through established shops. Many are sold cheaply in La Paz's Witches' Market but again quality can be variable. If you do buy here, make sure to ask the vendor to wrap it carefully as these items are notoriously fragile to transport.

WHERE TO BUY CRAFTS IN LA PAZ

Ayni Bolivia Calle Illampu #704 (Hotel Rosario); ✆ 245 1658; . Supporting over 300 artisans from poor, rural communities, many of them women on low incomes, this shop stocks over 300 items across a range of designs & styles. Credit cards accepted. *Open Mon–Sat 08.00–21.00, Sun 14.00–21.00.*

Jiwasankiri Galeria Gala Centro 1/F, Calle Sagarnaga. Stocking primarily ceramics, this shop works with local NGOs to support community artisans. *Open Mon–Sat 09.00–12.30 & 14.30–18.00.*

Artesanias Sorata Calle Sagarnaga corner with Calle Linares; no tel. Supporting women artisans from La Paz & Sorata, they specialise in llama-wool goods with original designs. Credit cards accepted. *Open Mon–Sat 09.00–12.30 & 14.30–18.00.*

Comart Calle Linares #958; no tel. Stocking a good variety of crafts from across Bolivia, the second floor is given over to a small museum showcasing Jalq'a & Tarabuco textiles. Credit cards accepted. *Open Mon–Sat 09.00–12.30 & 14.30–18.00.*

Artecampo Galeria Centro de Moda Subsuelo, Calle 21 de Calacoto. Best known for its bright colours & innovative use of natural materials, this shop focuses on artisan crafts from the Beni, Chaco & Amazon regions. *Open Mon–Sat 09.00–18.00.*

Ariadne Van Zandbergen

EQUIPMENT Although with some thought and an eye for composition you can take reasonable photos with a 'point-and-shoot' camera, you need an SLR camera if you are at all serious about photography. Modern SLRs tend to be very clever, with automatic programmes for almost every possible situation, but remember that these programmes are limited in the sense that the camera cannot think, but only make calculations. Every starting amateur photographer should read a photographic manual for beginners and get to grips with such basics as the relationship between aperture and shutter speed.

Always buy the best lens you can afford. The lens determines the quality of your photo more than the camera body. Fixed fast lenses are ideal, but very costly. Zoom lenses are easier to change composition without changing lenses the whole time. If you carry only one lens, a 28–70mm (digital 17–55mm) or similar zoom should be ideal. For a second lens, a lightweight 80–200mm or 70–300mm (digital 55–200mm) or similar will be excellent for candid shots and varying your composition. Wildlife photography will be very frustrating if you don't have at least a 300mm lens. For a small loss of quality, tele-converters are a cheap and compact way to increase magnification: a 300 lens with a 1.4x converter becomes 420mm, and with a 2x it becomes 600mm. Note, however, that 1.4x and 2x tele-converters reduce the speed of your lens by 1.4 and 2 stops respectively.

For photography from a vehicle, a solid beanbag, which you can make yourself very cheaply, will be necessary to avoid blurred images, and is more useful than a tripod. A clamp with a tripod head screwed onto it can be attached to the vehicle as well. Modern dedicated flash units are easy to use; aside from the obvious need to flash when you photograph at night, you can improve a lot of photos in difficult 'high contrast' or very dull light with some fill-in flash. It pays to have a proper flash unit as opposed to a built-in camera flash.

DIGITAL/FILM Digital photography is now the preference of most amateur and professional photographers, with the resolution of digital cameras improving the whole time. For ordinary prints a 6 megapixel camera is fine. For better results and the possibility to enlarge images and for professional reproduction, higher resolution is available up to 16 megapixels.

Memory space is important. The number of pictures you can fit on a memory card depends on the quality you choose. Calculate in advance how many pictures you can fit on a card and either take enough cards to last for your trip, or take a storage drive onto which you can download the content. A laptop gives the advantage that you can see your pictures properly at the end of each day and edit and delete rejects, but a storage device is lighter and less bulky. These drives come in different capacities up to 80GB.

A separate report by the Bolivian newspaper, *La Razon* (*www.la-razon.com*) in 2005 indicated that only 22.7% of the population have regular access to a fixed or mobile telephone connection, with around 2.5 million Bolivians on the phone. That compares with 75.1% owning a radio and 54% owning a TV, but only 3.4% having an internet connection.

One of the biggest challenges for the government, therefore, will be to improve the communications infrastructure of the country, especially in more rural areas.

USEFUL NUMBERS
Information 104
Domestic & international operator assistance 101

Bear in mind that digital camera batteries, computers and other storage devices need charging, so make sure you have all the chargers, cables and converters with you. Most hotels have charging points, but do enquire about this in advance. When camping you might have to rely on charging from the car battery; a spare battery is invaluable.

If you are shooting film, 100 to 200 ISO print film and 50 to 100 ISO slide film are ideal. Low ISO film is slow but fine grained and gives the best colour saturation, but will need more light, so support in the form of a tripod or monopod is important. You can also bring a few 'fast' 400 ISO films for low-light situations where a tripod or flash is no option.

DUST AND HEAT Dust and heat are often a problem. Keep your equipment in a sealed bag, stow films in an airtight container (eg: a small cooler bag) and avoid exposing equipment and film to the sun. Digital cameras are prone to collecting dust particles on the sensor which results in spots on the image. The dirt mostly enters the camera when changing lenses, so be careful when doing this. To some extent photos can be 'cleaned' up afterwards in Photoshop, but this is time-consuming. You can have your camera sensor professionally cleaned, or you can do this yourself with special brushes and swabs made for the purpose, but note that touching the sensor might cause damage and should only be done with the greatest care.

LIGHT The most striking outdoor photographs are often taken during the hour or two of 'golden light' after dawn and before sunset. Shooting in low light may enforce the use of very low shutter speeds, in which case a tripod will be required to avoid camera shake.

With careful handling, side lighting and back lighting can produce stunning effects, especially in soft light and at sunrise or sunset. Generally, however, it is best to shoot with the sun behind you. When photographing animals or people in the harsh midday sun, images taken in light but even shade are likely to be more effective than those taken in direct sunlight or patchy shade, since the latter conditions create too much contrast.

PROTOCOL In some countries, it is unacceptable to photograph local people without permission, and many people will refuse to pose or will ask for a donation. In such circumstances, don't try to sneak photographs as you might get yourself into trouble. Even the most willing subject will often pose stiffly when a camera is pointed at them; relax them by making a joke, and take a few shots in quick succession to improve the odds of capturing a natural pose.

Ariadne Van Zandbergen is a professional travel and wildlife photographer specialising in Africa. She runs The Africa Image Library. For photo requests, visit www.africaimagelibrary.co.za or contact her on ariadne@hixnet.co.za.

BUSINESS

Generally business hours are Monday to Friday 09.00–12.30 and 14.30–19.00, Saturday 09.00–12.30.

Some banks and government offices work through the lunch hour and most also operate on Saturday mornings, but downtown La Paz can feel like a graveyard on Saturday afternoons and Sundays.

When conducting international business, Bolivians tend to be well presented, courteous and respectful, addressing each other as *señor* (Mr) or *señora* (Mrs). They expect the same of their guests. They are, however, notorious for their poor time-keeping (see box, *Bolivia time*, page 32). By all means make appointments but don't

Bolivia has an active media sector, although newspaper readership is limited by low literacy levels; hence radio is the important medium to disseminate news in more rural areas. The media rights body, Reporters Without Borders (*www.rsf.org*), notes that threats and violence against the media can accompany social protests.

NEWSPAPERS

La Razon La Paz daily (*www.la-razon.com*)
Los Tiempos Cochabamba daily (*www.lostiempos.com*)
El Diario La Paz daily (*www.eldiario.net*)
El Deber Santa Cruz daily (*www.eldeber.com.bo*)
El Mundo Santa Cruz daily (*www.elmundo.com.bo*)
Correo del Sur Sucre daily (*http://correodelsur.net*)

TELEVISION CHANNELS

ATB Red Nacional (Canal 9) Private, La Paz-based (*www.atb.com.bo*)
Red P.A.T. – Private, national (*www.red-pat.com*)

RADIO STATIONS

Radio Fides – Catholic news, talk (*www.radiofides.com*)
Radio Panamericana – national news, talk network (*www.panamericana-bolivia.com*)
Radio Illimani – state-run (*www.comunica.gov.bo/illimani/indice.html*)

Finally, try to pick up a copy of the **Llama Express** (*www.theexpress.org*) around La Paz. This monthly English-language newspaper, run by volunteer staff from an office in the city's Sopocachi district, covers travel, politics and what's-on information.

be surprised if the other person is 30 minutes late, or be annoyed when they think this is a perfectly normal turn of events. The Latin *mañana* spirit, it seems, lives on in Bolivia.

Top tip: always try to carry an umbrella. La Paz is prone to flash rain showers and it will save you turning up to a meeting looking like a drowned rat.

The National Chamber of Commerce (*www.boliviacomercio.org.bo*) can offer further advice on doing business in Bolivia, as can the trade and investment section of the British Embassy in La Paz (*www.britishembassy.gov.uk*).

CULTURAL ETIQUETTE

Bolivia can be a deeply conservative country. Indeed, the further beneath the surface you scratch, the more conservative it can become. Of course some things will seem strange, but you are a guest in the country and have to keep this in mind. As such, your actions may sometimes be quite innocent but you can, in fact, cause major offence, albeit without even realising it. So how can you be a good tourist and respect the culture you are being welcomed into? Here's how.

• Do accept invitations with good grace when it comes to sharing food and drink. And if you really can't manage to get it down, then ask for a bag to take it away for later and then dispose of it with subtlety.
• Do join in with dancing, music or take part in festival activities when you're invited to do so. Even if you are terminally shy, or simply can't dance a single step, have a go then make your polite excuses.

- Do offer to share your own things, such as chewing gum or cigarettes, with people you meet. New friendships can be easily forged over a shared moment if you prove your openness to new people and situations.

BUT

- Don't start taking pictures of people in public places, especially those working in the market, without first asking for permission. Don't pay for the picture but, if they are pressing you, it's good form to offer to buy some of their wares before snapping away.
- Don't treat a visit to a local, indigenous community like a visit to the zoo. Discretion is the byword in these cases and blending in is the way to go – not pointing, gawping or showing obvious disrespect.
- Don't argue too much when negotiating over price as some prices are actually fixed, especially in more regular shops away from the street markets. Even in the market, there is generally a going rate and squabbling over a few centavos will make you no friends.

INTERACTING WITH LOCAL PEOPLE

Hang out around Calle Sagarnaga and stay in gringo-friendly hostels and, chances are, you'll do very little mixing with local Bolivians outside of asking for another beer or how much the llama steak costs.

Make a small effort, however, and your time in Bolivia could be much richer. There are opportunities to volunteer locally even on a short-term basis while homestays are growing in popularity for travellers seeking a more homely environment.

The key factor to consider is that, obviously, travellers tend to live in a travellers' world with the taste of home comforts that accompany it. There's nothing wrong with that but, sometimes, it's good to have a look at the world from the other side and the best way to do so is to indulge in a bit of cultural immersion.

GIVING SOMETHING BACK

Yes, of course, just by being there, you are making a financial contribution to the livelihoods of local people. But there are other ways to get involved: by volunteering your help and expertise, for example.

A few charitable organisations worthy of your help include the following.

Alma de los Andes (*www.spiritoftheandes.com*). This Bolivian co-operative has the best range of alpaca wool products and ensures profits go directly to the women who knit them. Visitors to the project are welcome and clothes can be made to order with prices from US$40 for an alpaca sweater.

Animales SOS Bolivia (*www.animalessos.org*) is really the only animal rights organisation in Bolivia. It is recognised by the Humane Society of the US (HSUS) and by the Humane Society International (HIS) as well as by the WSPA. As a volunteer organisation, it has been working for over five years in La Paz and has expanded in the last few years to most of the major Bolivian cities. They work with stray animals that are injured, sick, have been hit by cars, are ready to give birth in the street or animals that have been abused. They also confiscate wild animals from owners and rehabilitate them before sending them to a refuge in the Chapare. (It is illegal in Bolivia to own wild animals such as parrots and monkeys.) They currently have a small shelter that operates in a private house where there are

2

animals available for adoption, but the ultimate goal is to build a permanent, modern shelter which requires a large sum of money. There is a need for monetary donations and volunteers with veterinary experience. Contact Animales SOS, tel: 591 2 248 3333 or email: bolivia@animalessos.org.

Friends of Bolivia (*www.friendsofbolivia.com*). A great resource if you are looking for worthy organisations to donate to in Bolivia, it has links to charities throughout the country and lists of places where you can volunteer.

Hogar Mixto is a children's home in Sopocachi, working with runaway, orphaned, abused and abandoned children in La Paz. Home to about 50 boys and girls aged between six and 12, the running of the home is greatly assisted by donations of time and money. The volunteer programme includes creative activities, games, gardening and reading. There is a minimum eight-week commitment unless it's the flying visit of an impromptu juggling or theatre performance. Extra finances not only help the day-to-day running of the home, but also help to employ a family therapist. Hogar Mixto hopes to begin working with deaf and disabled children so there will shortly be a need for these skills as well. For information contact Diane Bellomy at cnsorata@ceibo.entelnet.bo or the volunteer co-ordinator at adh_volunteers@yahoo.com. Or telephone the director, Marina de Ascarrunz, on 243 1071.

Inti Wara Yassi gives volunteers the opportunity to work with wild animals that were injured or abused as pets, with the aim of returning them to the wild. The

TO GIVE OR NOT TO GIVE

Kristie Robinson of the Llama Express (www.theexpress.org).
It is estimated that there are some one million people in Bolivia today who make ends meet by begging, while it's obvious to any tourist that the number of beggars and street people is very high.

Considering that foreign travellers and residents are generally approached more than locals, how should we respond to requests for money? While it's obviously not possible to give to everyone, should you, in fact, give to anyone at all? Is giving money simply encouraging a culture of expectancy and laziness? Besides, giving money is just a temporary fix – it doesn't solve the root of the problem.

One of the biggest dilemmas concerns begging children. Many of the children who sell sweets or gum, or are shoe-shiners, are trying to better themselves and their position in society. Many of them, however, are sent out by their parents to make money. By giving to these children, their parents see they are successful and will be more inclined to send them out again, day after day. Some children sent out by their parents are not allowed to return home until they have made their quota of money.

The majority of people who do give prefer to help people who are actually working in some way to gain their money. It is relatively easy to set up a business, even just a small stall in the street, as Bolivia has one of the most advanced micro-finance sectors in the world. This is aimed specifically at helping poor women and men to set up their own businesses to support their families, with loans of as little as U$20, although the interest rates can be a little on the high side. That's why, if you wander through the streets in any large town or city in Bolivia today, there are people selling everything from shoelaces and sunglasses to fruit or flowers. In light of this, it's hard to justify giving money to those who simply hold their hands out.

Alix Shand

Bolivia is one of the poorest countries on the continent, hence the disparity between rich and poor can be overwhelming. The lack of government funding to help the poor, the handicapped and the dispossessed is evident as you walk the streets of any major cities. Furthermore, attention to environmental protection and animals hardly gets a mention in the government's annual budget.

If you have time, patience and a little money to keep you going then there are many organisations needing your help.

To be able to work with children you will need to go through the social services to get permission and register, but any volunteer organisation will be able to sort out this paperwork for you. You will, however, need a decent level of Spanish to be accepted. Most volunteer groups request that you commit to at least eight weeks to avoid the children becoming confused by many people coming and going.

Working with environmental organisations is a little more difficult, but looking them up on the internet and sending your CV usually yields results if you have the experience and knowledge they are looking for.

Whatever option you choose, volunteering will add a whole new dimension to your time in Bolivia and give you food for thought for your onward travel.

project is at Parque Machia, near Villa Tunari. Volunteers are asked to give a minimum of two weeks of their time.

SOS Children's Villages (*www.sos-childrensvillages.org*). This group offers support to local communities and villages in 131 countries throughout the world.

Volunteer, Study, Travel or Explore!
SOUTH AMERICAN
EXPLORERS.org
Going to South America is your business, making it a great trip is ours.

Andean condor

Part Two

THE GUIDE

64

3

La Paz

Tel code: 02; altitude: 3,577m; population: 793,293

The world's highest administrative capital city is, in fact, three cities in one, spanning a difference in altitude of over 1,000m and boasting the clearest blue skies in the Americas. The mountains that shroud the city, notably the majestic Illimani (6,400m), are less than one hour's drive away and ever-present on the horizon.

Straddled between the windswept Altiplano and the tropical Yungas region, La Paz has prospered as Bolivia's commercial centre ever since Simón Bolívar's army entered the city on 9 February 1825.

Today the city is a vibrant mix of indigenous Andean culture and post-colonial, big-city living. The legacy of the Spanish conquest is still evident in the façades of the parliament buildings around Plaza Murillo, but head south along Avenida Arce and the cityscape shifts to take in high-rise blocks and modern apartments.

OK, so Bolivia's largest city may lack the museums of Lima and the cultural life of Buenos Aires. It more than compensates, however, with its vibrant streetlife. Indeed, at ground level La Paz has lots to offer. From budget eats to the sprawling market area southwest of Plaza San Francisco, if you want to shop, eat, or do just about anything in La Paz, then simply head out onto the streets and take the city's pulse at grass-roots level.

You will need to get acclimatised first, however. Flying straight into the world's highest airport (4,050m) is potentially a one-way ticket to altitude sickness. You'll miss your usual share of oxygen at this altitude so take it easy at first and drink lots of coca tea – just like the locals do. Otherwise just popping out for a stroll can feel like running a mini-marathon.

La Paz's ethnic make-up is fantastically diverse. Everywhere you look you'll find people in traditional dress of bowler hats and layered skirts – a living testament to

SIX THINGS TO DO IN LA PAZ

1 Explore the market area around Plaza San Francisco: this is *the* place not just for bargains but to take the city's pulse (page 87).

2 Visit the Museo de Coca, La Paz's most rewarding museum, for a fresh perspective on the legendary leaf (page 87).

3 Treat yourself to a slap-up meal at one of La Paz's upscale eateries – all styles of local and international cuisine are represented (page 79).

4 Invest in a tailor-made suit, or a new ball gown, hand-crafted for a bargain price by one of La Paz's expert tailors (page 84).

5 Explore the city's cultural life with a classical concert, some local jazz or an exhibition at one of the city's cultural centres (page 83).

6 Sample the local *salteñas*, the local take on elevenses and a uniquely Bolivian treat (page 82).

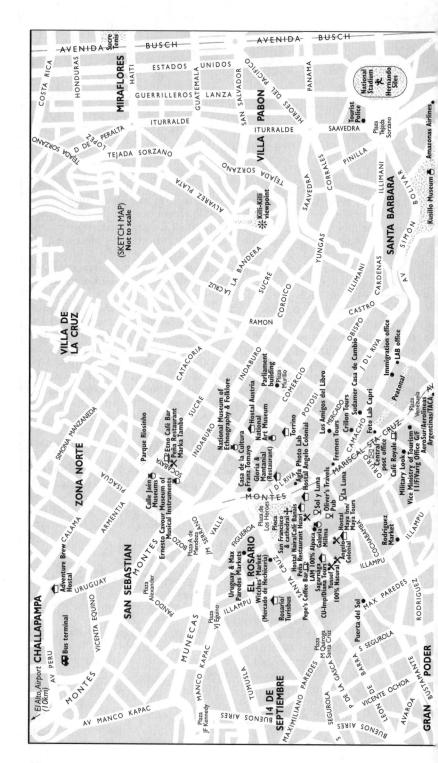

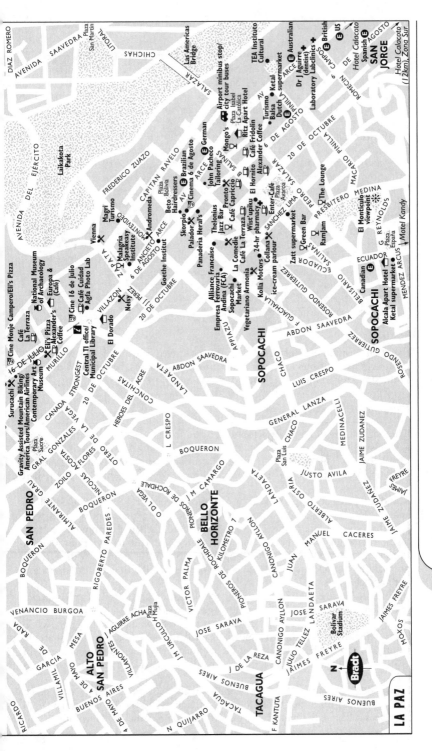

LA PAZ

the clash of cultures. But Bolivia's urban poverty is also never far away. While executives have business lunches in downtown restaurants, begging and drinking in the street is commonplace: a very Bolivian mix.

HISTORY

The original city of La Paz was founded 30km from the present location at Laja, a windswept Altiplano town on the old route from Potosí to Lima, on 20 October 1548. The Spanish moved lock, stock and barrel shortly after to the less climatically harsh valley of River Choqueyapu, where the city has flourished ever since.

Indeed, given its importance as a centre of commerce between the Altiplano and the Yungas regions, La Paz has developed into a major urban hub with suburbs sprawling out to the Zona Sur and El Alto, the latter forming the poorer districts towering above the city, which today forms a city in its own right. Indeed, El Alto is today the third most populous city in the country with a rising population of indigenous stock. It is set to overtake La Paz in terms of population within a few years.

Since the decline of the mining industry in Potosí (page 179), La Paz has grown to be Bolivia's most important city, although the residents of Santa Cruz, the arch-rivals of the residents of La Paz, also known as *Paceños,* would now disagree. While Sucre remains the official and judicial capital (it's still home to the Supreme Court), La Paz has been the seat of the national government since a civil war in 1899, with the majority of the administrative departments located around the city's Plaza Murillo.

Founded by Captain Alonso de Mendoza with the name Nuestra Señora de La Paz, it was the third city to be founded in Bolivia. Today the department's 20 provinces celebrate their anniversary on 16 July to mark the 1809 revolution.

GETTING THERE

BY PLANE El Alto International Airport (☏ *281 0120*) is located 12km from downtown La Paz and connected to the city by a motorway toll road. The airport is served by international carriers American Airlines and Aerolineas Argentinas, plus the local airlines Lloyd Aero Boliviano (LAB), AeroSur, Amazonas and TACA. There's a 15BS/US$25 airport tax payable on domestic/international flights.

Airport facilities include an ATM, Entel call and internet centre (10Bs per hour), an overpriced coffee shop, news-stand and some rather lacklustre gift shops. Upstairs there's a pricey Burger King and the Mirador restaurant, which has a set menu for a hefty 35Bs – best eat before you leave for the airport if you can.

Top tip: For a payment of US$8, you can use the LAB airline lounge with coffee and internet access. If you have your laptop with you, the whole airport is a wi-fi zone with free internet access.

BUS SERVICES FROM LA PAZ

The bus terminal in La Paz has had something of a facelift of late with new signposts and information boards located in the centre of the main concourse, making it a lot clearer now to find your correct bus.

There are 32 ticket offices operating from the terminal, many of them shared between several operators. Given this huge number of bus companies, and the cacophony of vendors hustling for business, it can be a disorienting experience for travellers. Keep an eye on your possessions, making sure to guard passport, money and tickets closely at all times, and you'll be fine.

The following table offers a guideline to bus services departing the terminal at regular intervals. Make sure to check with the information boards on the concourse for updated details of operators and changes to the schedule.

DOMESTIC DEPARTURES

Cochabamba	regular departures between 06.00–22.30
Copacabana	08.00 & 08.30
Oruro	regular departures between 04.30–21.30
Potosí	several departures between 18.00–21.30
Santa Cruz	several departures between 16.30–21.30
Sucre	several departures between 18.30–20.00
Tarija	16.30 & 17.00
Tiahuanaco	08.00 & 08.30
Tupiza	18.00, 19.00 & 19.30
Uyuni	15.30, 17.30 & 18.00
Villazon	18.00, 19.00 & 19.30

INTERNATIONAL DEPARTURES

Arica & Iquique	06.00, 07.00 & 13.00
Asuncion	20.00
Bogota	15.30
Buenos Aires	19.00 & 20.00
Caracas	15.30
Cusco	08.00, 08.30 & 09.00
Lima	08.30
Puno	08.00, 08.30 & 09.00
Quito	15.30
Sao Paulo & Rio	20.00

Airport transfers **Airport minibuses** depart every 15 minutes from outside the terminal building and head downtown to Plaza Isabel la Católica via the city's main thoroughfare, El Prado (3.80Bs). The last minibus leaves at 21.30, after which a taxi downtown costs a rather hefty 50Bs.

BY TRAIN Oruro is the rail hub of Bolivia while La Paz's train station is no longer in use. The La Paz-based offices for the rail company, **Empresa Ferroviaria Andina (FCA)**, are located at Calle Sanchez Lima #2199, Sopocachi (✆ 224 16545; www.fca.com.bo; open Mon–Fri 08.00–12.00 & 14.30–17.30), where you can buy tickets for forward journeys from Oruro.

BY BUS La Paz's **bus terminal**, Plaza Antofagasta (✆ 228 6061) has an ATM, exchange kiosk, post office and Entel call centre. There's food towards the back, where there are also some cheaper luggage stores than the one by the front entrance (open 05.00–22.30; 2Bs for 24 hours). There are English signs throughout and a 2Bs tax payable on all domestic departures.

GETTING AROUND

Much of downtown La Paz is negotiable on foot, but public transport is especially useful for those steep, uphill ascents.

Radio taxis, easily identified by their roof sign, charge a flat-rate 8Bs, but they are generally more reputable, especially after dark. Simply flag them down, always agree on fares upfront and make sure you have lots of small denomination coins – nobody ever, ever has any change.

Minibuses and *truffis* (like collective taxis) cost 1.50–2Bs for journeys in the centre, 2.20Bs for trips up to El Alto. Collective taxis charge a flat-rate 3Bs fare (per person), but will stop en route to pick up other passengers. Note: while these forms of transport are cheap, taking them is at your own risk as reports of robberies on busy public transport are on the rise. If in doubt, a radio taxi is always a safer bet.

For a **taxi service**, call Alpha Taxis (open 24 hours) in Sopocachi on 241 2525; Taxi City La Paz in the centre on 222 1212, or Taxi Movil del Sur in Zona Sur on 279 2222.

For those willing to brave the roads out of La Paz on a self-drive basis, **Kolla Motors** (Calle Rosendo Gutierrez #502; ✆ 241 9141; f 241 1344; e kollamotors@acelerate.com), hires out sturdy Land Cruisers. Bring your passport, international driving licence and credit card to finish the paperwork. Car hire is available to those aged 25 years and above only. Major credit cards are accepted and 24-hour service promised; prices start from US$79 per day, based on a mileage of 120km per day.

TOURIST INFORMATION

The government does its best to cater for tourists' information needs, but consistently suffers from a lack of resources. While the following will try to answer your questions, you may find some of La Paz's more reputable travel agencies (see below) are a better source of traveller information.

🚹 **Central Tourist Information Office** Plaza del Estudiante; ✆ 237 1044. Sometimes welcoming, sometimes simply closed; don't bother paying for the maps they hawk here as you can pick up free maps elsewhere. Open Mon–Fri 08.30–12.00 & 14.30–19.00. Allegedly.

🚹 **Vice Ministry of Tourism** 11/F Edificio Camara de Comercio, Av Mariscal Santa Cruz; ✆ 237 5129; f 235

BEWARE: ZEBRAS CROSSING

Urban La Paz is not best known for its range of wildlife. Indeed, with its constant deluge of belching bus fumes and lunatic drivers, the city's main drag, El Prado, is renowned as one of the worst spots in Bolivia for air pollution and a fair chance of not actually making it across the road.

Recently, however, the streets of Bolivia's de facto capital have been overrun with an invasion of zebras – humans dressed as zebras, that is. The reason? A new road safety campaign by the La Paz city council to promote awareness amongst *Paceños* about the dangers of congestion and pollution in this city of 800,000-odd people.

The human zebras, dressed in stripy black and white garb, congregate around the Prado, bringing a touch of colour to the drab urban cityscape and providing a safe passage for schoolchildren negotiating – wait for it – zebra crossings.

La Paz authorities have recently discussed ways to beat the city's crippling pollution with a proposal on the table for an elevated tramline around the central districts. Given the high estimated cost and the constant political instability in the country, however, the project looks unlikely to, ahem, get off the ground.

The zebra volunteers, meanwhile, are out in force. A group of 20-odd young people from underprivileged backgrounds, these human zebras all receive a token wage (a few dollars per day) for their efforts, plus enjoy the chance to prance around the streets dressed as a 6ft zebra every day between 08.00–10.00 and 14.00–16.00.

'I love being a zebra as it's a fun way to spread a serious message,' says Roseo Mamani of El Alto, close to La Paz. 'The only problem is the heat during summer – my head gets all sticky.'

0526; www.turismobolivia.bo. The body responsible for Bolivia's fledgling tourism industry co-ordinates

activities from their downtown office, although it's not officially open for visitors to just pop in.

LOCAL TOUR OPERATORS

Turisbus Av Illampu #704; ☎ 245 1341; f 245 1991; e turisbus@travelperubolivia.com; www.turisbus.com. A very reliable & friendly agency for organising bus tickets within & out of Bolivia, conveniently located downstairs in the Hotel Rosario (page 100). They also offer tours to the Salar & Madidi National Park amongst other itineraries across the country. *Open Mon–Fri 08.00–12.30 & 14.00–19.00, Sat & Sun 08.00–12.30.*

Magri Turismo Calle Capitan Ravelo #2101; ☎ 244 2727; f 244 3060; www.magri-amexpress.com.bo. This large agency has national coverage with offices across Bolivia & an equally wide range of tour options. The company owns the excellent ecolodge, La Estancia, on the Isla del Sol in Lake Titicaca (page 103), & they also act as the official American Express representatives in Bolivia. They don't, however, cash travellers' cheques. *Open Mon–Fri 09.00–12.30 & 15.00–19.00, Sat 09.00–12.30.*

Fremen Tours Edificio Handel, Calle Socabaya; ☎ 240 7995; e info@andes-amazonia.com; www.andes-amazonia.com. Best known for their floating hotel in the Amazon region, the Reina de Enin, Fremen also run a group of hotels in the Salar de Uyuni & a jungle lodge, El Puente, in the Chapare region. They have a good national coverage with branch offices in major cities & a large array of tours. *Open Mon–Fri 09.00–12.30 & 15.00–19.00, Sat 09.00–12.30.*

Turismo Balsa Calle Hermanos Manchego #2526; ☎ 244 0620; e info@turismobalsa.com; www.turismobalsa.com. A well-regarded agency with a range of tours covering the whole country, they specialise in tours to the region around Lake Titicaca. Indeed, they own the own lakeside hotel, Las Balsas, located at Puerto Perez, on the opposite side of the lake from Copacabana. *Open Mon–Fri 09.00–12.30 & 15.00–19.00, Sat 09.00–12.30.*

Crillon Tours Calle Camacho #1223; 🕾 233 7533; f 211 6481; e titicaca@entelnet.bo; www.titicaca.com. This upscale agency specialises in tourism around Lake Titicaca, where they own two properties & run a hydrofoil service (page 103). They also offer mystic tours, exploring the rituals of Aymara culture, particularly popular around the time of the new-year solstice (page 107). Prices, however, are rather high given the variable level of service & new ideas are sorely needed. *Open Mon–Fri 09.00–12.30 & 15.00–19.00, Sat 09.00–12.30.*

Maya Tours Calle Sagarnaga #339; 🕾 236 9052; e mayatoursopera@hotmail.com; www.mayatoursbolivia.com. This backpacker-targeted agency is located in the same small arcade as the Maya Inn (page 78). The range of standard but popular tours available to travellers includes visits to Chacalatya (50Bs) & Tiahuanaco (US$18). They may not offer the most complete service, but they're catering for the budget end of the market &, as such, are suitably cheap.

CITY TOURS

Viajes Planeta (*Av Montengero #1420, 1/F;* 🕾 *279 1440;* e *info@lapazcitytour.com*) runs daily bus tours in a giant, red, open-top double-decker, known as *Tocando el Cielo* ('touching the sky'). The city tour offers two daily departures in the morning and two in the afternoon, seven days a week. The two circuits last around 90 minutes each, with a ten-minute stop on each circuit. The ticket is valid for both circuits; allow around three hours for the complete journey.

Overall it's good for a bit of history and a nice, gentle introduction for a first-time visitor with a commentary in seven different languages. The audio system is, however, pretty old and sound quality a bit hit and miss.

The two circuits run as follows:

City Plaza Isabel La Católica – Plaza del Estudiante – Plaza Sucre – Prado – San Francisco Cathedral – Witches' Market – Calle Sagarnaga – Plaza Murillo – Mirador Killi Killi (rest stop) – Mercado Camacho – Miraflores/football stadium – Prado – Sopocachi/Plaza Avaroa – Plaza Isabel La Católica.

Zona Sur Plaza Isabel La Católica – Obrajes – Calacoto – Achumani – German District – Valle de la Luna (stop and option to enter the tourist information centre for 15Bs extra – don't bother) – Mallassa – Plaza Isabel La Católica.

Departures from Plaza Isabel La Católica Mon–Fri 08.30 & 16.00, Sat & Sun 09.00 & 14.30 (city circuit); Mon–Sun 10.30 & 14.00 (Zona Sur circuit); cost US$6. See map, *La Paz/bus tour* (page 74).

Meanwhile, for something a bit different, Calacoto Tours at the Hotel Calacoto in the Zona Sur can arrange a two-hour horseback or horse and carriage tour of the nearby Valle de la Luna, with the option of a picnic or barbecue lunch from US$25 per person.

WHERE TO STAY

The city offers a large variety of accommodation for all budgets with some great characterful boutique properties. The following properties are divided by budget category and listed in the order of the author's preference.

TOP OF THE RANGE

Hotel Europa (110 rooms) Calle Tiahuanaco #64; 231 5656; f 02 211 3930; e reserves@hoteleuropa.com.bo; www.hoteleuropa.com.bo. La Paz's leading international-standard, 5-star hotel has the pick of the facilities for those seeking home comforts & prepared to pay for them. The business centre & free in-room internet access make it a favourite for business travellers, while a coffee shop (open 08.00–midnight) & a piano bar (open 11.00–15.00 & 19.00–23.00) complete the catering facilities. But bargain hard on rack rates as, despite its pretensions, the rooms are now looking a bit old-fashioned. The Hotel Europa's Finn Club leisure centre (open Wed–Mon 13.00–21.00) is available for non-guests to use if they pay a fee. It offers deliciously hot showers, a large pool & steam room, with towels supplied. A day pass, great for a detox after a long hike, costs 80Bs & a massage a further 80Bs; a 1-week membership costs US$25, 1 month US$80. *Standard sgls/dbls US$135/155, inc buffet b/fast & use of leisure facilities.*

Ritz Apart Hotel (71 rooms) Plaza Isabel la Católica #2478; 243 3131; f 243 3080; e info@hotel-ritz-bolivia.com; www.hotel-ritz-bolivia.com. These smart serviced apartments, featuring small kitchenettes & all mod cons, are located on the square right opposite the spot where airport minibuses run to & from, making it ideal for a quick escape to the airport. *Junior/ Ambassador suites come with a US$120/230 rack rate, but ask about special rates.*

Radisson Plaza Hotel (239 rooms) Av Arce #2177; 244 1111; f 244 0402; e reservas@hn.radissonbolivia.com.bo; www.radisson.com/lapazbo. Sometimes you feel like splashing out (quite literally in the case of the Radisson spa), or simply having a night of luxury. Hence, this 5-star property is an ideal spot to sink into one of the king-size beds, soak in the tub & pig out on the all-you-can-eat buffet b/fast. Every evening the lobby bar hosts a happy hour until 21.00 with 2-for-1 drinks & a selection of snacks. & if you're heading for the airport, you can pick up a free minibus transfer & save yourself the taxi fare in the process. Wi-fi internet access in the lobby area & a well-equipped business centre ensure a loyal following with business travellers. *Standard/executive dbls US$180/260.*

Plaza Hotel (176 rooms) Av 16 de Julio 1789; 237 8311; f 237 8318; e plaza@plazabolivia.com.bo; www.plazabolivia.com.bo. The Plaza is, at least location-wise, hard to beat. Scratch below the surface, however, & this place feels a bit

THE AUTHOR'S FAVOURITE HOTEL

Hotel Rosario (42 rooms) Av Illampu #704; 245 1658; f 245 1991; e reservas@hotelrosario.com; www.hotelrosario.com. La Paz's best overall hotel for value & service is based in an adapted 19th-century colonial house built around a sunny courtyard. The rooms are tastefully decorated with good facilities & a nice, homely feel. Both the on-site Jiwhaki coffee & internet bar (open 15.00–19.00) & the Tambo Colonial restaurant (open for b/fast & dinner, live music Fri & Sat) offer good-quality snacks & meals. The tour agency, Turisbus (page 71), has a helpful office located downstairs within the hotel, as does Anyi, a community artisan project's shop. The owners also run the Hotel Rosario del Lago in Copacabana (page 100), which is of a similarly high standard. *Sgls/dbls/suite US$33/43/78, inc buffet b/fast, free use of internet & complimentary hot drinks found in the reception.*

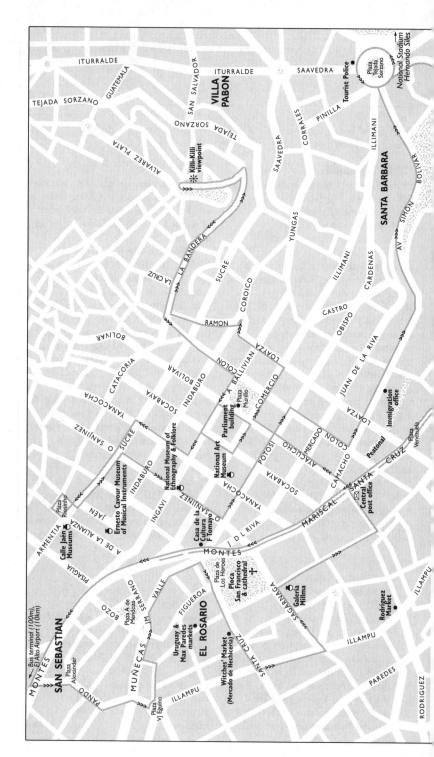

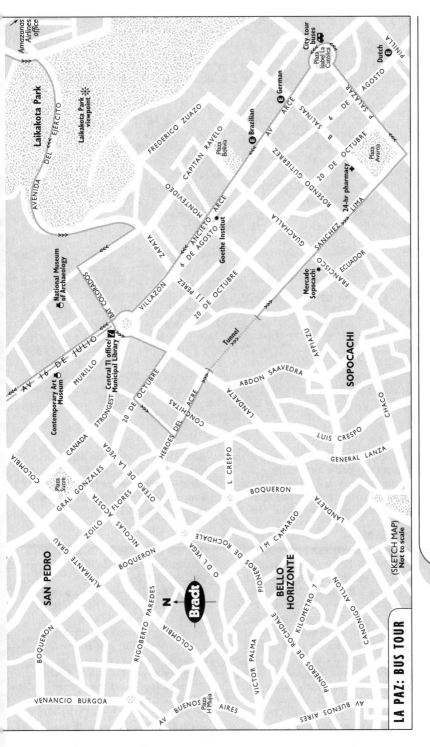

LA PAZ: BUS TOUR

(SKETCH MAP)
Not to scale

Rusty Young

A Bolivian prison might not be first on most people's list of holiday destinations, but that was exactly where I, along with thousands of other tourists, went while backpacking through Bolivia a few years ago. In fact, I loved it so much that I decided to stay a few months in order to better understand what must surely be one of the strangest places on the planet.

From the outside, with its high yellow walls that back onto the picturesque Plaza Sucre, San Pedro Prison might be any normal building in any city. But within its confines lies a city inside a city, a self-regulated prison society that mimics the outside world. This minimum-security facility caters to over a thousand male inmates – the most populated male prison in La Paz – as well as many of their wives and children who voluntarily move in with their convicted husbands and fathers, often taking the family pets with them.

Inside the scene is reminiscent of a small Bolivian suburb: think colourful umbrellas, market stalls as well as the obligatory Coca-Cola advertising lining a maze of passageways that link shops, restaurants, a child-minding centre, a church and even a football field – all this crammed into a single city block.

Each of the eight sections has a hotel-style rating. In San Pedro money is power – the rich live well and the poor suffer. In the five-star section, inmates enjoy cable TV, carpeted floors, personal libraries and views over the city. Inmates from the one-star sections live in windowless concrete hovels called *sarcophagi*. Admission to each section is based on economic means since inmates must buy or rent their own cells. Cell prices fluctuate according to supply and demand, but generally range from a one-off payment of a couple of hundred dollars in the poorer section to tens of thousands in the wealthier sections.

Very little is provided by the government, so inmates are responsible for catering for their own needs and controlling almost all aspects of their daily life – from washing, cleaning, cooking, buying food and clothing, to devising their own rules and punishments. Consequently, many are obliged to find work within the prison. There are convicted doctors, lawyers and dentists as well as cooks, waiters, shoe-shiners, messengers, and finally those who earn a living from the thriving black market.

jaded with only the well-regarded Utama penthouse restaurant, with some of the best steaks in town & amazing views across the city, helping it to stand out from the crowd. On the plus side, the serving of free coca tea in reception is a welcome addition,

especially for those worried about altitude sickness. Standards of service remain high & foreigner-friendly, while the in-house spa, with swimming pool, gym & jacuzzi, is a nice touch & open to non-guests for a daily charge. *Dbls US$119.*

MID-RANGE

🏠 **Hotel Calacoto** (42 rooms) Calacoto Calle 13 #8009; ☎ 279 2524; e info@hotel-calacoto-bolivia.com; www.hotel-calacoto-bolivia.com. Located out of town in the leafy Zona Sur district, this property offers a more tranquil alternative to the hubbub of the downtown hotels. There's a nice family atmosphere & a pleasant setting with a garden, spa & bedrooms built around a colonial courtyard. It's a bit of a trek into the city, but the self-catering apartments are popular with families, while the in-house travel agency, Calacoto Tours, offers some alternative takes on traditional sightseeing trips (see *City tours*, page 72). Hotel Calacoto offers a local mobile phone hire service for

$2 per day, plus it prides itself on being La Paz's most pet-friendly hotel. *Sgls/dbls US$32/38; apts for 2/4 people US$45/60.*

🏠 **Hostal Naira** (22 rooms) Calle Sagarnaga #161; ☎ 235 5645; f 231 1214; e info@hostalnaira.com; www.hostalnaira.com. At the smarter end of Sagarnaga's strip of budget properties, the rooms are a bit dark, but surroundings generally a cut above at this property. Private bathrooms, cable TV & heaters complete the range of mod cons. *Sgls/dbls US$25/32 with a good b/fast served downstairs in backpacker-friendly Café Banais* (☎ 231 1214; open 07.00–22.00, a reliable spot for drinks,

Women play a vital role in the daily prison economy, while children leave to attend school or play inside the prison. The guards enter only to mark the roll in the morning. San Pedro is home to an estimated 200 children, while the Palmasola prison, in the eastern city of Santa Cruz, holds around 400 women. The number of children living in prisons has increased dramatically since the 1980s, when the government took a tougher line against drug-trafficking. Entire families ended up in jail because children had nowhere to go when their parents were arrested.

Contrary to what one might expect, however, this law of the jungle-style system does not necessarily lead to chaos and violence. The presence of women and children has a pacifying influence on the prisoners; fighting in front of them is strictly forbidden. Section delegates, voted for in annual elections, are empowered to send misbehavers to solitary confinement, while persistent offenders are transferred to Chonchocorro, a US-style maximum-security penitentiary in El Alto. Few inmates break these rules or try to escape. In fact, many claim that life inside is better than on the outside.

Until recently tourists were allowed to tour the prison and sometimes spend the night in one of the cells. These days, a menacing sign reading 'No Foreign Tourists Allowed' adorns the main entrance. But that has not deterred the more foolhardy tourists from seeking admittance to this bizarre cross between flagrant capitalism and Latin American family values, between government neglect and human compassion. From time to time, they are successful, but these days, given the prison's infamy as a centre for dealing drugs and the over-zealousness of some travellers to take advantage of the cheapest prices in La Paz, San Pedro has become too high-profile. As such, the authorities try to ensure that admittance is now reserved for the criminals, not curious backpackers. Besides, if you are caught buying drugs in Bolivia, there is a mandatory six-year prison sentence for possession.

Rusty Young is the author of Marching Powder *(Macmillan, 2002) about life in San Pedro. For photos and more information, visit www.marchingpowder.com. There are also more pictures of San Pedro from www.niels.com.*

vegetarian pitta wraps (8–12Bs) & internet access (4Bs/hr).

⌂ **Alcala Apart Hotel** (20 rooms) Calle Victor Sanjines #2662, Sopocachi; ☎ 241 2336; f 241 1113; e alcalapt@zuper.net. With a great location overlooking leafy Plaza España & situated right next to a Ketal supermarket, these serviced apartments may be set away from the hubbub of the centre, but they are easily accessible by public transport. The on-site restaurant, La Castellana, offers a good set lunch (17Bs). *Well-equipped sgls/dbls US$50/60 with kitchenette.*

⌂ **Hotel Diamante Azul** (60 rooms) Pasaje Aroma 40; ☎ 245 7576; f 245 8976; e hoteldiamanteazul@hotmail.com. Brand new, spotlessly clean & very welcoming, this is a real little find at the mid-range/budget category. Tucked away up a sidestreet & little known up until now, while not flash, it's a very reliable option &, being new, is currently one place where you can find a room at a fair price when other places are booked

out. Better still, it's ideally located for exploring the sprawling street markets located nearby. The rooms are nicely furnished with comfy beds & private bathrooms, plus they come with cable TV & a continental b/fast (small, but adequate to start the day) is served in the downstairs dining hall. *Dbls US$36.*

⌂ **Hotel El Dorado** (80 rooms) Av Villazon; ☎ 236 3355; f 239 1438; e eldorado@ceibo.entelnet.bo; www.hoteleldorado.net. A great central location but rather dark & lacklustre décor lets down the overall standard at this very centrally located mid-range property. The rooms have decent facilities while the in-house restaurant offers excellent views across the La Paz cityscape, but the whole place needs freshening up. *Sgls/dbls US$32/40, with b/fast.*

⌂ **Hotel Gloria** (92 rooms) Calle Potosí #909; ☎ 240 7070; f 240 6622; e titikaka@ hotelgloria.com.bo; www.hotelgloria.com.bo. A long-established, 3-star property on the traveller scene, the Gloria group includes sister properties in Copacabana (page 100) & Umiri (see box, *Something for the weekend?*, opposite). The rooms, sadly, are a bit faded, but the range of in-house facilities — a money exchange, the Pierot coffee shop & the Gloria Tours travel agency, all opening Mon–Fri 09.00–12.30 & 14.30–19.00, Sat 09.00–12.00 are all useful additions. The Mantanial restaurant (page 81), meanwhile, is a real haven for hungry vegetarians. *Sgls/dbls US$36/47 with buffet b/fast & free use of the internet; ask about low-season deals.*

BUDGET

🏠 **The Adventure Brew Hostel** (12 rooms) Av Montes #533; 📞 231 3849; e gravity@ unete.com; www.theadventurebrewhostel.com. This hostel has been established by the people behind the tour agency, Gravity Assisted Mountain Biking (page 72). As such, it's a hostel for travellers run by travellers, which takes the traditional hostel experience & ups the stakes to offer the full traveller package. The communal areas on every floor include kitchen, DVD lounge, internet & internet telephony room, plus a chill-out zone. The owners really thought this place through with free hot-water bottles & lockers under the beds to keep your backpack secure. Plus they arrange a regular programme of events, bar crawls & outings, so just check the list each morning, sign up & hitch a ride. The micro-brewery downstairs with its Saya beer keeps the party in full swing each night. *Private/shared rooms US$10/7.*

🏠 **Casa de Huespedes Arthy's** (7 rooms) Av Montes 693; 📞 228 1439; e arthyshouse@hotmail.com; http://arthyshouse.tripod.com. Tucked away & delightfully peaceful, this small guesthouse is a real little find at the budget end of the market. Homely & friendly, it prides itself on personalised service & a reputation spread by word of mouth. You could so easily walk past without even noticing it, but the owners like it that way. The rooms are simple but comfortable with double-glazed windows to keep noise levels down: I room for 4, I sgl & 5 dbls, all of which share the bathroom. Downstairs the TV room, with cable & DVDs, & a communal kitchen for guests to use, give the places a real homely feel. Sure it's no-frills, bus it's really handy for the bus terminal. *Rooms 40Bs pp.*

🏠 **Hostal Maya Inn** (20 rooms) Calle Sagarnaga #339; 📞 231 1970; www.mayatoursbolivia.com. The Hostal Maya Inn makes for a reliable standby at the budget end of the market. It's a cheap & cheerful spot with basic but functional rooms, some with private bathrooms, & the convenience of a tour agency & laundry all within stumbling distance of the front door. The central location & budget rates keep travellers coming back, but do make sure to ask for a room on the back as the reverb from the folk-music venue practically next door, Peña Restaurant Huari (page 83), will have your bed shaking well into the early hours. *Rooms with private/shared bathroom 70/50Bs pp.*

🏠 **Hotel Sagarnaga** (48 rooms) Calle Sagarnaga #326; 📞 235 0252; e reserves@hotel-sagarnaga.com; www.hotel-sagarnaga.com. A basic but comfortable budget hotel, it is located right in the thick of the main traveller district. The rooms are simple but do, at least, come with private bathrooms. This place is highly popular with budget-conscious Israeli travellers. Indeed, sometimes eating b/fast at the downstairs café can feel like stepping into a scene from downtown Tel Aviv rather than La Paz. The in-house agency Diana Tours caters accordingly to the budget market. *Dbls US$30 with b/fast.*

🏠 **Hostal Angelo Colonial** (12 rooms) Av Mariscal Santa Cruz #1058; 📞 212 5067; e hostalangelocolonial@yahoo.com. A popular backpacker haunt, the rooms here are simple but adequate for budget travellers, while a communal kitchen & TV room (but no cable TV) are good places to meet other travellers. There's no b/fast & no private bathrooms, but the café next door, La Fiesta, is a good bet for drinks & snacks & provides an ideal venue to cement new friendships. The owners also run the Angelo Colonial restaurant in Calle Linares, located 2 blocks parallel to the hostel. *Sgls/dbls/tpls 35/65/90Bs.*

🏠 **Hostal Austria** (12 rooms) Calle Yanacocha #531; 📞 240 8540; e hotelaustria@ accelerate.com. Cheap & sometimes cheerful, this long-standing backpacker crash-pad has some of the cheapest rooms in town — just don't go expecting too many homely touches. It's handy for Plaza Murillo & the museum district, but the rooms are basic, some with hand basins but no private bathrooms. There is, however, on-site internet access (4Bs/hr), laundry (7Bs per kg) & a communal kitchen to mix with other travellers. Note: the place is locked between 23.00 & 06.00 — & the curfew is enforced. *Rooms/sgls 25/35Bs pp, no b/fast.*

Whether romance blossoms across the dance floor at Mongo's, (page 82), or you fall for your next-door neighbour in a dorm room, love-struck couples do have some red-blooded options to escape the prying eyes of Bolivia's rather conservative society.

Discreetly positioned around La Paz, a slew of love hotels open their doors most days from lunchtime till late. Although not quite as brash as their Japanese counterparts, they often do feature jacuzzi baths, water beds and, crucially, complete anonymity.

In La Paz, **Motel Kandy** (*Prolongacion Fco. Bedregal #802;* ✆ *241 6942*) leads the field both for its discreet service and comfortable rooms: 100Bs for 90 minutes – ask for jacuzzi room.

For an unusually clean dirty weekend, otherwise, try a trip to the hot-springs resort of Urmiri, located three hours from downtown La Paz. Buses leaves early on Saturday mornings from the Hotel Gloria (page 277). From the Oruro highway a signpost marks the 28km bone-shaking trek down a dirt track to the historic **Hotel Gloria Umiri** (*reservations in La Paz* ✆ *240 7070;* e *titikaka@hotelgloria.com.bo*). The sauna has seen better days and the public pool gets very crowded, but the waterfall pool is a great place to wash away stress, while rooms with a private sunken bath – big enough for nudge, nudge – are worth paying the extra for. Massage is available, too – but only when the masseuse can be bothered to turn up.

Aimed at families and couples, Urmiri makes for a decent weekend break within easy reach of La Paz without breaking the bank. Take towels and wash kit, but drinking water is available free on site. Full-board weekend packages (without drinks) cost US$33 per person; discount deals are available for mid-week stays.

✖ WHERE TO EAT

RESTAURANTS

✖ **Restaurant Vienna** Calle Frederico Zuazo #1905; ✆ 244 1660; e info@restaurantvienna.com; www.restaurantvienna.com. The best international-standard restaurant in town has an impressive old-Europe setting & a strong Germanic influence with mains 35–42Bs & entrees 12–42Bs. It's not cheap, but a good excuse to dress up & mix with the local intelligentsia, all brokering deals with their clients or mistresses over lunch. The set lunch (30Bs) makes for a particularly good-value way to soak up the atmosphere, while a large selection of international magazines offer great browsing material over a coffee. American Express cards accepted. *Open Mon–Fri 12.00–14.00 & 18.30–22.00, Sun 12.00–14.30.*

✖ **Pronto** Calle Jauregui #2248; ✆ 244 1369. Good homemade pasta & some very decent vegetarian options – try the spinach ravioli (30Bs) – make this place a popular spot for travellers looking for a taste of class. Prices are higher than average with pastas (22–39Bs) & antipasta (12–22Bs), but the quality is excellent & surroundings really pleasant. *Mains 25–40Bs. Open Mon–Sat 18.30–22.30.*

✖ **La Comedie** Pasaje Medinacelli #2234; ✆ 242

3561; e lacomedie-lapaz@mixmail.com. This smart, international-style restaurant has an arty, French motif & an interior to match. Seriously upscale, the meals are all à la carte with mains around 50Bs & drinks around 10Bs. &, if you feel like splashing out, a bottle of French wine costs around 250Bs. *Open Mon–Fri 11.30–23.00, Sat & Sun 19.00–22.00.*

✖ **Elis's Pizza** Av 16 de Julio #1497; ✆ 233 5566. This popular pizza joint is conveniently located right next to the Cine Monje Campero (page 83) for meals around 20Bs, while the owners also run a cafe-style sister restaurant lower down the Prado in the Edificio Cosmos (✆ 231 8171), which offers a 15Bs set lunch. *Open Mon–Fri 11.00–23.00, Sat & Sun 11.00–21.00.*

✖ **100% Natural** Calle Sagarnaga #345; no tel. The ultimate traveller hangout, this organic juice & snack bar has some of the healthiest, natural food in La Paz with jumbo sandwiches a perennial fave (11Bs), fresh juices (7–9Bs) a winner & the best llama steak in town (22Bs). Unfortunately, service can be, at times, rather frosty. *Open Mon–Fri 08.00–22.00, Sat & Sun 09.00–21.00.*

3

Set lunch is the way to go: reliable, filling and good value, it is an essential La Paz experience. A 10Bs *almuerzo* guarantees a decent standard; 6Bs *almuerzos* exist, but your stomach may later regret economising for the sake of a few Bolivianos.

1 Hotel Torrino (*Calle Socabaya #457;* ☏ *240 6003; open daily 11.30–15.00*). A great setting on a colonial patio and a generous set lunch make this a popular lunch spot for the seriously hungry with a taste for the good life. The set lunch, served daily (15Bs), comes with a self-service salad bar and a choice of mains. At weekends the lunch (22Bs) is accompanied by a tango performance.

2 Café Capriccio (*Belisario Salinas #380;* ☏ *244 4274; open daily 09.30–22.00*). A rustic café/bar with an Italian influence, it has classical music to soothe the lunchtime rush from offices around nearby Plaza Avaroa. By night it takes on more of a cocktail-bar feel. Set lunch 10Bs, à la carte pasta mains 20Bs, small pizzas 15Bs.

3 Restaurant Surucachi (*Av 16 de Julio (Prado) #1598;* ☏ *231 2135; open daily 11.30–21.30*). Set in a fantastic old building with a rambling staircase, it's reliable, central and staffed by waiters in black ties. Set lunch 10Bs, à la carte evening mains 20Bs; there's also a café downstairs for coffees and cakes.

4 Restaurant Nelsy (*Edificio Villazon, Av Villazon #1958;* ☏ *231 9935; open daily 11.30–15.00*). A really popular locals' hangout for a generous four-course lunch, topped with coffee and a chance to catch the lunchtime news on a giant-screen TV in the back room. Set lunch 12Bs. There's a Nelsy café next door for cheap coffees and snacks.

5 Restaurant Palador (*Calle Fernando Guachalla #359;* ☏ *244 1812; open daily 11.30–15.00*). Popular with the business crowd for its a formal atmosphere and smartly-dressed waiters, this is one of the smartest *almuerzo* options in town. A filling set lunch costs 14Bs, including desert, coffee and a side dish of the closest thing to baked beans in La Paz; mains 30Bs with Brazilian specialities.

6 Hotel Europa, Café Europa (*Calle Tiahuanaco #64;* ☏ *231 5656; www.hoteleuropa.com.bo; open daily 06.30–22.30*). If you're feeling both flushed *and* hungry, the hotel's Café Europa offers a blow-out buffet set lunch with a huge range of dishes from salads to steak. It's La Paz's most waist-expanding and expensive *almuerzo* at 45Bs a pop but excellent quality.

✗ **Yussef** Calle Sagarnaga #380, 1/F (marked 'Fotocopias'); ☏ 231 7099. The favourite hangout for hungry Israelis, this Middle Eastern restaurant does the best couscous in La Paz (28Bs), plus offers some excellent options for vegetarians (try the huge vegetarian mixed plate for 35Bs). It's quieter at lunchtimes but, if you're after making a night of it, there's mint tea (4Bs) & hubble-bubble pipes (35Bs) for a post-prandial *digestif*. Open daily 11.30–15.00 & 19.00–22.00.

✗ **Le Pot-Pourri des Gourmets** Calle Linares #906, ☏ 715 40082. Located opposite the Museo de Coca, this tucked-away, first-floor restaurant is quite a little gem with b/fast served 07.30–12.00 & a great-value set menu (19Bs) served 12.00–22.30. Mains range 30–35Bs & there's a daily changing menu with a good range of Bolivian & international options. Open daily 07.30–22.30.

✗ **Restaurant Angelo Colonial** Calle Linares #922, tel 215 9633. The Angelo Colonial complex, located just off Calle Sagarnaga, is a traveller-friendly behemoth with a good café (*open 09.00–21.00*), a post office (*open Mon–Fri 08.00–20.00, Sat 08.00–16.00, Sun 09.00–12.00*), an internet café (3Bs/hr) & a tourist information office (*open daily 10.30–12.30 & 15.30–19.00*). The owners also run Hostal Angelo Colonial (page 78).

CAFÉS If you fancy reading the local papers over a decent coffee, the chain of coffee shops, **Alexander Coffee**, is Bolivia's answer to Starbucks with decent-quality coffee (from 6Bs). Best for muffins (5Bs) or wraps (20Bs), they have branches on the Prado (*Av 16 de Julio #1832;* ↘ *231 2790*) and Plaza Avaroa (*Av 20 de Octubre #2463;* ↘ *243 1006*) and in the Zona Sur. Open 07.00–23.00. By night it becomes Alexander Pub (*open until 02.00 Fri & Sat*). The following individual cafés are recommended:

Café Cuidad Plaza Estudiante; ↘ 244 1827. Not the cheapest café in town, but a handy one to know as it's the only place open 24hrs a day for a range of snacks, drinks & meals. The best seats are to be had by the windows – an excellent people-watching vantage point – & on the breezy terrace out back for some fresh air. *Coffee around 5Bs, set b/fasts & sandwiches 10Bs, mains around 30Bs.*

Enter-Cafe Calle Belisario Salinas #482; ↘ 720 93261. If you want a decent coffee (7Bs) or snack (sandwiches 17–20Bs) while you surf, then this internet café is a good, central bet. There's even a loyalty scheme to earn free internet access & b/fast (8–18Bs) served daily. *Open daily 08.00–midnight.*

Pepe's Coffee Bar Calle Jimenes #894; ↘ 245 0788. A popular traveller's coffee bar for snacks, shakes & great all-day b/fast (12–25Bs); it's also one of the few places offering take-away coffee (5–8Bs) & sandwiches (12–16Bs) in town – try the

Pepe's Burger (17Bs) with bacon & cheese & look out for the coca leaf & coffee bean table design. *Open daily 08.00–21.00.*

Fridolin Av 6 de Agosto #2415; ↘ 215 3188. An Austrian-style coffee & cake shop with a nice terrace for people-watching; try the lemon pie (6Bs) & coffee (from 5Bs). *Open daily 08.00–22.00.*

Café Royale Calle Colon corner with El Prado; ↘ 233 5932. A handy coffee shop located on a people-watching corner of the Prado. It offers coffees (3–10Bs), sandwiches (6–10Bs) & brownies (2–5Bs). *Open daily 08.00–22.00.*

Etno Café Bar Calle Jaen #772; ↘ 228 0343; e etnoproduccions@gmail.com. A hole-in-the-wall café bar on colonial Calle Jaen, Etno is a good spot for a coffee hit while visiting the museum strip. It's an arty café with music & friendly service, offering drinks (4–8Bs), b/fast (8–12Bs) & cocktails at night (10–25Bs). *Open Mon–Sat 09.00–late.*

Top Tip: if you've brought your laptop with you, seek out the **Café La Terraza** chain of coffee shops with branches on the Prado (*Av 16 de Julio,* ↘ *231 0701*) and in Sopocachi (*Av 20 de Octubre #2331;* ↘ *242 2009*) for free wi-fi internet access.

SUPERMARKETS

Zatt Av Sanchez Lima #2362; ↘ 241 4222; open 08.00–22.00. Upstairs there's a useful, although often packed, food hall, La Jungla Plaza de Comidas, with

a range of eateries from pizza to Tex-Mex & sandwiches (*open Sun–Thu 10.30–22.30, Fri & Sat 10.30–23.30*).

VEGETARIAN LA PAZ

In a country where the staple diet is meat, meat and more meat, finding a good nut cutlet is no easy task. But don't despair, there are a few hidden gems out there for tofu fans. Both 100% Natural and Yussef, located on Calle Sagarnaga (page 79), have good vegetarian options on the menu. Meanwhile, the reopened **Andromeda** (*Av Arce #2116;* ↘ *244 0726; open Mon–Fri 12.00–15.00*) has a great set lunch (30Bs) with French and Bolivian influences and some particularly creative vegetarian options. .

For serious vegetarians **Restaurant Vegetariano Armonia** (*Calle Ecuador #2286, Sopocachi;* ↘ *241 2858; open Mon–Sat 11.30–14.30*) offers an all-you-can-eat vegetarian lunch buffet for 21Bs. The pick of the bunch, however, is **Restaurant Manantial** at the Hotel Gloria (page 77), which has an enormous vegetarian buffet lunch (17Bs) and the only reported sightings of tofu in La Paz. Only go if very, very hungry. Lunch served daily 11.30–14.30.

They're small, yellow and dribble hot gravy down your chin. In La Paz alone thousands are consumed daily with shops producing 1,500 each morning. They are *salteñas*, Bolivia's favourite mid-morning savoury fix. They may look like a deformed Cornish pasty but are, in fact, a national obsession.

Served piping hot from street carts, they come in meat or vegetarian varieties. 'Good chefs are more skilled than architects. Making the perfect *salteña* is,' explains Emilio Loayza, a local baker and cooking school instructor, 'truly an art form.'

For the best-quality *salteñas* in La Paz, try **El Hornito** (*Av 6 de Agosto #2455*; no tel) for top-notch *salteñas* with both meat and vegetarian varieties (2.50Bs); **Wist'upiku** (*Calle Belisario Salinas corner with Calle 20 de Octubre;* ✆ *242 4891*) has authentic *empañadas*.

Ketal Av Arce, corner with Calle Macario Pinilla; ✆ 243 2943 & Plaza España; ✆ 242 3630; open daily 07.30–22.30. Both have a small café section offering lunches & dinners on the run (mains around 15Bs).

There's a great little bakery, **Panaderia Heral's** (*Calle 6 de Agosto #2289; no tel*), which serves up fresh bread, pastries and biscuits straight from the oven several times daily. There's also a great little hole-in-the-wall ice-cream parlour, **Collana**, on Avenida Sanchez Lima, located just before the Zatt supermarket.

ENTERTAINMENT AND NIGHTLIFE

BARS

♀ **RamJam** Calle Presbitero Medina #2421; ✆ 242 2295. The latest hotspot in town, run by an expat Englishwoman, RamJam is a funky bar/café/eatery with Saya micro-brewery beers (from 10Bs) & a good range of mains, inc curries & roasts for a taste of home (from 20Bs). There's live music during the week &, at weekends, DJs spin the place into a full-on fiesta with the dance floor packed after midnight. *Open nightly 19.00–03.00.*

♀ **Mongo's** Calle Hermanos Manchego #2444 Sopocachi; ✆ 244 0714. A popular gringo hangout, this bar & restaurant has candles on the tables & occasional live music to foster the expat & Bolivian mingling — only the constant football on TV dominating the first room tends to spoil the ambience. Beers 10–18Bs & cocktails 18–24Bs. The food is of good quality, notably the chicken cordon bleu (28Bs), beef stroganoff (38Bs) & fish & chips (30Bs). *Open nightly 18.30–late.*

♀ **Sol y Luna** Calle Murillo #999; ✆ 720 97932. A popular traveller bar with a great CD collection, this place has a candlelit ambience & an extensive bilingual menu with a strong Dutch motif (the owner is from the Netherlands). Mains (20–28Bs) are generous & inventive, especially the chicken in chocolate — yes, chocolate — sauce, while vegetarian mains (20–26Bs) & the mixed plates for sharing

(24–32Bs) are good value. Beers come by the pint (10–14Bs), while house cocktails range 14–25Bs — try the house cocktail, the Mojito Boliviano with singani & coca leaves. *Open Mon–Sat 18.00–late.*

♀ **The Lounge** Calle Presbitero Medina #2527; ✆ 241 0585; e theloungeartbistro@yahoo.com. This arty café/bistro is a welcome new addition to the La Paz scene with art exhibitions, cocktails & supper served nightly. The best option is to share plates of tapas (16–30Bs) with a glass of wine or beer (10Bs) — try the sushi made with trout from Lake Titicaca (30Bs). A fireplace & jazz music backdrop complete the cosy feeling. *Open nightly 19.00–midnight.*

♀ **Oliver's Travels** Calle Murillo #1014; no tel. Rapidly becoming the favourite gringo hang-out in town, this '100% fake English pub' claims to be the 'fifth-best bar in La Paz, except on Sundays when Sol y Luna is closed'. A sense of humour, live sports coverage & the likes of beans on toast (12Bs) & bacon & eggs (15Bs) cement the reputation. The steaks are particularly good (25Bs) & a pint of lager costs 14Bs for a taste of home. *Open daily 08.00–01.00.*

♀ **Green Bar** Belisario Salinas #596; ✆ 242 0690. A smoky, divey bar with a good mix of locals & travellers all just a few mins' stumble from Plaza

Avaroa. It's a no-frills but authentic joint – think loud music, pictures of the Beatles on the walls & jugs of draught beer a-plenty. *Open Mon–Sat 18.30–late.*
♀ **La Luna** Calle Oruro #197; ✆ 233 5523;

e publalunabolivia@hotmail.com. Divey & slightly run-down, this is the place where most pub crawls end up, knocking back shots until the last man falls over. *Open daily 19.00 until late; happy hour 20.00–21.00.*

LIVE MUSIC

♀ **Puerta del Sol** Calle Max Paredes corner with Sagarnaga; ✆ 245 7978. This so-called *peña* (folkloric music) pub is one of La Paz's leading live music venues with local bands playing every Fri & Sat night. This may be a folk club, but don't expect real ale & Arran sweaters — Bolivian folk music is an even more acquired taste. *Open 19.00–late; entrance from 15Bs upwards according to the popularity of the act.*
♀ **Thelonious Jazz Bar** Av 20 de Octubre #2172; ✆ 242 4405. Dark & smoky, this cool jazz bar has live music Wed–Sat & jazz concert videos every Tue (when entrance is free). Book ahead for big-name shows. *Open Tue–Sat 19.00–02.00; entrance from 30Bs.*

♀ **Peña Restaurant Huari** Calle Sagarnaga #339, 1/F; ✆ 231 6225. This huge restaurant caters very much to large tour groups with its nightly *peña* music show starting at 20.00. The entrance fee includes 1 drink, but all food is extra with mains from 70–100Bs, making it one of the priciest nights out in town. *Open daily 19.00–late; entrance US$10.*
♀ **Peña Restaurant Marka Tambo** Calle Jaen #710; ✆ 228 0041. This place is also pretty much geared towards the tourist dollar, but well known for its peña shows, staged Thu–Sat at 22.00, which attract some well-known local musicians. There's a 30Bs pp entrance fee while à la carte mains start from 35Bs. *Open Thu–Sat 19.00–late.*

CINEMAS Screenings generally cost around 20Bs for the main features with off-peak prices available.

Cine Monje Campero Av 16 de Julio #1495; ✆ 233 3332. The city's most modern cinema presents the recent international film releases with screenings 3 times daily.

Cine 16 de Julio Av 16 de Julio #1807, corner with Plaza Estudiante; ✆ 244 1099. Screenings 3 times daily.
Cine 6 de Agosto Calle 6 de Agosto #2284; ✆ 244 2629. Screenings twice daily.

CULTURAL CENTRES Both of the following have small language libraries and offer language courses, plus stage occasional cultural events.

Alliance Francaise Calle Fernando Guachalla #399 corner with Av 20 de Octubre; ✆ 242 3660; www.afbolivia.org. This place is also home to the

pricey but cosy French-style café bar, **Le Bistrot** (✆ 211 8060).
Goethe Institute Av 6 de Agosto 2118; ✆ 244 2453; www.goethe.de/lapaz

Cultural events for the month ahead are posted outside the **Municipal Library** in Plaza del Estudiante (*www.bibliotecamunicipal.gov.bo*) and in the foyer of the **Casa de la Cultura Franz Tamayo** (*Corner Av Mariscal Santa Cruz & Calle Potosí;* ✆ 240 6816) The **Museo y Centro Cultural San Francisco** (*located to the side of the cathedral,* ✆ 231 8472) hosts occasional exhibitions, such as the World Press Photo exhibition; open daily 09.00–21.00.

The **TEA Instituto Cultural** (*Av Arce, Parque Zenon Iturralde #110;* ✆ 243 2185) study centre offers a range of dance classes, ranging from the folkloric to modern styles, such as salsa, hip hop and even – intriguingly – one called *robotico*. There are also aerobics, ballet and martial arts classes. Cost per lesson 50Bs with eight 1-hour-long classes per month; classes run 10.00–12.00 & 15.00–21.00.

The huge number of cloth shops are one of La Paz's best-kept secrets and **John Pacheco Tailoring** (*Edificio Florida, Calle Rosendo Gutierrez #255;* ☎ *244 0500; open Mon-Sat 10.00–19.30*) is one of the best. A man's shirt costs US$8, a dress US$12, a women's two-piece suit US$25 and a man's three-piece suit US$50. Three days are required for completion and you need to buy your own material first (US$2.50–5, depending on the quality). Market stalls to the north of Calle Santa Cruz make for the best hunting ground for the latter.

SHOPPING

Military Look Calle Almirante Grau #165; no tel. This hidden gem of a shop has recycled ex-military gear at good prices – ideal for camping gear, waterproof ponchos (US$10) & canvas backpacks (US$3) if you're planning a jungle trip, or an excursion to the Salar de Uyuni. Russian soldier hats for fancy dress fans are a bargain at US$8–12. *Open 09.30–13.00 & 15.00–19.00.*

LAM 100% Alpaca Calle Sagarnaga #295; ☎ 231 6871; e artesanias_lam@yahoo.com. A chain of craft shops dotted around Calle Sagarnaga, they sell good-quality alpaca goods but aim squarely at the tourist market; prices from 395–530Bs for sweaters, ponchos & cardigans. *Open 09.00–12.30 & 15.00–19.00.*

Galeria Millma Calle Sagarnaga #225; ☎ 231 1338; e millma@adslmail.entelnet.bo; www.millmaalpaca.com. The owners of this upscale alpaca-wear shop make a great selection of quality textiles & alpaca goods in their own factory. Again they are catering very much for the tourist market. Prices from US$97–150, credit cards accepted. *Open 09.30–12.30 & 15.00–19.30.*

Los Amigos del Libro Calle Mercado #1315; ☎ 220 4321. La Paz's favourite foreign-language bookshop has a good range of titles in English, inc guides, maps & dictionaries. *Open Mon–Fri 09.30–12.30 & 15.00–19.30, Sat 09.30–12.30.*

Caroline Calvert of the Llama Express (www.theexpress.org)
La Paz has often been described as one big street market and the markets are without doubt one of the most vibrant and interesting aspects of La Paz daily life. Indeed, practically anything can be found at very competitive prices – especially after a little haggling. Refine your skills at the following.

FERIA DEL ALTO La Paz's largest street market sells the most random and eclectic selection of items. It takes some hunting but there are bargains to be found; the selection of second-hand and imported wear is particularly good. Open Thursdays and Sundays; take any bus from the city to El Alto.

MERCADO RODRÍGUEZ This is the best and cheapest food market in La Paz. As well as great fruit and vegetables, Rodriguez is the place to buy fresh fish from Lake Titicaca and seafood from Peru. But get there early to pick up the freshest produce possible. This market is perhaps the best place to observe the street life and the workings of a busy, functioning market. Open daily at Calle Rodriguez. Similar, but more expensive, is the **Mercado Sopocachi** in Sopocachi.

MERCADO DE HECHICERIA (WITCHES' MARKET) Locals joke you can buy anything in La Paz's sprawling street market area, but where Sagarnaga crosses Linares, you *really* can. Here the merchandise takes a more sinister turn with potions and charms designed to placate the Aymara spirit world. Earthenware figures each represent a request for

OTHER PRACTICALITIES

AGFA PHOTO LAB (*Branches on Plaza Estudiante & Plaza San Francisco;* ✆ *240 7030; open daily 09.00–20.00*) They develop slide film for 15Bs without mounts, 33Bs with, and will burn images to CD for 30Bs.

BETO HAIRDRESSERS (*Av 6 de Agosto #2216;* ✆ *244 4025; open 09.00–20.30*) This salon for both men and women is run by a stylist trained by Vidal Sassoon in London; a wash and cut costs 90Bs.

CENTRAL POST OFFICE (*Open Mon–Fri 08.00–20.00, Sat 08.00–18.00, Sun 09.00–12.00*) The office downstairs for weighing and packaging large packets opens 08.00–12.00 & 14.30–18.30.

FOTO LAB CAPRI (*Av Mariscal Santa Cruz corner with Calle Colon;* ✆ *237 0134; www.tecnologiafotografica.com; open 09.00–13.00 & 15.00–19.00*) The best bet in town for camera repairs and parts – but not yet for digital cameras. Ask for Señor Rolando Calla, available mornings only from 11.00.

IMMIGRATION OFFICE (*Calle Camacho #1480,* ✆ *237 0475; open 08.30–13.00 & 13.30–16.00*) This is where to enquire about visa extensions. Don't join the normally huge queue outside, simply go to window number 12, marked *Tramites de Extranjeria*. Top tip: If you arrived overland and only got a 30-day visa, you can extend to 90 days without charge at the sister office across the road (*Calle Camacho #1433; open 09.00–12.30 & 14.30–17.00*). Take a photocopy of your passport and current green entry form.

good luck in different contexts. The monkey promises good fortune and prosperity, the tortoise signifies a long life and the owl, perhaps more obviously, symbolises wisdom. The perennial bestseller is, however, the dried llama foetus, a ghoulish charred skeleton to be buried in the foundations of new homes or offices to ensure future prosperity. Best of all, this is a working market and, if you're lucky, you may even stumble across a *yatiri* (faith healer). Offer him a financial incentive (just a few Bolivianos is enough) and he'll bless your new purchase on the spot. Open every day, but they say you have better luck on a Tuesday or Friday; Calle Linares between Calles Santa Cruz and Sagarnaga.

MERCADO URUGUAY Second-hand clothes and artisan handicrafts are de rigueur in this sprawling street market. The stalls near the plaza are largely an overspill of the shops on Calle Sagarnaga, selling scarves and ponchos, while meandering up Calle Graneros, the stalls are dominated by copies of brand-name clothes. Beware: quality can be variable. Open Fridays and Saturdays; Plaza San Francisco environs and Calle Graneros.

MERCADO MAX PAREDES The most typically Bolivian of the markets in La Paz, this is a real local's favourite for traditional garb and coca leaves. The streets branching off have pots, pans and kitchen accessories, plus electrical goods, but make sure such items are in good working order and come with all the necessary accessories before parting with your cash. Best on Saturdays; Calle Max Paredes.

La Paz OTHER PRACTICALITIES

3

SKORPIO HAIRDRESSERS (*Galeria Postal, Av 6 de Agosto;* ✆ *244 2024; open Mon–Fri 09.00–13.00 & 15.00–20.00, Sat 09.00–16.00 without a lunch break*) A barber's shop-style place offering a cut from 40Bs.

SPEAKEASY INSTITUTE (*Av Arce #2047;* ✆ *244 1779;* e *speakeasyinstitute@yahoo.com; www.speakeasyinstitute.com*) A well-regarded language school offering Spanish classes taught by native speakers and courses starting from 20 hours' tuition. There's also a book exchange and the ex-pat owner is a vital source of general advice for travellers.

SUDAMER CAMBIO (*Calle Camacho #1311;* ✆ *220 3148*) This is the currency exchange house everyone uses. They accept Visa, Amex and Thomas Cook travellers' cheques (expect a 1.5% commission charge), plus offer fair rates for other Latin American currencies, so plan ahead and don't lose out on those border-crossing exchanges.

TOURIST POLICE (*Plaza del Estadio, Miraflores;* ✆ *222 5016*) This is where to fill in the theft form you'll need to make an insurance claim.

MEDICAL SERVICES
24-hour pharmacy Super Drugs Plaza Avaroa; ✆ 243 4444
Dentist Dr Jorge Aguirre, Edificio Illimani II, Av Arce #2677; ✆ 243 0496
Hospital Clinica del Sur Av Hernando Siles, Obrajes, Zona Sur; ✆ 278 4001
Laboratory results Labclinics at Unimed Av Arce #2630; ✆ 243 1133. Open Mon–Sat 08.00–22.00

EMBASSIES
⊖ **Australia** Edificio Montevideo, Av Arce #2081; ✆ 244 0459; f 244 0801; www.chile.embassy.gov.au. Open Mon–Fri 08.30–13.00.

⊖ **Brasil** Edificio Multicentro Torre B, Av Arce #2229, ✆ 244 0202; e embajadadobrasil@accelerate.com. Open Mon–Fri 09.00–12.45.

⊖ **Canada** Edificio Barcelona 2/F, Plaza España; ✆ 241 5021; f 241 4453; e lapaz@dfait-maeci.gc.ca; www.dfait-maeci.gc.ca/latinamerica/bolivia-en.asp. Open Mon–Fri 08.00–12.00.

⊖ **France** Av Hernando Siles #5390, Obrajes; ✆ 278 6114; f 278 6746; e information@ambafrance-bo.org; www.ambafrance-bo.org. Open Mon–Fri 08.30–12.30.

⊖ **Germany** Av Arce #2395; ✆ 244 0066; out of hours emergency ✆ 244 1166; f 244 1441; e info@embajada-alemana-bolivia.or; www.embajada-alemana-bolivia.org/de/home/Default.htm.

Reception open Mon–Fri 09.00–12.00.
⊖ **Great Britain** Av Arce #2732; ✆ 243 3424; out of hours emergency ✆ 715 55557; f 243 1073; e ppa@megalink.com; www.britishembassy.gov.uk/bolivia. Desk service Mon–Fri 09.00–12.00.

⊖ **Italy** Calle 5 Jordan Cuellar #458; ✆ 278 8507; f 278 8178; e ambitlap@ceibo.entelnet.bo. Reception open Mon–Fri 09.30–12.30.

⊖ **Netherlands** Edificio Hilda 7/F, Av 6 de Agosto #2455; ✆/f 244 4040; f 244 3804; e nllap@caoba.entelnet.bo; www.embholanda-bo.org. Open Mon–Fri 08.30–17.00.

⊖ **Spain** Av 6 de Agosto #2827; ✆ 243 1203; f 243 2386; e embespa@ceibo.entelnet.bo. Open Mon–Fri 09.00–12.30.

⊖ **United States** Av Arce #2780; ✆ 216 8000; f 216 8111; e consularlapaz@state.gov; http://bolivia.usembassy.gov. Reception Mon–Fri 08.30–13.00 & 14.00–17.30.

AIRLINES
✈ **AeroSur** Av Mariscal Santa Cruz #616; ✆ 243 0430; e aerosur@aerosur.com; www.aerosur.com. In the same building (11/F) you can join the Club AeroSur loyalty scheme. Open Mon–Fri 08.30–12.30 & 14.30–19.00.

✈ **Aerolineas Argentinas** Edificio Petrolero Av Mariscal Santa Cruz #1616, ✆ 235 1711; f 239 1059: e interfly@acelerate.com; www.aerolineas.com.ar. Open Mon–Fri 09.00–12.00 & 14.30–18.30, Sat 09.30–12.30.

✈ **Amazonas** Av Saavedra #1649, Miraflores, ☎ 222 0848; www.amazonas.com. *Open Mon–Fri 09.00–12.30 & 14.30–19.00, Sat 09.00–12.00.*
✈ **American Airlines** Edificio Hermann, Av 16 de Julio # 1440; ☎ 235 1360; www.aa.com. *Open 09.00–18.30, Sat 10.00–12.00.*
✈ **Lloyd Aereo Boliviano (LAB)** Calle Camacho #1460; ☎ 237 1020; toll-free reservations ☎ 800 10 3001; toll-free customer service ☎ 800 10 1007. *Open Mon–Fri 08.30–12.30 & 14.30–18.30, Sat 09.00–12.00.*

✈ **TACA** Edificio San Pablo 4/F, Av 16 de Julio #1479; ☎ 231 3132; www.taca.com. Has introduced services from La Paz & Santa Cruz to Lima with onward connections within Latin America. *Open Mon–Fri 09.00–12.30 & 14.30–18.30, Sat 09.00–12.30.*
✈ **Varig** Edificio Camara de Comercio, Av Mariscal Santa Cruz, ☎ 231 4040; www.varig.com.bo. *Open Mon–Fri 09.00–12.00 & 14.30–19.00, Sat 09.30–12.00.*

WHAT TO SEE AND DO

While Plaza Murillo, with its cathedral and parliament building, is the historic hub of the city, the main sights are as follows.

MUSEO DE COCA (*Calle Linares #906,* ☎ *231 1998; www.cocamuseum.com; open daily 10.00–19.00; entrance 8Bs*) The city's best museum tackles the thorny issue of coca with an informed and objective jaunt through the history of the much-maligned coca leaf. Surprisingly insightful, it leaves you to make up your own mind about a continually contentious topic, starting with the historical context – coca has been chewed by indigenous tribes in the Andes for over 4,000 years – and moves on through a scientific explanation of the production of cocaine to its subsequent effects on humans.

There are some revelations for trivia fans too: did you know, for example, that in 1859 the active ingredient of the leaves – yes, that is cocaine – was isolated and used to give Coca-Cola drinkers a little spring in their step right up until 1906.

In the same courtyard is the less compelling but suitably anthropological **Museo del Arte Textil Andino Boliviano** (☎ *231 6396; open daily 08.00–19.00; entrance 8Bs*).

MUSEO DE ARTE CONTEMPORÁNEO (*Plaza Av 16 de Julio #1698;* ☎ *233 5905; open Mon–Sun 09.00–21.00; entrance adult/child 10/3Bs*) Set in a striking 19th-century colonial building (Gustave Eiffel had a hand in the design), there are three floors of modern artworks. The standard of the works can be variable, but the setting is always attractive.

MUSEO NACIONAL DE ARQUEOLOGÍA (*Calle Tiahuanaco #93;* ☎ *231 1621; open Mon–Fri 09.00–12.30 & 15.00–19.00; Sat 10.00–12.30 & 15.00–18.30; entrance 10Bs*) This is an hour well spent for anyone planning a trip out to the Inca ruins of Tiahuanaco.

MUSEO NACIONAL DE ARTE (*Calle Comercio corner with Calle Socabaya #432;* ☎ *240 8640; www.mna.org.bo; open Tue–Sat 09.30–12.30 & 15.00–19.00, Sun 09.30–12.30; entrance foreigners/Bolivians 10/5Bs*) La Paz's finest baroque building includes a collection of Andean art classics spread across three floors, including works by Bolivia's best-known artist, Melchor Pérez de Holguin.

MUSEO NACIONAL DE ETNOGRAFÍA Y FOLKLORE (*Calle Ingavi #916;* ☎ *235 8559; open Tue–Sat 09.30–12.30 & 15.00–19.00, Sun 09.30–12.30; free entry*) Housed in a historic building, this museum explores indigenous Indian culture through its arts and crafts, such as weavings and masks – one for the anthropology buffs.

Emma Carr of the Llama Express (www.theexpress.org)

The Bolivian culture is rich with superstition, mystical beliefs and bizarre rituals, many of which date back to pre-Inca times. One of the strangest of all is the *fiesta de las ñatitas* (festival of skulls), which falls on 9 November and closes the week-long celebration for All Saints.

Skulls are brought to the chapel at La Paz's general cemetery to be given a Catholic blessing. It has only been in the past few years that the ritual has been recognised by the Church, but priests still will not associate the rite with mass. Previously, this Ayamaran custom was practised in secret, although the ritual now attracts hundreds of faithful believers every year.

While some families possess the skulls of their deceased relatives and friends who they believe to still be watching over them, a vast number are complete unknowns that have been purchased at morgues or medical facilities. The skulls are placed in empty niches in the walls of the cemetery chapel and are adorned with garlands, petals, candles and coca leaves. After the blessings, the skulls are returned to the owners' homes, where it is believed that they will bring the family protection and good fortune for the rest of the year.

CALLE JAÉN MUSEUMS La Paz's best-preserved colonial street is home to four museums accessed by a single ticket (foreigners/Bolivians 4/3Bs) and all open Tues–Sat 09.30–12.30 & 15.00–19.00, Sun 09.00–13.00.

Of these, the **Museo Costumbrista Jean de Vargas** (✆ 237 8478) with displays on La Paz's colourful history and characters, is the most rewarding. The **Museo de Litoral Boliviano** is also worth a look for its maps detailing the coastline Bolivia lost to Chile in the War of the Pacific, while the **Museo de Metales Preciosos** and **Museo Casa de Murillo** are less exciting.

MUSEO DE INSTRUMENTOS MUSICALES ERNESTO CAVOUR (*Calle Jaén #711;* ✆ *240 8177; Open Tues–Fri 09.30–13.00 & 14.30–18.30, Sat & Sun 09.30–13.00; entrance adults/children 5/1Bs*) Cavour, one of Bolivia's leading folk musicians, hosts visits and offers guitar and *charango* (a ukelele-style instrument, see page 30) classes at this small but worthwhile little museum. Lessons can also be arranged for the *zampoña* (pan pipes) and the *quena* (a wooden flute-like instrument). Three one-hour lessons a week, spread over the course of a month, cost 150Bs.

EXCURSIONS FROM LA PAZ

CHACALATYA Once the world's highest ski resort (5,300m), **Chacaltaya** has subsequently become Bolivia's highest-profile victim of global warming. Located 36km from La Paz by a bumpy bus journey, the site was founded by the Club Andino Boliviano (CAB) in 1939 and once boasted a 2km piste at an altitude that leaves most ski resorts gasping for breath.

It was a British engineer, Raul Posnansky, and his fellow ski enthusiasts, who built the first refuge on-site and helped skiing to blossom in Bolivia before he died in an avalanche in 1945.

In 2002 scientists predicted that Chacalatya had less than five years of active skiing left before all the snow melts away. It's still hanging on in there but, today, it's mainly the ghosts of fallen skiers who frequent the piste.

On-site there's a small and rather overpriced café with hot chocolates (10Bs), hot coffee with rum (10Bs) and sandwiches (6Bs). There are very basic bathroom facilities and a relatively easy-going one-hour walking trail around the site with great views across the Andean range. From December to March you can still just about get a ski run. The lodge will hire out skis and boots for 100Bs per person/day, including use of the ski lift.

Visits can be arranged in La Paz with the **Club Andino Boliviano** (*Calle Mexico #1638;* ✆ *231 0863;* f *231 2875;* e *fecab@bolivia.com*). Tour agencies, such as Maya Tours (page 72), charge 50Bs for a half-day visit, excluding lunch and the entrance fee to the Chacaltaya ski lodge (10Bs).

FROM CHESTER TO LA PAZ

Stephen McKeown

Mallasa Zoo, set in the La Paz suburb of the same name, is the highest zoo in the world. For a very modest entry fee you can easily spend a whole day relaxing in spectacular scenery and getting close up and personal with some equally spectacular Andean wildlife. Although Mallasa Zoo faces the same challenges as other zoos in developing countries, the director and staff, with the support of city politicians, are committed to making it a five-star conservation centre and tourist attraction. To help them realise their ambitious plans they engaged the help of staff from Chester Zoo, the UK's most popular animal attraction.

Chester Zoo's Director, Gordon McGregor Reid, travelled to La Paz assisted by a grant from British Executive Service Overseas (BESO; now merged with VSO) and produced a report on the zoo with a list of recommendations for the way forward. This sowed the seeds for an ongoing relationship where education and conservation specialists from Chester went on a follow-up visit accompanied by colleagues from Spain and Colombia. After ten days of intensive workshops and discussions, enough information had been gathered for a second, more detailed report to be produced with action plans for all areas of the zoo's activities.

The zoo certainly has potential. The setting is an attraction in itself and there's plenty of space for expansion. A smelly rubbish dump next to the zoo has been closed down and cleaned up and a litter recycling scheme for visitors introduced. Birdwatchers get some easy ticks here as wild birds flock to the zoo to take advantage of leftovers from feeding time. Hummingbirds, including the giant variety, are all over the place sipping nectar from the zoo's gardens.

The education team at Mallasa is hoping to set up feeding stations for wild birds with identification panels to help locals appreciate their own wildlife and, hopefully, attract tourists to the zoo. Probably the most spectacular exhibit in the zoo, certainly its most dominant feature, is the huge condor aviary. These birds actually look prehistoric at close quarters – a rare view because elsewhere you'll probably only see them as a speck soaring over the mountain.

The zoo also has one of the biggest collections of jaguars in the world. This cat, almost impossible to see in the wild, breeds quite readily in zoos and Chester Zoo helped the Mallasa team to set up a family planning programme (complete with contraceptives) for the jaguars, to stop the several dozen who live here taking over the whole zoo.

This kind of partnership works for everybody given that saving species from extinction is the intended result. And if a visit to Mallasa zoo becomes part of the La Paz tourist circuit, the extra funds that generates can only help the zoo realise its vision for the future.

Stephen McKeown is Head of Education at Britain's Chester Zoo (www.chesterzoo.org)

THE VALLE DE LA LUNA At the far south of the well-to-do suburbs of the Zona Sur, the **Valle de la Luna** (Moon Valley) makes for a half-day escape from the noise and pollution of downtown La Paz. Despite the name, however, don't go expecting a lunar landscape, rather a warmer and drier landscape dotted with large rocky outcrops gnarled into bizarre, futuristic formations by thousands of years of erosion – and lots of cacti. To enter the main park area, where most bus tours stop off, there's a 15Bs entrance fee payable.

A visit can be combined with a trip to Mallasa (entrance 3.50Bs, see page 89), where lowlights include a room full of fairly dormant reptiles, a tiny condor enclosure and a section devoted to big cats that pace up and down their cages in vain search of an escape hole.

More worthwhile is a hiking excursion to the **Muela del Diablo** (The Devil's Molar), a huge rock towering over the whole of Zona Sur, using rocky paths to scramble over the landscape. The reward is some pretty impressive views across the area.

The area can be visited as part of an organised tour with any of the agencies on Calle Sagarnaga, although most just pass through for a photo stop. Alternatively, for a more leisurely pace, catch a minibus marked 'Zoológico' or 'Valle de la Luna' from the corner of Calle Mexico and Plaza del Estudiante – it's a 45-minute ride; a return taxi ride will cost about 50Bs with waiting time.

Tourists are not advised to try camping in this area since reports of after-dark thefts and muggings in recent years. You should follow the example of the tour groups and return to the main downtown area before nightfall.

TREKKING *with James Brunker (www.magicalandes.com)*

The 150km of Bolivia's Cordillera Real stretch from the Sorata Valley to Río La Paz (Río Choqueyapu), providing a splendid backdrop for the world's highest capital city. There are six peaks over 6,000m, and many more above the 5,000m mark. This mountain range is perfect for backpacking, offering days of hiking above the treeline with snow-capped mountains appearing round almost every bend, and steep descents to the tropical vegetation of the Yungas.

The trails described in this section start within a day's journey of La Paz, and a couple of them are only a few hours away. There is no problem acclimatising for the hikes: a few days' sightseeing in La Paz will take care of that.

ZONGO TO LA CUMBRE OR COROICO This is a high-altitude walk – between 3,900m and 4,880m – partly along a good trail and partly cross-country, taking you parallel to the glaciers of Huayna Potosí, past a series of lakes, and connecting with the La Cumbre–Coroico trail. There are plenty of options for well-prepared and adventurous backpackers. Allow three to five days, bring all the warm clothes you've got, as the first two nights will be bitterly cold. Stock up well with provisions before departure.

The route starts from the comfortable Huayna Potosí Refuge by the reservoir at Zongo Pass. A taxi there from La Paz will cost around US$20; alternatively contact the Huayna Potosí Travel Agency in La Paz who own and run the Refuge (*Calle Sagarnaga 398 corner Calle Illampu, ℡ 2317324/2456717, www.huayna.com*). They can also provide up-to-date information and offer hikes and climbs in the area.

The trail follows the Zongo road as it continues down the valley in a series of zigzags. After 2km, just after the second hairpin bend, your trail leads off to the right and across a small stream. The path is faint at times, disappearing altogether across open pasture, but you should have little difficulty following it along the contours of the mountain, above and parallel to the valley road. The views of Huayna Potosí are splendid, and soon the snowy peak of Telata comes into view.

After 90 minutes you'll pass a small lake, and three or four hours after leaving the road the path swings round a lower peak called Chekapa and heads towards an unnamed pass at 4,880m. Beyond the pass is a well-watered valley with a series of dammed lakes, part of another hydro-electric scheme. There's good camping all along this valley.

From the dam at the first lake, continue east to the second lake, taking a path along the south (right) shore and uphill towards Laguna Telata, whose dam is just visible. There are marvellous views of the dramatic snow-covered peak known as Tiquimani (the peak is incorrectly marked Illampu on IGM maps). The last possible camping places for several hours are near this lake, either below the dam or at the far shore. This is where the cross-country stretch begins.

Walk across the dam and make your way over rocks and cliffs, guided by cairns, above the northern shore of the lake. This involves scrambling but no technical climbing. At the eastern end of the lake, start up the scree slope towards the lowest point on the shoulder above you to your left (northeast). This climb, again guided by cairns, isn't difficult and will take about an hour.

From the top you'll see three lakes and a shoulder to your right. From this shoulder you should make your way down towards the southeast and over a wall, then pick up a very faint path to the right of a stonefall. Continue steeply downhill to a swampy area studded with Andean gentians. Go down to the valley bottom and the river. As you veer east beneath the crags of Jishka Telata you'll pass a large cave beneath some monstrous fallen boulders – an excellent shelter if the weather is bad. Continue to follow the river on its left bank until the trail at last asserts itself and you can follow it easily to a hacienda, Sanja Pampa, and the bridge beyond.

After crossing the river you'll pass through a scattering of houses and up a steep but good path skirting round the end of a ridge called Waca Kunca. As it levels out, the trail passes several ponds, crosses a stream, then heads south, descending steeply before turning southwest to the village of Achura (Chucura). There's a bridge across the river and it is a short climb to reach the main trail just above the village.

Here you must make the decision either to go up to La Cumbre, about six hours away, or to continue down to Coroico which will take you two more days.

The Zongo Valley The Zongo Valley provides an alternative, yet not necessarily easy, route to the North and South Yungas. As with all journeys through these valleys east of the Andes, you experience rapid and surprising changes in climate and vegetation. Just below the pass you might see small herds of llamas grazing on esparto grass and glaciers spilling over high cliff edges. Then slightly lower down you will notice a few shrubs and trees covered with moss, which will give way to forest and, eventually, sub-tropical broad-leaved plants and hardwood trees. It's hard to find a more dramatic change in scenery in such a short distance.

The approach to the valley is the same as going to Zongo Lake and the beginning of the trailhead to the Cumbre, except you continue along the well-reinforced and maintained road zigzagging dizzily down (you drop over 1,500m in a few kilometres) through a valley of waterfalls, rivers and hydro-electric stations.

Simply follow the road, keeping right at any branches and continue steadily down past the hydro-electric stations including Zongo, Botijlaca and Cuticucho. After the Santa Rosa station you will pass by an outdoor cement football court on your right; then, further down, a small school on your left. Just below these, to the right of the road, is a large open area of grass with a small building (bathrooms) and a thatched gazebo. This is the Scout Camp, established several years ago for camping.

ALTERNATIVE ROUTES AROUND ZONGO

There are several variations on the above route in the Zongo area for the keen trekker. The first starts a few minutes after the trail leaves the Zongo road; a path branches right up the side valley and arrives at a small dam and lake, Laguna Canada, after an hour. From the far end climb up to meet a small aqueduct and follow it upstream to a couple of smaller lagoons (rapidly drying as the glaciers in the area recede). Follow the faint trail and cairns up the valley behind and left of these lagoons to arrive at a pass in another hour. From the pass you can scramble up the ridge to your left to the 5,090m summit of Cerro Huayata for great views of Huayna Potosí and down the Zongo valley. From the pass the trail drops steeply down to the right side of the next valley and follows it down to Samana Pampa, the first village on the La Cumbre – Coroico trail. La Cumbre is five hours uphill, Coroico two or three days down the trail.

A second option starts from the first lake below the unnamed 4,880m pass described above. From the dam at the end of this lake, follow round the left (west) shore of the second lake to another dam; a path drops steeply below the dam to a third bottle-green lake below you. Steps have been cut into some of the steep slabs, so take care if it's icy. Drop down the left side of the outlet stream of this third lake and into the main valley heading roughly north. As this valley opens out (the stream temporarily disappears under an old landslide) head across this valley and up into the side valley coming in from the right (southeast) before some large black rocky slabs. The path is very faint at first but soon becomes clearer before it climbs past and above two beautiful lakes with superb views back to the looming black bulk of Mount Tiquimani. Cross a pass about 45 minutes above the second lake, then head straight ahead to the right of a conical hill before dropping in stages to meet the main valley. Follow this valley down to the small hamlet of Sanja Pampa; you have now rejoined the route described in the main text.

A variant on this second option is to keep heading down the main valley below the third lake. This brings you to the hamlet of Uma Palca in around an hour, in a dramatic location beneath the walls of Tiquimani. From Uma Palca follow the valley up to the west directly below the flanks of Tiquimani; this valley leads to Lake Warawarani in a couple of hours. Shortly after the lake you cross a pass. Below here a road connected with hydroelectric works takes you down to the main La Paz – Zongo road passing a couple of lakes, coming out at Estancia Botijlacta. Look for paths to cut off the hairpins. Transport from Zongo to La Paz passes Botijlacta in the mornings from around 09.00.

The Zongo, like each of the Yungas valleys, is a micro-ecosystem and you have a good chance of sighting plants or birds that can be found only in these valleys.

Perhaps one of the most interesting activities in the area is to explore the numerous maintenance trails that lead both east and west into the mountains from the River Zongo at the base of the valley. One of these trails begins after crossing a narrow iron bridge just opposite the Scout Camp and leads you up along a steep, forested hillside, then across a large steel pipe and up the spine from where you can catch glimpses of the jungle valleys far below. Be careful: when it is rainy the pipes are very slippery. If you don't mind heights and are sure-footed, it's a thrill to follow the aqueduct that runs from Planta Harca along the side of a cliff to a village beside the Río Yohuilaque. Higher up in the valley there are canals cutting through the rock in long tunnels that are worth a look.

After the last hydro station (Planta Huaji) a rough trail leads farther down the valley until it meets with the Río Coroico. This portion of the hike might take two to three days, depending on the weather. Once you arrive at the Río Coroico, follow the path going left for several kilometres until you come to the village of Bella Vista. Here you can cross over to the town of Alcoche where transportation back to La Paz, or deeper into the lowlands, can be found.

The Condoriri circuit The Condoriri group of mountains is well known to climbers as offering some of the best scenery in Bolivia and plenty of peaks to climb, varying from very easy to extremely difficult.

For hikers and backpackers Lake Chiar Kota (4,600m) is a lovely natural lake where you can stay to enjoy the scenery, a route which takes you to the Zongo area and possible links with other treks. The lake is used as a base camp for mountaineers to explore the nearby peaks.

The base camp for the three-day Condoriri circuit and other hikes is easily reached from the small village of Tuni. There is no public transport to Tuni, but a group could easily organize transport through an agency in La Paz; this will cost around US$30 for a taxi, or US$80 for a 4x4. Alternatively there is often space in vehicles taking mountaineering groups; agencies normally charge US$10–15 per person for the trip. If you prefer to use public transport, take any transport in the direction of Lake Titicaca and get off at the first village, Patamanta, some 10–15km beyond the tranca (toll-gate). You will see a dirt road leading off to the right. Follow the dirt road to the top rim of a broad river gorge. Ask villagers for Tuni-Condoriri, the name of the reservoir just beyond Tuni village. You may get a lift but otherwise it is a dull, 21km walk along the jeep track to Tuni. The road climbs to the emerald-green reservoir a few minutes above Tuni, though vehicles can rarely pass due to a locked gate. There are splendid views of Huayna Potosí from here. Keeping the lake to your right, follow the road along its shores until you come to the far end where there is a small dam and spillway. A track branches right off the main road, crosses the spillway and heads up the valley following a canal, giving you beautiful views of Condoriri (which resembles a condor with outstretched wings) as you head directly towards it. One hour after the spillway you will reach the end of the canal and the road at another small reservoir.

From here the trails climbs to your right then follows the valley towards Condoriri, and after another hour (passing another small lake with a tiny island in the middle en route) you will arrive at Lake Chiar Kota, a beautiful spot with the peaks of the Condoriri range ahead of you. This is an ideal base for exploring the area. Villagers from Tuni (who own the land) will probably charge you a few Bolivianos to camp here and have built a few basic latrines in old llama corrals. They can also hire mules and act as guides if you wish.

One of the 'easy' peaks is El Diente (5,200m) but this still needs proper equipment (crampons and rope) and glacier experience. The mountain lies at the far end of the valley, to the right of Condoriri. Another popular climb behind El Diente is Pequeño Alpamayo (5,370m), often climbed by agencies as a warm up for Condoriri (5,648m) itself. Again, glacier experience and equipment is needed.

There are a couple of options for continuing from Lake Chiar Kota to save retracing your route to Tuni. Climb southeast up the ridge below the black triangular peak of Aguja Negra and follow the mule track across a plateau to reach the first pass proper and a cairn after about 90 minutes. There are great views of Huayna Potosí from here. The path follows the stream down into the next valley then climbs ahead to reach a second pass in another 90 minutes. You could alternatively follow the valley all the way down and back to Tuni. From the second pass head down and across towards the far side of the valley; the trail is faint at first but gets clearer as you head down the valley. Follow it all the way down to reach the village of Chacapampa in the Zongo valley in three to four hours. Chacapampa was built to house hydroelectric workers and has no facilities. Minibuses back to La Paz from Zongo pass along the road just above Chacapampa at around 08.30, so if you are arriving late you may wish to camp shortly before Chacapampa.

From the second pass you could also return to Tuni. Instead of heading down and across the valley, keep following the ridge round to your right until you reach a notch, head through it and then follow the trail steeply down into the valley and back to Tuni.

From Tuni you can either meet pre-arranged transport, walk out the way you came in to the Titicaca road or follow an old mining road left (east to southeast) to Milluni on the La Paz–Zongo road. This road parallels the Cordillera Real, passes a few disused tin mines and gives great views of the peaks of Maria Lloco, Pico Milluni and Huayna Potosí in its later stages; there are camping possibilities, especially in the valley below the west face of Huayna Potosí. From Tuni to Milluni takes around six hours using this route. Milluni these days is a ghost village. In its heyday it housed around 4,000 people and was the main smelter for the tin mines in the area. On the La Paz side of the village by a police checkpoint is an interesting old cemetery. The lake below the village is still heavily contaminated by mining chemicals. There is regular transport back to La Paz from here, more frequent in the mornings.

4

The Altiplano

LAKE TITICACA AND COPACABANA
Tel code: 02; altitude: 3,841m; population: 14,586

Mystic, serene and entrancing, sacred Lake Titicaca is the world's highest navigable lake and straddles the Bolivian and Peruvian borders at an altitude of 3,820m. The lake is regarded as the birthplace of the Inca civilisation and, as such, is the most sacred site in Bolivia. These days the lake is divided across its centre by an invisible border separating the northwestern shores of Peru from Bolivia.

Legend has it that, when the Spanish conquistadors ransacked the Inca wealth in the mid 16th century, defiant locals threw their treasures into the lake. Some even suggest that the lost city of Atlantis lies beneath its calm waters. The French scuba diver Jacques Cousteau came in search of it, but returned home with only a large frog collection to show for his trouble.

Today the lake is now a bustling centre for travellers between Bolivia and Peru. Boat trips out to the Isla del Sol and Isla de la Luna are a great way to soak up the scenery of the cradle of ancient traditions.

The main hub for travellers to the lake region is Copacabana, located at the water's edge. More recently, Copacabana has developed as a stopover hub en route to Peru (see *Border crossings*, page 41).

In early August the festival of the Virgin of Copacabana, coinciding with Bolivia's national day celebrations, sees Copacabana packed to capacity, prices hiked and pickpockets queuing up to prey on camera-wielding tourists. If you're going to go, make sure to book well ahead and be very careful with your backpack.

HISTORY Copacabana has long been a hotbed of religious activity with pilgrimages and rituals dating back to ancient times. First the Tiwanaku culture had its sacred sites near here, then the Incas, and now Bolivia's patron saint, the Dark Lady of the Lake, is housed in the church. The town's cathedral has historically been one of the most important religious sites in all of Bolivia with pilgrimages and rituals dating back to ancient societies. Even today worshippers gather every Sunday outside the cathedral to make colourful offerings to Pachamama, the mother earth.

The Altiplano LAKE TITICACA AND COPACABANA 4

THREE THINGS TO DO AROUND LAKE TITICACA

1 Feast on fresh, lake-caught fish at one of the great local eateries in Copacabana (page 100).

2 Go in search of tranquillity with an overnight sojourn on the mythical Isla del Sol (page 102).

3 Take a hike around the world's highest navigable lake to breathe in some fresh lake air and soak up the spectacular views (page 101).

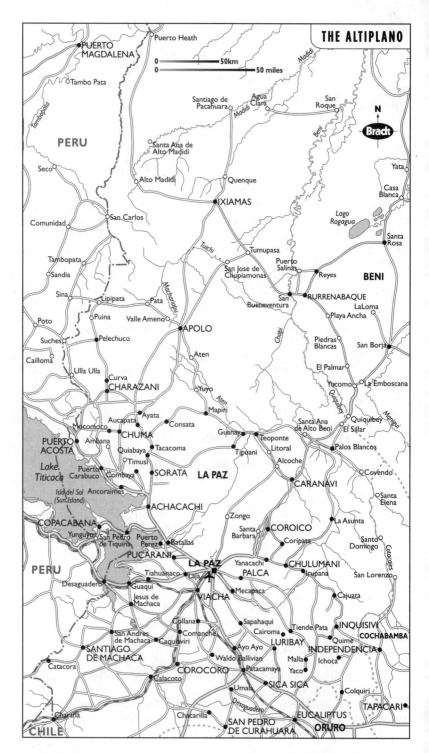

THE ALTIPLANO

0   50km
0   50 miles

Bradt

N

PERU

Puerto Heath
PUERTO MAGDALENA
Tambo Pata
Seco
Comunidad
Tambopata
Sandia
Sina
Poto
Suches
Cailloma
Ulla Ulla

Santiago de Pacahuara
Agua Clara
San Roque
Santa Ana de Alto Madidi
Alto Madidi
Quenque
IXIAMAS
San Carlos
Tumupasa
San José de Chupiamonas
Puerto Salinas
Reyes
BENI
Lago Rogagua
Santa Rosa
Casa Blanca
Yata
San Buenaventura
BURRENABAQUE
LaLoma
Playa Ancha
Piedras Blancas
San Borja
El Palmar
Yucomo
La Emboscana
Lipipata
Pata
Puina
Valle Ameno
APOLO
Aten
Pelechuco
Curva
CHARAZANI
Yuyo
Mapiri
Ayata
Consata
Guanay
Santa Ana de Alto Beni
Quiquibey
El Sillar
Palos Blancos
Aucapata
Mocomoco
CHUMA
Ambana
Quiabaya
Tacacoma
Tipuani
Teoponte
Litoral
Alcoche
Covendo
PUERTO ACOSTA
Lake Titicaca
Puerto Carabuco
Timusi
Combaya
SORATA
LA PAZ
CARANAVI
Santa Elena
Isla del Sol (Sun Island)
Ancoraimes
ACHACACHI
Zongo
COROICO
La Asunta
COPACABANA
Yunguyo
San Pedro de Tiquina
Puerto Perez
Batallas
Santa Barbara
Coripata
Santo Domingo
PERU
PUCARANI
Yanacachi
CHULUMANI
Tiahuanaco
LA PAZ
PALCA
Irupana
San Lorenzo
Desaguadero
Guaqui
Laja
VIACHA
Mecapaca
Cajuata
Jesus de Machaca
Collana
Sapahaqui
Cairoma
Tiende Pata
INQUISIVI
COCHABAMBA
San Andres de Machaca
Caquiaviri
Comanche
LURIBAY
Quime
INDEPENDENCIA
SANTIAGO DE MACHACA
Ayo Ayo
Waldo Ballivian
Patacamaya
Malla
Yaco
Ichoca
Catacora
COROCORO
Umala
SICA SICA
Colquiri
TAPACARI
Galacoto
Charaña
Chacarilla
SAN PEDRO DE CURAHUARA
Desaguadero
EUCALIPTUS
ORURO
CHILE

The soul of the Aymara is *Ajayu*, roughly translated as spiritual welfare. This is in two parts, *Ajayu mayor* and *Ajayu minor* (*Jacha Ajayu* and *Jisk'a Ajayu* in Aymara). *Ajayu minor* is more subtle; it could be compared, perhaps, to the aura of New Age believers, or to an intangible fluid. Like the body it can become dirty, not through outside agents but through 'dirty deeds' – one's own actions or the actions of others. The *Ajayu minor* can also be lost, for instance if a child falls over or an adult receives a profound fright. The shock of such accidents can cause the *Ajayu minor* to leave the body.

If the *Ajayu minor* departs or becomes dirty, a *brujo* (wise man or witch-doctor) can clean and restore it with smoke and incense or with water. This is the significance of the quiet groups of people and the puffs of incense on the hill of the Seven Stations of the Cross, behind Copacabana. It hardly need be said that to take a photo of this ceremony would be seriously intrusive.

An Aymara guide in Copacabana explains how his grandfather would take a cup of water from Lake Titicaca and tell his grandsons: 'This is only a tiny part of the lake, but an essential part of it; so are we in relation to all of Creation.' He taught them the ceremony of giving thanks to the sun, the rain and the earth for working together to produce crops. 'We need to thank them,' he said, 'and likewise we ourselves must work together in harmony.'

Legend has it that in 1580 the Virgin first appeared to a man called Tito Yupanqui in a dream. He became obsessed with this figure and subsequently embarked on a 400-mile journey to Potosí to learn to sculpt. Armed with his new-found skills, he returned to Copacabana to carve a beautiful model of the Virgin, which was subsequently housed in the cathedral. The chapel (in the main church) is well worth a visit because of the devotions of the people, but even more rewarding is the Capilla de Velas, to the left-hand side of the church, where people burn candles in support of their prayers. They used to press home their requests to the virgin by writing or drawing on the walls with melted candle wax.

Today, Catholic pilgrims besiege this normally tranquil town to pay homage to Bolivia's patron saint, the Virgen de La Candalaria, for one week every year in August. They pay homage to the miracles that the 'Dark Lady of the Lake' performed during her lifetime in the hope that similar good fortune will befall those who worship her.

Indeed, Copacabana's inhabitants and non-gringo visitors seem to spend much of their waking and praying hours thinking about rituals, especially those involving trucks. There are drawings of trucks in the chapel and models of trucks that you can carry past the Stations of the Cross hoping they will be changed by divine intervention into something larger and more practical, and, when the miracle has come to pass, there is a ceremony to bless the new truck. On Sundays and holy days there is a *challa* or blessing of cars outside the church. A priest officiates, and large quantities of alcohol and smaller quantities of holy water are sloshed or sprinkled over the engine and other vital parts. The vehicles are wonderfully decorated with flowers for the occasion

GETTING THERE There are two **bus operators** plying the route between Copacabana and La Paz's cemetery district, via Tiquina, where there's a 1.50Bs lake crossing. Trans Tur 2 de Febrero (✆ *862 2233*) has daily departures 08.00–18.30, while Manco Kapac (✆ *862 2234*) leaves daily 07.00–18.00; both have ticket offices on Copacabana's main square, Plaza 2 de Febrero, and charge 15Bs one way. If

The Altiplano LAKE TITICACA AND COPACABANA

4

possible try to take one of the smaller minibuses, which are marginally more comfortable.

The journey from La Paz to the lake is full of interest. You climb out of the bowl of La Paz to the dusty, bleak Altiplano where the traditional way of life is maintained; indigenous Indians herd their llamas, till the soil and the sun shines in a relentlessly blue sky.

To reach Copacabana you have to cross the narrow Strait of Tiquina by ferry, and then comes a spectacular drive along an arm of the peninsula and over the headland on a newly surfaced, twisting road to arrive high above Copacabana. The views of the lake and of the town are stunning.

Buses for Peru leave from Avenida 16 de Julio in Copacabana, while buses back to La Paz leave from Plaza Sucre in Copacabana.

GETTING AROUND Copacabana is easily covered on foot with Avenida 9 de Agosto the main gringo strip for tour agencies and places to eat. Down by the harbour, lakeside stalls offer hire of pedallos (40Bs per hour), motorbikes (40Bs per hour) and bicycles (15Bs per hour) to circumnavigate the lake.

For the 90-minute **boat trip** to the Isla del Sol, public (read 'crowded') boats leave from the harbour daily at 08.30 and 13.30 (15Bs each way). If you miss these, or if you want to avoid the crowds, you have to rely on hiring a private boat – negotiate prices down to 100Bs each way, or 200Bs for a same-day return.

Top tip: public boats arrive at Yumani from where the large and very, very steep Escalera del Inca steps climb up to the main island. If you hire a private boat, however, you can ask to stop at Pilko Kania, from where the climb is far gentler.

Numerous tour operators run cruises on Lake Titicaca with half/full-day options, plus extensions to Puno in Peru. The pick of the bunch is **Transturin** (*Av 6 de Agosto;* \ *862 2284;* e *info@transturin.com;www.transturin.com; for bookings in La Paz, Calle Alfredo Ascarrunz #2518;* \ *241 1922;* f *242 2222*). A high-end company aimed firmly at the tourist market, they offer very comfortable catamaran cruises with an option to overnight on board in a small but comfortable cabin. The visit includes a three-course lunch, a guided visit to the Inti Wata Cultural Complex, with its collection of artefacts and Tiwanaku ceramics, and a short reed-boat ride. Transfers to/from La Paz are available as part of the package. Open daily 08.00–12.30 & 14.30–18.00. Half/full-day/overnight US$45/60/90 pp.

TOURIST INFORMATION There's a **tourist information office** on the west side of Plaza 2 de Febrero next to the police station, but opening hours (allegedly 09.00–12.00 and 15.00–18.00) are irregular, staff unhelpful and quality information scarce. Better to enquire at the Transturin office (see above).

 WHERE TO STAY A popular spot to overnight, there's something for everyone here, plus a couple of great upscale options if you fancy splashing out a little (see *Top of the range*). The following properties are divided by budget category and listed in the order of the author's preference.

Top of the range

🏠 **Hostal La Cúpula** (18 rooms) Calle Miguel Perez 1–3; \/f 862 2029; e bolivia@hotelcupula.com; www.hotelcupula.com. The smartest property in town is located a bit away from the centre, set on a hillside with a spectacular view across the lake. Rooms are comfortable with some nice homely touches, there's free use of kitchen & washing facilities, while the gardens feature hammocks for a blissful post-lunch snooze. Rooms 11, 15 & 18 have the best views & facilities. *Standard sgls/dbls with private bathroom US$14/20; with shared bathroom US$10/14; sgl/dbl suite with living room & lake views US$20/32. Note: the rates are hiked slightly Jul–Aug & do not inc b/fast.*

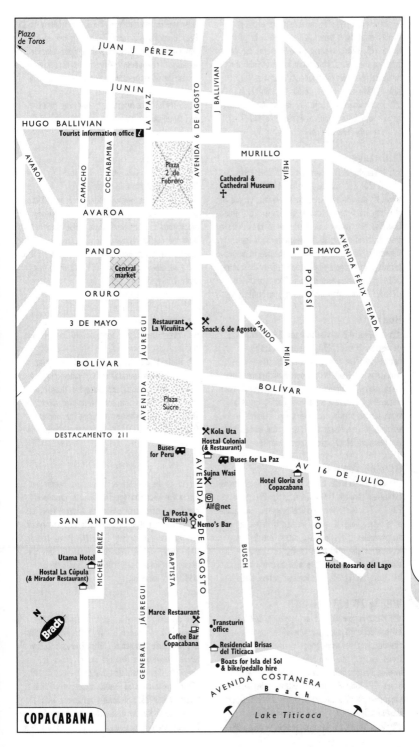

Plaza
de Toros

JUAN J PÉREZ

JUNIN

HUGO BALLIVIAN
Tourist information office

AVAROA

CAMACHO

COCHABAMBA

LA PAZ

AVENIDA 6 DE AGOSTO

J BALLIVIAN

Plaza
2 de
Febrero

MURILLO

MEJIA

Cathedral &
Cathedral Museum
†

AVAROA

PANDO

Central
market

1° DE MAYO

AVENIDA FÉLIX TEJADA

ORURO

POTOSÍ

3 DE MAYO

Restaurant
La Vicuñita

Snack 6 de Agosto

PANDO

BOLÍVAR

JÁUREGUI

AVENIDA

Plaza
Sucre

MEJIA

BOLÍVAR

DESTACAMENTO 211

Kola Uta
Hostal Colonial
(& Restaurant)

Buses
for Peru

Buses for La Paz

Sujna Wasi

AV 16 DE JULIO

Hotel Gloria of
Copacabana

AVENIDA 6 DE AGOSTO

Alf@net

La Posta
(Pizzeria)

Nemo's Bar

POTOSÍ

SAN ANTONIO

MICHEL PÉREZ

Utama Hotel

Hostal La Cúpula
(& Mirador Restaurant)

BAPTISTA

BUSCH

Hotel Rosario del Lago

N
Bradt

JÁUREGUI

GENERAL

Marce Restaurant

Coffee Bar
Copacabana

Transturin
office

Residencial Brisas
del Titicaca

Boats for Isla del Sol
& bike/pedallo hire

AVENIDA COSTANERA
Beach

COPACABANA

Lake Titicaca

4

La Cupula's Mirador restaurant has excellent quality meals with b/fast (12/18Bs) & à la carte mains (25–30Bs); it offers packed lunches for day trips on the lake (25Bs). Given its international influence, there are also fondues available (80–120Bs); open 07.00–15.00 & 18.00–21.00.

🏠 **Hotel Rosario del Lago** (32 rooms) Av Costanera corner with Calle Rigoberto Paredes; ☎ 862 2141; e lrosario@ceibo.entelnet.bo;

www.hotelrosario.com/lago. The sister property to La Paz's Hotel Rosario (page 73), this is one of the smarter addresses in town with a great lakeside location & seafood specialities at its Kota Kahuaña restaurant. In-house agency, Turisbus, will arrange boat excursions to the islands. *Sgls/dbls US$33/43.50, inc b/fast. Note: rates are hiked slightly Jul–Aug.*

Mid range

🏠 **Utama Hotel** (24 rooms) Calle Miguel Perez; ☎ 862 2013; e utamacopacabana44@hotmail.com. Don't let the kitsch murals on the walls put you off; this may be a budget option but it's a great little find. The best rooms have sea views & come with a free bottle of water; all have private bathrooms. Downstairs, free fruit & tea are available from mid-morning. Its location, slightly uphill from the centre, adds to an atmosphere of calm. *Rooms with sea view & TV/street view US$10/5 pp, inc buffet b/fast.*

🏠 **Hotel Gloria** Copacabana (32 rooms) Av 16 de Julio; ☎/f 862 2094; e titikaka@hotelgloria.com.bo; www.hotelgloria.com.bo. A sister property to La Paz's Hotel Gloria, this imposing block hotel is more comfortable inside than it looks from the outside, especially in those rooms with a sun terrace. Check out the in-house Café Sol y Luna for a sundowner. *Sgls/dbls US$35/42, inc b/fast; lunch US$4, dinner US$3.*

Budget

🏠 **Residential Brisas del Titicaca** (36 rooms) Av 6 de Agosto; ☎ 862 2178; e brisastiticaca@hotmail.com. The town's Hostelling International affiliate is a decent budget option with simple but clean rooms benefiting from a fresh breeze off the water. Better rooms have private bathrooms & a small terrace offering sea views. But a word of warning: in true youth hostel style, the owners lock the doors at 22.00 sharp. *Rooms with sea*

view/street view/shared bathroom 40/35/25Bs, inc b/fast.

🏠 **Hostal Colonial** (29 rooms) Av 6 de Agosto; ☎ 862 2270; e titicacabolivia@yahoo.com.ar. A reliable budget option, this place has clean rooms with private bathrooms, some with lake views. There's also an in-house restaurant for lunches (mains 30Bs). *Rooms 35Bs/person, inc b/fast.*

Outside Copacabana

🏠 **Inca Utama Hotel & Spa** (63 rooms) Reservations exclusively through Crillon Tours in La Paz (page 72); ☎ 213 6614. This lakeside property touts itself as a 5-star hotel & spa. In reality, it has a rather disappointing 1970s feel & a rather out-the-way location on the road from La Paz to Huatajata. The rooms are at least en suite with electric blankets, but there are no TVs, nor internet access. Meals

served at the in-house restaurant are decent but pricey for what you get. The grounds include a clutch of museums of which the Andean Roots eco-village has a rather uncomfortable Inca Disneyland feel. Far more rewarding is the Alaj Pacha Andean Observatory with its retractable roof to study the ancient art of Andean astronomy. *Sgls/dbls US$76/48, inc b/fast.*

✗ WHERE TO EAT

🏠 **Marce Restaurant** Av 6 de Agosto; ☎ 862 2244; e marcelboliv@yahoo.com. One of the smarter eateries along the main gringo straight, this place serves its meals on linen tablecloths amid a rustic interior. The set menu (15Bs) is good value while mains (20–30Bs) & vegetarian dishes (10Bs) are complemented by a salad bar. Drinks 7–10Bs. *Open daily 08.00–22.00.*

🏠 **Sujna Wasi** Calle Jauregui #127; ☎ 862 2091.

This cut-above eatery has a nice feel & a good menu (in English) with b/fast (15Bs), mains (30Bs) & a vegetarian set lunch (15Bs). There's a sunny terrace & live peña (folklore music) shows at weekends. *Open daily 08.00–22.00.*

🏠 **Kola Uta** Av 6 de Agosto corner with Plaza Sucre; ☎ 862 2332. A homely restaurant with a great line in healthy b/fast (try the 'Happy Good Morning' fruit/yoghurt/muesli combo for 15Bs) & a vegetarian set lunch (12Bs), plus mains from the English-language menu (26Bs). *Open daily 07.00–22.00.*

⌂ **Restaurant La Vicuñita** Av 6 de Agosto; ⋏ 715 16081. A decent all-rounder for meals & snacks set away from the hubbub of the main tourist drag. Best for lunch, try the fresh fish mains (25Bs),

chicken (20Bs) or pizzas (25Bs); less exciting is the set lunch/dinner (10Bs). *Open daily 09.00–22.00.*

⌂ **La Posta** Av 6 de Agosto. Located next to Nemos Bar for the late-night nibbles crowd, this pizzeria (small 12–17Bs & large 23–33Bs) is a gringo-friendly spot with street-side tables. *Open daily 11.00–22.00.*

For a snack, try **Snack 6 de Agosto** (*Av 6 de Agosto;* ⋏ *862 2114*), which has a set menu (10Bs) and 25Bs pastas. For drinks, head for the terrace of **Coffee Bar Copacabana** (*Av 6 de Agosto; no tel*) with coffee (5Bs) and juices (8Bs).

NIGHTLIFE Nemos Bar (*Av 6 de Agosto; no tel; open daily 18.00–late*) has beers and cocktails for the backpacker crowd in a dim, late-night setting.

OTHER PRACTICALITIES Alf@Net (*Av 6 de Agosto; open daily 09.00–22.00*) has internet access (14Bs per hour), plus a book exchange, money exchange and a café cum bar.

Avenida 9 de Agosto, the main strip for traveller-friendly facilities, boasts money exchange facilities and an Entel call centre, while restaurants along this strip also offer a laundry service (around 10Bs/kg).

WHAT TO SEE AND DO Copacabana Cathedral (*open 11.00–12.00 & 14.00–18.00; free entry*) is the town's main attraction. Visitors flock each weekend to visit the black statue of the Virgin of Candelaria encased above the altar. The Museo de la Catedral (*open 08.30–12.00 & 14.30–17.30*) hosts religious artworks, while every weekend drivers come to bless their vehicles with colourful cha'llas (blessing ceremonies) to ensure future safe passage. You can buy a bottle of holy water to complete your own cha'lla for 3–5Bs from the museum.

A STROLL AROUND THE LAKE: WALKS AROUND TITICACA

On the hill behind town are the Stations of the Cross; pilgrims climb up here not only with model trucks, but with model houses or animals, to pray for a little materialism. It's easy to mock, but when you climb with them and witness the seriousness and yearning behind the prayers for possessions that we would take for granted, it is no laughing matter.

On the other side of the town, away from the lake, is the path leading to the Horca de Inca, an impressive site, genuinely Inca, which is more likely to have had an astronomical significance than to have been the gallows that the name implies. The structure appears to be aligned to the winter solstice and the view from here is spectacular.

The Inca road to Yampupata, meanwhile, leads along the Copacabana peninsula and is the nearest land to the Island of the Sun. The four-hour walk, along an old Inca road (mostly destroyed, however, for the construction of a seldom-used vehicular road), is highly enjoyable.

Follow the road out of town and along the lake; there are very occasional vehicles, but mostly other foot travellers and their animals. One and a half hours after Copacabana the main track goes up a hill but a lower path to the left crosses a meadow with a stream (bridged by logs), near a house and a shrine, to climb steeply up an obviously Inca road (stone paved) to rejoin the road again. A tiring but scenically rewarding short cut. Yampupata is about two and a half hours after the log bridge.

Bolivia's patron saint, the Dark Lady of the Lake, is housed in the church. Her chapel (in the main church) is well worth a visit because of the devotions of the people, but even more rewarding is the Capilla de Velas, to the left-hand side of the church, where people burn candles in support of their prayers. They used to press home their requests to the virgin by writing or drawing on the walls with melted candle wax; this practice has now been forbidden. A few years ago there was hardly a bare space left on the walls.

THE ISLANDS OF LAKE TITICACA

Incan mythology blesses the lake as the focal point for all worship to Pachamama, the mother earth. The mysticism and spirituality of the area is still evident in the countless ruins and traditional communities that occupy the shores and islands.

ISLA DEL SOL (SUN ISLAND) The Isla del Sol, measuring just 9km by 6km, is one of the most sacred places in Bolivia. The two main villages are Yumani, home to the largest town and the main transport hub for boat excursions at the southern tip of the island and, on the northeast side of the island, Challapampa, which is quieter, more rural and home to some fascinating Inca ruins.

Arriving by boat at Yumani, travellers have to walk up the 206 very steep Inca steps to reach the main part of the town. These steps are original Inca constructions and lead up to a sacred stone fountain with three separate springs, which are said to be a fountain of youth. Close to the latter is the sacred rock labyrinth at Chincana. According to legend, this is where the sun god Viracocha brought his son and daughter, Manco Capac and Mama Ocllo, up from the depths of the water to found the Inca race.

With a network of trails covering the island and the ready availability of fresh water, the island is an ideal base for walkers. Arriving on the island at the Inca steps, a short walk to the southeast leads you to the ruins of Pilkokaina – it's easily spotted when arriving on the island by boat (but not signposted, so easily missed). An alternative for campers is to head directly for the ruins of Pilkokaina. Also known as the Temple of the Virgins of the Sun, the ruins are Tiwanaku in style with early Inca influences. The stonework is crude, but there are some well-preserved and interesting adobe doorways moulded in the step-pattern that is typical Tiwanaku and also seen in Ollantaytambo in Peru. Illampu, a *nevado* (snow-covered mountain) sacred to the Incas, is framed by one of the trapezoid windows.

From Pilkokaina the path continues in a northwesterly direction to Yumani, along the spine of the island, taking you to the northwestern tip of the island towards Challapampa. The walk from Yumani to Challapampa takes around three hours and provides stunning views of the lake, Peru to the southwest and the Cordillera Real to the northeast. Before descending to the town, it is worth visiting ruins close by on the northern part of the island.

The path leads to Chincana, popularly known as El Labarinto (the Labyrinth), and La Piedra Sagrada (the Sacred Rock). El Labarinto is a site given an explanatory name that needs no explanation. Originally pilgrims to the island would enter the

STAYING ON THE ISLA DEL SOL

The Isla del Sol is developing rapidly with several La Paz-based operators owning ecolodge-style properties on the island (see below), which have been developed in collaboration with the local indigenous community.

There is also now a slew of small hostels, restaurants and simple lodgings springing up across the island, with the majority clustered around Yumani, on the island's southern tip. Many of these come and go but one budget option for independent travellers taking boats from Copacabana (page 97) is the Hostelling International-owned Hostal Inka Pacha (↘ 719 80468; e inkapachaecologico@ hotmail.com), which has simple rooms from 40Bs per person; meals extra.

There is an Entel call centre on the island for phone calls (although opening hours are variable at best), but there is no internet connection. Plan on being out of contact and just enjoy your stay. There are no accommodation options on the Isla de la Luna.

⌂ **Albergue Ecológico La Estancia** (11 rooms) Reservations exclusively through MagriTurismo in La Paz (page 71); hotel ↘ 715 67287;. The smartest of the properties on the island, this ecolodge has well-designed rooms with attractive rustic fittings, solar-powered heating & showers. It's set in attractive grounds with a central dining hall serving decent quality meals. Better still, this is one project that genuinely lived up to the 'ecolodge' tag as it's very environmentally friendly & provides a valuable source of employment for the local community. *Sgls/dblsUS$40/56 inc dinner & b/fast; full-board packages with excursions also available – ask for details.*

⌂ **La Posada del Inca** (17 rooms) Reservations exclusively through Crillon Tours in La Paz (page 72); hotel ↘ 715 28062. A converted, terracotta-tiled hacienda set around a series of small courtyards in private grounds, this cosy lodge has superb views across to the Isla de la Luna & Cordillera Real. The bedrooms feature attractive wooden fittings & heaters, plus private bathrooms with solar-powered showers. *The fixed menu meals are generous though expensive (US$10), as are the overnight cruise/lodging packages at US$218.50 pp, based on 2 sharing. Nice but pricey.*

According to legend, the Inca Empire was founded on the lake. Incan mythology blesses the lake as the focal point for all worship to Pachamama, the mother earth. The mysticism and spirituality of the area can be seen in the countless ruins and traditional communities that occupy the shores and islands, taking you back to the 14th century. The remains of the city of Tiwanaku are just 15 miles (24km) northeast of the lake.

Metaphysical laws explain that there are two main sources of power on earth: male and female. This concept is considered relevant, since it represents the two antagonistic meanings of life. Good and Bad, Night and Day, Light and Dark, the Physique and Psychic, emphasising the complete circle of nature representing the two faces of our daily existence. During thousands of years, these two sources, characterised by two magnetic rays, have been in the Himalayas. But now, as we enter the Age of Aquarius, the source of power has moved from Tibet (northern hemisphere – male) to Lake Titicaca (southern hemisphere – female). Six different levels of spirituality (and cultures) arose in the northern hemisphere under the male sign, but this seventh level is for the first time in the southern hemisphere under the female sign, Pachamama. According to ancient prophecies, a new beginning commences and the Pachacuti in the Andes represents the 'awakening' of a new and better world. From now on, the positive energy of the world will be generated by Lake Titicaca, while serenity will be guarded by the Himalayas. It is said that most of the problems the world has been through have been impelled by a lack of equilibrium, and the dramatic changes in the last years are supporting this theory, and that the time of joy for mankind has finally arrived with the harmony of this shared balance of power.

complex of tiny rooms from the downslope. As they had been requested to be truthful at an earlier 'gate', this second test ensured that only honest pilgrims successfully emerged from El Labarinto. Travellers then move on to La Piedra Sagrada, the resting home of the sun and the moon, and the last point on the pilgrimage.

Challapampa is a small town to the east of Piedra Sagrada with a few basic facilities. From Challapampa a path follows the shoreline. Rising along the cliff edge, the path drops to pass through the town of Challa before rising again to join the main island path. Tourist boats stop at Challapampa on the way to the Island of the Moon.

ISLA DE LA LUNA (MOON ISLAND) During the time of the Incas the island is believed to have been used as a convent to house 'chosen' women, who wore hand-woven alpaca garments and performed special ceremonies dedicated to the sun. As you first walk onto the island, keep an eye out for the polished stones. These stones, similar to those found in Machu Picchu, illustrate how the Incas used hinges to hold rocks together.

TIAHUANACO

Tiahuanaco is full of mystery. Bolivia's answer to Machu Picchu, albeit on a much smaller scale, and nestled in the plateau of the Andes, it is one of Bolivia's most important archaeological sites, with monumental stone statues over 1,000 years old. The ruins, and the accompanying modern museum, are located 80km west of La Paz, strung out along the windswept Altiplano in the direction of Lake Titicaca.

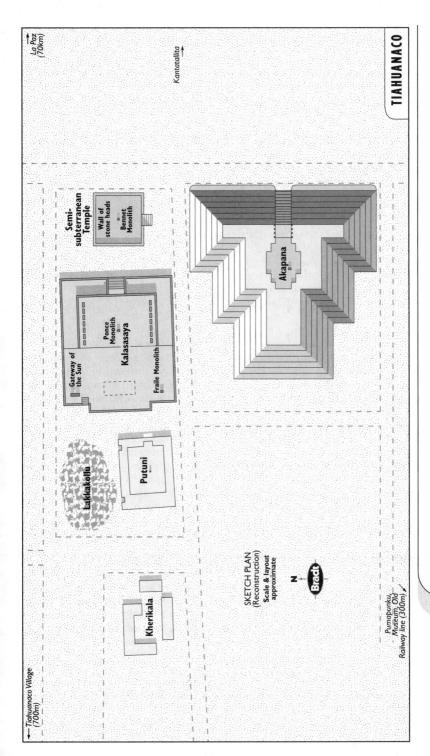

← La Paz
(70km)

Kantatallita

TIAHUANACO

Semi-
subterranean Temple

Wall of
stone heads

Bennet Monolith

Gateway
of the Sun

Ponce
Monolith

Kalasasaya

Fraile Monolith

Akapana

Lakkakollu

Putuni

← Tiahuanaco Village
(700m)

Kherikala

SKETCH PLAN
(Reconstruction)
Scale & layout
approximate

N

Bradt

Pumapunku,
Museum, Old
Railway line (300m) ↙

4

During 2005 the historical-archaeological research team of the University of Helsinki discovered a ritual offering site with well-preserved pieces of ceramics during excavations on Pariti Island in Lake Titicaca. The relics are considered to be some of the most significant to be found in years and add substantially to what is known about the Tiahuanacu culture, which flourished before the Incas and for which the island was probably an important religious site.

Many types and ornamental elements of vessels discovered on Pariti were completely new to scientists. People are depicted very realistically on the objects, providing a rare insight into the Tiahuanacu culture.

Little is known about the Tiahuanacus because they left no writings and their culture died out in the 11th century AD. Records show they settled on the Bolivian side of Lake Titicaca in the Andean mountains around 400BC. They built their administrative centre, the city of Tiahuanacu (page 104), west of La Paz from AD300–500, and their influence on the region continued to grow for several centuries.

Surveys of the island, which took place over the summer, uncovered a cache of about 300kg of deliberately broken ritual ceramics. Radiocarbon dating reveals they were buried some time between AD900 and AD1050.

More details from www.helsinki.fi/hum/ibero/research/andes/.

Tiahuanaco encapsulates the strength of the indigenous Aymara culture that remains a powerful part of Bolivian culture today. The residents of Tiahuanaco were extremely advanced for their time in that they managed to thrive on the barren, demanding land of the Antiplano and went on to become totally self-sufficient. In fact, the American anthropologist Alan Kolatu discovered in 1986 that once the harvests of Tiahuanaco had miraculously fed over one million people, supported by a highly advanced and complex agricultural system.

Today Tiahuanaco is a major tourist attraction and a mainstay of any Bolivian tour itinerary. In recent years it has become a site of pilgrimage for the Aymara New Year celebrations with swarms of New Age types, students and curious travellers alike descending on the site on 21 June for the Bolivian winter solstice celebrations with hands outstretched to catch the first rays of sunlight of new year (see *New year Bolivian style* opposite). Some treat this as a spiritual pilgrimage, others come to worship at the altar of alcohol. Either way, it's always guaranteed to be the coldest night of the year – bring lots of warm clothes and a sense of irony.

HISTORY Tiahuanaco was once home to one of the most important civilisations in the Americas, its huge stone monoliths built in 600BC and left to crumble after the mysterious collapse of the society around AD1200. The principal structure is the huge sun gate, which is thought to be similar to a solar calendar and part of a larger observatory complex that complemented the Andean worship of gods and spirits based around the earth. The story of the rise and fall of Tiahuanaco has continued to puzzle historians and anthropologists for years – and will probably continue to do so for many generations to come.

GETTING THERE AND AROUND Frequent **minibuses** leave from La Paz's cemetery district each day 07.00–19.00 with Tiahuanaco as their destination (90 minutes, around 10Bs). All buses heading for Desaguadero also pass by Tiahuanaco. Heading back to La Paz, buses depart from Tiahuanaco's main square at regular intervals daily 07.00–18.00.

Alternatively, any of the agencies along Calle Sagarnaga in La Paz will sell you a day trip, including lunch and the entrance fee to the museum. Try Maya Tours (page 71) for a gringo-friendly deal.

On the way to Tiahuanaco you pass through the small town of Laja which was the original La Paz, founded in 1548 by Alonzo de Mendoza. The town is dominated by its church, across a large plaza with bizarre-looking giant cacti interrupting the view. The church is usually locked (it is said to have a solid silver altar) but there are some interesting stone carvings on the outside pillars, including a monkey. The walls, as with all Catholic churches, are decorated with the 14 stations of the cross. The paintings are radical, contemporary and reflect the torments that may have faced a late 20th-century Christ in Latin America. The works go unsigned.

TOURIST INFORMATION There seems to be a major dearth of written material about the site, so you need a good guide to visit the ruins. It may also be worth heading to the Museo Nacional de Arqueología in La Paz (page 87) to swot up on details before making a visit.

Note: there is no tourist office, no ATM, no Entel call centre and no internet access (yet) in Tiahuanaco. In fact, after about 17.00 when the museum closes, there's pretty much nothing going on in Tiahuanaco at all.

NEW YEAR BOLIVIAN STYLE

At the archaeological ruins of Tiahuanaco, a site created by a civilisation so ancient it makes the Incas looks like Johnnies-come-lately, the festivities to see in the new year are already in full swing. According to the Aymara astrological calendar, the annual winter solstice on 21 June heralds the start of the Aymara new year. The event is now increasingly seen in with a fiesta that blends ancient mysticism with contemporary drunken revelry.

For a small group of vaguely bewildered Brits, then, there's nothing to do but join in. So we buy ourselves a bottle of cheap rum, top up the flask of hot coffee to fend off the official arrival of winter and wade into the middle of the dancing.

The concept behind the solstice focuses on good fortune for the harvests ahead, with rituals performed to bring renovation and purification to the land. It's a time of hope and for thanking the Andean deities for the favours they granted during the previous year.

The highlight of the festival is to greet the sun at the entrance of the temple at dawn with open palms, the theory being that the nearer you are to the sun, the greater the power and blessing will be. The sun gate has been astronomically oriented so as at the exact moment the New Year sun breaks the peaks of the mountains, it produces a spectacular burst of light through the sun gate.

As the first rays of dawn are filtering through the Andean mists and the 6,000-odd crowd, a mixture of curious tourists, New Age chakra-chargers seeking to soak up cosmic energy and local *kallawayas* (the local medicine men identified by their brightly coloured ponchos) supervising the first llama sacrifice of the new year, start surging towards the sun gate for the 07.00 start of the annual ceremony.

We've huddled around makeshifts bonfires in the main square all night, paid our 40Bs each to enter the ancient site and now we're ready to raise our hands towards the east and welcome the heat of a new dawn. That is, however, until the local police decide the best way to stop people without tickets pushing though the entrance gate is to tear gas the whole crowd.

Happy new year indeed.

THE TIAHUANACO PYRAMID

Matt Hindley of the Llama Express (www.theexpress.org)

In 1934 the archaeologist Wendell C Bennett was credited with first 'discovering' the main site of Tiahuanaco. Even though, by the time he began excavations, Tiahuanaco had already suffered from many centuries of plunder, Bennett still managed to uncover fresh ruins, indicating that Tiahuanaco had risen from a collection of small independent agricultural states to having a self-supporting, fully formed, regional government and army.

One of his greatest discoveries was the Akapana Pyramid, built around AD300 by the Tiahuanacan people as a ceremonial centre. This truncated pyramid is 194m long by 184m wide and just 18m tall. It has seven different levels and no peak, making it quite different from the typical Egyptian model, which is much taller, with four sides and a peak.

By the end of the Tiahuanaco era around AD1000, it was allegedly covered in sand and hidden from the world by later civilisations. When, in 1540, the Spanish found Tiahuanaco, they destroyed the back of the pyramid in their search for gold. They later tried to repair the damage they caused, using stones from the top, which were all of a different shape and material.

Although new excavations are now in the early stages, there have already been a number of discoveries, including an Andean Cross on top of the pyramid, which is thought to have served for elementary star-gazing.

Pablo Rendon, head archaeologist on the east wing of the pyramid says, 'We also think that it was used for astronomy. We think that it might have been filled with water so that they could get a better look at the stars.'

One of the main problems that the archaeologists have encountered has been with the 3,000 cubic metres of earth that they are expected to clear during the excavation. Still, it is hoped that, by 2010, the whole pyramid will have been excavated, depending on financing. At the moment, however, only 3% of the Tiahuanaco site is visible.

According to businessman and former presidential candidate, Samuel Doria Medina, who has been helping to fund excavation work: 'I think the idea that Bolivia has the second-biggest pyramid in the world is emblematic of the potential for tourism in this country.'

WHERE TO STAY

Hotel Tiahuanaco (15 rooms) Calle Bolivar #803; ☎ 289 8548. The only real option to overnight in town has simple but comfortable rooms, a public phone & plans to install an internet connection. The in-house restaurant does a good, 3-course set lunch (25Bs) & à la carte mains (30Bs). The owners are very knowledgeable about the ruins & offer day tours from US$20. *Rooms US$10 pp, inc b/fast.*

WHERE TO EAT

La Cabaña del Puma Located next to the museum; ☎ 289 8541. This is still the favourite place for lunch for visiting tour groups with sofas & a sun lounge area. It's strictly lunch only here but the set menu (25Bs) has 3 courses, while mains (25Bs) offer the usual llama meat amongst other 'carnivore' staples. Drinks 5–10Bs. Book ahead if possible as it's always full of coach parties. Reliable, albeit a little overpriced. *Open daily 11.30–14.00.*

The plaza has some very basic stalls hawking water and snacks, as they are situated opposite the museum. Trying any of these stalls is only for those with genuinely cast-iron stomachs.

WHAT TO SEE AND DO

Museo Regional Arqueológico de Tiahuanaco (*just off main square in centre of village; no tel; entrance 80Bs/Bolivianos 10Bs/children under 7 free; private guide extra 50Bs; open daily 09.00–17.00*) This sprawling museum complex is the main draw in town and, as such, attracts large numbers of coach parties during peak hours. It comprises four elements: the Puma Punka ruins, Kalasasaya archaeological site, Museo Convencional y Centre de Atención, featuring mainly ceramic exhibits, and the Litico Museum with its collection of stone exhibits.

SORATA *Tel code: 02; altitude: 2,677m; population: 18,932*

Sorata gets a bad rap. In 2003 severe roadblocks and social conflict led to a siege situation in the town with up to eight fatalities (none were tourists). Ever since, Sorata has all but fallen off the itineraries of the major La Paz operators and its reputation as a trekking destination has taken a severe knock.

It's a shame because Sorata is actually a nice little place with a vague alpine feel and great walking to be enjoyed around the mountains close by. There is hope on the horizon, however, with a new asphalt road between the Altiplano and Sorata mooted to open up the destination as a place for weekenders from La Paz to enjoy some alpine air. It's due for completion in late 2007, but don't hold your breath. This spark of hope also depends, of course, on the locals keeping a lid on potential blockades and social unrest. If they can achieve this, Sorata has the potential to overcome its jaded reputation and become an excellent weekend escape for trekkers, hikers and bikers.

It's also worth noting that Sorata is one place where you really need to come prepared: bring maps for trekking and make sure you've got enough cash – there's no ATM in town, and only the restaurant, Pete's Place (page 113), can help you out if you're stuck trying to change money.

HISTORY With its alpine feel and overlooked by the towering majesty of Mount Illampu (6,368m), Sorata has traditionally been suggested as the location for the original Garden of Eden. The town, laid out in a classical Spanish design, was formerly a major commercial centre and a gateway to the goldfields and rubber plantations. But since the trade route was diverted through the North Yungas, Sorata's colonial elegance has taken on an increasingly faded air. Today, Sorata awaits an upturn in its fortunes expectedly and celebrates happier days with a week-long festival. The most spectacular of these celebrations tends to fall on the Sunday before 14 September. During this time the sleepy main square is awash with colourful dance troupes and brass bands in full fiesta mode.

GETTING THERE Buses leave from the cemetery district in La Paz and return from Sorata's main square, Plaza General Enrique Peñaranda, for a standard fare of 13Bs one way. On the west side of Sorata's main square, **Buses La Recaja** (\ *238 5245*)

4

THREE THINGS TO DO IN SORATA

1 Take a hike, or even a bike, and get active with an adventure trip into the spectacular trekking country around Sorata (page 111)
2 Pile on the pounds at Pete's Place, one of the friendliest café bars in the Altiplano and a great taste of home for weary travellers (page 113)
3 Soak up the mountain scenery from the terrace of Camping Altai Oasis and breathe in that fresh Sorata air (page 112)

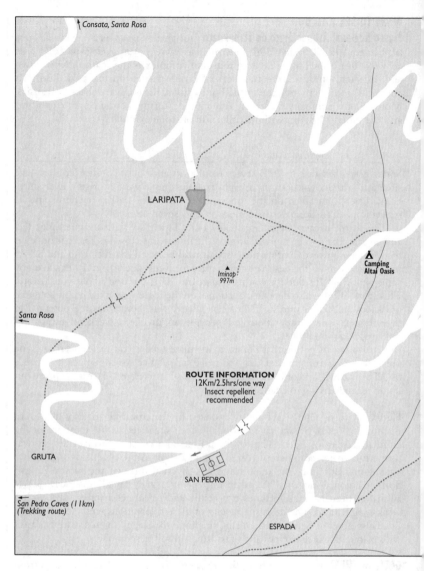

Consata, Santa Rosa

LARIPATA

Iminap
997m

Camping
Altai Oasis

Santa Rosa

ROUTE INFORMATION
12Km/2.5hrs/one way
Insect repellent
recommended

GRUTA

SAN PEDRO

San Pedro Caves (11km)
(Trekking route)

ESPADA

has daily departures to La Paz running 04.00–16.00, except on Thursdays, Saturdays and Sundays when the last bus leaves at 17.00. Buses on Sundays tend to be particularly crowded.

GETTING AROUND Most of the action in Sorata is located within a stone's throw of the main square. For outlaying hotels and cafés, it's generally just a gentle stroll, but taxis can also be found around the plaza with 15Bs flat-rate fares out to your lodgings.

TOURIST INFORMATION There's no official tourist information office in Sorata but both the expat-run Pete's Place (page 113) and Residencial Sorata (page 112) are great sources of advice and information for travellers.

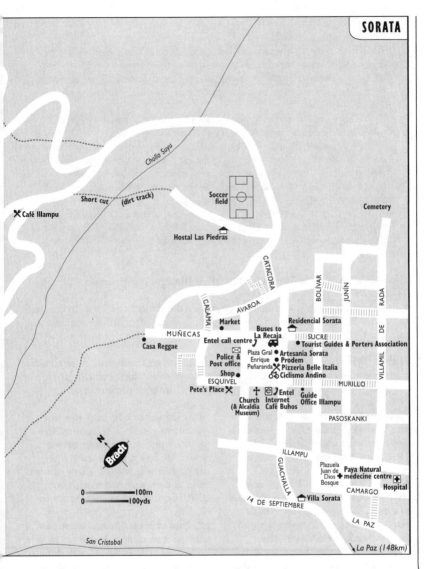

Short cut (dirt track)

Cholla Suyu

✕ **Café Illampu**

Soccer field

Cemetery

Hostal Las Piedras

CATACORA

BOLIVAR

JUNIN

RADA

CALAMA

AVAROA

Market

Residencial Sorata

MUÑECAS

Buses to La Recaja

SUCRE

DE

Entel call centre

Casa Reggae

Police & Post office

Plaza Gral Enrique Peñaranda

Artesania Sorata

Tourist Guides & Porters Association

● **Prodem**

VILLAMIL

✕ **Pizzeria Belle Italia**

Shop ●

ESQUIVEL

👓 **Ciclismo Andino**

MURILLO

Pete's Place ✕

✝ **Church (& Alcaldia Museum)**

🄴 🎵 **Entel**

Internet Café Buhos

Guide Office Illampu

PASOSKANKI

N
Bradt

ILLAMPU

GUACHALLA

Plazuela Juan de Dios Bosque

✚ **Paya Natural medecine centre**

✚ **Hospital**

0 ▬▬▬ 100m
0 ▬▬▬ 100yds

14 DE SEPTIEMBRE

🏠 **Villa Sorata**

CAMARGO

LA PAZ

San Cristobal

↘ **La Paz (148km)**

Also worth seeking out is **Ciclismo Andino** (*east side of Plaza General Enrique Peñaranda;* ☏ *712 76685; www.ciclismoandino.com*). This small, specialist adventure tourism agency, run by adventure guide, Travis, formerly of Gravity Assisted Mountain Biking in La Paz (page 72), is trying to develop Sorata as an adrenalin-sports destination. There are two main trips currently on offer: biking from Sorata to Charazani (US$50 per person, based on a minimum group of four) and a five-day biking and rafting trip from Sorata to Rurrenabaque (US$230 per person, based on a minimum group of four). Travis can also help advise on wider adventure options in the area.

Trekkers should check with the two official trekking agencies in town (listed below), which both have small offices just off the main square. They are **Asociation de Guias Turisticas y Porteadores** (*Calle Sucre #302;* ☏ *715 94612;*

There are three main treks around Sorata: the Gold trail, the Glacier trek and the demanding Illampu circuit. The Mapiri trail is now severely neglected and overgrown, but other smaller day treks can be arranged via local trekking agencies, notably the Laguna Chillata trail, an eight-hour day trek with great views of Lake Titicaca.

The going rate for a trekking guide is US$12–15 per day, based on a group of two, plus US$9 per day for a mule and US$10 per day for a porter.

Trekkers need to be aware that there have been consistent reports of problems on the Illampu circuit. On the morning of the last day trekkers have been violently robbed by llama herders from the community around Laguna San Francisco. Many reputable agencies now refuse to run this trek, or make a deliberate detour to avoid this lawless settlement.

Before starting any trekking journey, try to have a chat with Louis Demers, owner of the Residencial Sorata (below), and with Pete of Pete's Place (see opposite page), who keeps a good source of reference maps for trekkers.

e *guiasorata@hotmail.com*) and **Guide Office Illampu** (*Calle Murillo #212;* ↘ *719 34528*).

It's also well worth your while dropping into the Residencial Sorata to chat with the owner, Louis Demers, who is an absolute mine of information about local trekking routes.

WHERE TO STAY While the guesthouses in the centre are functional for the trekking trade, the most welcoming spot is located out of town along country lanes. The following properties are listed in the order of the author's preference.

Camping Altai Oasis (13 rooms, 2 chalets & space for camping) Located 1.7km northwest of the main square on the road to San Pedro; ↘ 715 19856; e resaltai@hotmail.com. This rustic but comfy spot is a friendly place with a good range of facilities, inc a book exchange & laundry service (8Bs). The in-house restaurant serves excellent meals on a balcony with superb views out across the mountains. It's not the cheapest place to eat, but of far superior quality with b/fast (18–25Bs), vegetarian mains (18–30Bs) & house specials, such as Hungarian goulash & Polish borsch (40Bs). *Rooms with private bathroom 80Bs/dorms 20Bs/camping 10Bs. Cabins for 3/5 people with a self-contained kitchenette & fireplace cost 150/300Bs.*

Residencial Sorata (27 rooms) Corner of Plaza General Enrique Peñaranda; ↘ 213 6672; f 213 5664; e resorata@entelnet.bo. This Canadian-run hotel is located in a sprawling colonial mansion with antique furniture & a huge sense of history. Indeed, built in 1895 to house the Richter family, it was later taken over by the Günther family, who were involved in the local rubber industry until the mid 20th century. Hence the building is also now known as the Casa Günther. Sadly, though, while full of character, the place is now looking rather faded in its glory. Nevertheless, it's a popular spot with trekkers, who come to pick the brains of the knowledgeable owner, while the in-house restaurant serves up decent b/fasts/lunches/dinners for 12/14/14Bs. *Rooms with private/shared bathroom 40/20Bs.*

Hostal Las Piedras (10 rooms) Located 500m southwest of the centre on the road past the soccer pitch; ↘ 719 16341. Popular with weekenders from La Paz, this German-run guesthouse has light & airy rooms in a small house heading down a track towards the river. Friendly & arty, it offers b/fast 10–20Bs & sandwiches 8–10Bs in a cosy ambience. *Sgls/dbls with private bathroom 40/60Bs; shared rooms with shared bathrooms 15Bs.*

Villa Sorata (3 rooms) Guachalla #238; ↘ 213 5241. At the top of the price range, this converted colonial property has a sunny terrace & great views, but rooms look a bit neglected considering the above-normal prices. *Sgls/dbls/tpls with private bathroom & b/fast 50/75/90Bs.*

WHERE TO EAT

✗ **Café Illampu** Located 1km northwest of the centre on the road to San Pedro; ☎ 289 5009. Out in the sticks en route to the San Pedro cave, this Swiss-run bakery-cum café has a fantastic selection of homemade cakes & pastries (8—10Bs), which makes it an essential stop for hikers. The Illampu b/fast (22Bs) will set you up for the day, while there's yoghurt & fruit (6Bs) for the more health conscious, plus homemade bread for 15Bs per kg. You can also camp in the grounds of the café from 8Bs pp per day. *Open Wed–Sun 09.00–19.00.*

✗ **Pizzeria Bella Italia** East side of Plaza General Enrique Peñaranda; ☎ 289 5009. Of the slew of pizzerias dotted around the plaza, this one stands out for its higher quality, with b/fast (10–15Bs), pastas (25–30Bs) & a big choice of pizzas (small/medium/large 23/45/60Bs). There are tables overlooking the plaza & cocktails served nightly for those seeking a flicker of nightlife (10–13Bs). *Open daily 08.00–22.00.*

ENTERTAINMENT AND NIGHTLIFE There's no main drinking den in town for gringos since the Spider Bar closed (ignore the café on the main square that has stolen the name).

You can get a beer at restaurants around the plaza, otherwise you could try **Casa Reggae**, an Argentinian hippy commune on the western fringe of town, for the latest alternative happening. Chances are, however, they'll just try to sell you some alternative stimulation.

SHOPPING

Artesania Sorata Plaza General Enrique Peñaranda; ☎ 213 6677; e cnsorata@ceibo.entelnet.bo. This quality souvenir & gift shop sells artisan goods from its base on the main square. Natural dyes & pure alpaca wool are used to create beautiful hats, scarves & jumpers. Check out the range of woven hats (90Bs).

Open Wed–Sun 09.00–12.30 & 15.00–18.00.
Centro de Medicina Natural Paya Plaza Obispo Bosque #584; ☎ 213 6675. This quirky little natural remedy shop has a range of pomades to cure all ills (5Bs). *Open Tues–Sat 09.00–12.00 & 14.00–18.00, Sun 09.00–16.00.*

OTHER PRACTICALITIES

Buhos internet café (*Plaza General Enrique Peñaranda; open daily 09.00–21.00*) has very slow internet access for 20Bs per hour..

Entel call centres (*open daily 08.00–22.00*) Two locations on Plaza General Enrique Peñaranda.

Post office (*Plaza General Enrique Peñaranda*) Prone to seriously irregular opening hours – if it actually opens at all.

Prodem (*Plaza General Enrique Peñaranda; open Mon–Fri 08.30–12.00 & 14.30–18.00, Sat 09.00–12.00*) will change money but charges a hefty 5% commission on Visa and MasterCard advances.

THE AUTHOR'S FAVOURITE EATERY

Pete's Place Calle Esquivel #108; ☎ 712 06853. Run by a friendly Londoner, Pete, who writes books on Bolivian politics on the side, this is the traveller's favourite place for a pot of Earl Grey tea (10Bs) & a chance to read the back copies of the *Guardian Weekly* newspaper. The house b/fast (20Bs) is a winner, while the vegetarian set lunch (14Bs) & dinner (17Bs) are served 12.00–18.00 & 18.00–21.30 respectively. Friendly & relaxed, this place is also a good source of traveller information as the owner keeps a supply of hard-to-come-by local trekking maps. Pete's will also change money & charges 3% commission on travellers' cheques – handy to know if you're stuck without cash as Sorata has no ATM. *Open daily high season 08.30–22.00, low season 12.00–21.00.*

Shop (*Northeast corner of Plaza General Enrique Peñaranda opposite Residencial Sorata; open daily 08.30–21.30*) This is a good place to stock up on supplies.

WHAT TO SEE AND DO

Alcaldia Museum (*Open Wed–Mon 08.00–12.00 & 14.00–17.00; free entrance*) This small, musty museum on Plaza General Enrique Peñaranda contains Inca artefacts and examples of traditional festival garb.

San Pedro Cave (*open 08.00–17.00; entrance 8Bs*) Located 11km from town along a gentle hiking path, this is the main day hike in the area and, rather conveniently, passes by Café Illampu (page 113) for a post-hike slab of cake. It's a five-hour round trip on foot, although it's often possible to hitch a ride back into town, and otherwise a taxi only costs around 40Bs. Take a swimming costume if you're planning to catch a dip in the tepid cave waters. The legends surrounding the cave are also interesting: the conquistadors are said to have buried a large treasure somewhere deep inside the cave and some say the cave was deliberately flooded to conceal the treasure. Probably the lake inside the cave is natural, but El Dorado is still in the minds of the local people. Divers have been discouraged from exploring the cave to its limits after a fatal accident (attributed to an Inca curse).

At the time of writing, local authorities were planning to install electricity in the cave and build a refuge for hikers close by. Enquire locally for the latest details.

MOUNTAINEERING IN BOLIVIA

For travellers looking for scenery, the mountain ranges of Bolivia offer spectacular vistas. From the towering snow-capped peak of Mount Illimani to the looming majesty of Mount Illampu, La Paz is one of the few cities on the globe where the mountains are situated close by. Indeed, the whole Altiplano region is encircled by majestic Andean peaks.

Adventurous travellers can arrange trekking and mountaineering trips to conquer these sleeping giants with prices typically starting from US$140 per person for a three-day trip. Others may just prefer to admire the view from a distance. But either way, the geography of Bolivia leaves an indelible impression. For a personal account, see *A non-mountaineer's guide to climbing Huyana Potosí*, page 119.

Bolivia is composed of four mountain ranges starting with the Cordillera Apolobamba in the northwest, the Cordillera Real that passes La Paz, the Quimza Cruz in the southeast, and the Cordillera Occidental near Chile. These mountains offer countless options for a variety of climbers, from the casual enthusiast who usually sticks to trekking, to the advanced mountaineer looking for a first ascent on a new route in an obscure location. The easiest range to get access to, and the one with the best infrastructure to support climbers, is the Cordillera Real based out of La Paz.

The prime climbing season for Bolivia is May to September, although it is occasionally possible to get decent climbing conditions and weather outside that window. However, if you are hiring a guide service, stick with the more reliable months as they don't give weather refunds. Of course, the South American winter starts 21 June, so the nearer you are to that date, the colder it will be. Usually, in late September, the snow starts to fly as the rainy season begins again. But usually it does not get cloudy until the afternoon and it will always be clear and sunny in the mornings.

There are no sophisticated mountain rescue facilities in Bolivia, so be prepared and, most of all, be careful. If you get into difficulties, help is a long way away. For

Matthew Parris

Many travellers treat Sorata as a dead-end: a pretty town to be reached by bus from La Paz, used as a base for some smashing local walks and climbs – and then left by the same bus, back to La Paz.

But there is another way out of Sorata, as beautiful as it is plain-sailing even for the more timid. Try going down to the Yungas via Consata and Santa Rosa – then Mapiri, Guanay (by canoe-bus) and back up to La Paz by bus or onward towards Brazil. A motorable track leads down the mountains from Sorata to Consata, and Louis Demers at the Residencial Sorata (see page 112) can help find transport – though, walked over two days, the journey would be lovely on foot.

I went by Toyota, reaching Consata, a tropical village in the foothills of the Andes, after lunch. We pulled ripe oranges off trees where we lodged – a tiny but friendly hostal, Don Betus, run by an immensely attentive elderly couple, the hospitable Rosa and her friendly husband. The hostal is on the left before you enter the village. Should we lock our valuables? No. There was a thief here once but they shot him.

Santa Rosa is 30 miles on down the river. The dawn brought no transport so we started to walk. It did not matter that nothing came. Our morning stroll – along a jungle track through hills, alongside rivers, overflown by shattering green parrots, attended by butterflies the size of handkerchiefs, observed by bird-spiders from giant webs and ignored by armies of leafcutter ants on the march, and surrounded by flowering trees and waterfalls – was like paradise.

Lunch was at Incachaka after 15 miles; rice and fried egg (they never have less in Bolivia, and rarely more), and we marched on into the afternoon sun. Suddenly there was a swimming pool – a big, roadside, concrete pool fed by cool clear water from a nearby stream – so we stripped off and swam. Then onward, the forest trees growing more huge as we descended into the heat. Next, at a bend in the track, a giant mahogany, and a liana rope hanging from 50ft above. We all swung and shrieked like kids.

Then on. All at once a swarm of black hornets attacked from the trees. We fought them off. Our losses amounted to five stings: six hornets bit the dust.

Another corner: and a river to cross. A wide, deep and turbulent river. Boots off, we waded over with sticks. The track began to climb. We began to tire. After climbing a thousand feet, we were strung out single over a mile, all exhausted.

Lights! A bar! Music! We had reached a mining settlement called (confusingly) Consata Limitada. From here it was only a few miles through gullies by Land Rover to Santa Rosa and the Hotel Ruth – the noisiest hotel in the world. But that's another story.

Matthew Parris is the author of Inca Kola (Phoenix Press, 1993)

4

the latest information on mountaineering in Bolivia and advice on guides, maps and equipment, contact The South American Explorers Club in Cusco (*www.saexplorers.org*).

TOPOGRAPHICAL MAPS Maps can be purchased from some tour agencies, occasionally the local bookstores, or from the **Instituto Geográfico Militar (IGM)** in La Paz (*Estado Mayor, Av Bautista Saaverdra #2303, Miraflores;* 222 9786; e *open Mon–Fri 08.30–12.00 & 14.30–17.00*), although the IGM can be a bit of a bureaucratic process and often has only black and white photocopies of the map sheets.

The IGM map sheets are usually 1:50,000 scale maps similar to the USGS (United States Geological Survey) maps in that they are arranged to cover the entire country sequentially. In this manner, it is often necessary to buy several sheets to cover an entire mountain route because the area you want can be on the edge and overlap with the next map in the sequence. It also can be confusing using the various maps available because names and spellings can be wrong, different, or a mix between Aymara and Spanish.

There are some alternatives to the IGM sheets:

- A New Map of the Cordillera Real de los Andes (scale 1:135,000), 1995, by Liam O'Brien, covers the entire range from Illampu to Illimani and provides an excellent big picture for route planning and driving to the trailheads. It is not quite detailed enough to be useful for navigating by foot. These are, however, fairly easy to find around in many book shops.
- The DAV (Deutscher Alpenverein or German Alpine Club) maps (scale 1:50,000) cover specific popular mountains, such as Illimani, and make life easier by not having to buy several IGM sheets to cover one mountain. Usually these are easier to find in the agencies.
- Walter Guzmán Córdova maps (scale 1:50,000) also make nice maps for specific peaks – look for them at Los Amigos del Libro book store (page 84).

CLIMBING ROUTES Bolivia has several peaks over 5,000m that can safely be climbed with no mountaineering experience. However, current conditions should always be checked before you set off and you should always go with a reliable guide. Two of the more manageable are described below.

Japu Japuni (5,088m) This peak can be accessed from the 4,880m pass on the first day of the Zongo to La Cumbre hike. Follow the rocky ridge north of the col, keeping slightly to the right, and about a third of the way up you'll find a large cairn. The summit (reached in about one hour from the pass) affords an incredible view of the Cordillera beyond Huayna Potosí. The ascent doesn't require any special equipment or climbing skills; avoid it in bad weather as there are cliffs below the ridge.

Huiata (5,092m) Starting from Achura, take the steep path going north up the valley side past Waca Kunca and following the Zongo route in reverse up the wide, gentle Illampu Valley. There are several excellent camping sites along the river as far as the 4,100m contour below Jishka Telata.

Continuing southwestwards, head up the Illampu, first on its north side, then crossing on a small footbridge before passing some big boulders and eventually climbing up the left hand of two tributaries to a flat area southeast of Huiata at about 4,600m. From here you head straight for the steep buttress of the lower, eastern part of the mountain. The path leads to the right of this, giving a splendid view of the topaz-green waters of Laguna Chaco Kkota with the Telata glacier behind.

Keeping the elevation above the lake, head due west up the valley beyond, heading to the left (south) of the peak ahead, climbing a steep snowfield to a ridge, then gaining the summit from the rear (west) side. Huiata gives excellent views of Huayna Potosí, the Telata Massif, the Huarinilla Valley towards the Yungas, and more.

This climb can be easily tackled by ordinary trekkers and without special equipment. Trucks also make the journey. The 96km road to La Paz meets the one from Chojlla at Unduavi. Until then it's little more than a track, winding under waterfalls (have your rain gear ready if you are travelling by truck) and alongside vertical cliffs.

There is an unlimited supply of agencies in La Paz willing to provide you with everything you need to climb the popular local peaks. In fact, many tour agencies have regular departures once or twice a week to Huayna Potosí, and less frequently, to Condoriri and Illimani. But beware: make sure to shop around and ask a lot of questions before you hand over any money.

As Huayna Potosí is so popular, some agencies pair glorified porters who speak little English and have few survival skills with tourists who don't know any better. So, if you don't speak any Spanish and/or have little mountaineering experience, see if you can speak with the guide before you go to test his English and find out how much practical instruction will be included in the trip.

Even though Huayna Potosí and Illimani are regarded as relatively easy 6,000m peaks, high altitude illnesses, such as pulmonary or cerebral oedema, can and do occur. Moreover, some sections on these mountains can be very hard. This is especially true if you do not have a lot of climbing experience. Factor in bad weather or bad conditions and accidents can easily occur.

You should definitely also inspect all of your gear before leaving, especially your double plastic boots to ensure you have a comfortable fit – don't make the mistake of turning up at the trailhead to discover the shoelaces are worn out or the eyelets are broken.

Two recommended mountaineering agencies are:

Andean Summits Calle Sagárnaga #189; ☏ 242 2106; e andean@latinwide.com; www.andeansummits.com. They have excellent experience of climbing in Bolivia in almost any range, hence the kind of reputation that pitches them at a much higher price than other agencies on Calle Sagárnaga.

Bolivian Journeys Calle Sagárnaga #363, 1/F, ☏ 235 7848; e boljour@ceibo.entelnet.com. Run by a former guide, this company has guides that speak English & German. They know a lot of people along the more popular routes, hence can arrange mules or porters; they also carry a decent array of maps of the area.

The South American Explorers Club in Cusco (*SAE; www.saexplorers.org*) produces a series of trip documents about climbing and trekking in Bolivia.

CLIMBING IN THE CORDILLERA APOLOBAMBA

Paul Hudson, updated by John Pilkington & Peter Hutchison

The attractions of the Cordillera Apolobamba for a climbing expedition were its feeling of remoteness, mostly good weather, alpine-like peaks and high base camps.

The area has been visited by British climbers on various occasions and 47 of the 101 identified peaks had been conquered by British climbers. We climbed 13 peaks in the southern part of the range, ten of which were first British ascents. Our first camp was at Paso Osipal, from where we climbed Sunchuli (5,306m), Cololo (5,916m) and Iscacuchu (5,650m). From the next camp, near the village of Sunchuli, we ascended Chuchillo 1 (5,655m), Corohuari (5,668m), Yanaorco (5,600m), Cavayani (5,700m) and Chuchillo 2 (5,450m) together with a number of unnamed summits. The best excursion was a two-day trip, which started high up the valley west of Sunchuli, and saw us climbing on to the ridge via one of its side valleys. The trip west along its spine was excellent despite its difficulties and saw us bivvying east of Cavayani itself.

Our equipment included snow stakes which were invaluable both as abseil anchors and running belays, the 3ft ones being better than the shorter ones. The glaciers we encountered were straightforward and the difficult and dangerous sections could easily be avoided. We employed only a few ice screws so there is no need to take too many; the rock gear remained unused mainly due to the poor rock. Our 9mm Cairngorm ropes were employed on a ratio of one to two people. We bivvied out on two occasions without sleeping bags, our duvets and Phoenix bivvy bags being adequate, although for real comfort extra layers and a Karrimat would have been good.

It is a good idea to bring mountain food from home; this is essential if you are planning to stay up high on a multi-day route. We took multi-fuel stoves and bought paraffin from a garage in La Paz.

Pelechuco is quiet and pretty, with a strong Spanish flavour. There are cobbled streets, colonial-style courtyards and a general air of decay. The church clock and the splendid wrought-iron fountain in the plaza were donated by Karl Francke, a 19th-century immigrant who made a fortune mining the area's gold.

To begin the walk, climb the steps by the church and turn left at the top. After crossing a small stream make a right turn and follow this path out of town towards the first pass. Where the path forks, take the higher right-hand branch. After about 2½ hours a small house will come into view. Bear right here and continue for 75 minutes to an excellent campsite. The path is clear and well used, and another 75 minutes will bring you to the top of the pass at 4,800m. A steep half-hour descent follows to the Río Illo Illo and good camping.

Follow the river downstream past more good campsites, ignoring the path that, after half an hour, ascends to a couple of hamlets on the right. After a further 30 minutes, cross a side stream on a stone bridge and climb gently up the valley side to the village of Illo Illo, where shops sell basic provisions.

From Illo Illo a jeep track leads over the next pass towards the mining settlement of Sunchuli. You can join it above the village, but the most direct route leaves the plaza by the church and descends to a stream before climbing steeply to join the jeep track in half an hour. Follow this track for a further hour to the village of Piedra Grande, then continue for another half hour, and after fording a stream turn left up a steep path to join an old, possibly pre-Hispanic, route. A further two hours of climbing, with ever-improving views of Chuchillo II (5,450m), will bring you to a pleasant camping area. The Sunchuli Pass is now in view straight ahead, with the road leading diagonally down from it to the right.

The path heads straight for the pass, crossing a marsh before zigzagging steeply up to the road. From the summit (reached 1½ hours after leaving the camping area) follow the road down to the Sunchuli Gold Mine, once abandoned but reopened in 1992 and now clearly prospering. The rough-and-ready village nearby has shops selling basic supplies.

From the mine take the well-used jeep track, which zigzags up the right-hand valley side. After perhaps half an hour it levels out, and at this point look for a minor track leading uphill and to the right. This doubles back above the mine before crossing the ridge via a 4,900m pass with stunning views of the Cordillera Real to the south. You may see condors here. You can reach this point without descending to the mine by striking out southwest after the Sunchuli Pass, contouring round the valley above a prominent aqueduct.

From the pass the track descends steeply to Viscachani, a mining village that has seen better days, which you'll reach 2–2½ hours after leaving the Sunchuli Pass. You can camp beyond the village. There is a deserted gold mine here, which may be fun to explore.

From Viscachani your route heads up the right-hand side of the valley beneath the village and drops down into a neighbouring valley where you'll find a small lake. A short climb takes you into a third valley, with a village away to the left. Go down to

Robert Conway of www.blueventures.org.

Huyana Potosí (located just 25km from La Paz) is said to be an ideal climb for beginners, and there truly couldn't have been anyone who was more of a beginner than me. To say this was going to be a new experience for me would have been somewhat of an understatement. Hailing from rural Surrey and never having been above sea level before this trip, my background for mountain climbing was less than ideal.

Huyana Potosí is in Bolivia's Cordillera Real and looks something like a large horn sticking out of the ground. It may look easy and direct, but don't let that fool you as at 6,088m above sea level, anyone would feel somewhat light-headed even if fully acclimatised; and a lot worse if not.

There are always companies willing to offer this climb and there'll always be someone who's willing to undercut another. But be careful: you never know where those cuts could have been made. We shopped around and took a three-day trek in which the first day was glacial climbing and teaching us how to walk in crampons. This, as well as being an awesome experience, is also ideal for those who've never walked on ice before.

Afterwards it was back to our mountain lodge, where there were hot showers, warm food and ample coca tea to sup while we rested our aching limbs. That was the good news. The bad news was that the really hard stuff would start tomorrow.

I say 'hard', but the day itself only started at 12.00, after which it was the trek up to high camp. This didn't involve any ice climbing, but we did have to carry our rucksacks, arriving around 17.00 in time for dinner and bed by 18.00.

The reason? The final day started with a wake-up call at midnight to begin the long ascent to the peak, with the aim being to make it there for sunrise at 07.00. We were attached to our guide in groups of one, two or three and, after an initial trek, it was time to put the crampons on and start snow walking all the way to the top. The views on this leg were breathtaking with La Paz's distinct basin shape giving its silhouette a unique appearance.

A colleague had told me prior to departure that 'climbing a mountain is like banging your head against a brick wall'. The whole horrible truth of this is only truly apparent, however, when you reach the last 200m. Although the rest of the climb is physically and mentally exhausting, it was only once we looked upon that final stretch that we could appreciate what a daunting task still lay ahead.

It may only be 200m and the incline may only be 45 degrees, but with a combination of severe altitude and ice stalagmites the size of small children, the last stretch makes for the closest thing to hell you can imagine. There was nothing for it but to take my trusty ice axe and do my best to pull myself to the top.

Those last few steps were possibly some of the most rewarding that I have ever experienced. The feeling of joy, relief and exhaustion is truly something that everyone must experience. That is, until we realised, of course, that now we had to go back down.

Rob Conway and Deshan Weeraman were part of the St George's, University of London Expedition to undertake research into the use of coca and altitude sickness in Bolivia. To find out more, please visit the website www.altituderesearch.org.

The Altiplano **MOUNTAINEERING IN BOLIVIA**

4

the right towards a gap between two crags, and about an hour from Viscachani you'll come to a magnificent viewpoint from where the next and final pass can be seen. An hour of hair-raising descent from here will bring you to a river at a place called Incacancha. This is an enchanting spot with a stone bridge, a waterfall nearby and a wonderful campsite from where you can contemplate the mountains all around.

The next climb takes some two hours and is bedevilled by false summits. Akamani (5,700m) is in view to the right. From the true summit it's mostly downhill for the rest of the walk (watch out for more condors). First descend to the right, traversing round the head of the valley to a gap. Pass through this and drop straight down the next valley to another good campsite, an hour from the top, at a place called Jatunpampa. If it's late in the day you should consider stopping here, because the countryside ahead is intensively farmed and campsites are harder to find. Otherwise continue descending through stone enclosures, cross the main river and climb diagonally to the left onto a spur. Descend again to ford a second river (an hour from Jatunpampa) and follow the path up the valley side to meet a disused irrigation channel. Follow this for 15 minutes before turning off to the right, from where a further hour of gradual ascent will bring you to a jeep track. When you come to a junction carry straight on, and Curva will almost immediately come into view on top of a small hill.

With no accommodation and very limited food supplies, Curva will offer little encouragement to stay. Luckily, an excellent ancient path leads down from its main square, giving magnificent views of the terracing opposite, and after descending for an hour and climbing for a second hour you'll find yourself at a fork. The route to Charazani goes vertically up from here. When, after half an hour, you reach a church, look back for a final view of the Akamani massif and forward for your first sight of Charazani. From here the direct route drops down steeply to a road, which you follow for a short distance before turning left towards a cross and descending to the river. The more obvious path descends gently to the road, which you can then follow round the valley to Charazani. Either way, the town is reached about 75 minutes after leaving the church.

Buses back to La Paz leave from the plaza in Charazani daily at 20.00 – the journey takes about ten hours.

BACKPACKING AND TREKKING IN BOLIVIA

Bolivia has some great trekking with spectacular vistas, a range of trails from easy to challenging and a chance to mix with indigenous culture en route. Best of all, compared with trekking in some other South American countries, such as Peru, travellers are surprised to find just how much lower the prices are and how less crowded the trekking trails can be – a real treat for those who have already fought the crowds on Peru's Inca Trail.

Trekking is best from April to November (dry season), although you will need suitable gear for cold night temperatures. From December to March (rainy season) trails can be washed out and progress very, very slippery.

Whatever your destination, make sure to be prepared for some very basic camping facilities and take lots of water, insect repellent, sunscreen, a hat and a torch. Allow plenty of time and set off early each day to give yourself decent rest breaks.

Bradt's *Peru & Bolivia: Backpacking and Trekking* guide has detailed descriptions of routes and trails (see *Appendix 2*).

A TOUR OPERATOR'S VIEW

Jorge Cardenas, who heads up the trekking department at La Paz-based tour operator, Magri Turismo (www.magri-amexpress.com.bo)
Bolivia is a pristine destination for trekkers, with huge natural biodiversity. As such, the country boasts a wide range of trekking options to explore the Andes, one of the main tourist attractions. The trailheads for many of these Andean treks are situated close to Bolivia's administrative capital, La Paz, which is set in the foothills of the range and overshadowed by some of its more majestic mountains.

As a trekking hub, La Paz is ideally located – less than one hour to reach the trailhead for some of the best pre-Inca routes, or to find yourself amid mountain scenery at an altitude of over 6,000m. Trekking options range from a one-day trek, enjoying the surroundings of the city of La Paz, through to a tough but rewarding 21-day hike, crossing part of the Cordillera Real from Sorata to Coroico.

As well as the element of adventure, trekking in the region makes for a great way to connect with the rich Andean culture. Elements of the indigenous culture remain vibrant and alive today; they form an interface between the country's natural wonders and its people, who continue to preserve the traditions, language and skills of the indigenous community.

When choosing a trek, you need first to decide between Altiplano and jungle trails. Which of these two types is best suited to your own preferences and physical ability? The first, based among the high peaks of the Andes range, explores lagoons and high wetlands, and is ideal for spotting llamas, alpacas and vicuñas. The second, passing the Andes to its eastern flank, traverses the subtropical rainforests of the Yungas and makes for a more jungle-based trek.

Many of the treks around La Paz follow old llama caravan routes, used by ancient Andean cultures to transport goods and wares. Some date from around the time that Tiahuanaco, one of the oldest cultures of the central highlands, was first founded in Bolivia. However, it was the Incas, the most important culture to flourish in Latin America, who built the great Kápac ñan or Inca Route that traverses the continent even today.

For a chance to acclimitise before embarking on one of the tougher Andean treks, Lake Titicaca and its surroundings make for an ideal base with an elevation around 4,000m and some fine stamina-building trekking to be had on the Isla del Sol. For an adventure trip with a bias towards a more diverse natural environment, the central valleys and tropical lowlands of the Amazon and Chaco forests are as rich in their natural biodiversity as they are in native culture.

TREKKING THE CHORO TRAIL: A FIRST-PERSON ACCOUNT It starts, like every
journey in Bolivia, with a ch'alla, or offering to Pachamama, the mother earth, to ask for her blessing on the journey ahead. So we gather at the statue of Christ at La Cumbre, 28km from downtown La Paz at the entrance to the Cotapata National Park. The trail stretches out ahead of us, shrouded in mountain mist, while coca leaves and splashes of alcohol left by trekkers at the start of the trail mark the point of no going back.

The Choro (thieves') trail, leading 52km east from La Paz, is the best known of Bolivia's pre-Columbian routes. The route actually dates from Bolivia's Tiahuanaco era (1580BC to AD1200) and has been identified as a probable transport route between Coroico and La Paz during Tiahuanaco's classical period (AD0 to AD300). Christopher Columbus arrived in Cuba in 1492 and the Spanish conquered Potosí in 1545 – hence the trail is known is a 'pre-Columbino'.

Choro, like most of Bolivia's treks, is managed by the ever under-funded Bolivian National Parks Authority (SERNAP; *www.sernap.gov.bo*) with occasional initiatives to maintain the route and a small toll (generally 10Bs per person) collected at various pueblos along the route. Tourist groups actively started walking the trail 15 years ago and it now attracts around 2,000 per year. Compared with the 500 per day currently walking the Inca Trail in Peru, that means they have plenty of space to soak up the scenery without bumping into large groups and often have the run of the campsites at night.

The first day of the hike is a classic Altiplano trek with a windswept path across rough-hewn rocks and open pasture, passing the occasional adobe shack and farmers tending their flocks of llamas en route. As we approach the lunch stop at

Samaña Pampa, we encounter the first tributaries of the rivers that will run on to the Amazonian rivers Beni and Tuichi.

The afternoon leg, despite the well-preserved trail, makes for steep, downhill progress at times, so be prepared for blisters and aching knees. We rest a while in Chucura, a huddle of village huts with a lost-in-time feel. The local toll collector, Don Miguel, clearly isn't too keen on having his photo taken by a gringo with ill-fitting hiking boots. That is, until I explain that hordes of British girls will come to find him after seeing his picture and he promptly breaks into a toothless but radiant ear-to-ear grin.

The last hours of day one are tough with rough stones to clamber over to reach the campsite at the small village of Challapampa. Worse still, by the end of the afternoon, my blisters are killing me with the friction of the constant descent grinding against my boots.

The second day sees a drastic shift of vegetation from the high-altitude, windswept Altiplano to the tropical environment of the jungle-like Yungas. We set

WHAT I LOVE ABOUT TREKKING IN BOLIVIA

Hilary Bradt

Well, it could be something to do with the way I was introduced to it. When we arrived in Bolivia in 1973 we met an American who passed on the information told him by an inebriated member of the Costa Rican National Orchestra: that if he went to a "Jesus Cross" near La Paz and followed the outstretched left hand, he would find an Inca trail leading into the jungle. We had to try it! The tourist office staff were amused – and bemused – at the idea of anyone wanting to walk into the Yungus, and had never heard of an Inca trail. Or indeed of any trail, come to that. However they did identify the statue of Jesus as standing at La Cumbre.

Jesus did indeed point out the way, aided by llama prints in the snow, and as we dropped below the snow line the warm air of the Yungus embraced us, flowers brushed our legs, and the rough track broadened into a typical Inca road of precisely-cut blocks of stone. A day's descent, and we were picking wild strawberries, watching flocks of parakeets and disturbing brilliant blue Morpho butterflies the size of saucers. By the time we reached Coroico we'd decided to write a book.

I returned to Bolivia many times, both independently to explore new routes, and as a trek leader. Each year I would escort groups through the Cordillera Real and once – magically – to the Cordillera Apolobamba, a region so remote that the *arrieros* splashed our donkeys' hoofs, and the truck tyres, with *aguardiente* to ensure the *apu* (spirits) granted a safe journey. We hiked up snowfields, under turquoise glaciers, down scree slopes and through tunnels of vegetation as we reached the lower altitudes. We saw condors so close that we could see the white fluffy neck ring and heard the buzz of tiny hummingbirds as they zipped past to enjoy the red fuchsias. And we met the descendants of the Incas and Aymaras who exchanged greetings in a language unchanged since before the Spanish conquest. Just as their foot-ploughs and llamas are unchanged.

Perhaps all mountain dwellers are like this: calm and courteous, drawing their strength from the mountains and the spirits that dwell there, and ignoring the modern world even as it jostles at their doorstep. So trekking in Bolivia is not just about nature, it's about people too. But sometimes it's hard to separate one from the other.

Hilary Bradt is the founder and managing director of Bradt Travel Guides (www.bradtguides.com).

off with the sun at 08.00 and head downhill following the River Chucura. It's a hot and sweaty descent, but the scenery more than compensates, while orchids and butterflies bring exotic splashes of colour to the trail.

The lunch stop is Choro, where four peasant families live in a cluster of broken-down shacks by the river, where they dry their llama meat over stones. An old crone who hasn't seen a bar of soap in ten years hawks greasy bottles of soft drinks to passing trekkers, while some walkers plunge into the river for a post-prandial refresher.

The afternoon of the second day feels like more of a slog with less compelling scenery and a tough, uphill trail leading to San Francisco, a tiny, rural pueblo, where we bed down early for the night after a supper of soup, macaroni and sugar-coated bananas. This small group of huts is home to a bunch of friendly locals, who have rigged up a makeshift shower for trekkers with a drip of water and a platform overhanging the valley. The water may be cold and the water pressure inferior to a basic dribble, but the view as I'm sluicing my aching feet is quite spectacular.

The final day starts with scrambling over slippery rocks under a cascade of water. After crossing the River Coskepa, we start the steep incline of the Devil's Hill, a 45-minute yomp over ancient steps with a great view across the increasingly subtropical plantations of bananas and citric fruits that pepper the Yungas landscape. At the top of the hill there's a rest point at Bella Vista, two hours into the trek, where a small shop with soft drinks offers a welcome respite after the uphill crawl.

Mid-morning and we make a rest stop for tea and snacks at Sandillani, a gorgeous Yungas village and home to Tamiji Hanamura, an eccentric Japanese hermit, who runs a small campsite (5Bs per person) from his orderly back garden, replete with picnic tables for passing trekkers. Locals say that 70-year-old Tamiji-san hasn't been to Coroico in 15 years, or to the nearest village in ten. But his relative isolation is soon to be disturbed as construction work is now under way for a new refuge with 50 beds right opposite his simple home.

The last leg of the trek descends into Chairo (from where buses and trucks connect to Coroico, the transport hub of the Yungas). It's a soft decline for the first hour but then, just when you think it's all over, there's one final crushing irony: the last hour is hell with a repeat of day one, namely a steep descent over loose stone fragments in a zigzag formation. Halfway down, a sign sums up perfectly the pain in my knees and feet. It reads: 'I'd prefer to die of the pain in my feet than to continue walking on my knees.'

Chairo, a village on the shores of the River Huarinilla and rich in tropical agriculture, is the holy grail for trekkers. The reason? The sacred fridge that awaits you at the village shop, where you can buy your first genuinely cold soft drink in three days. It's a biblical moment for many. Some cast themselves into the water to be reborn; others fall to their knees sobbing and clutching their blisters in fear they may never play football again.

Me? I handed over 5Bs and swallowed my principles down in three mouthfuls. After three days, 52km and two blistered feet, 75cl of branded corporate America had never tasted so good.

THE ILLAMPU CIRCUIT
Kathy Jarvis (www.andeantrails.co.uk)
Security warning: over the past few years several tourist have been robbed in the area around Lake San Francisco. It is best to avoid taking any valuables with you on trek and to use local guides and *arrieros*. It is also possible to leave the trek via a different route.

This is a spectacular, tough seven-day trek with a distance of some 90km, starting out from subtropical Sorata at 2,695m and passing high around the flanks

BOLIVIA'S BEST-KNOWN TREKS

Trek	Duration	Difficulty	Highest Point
Choro Trail *See description, page 121*	3 days	Moderate	4,850m
Condoriri Trail	2–3 days	Moderate	5,000m
Gold Trail	7 days	Difficult	4,658m
Illampu Circuit *See description, page 123*	5–7 days	Difficult	5,045m
Illimani Circuit	5 days	Difficult	4,850m
Sorata Glacier	3 days	Moderate	4,200m base camp climbing to 5,100m
Taquesi Trail *See description, page 126*	3 days	Moderate	4,650m
Yunga Cruz	4 days	Moderate	4,900m

of Illampu and Ancohuma, before returning to the starting point. There are four passes on the trek, the fourth and highest, Abra de La Calzada, taking you up to a breathtaking, heart-pounding 5,045m. Other highlights are the remote highland villages, herds of grazing llamas, awe-inspiring mountain scenery, stunning views over shimmering Lake Titicaca to Peru on the far shores, and the chance of seeing viscachas, Andean geese and soaring condors overhead.

The trek is best done in the dry season between April and October, but be prepared for cold and wet at any time. You can stock up on basic provisions in Sorata before setting out. With a good map and compass you can of course go it alone, but the frequent difficulty in choosing the right trail from among a myriad of tracks, or choosing the right direction when there is no sign of any track, can be very confusing. You can, however, easily hire guides in Sorata (see page 112).

Set off from Sorata heading past Residencial Sorata (see page 112) up Calle Sucre. Turn right at the top and then left up Calle Illampu, leaving Sorata on a wide path heading southeast. After approximately 30 minutes take a steep path left (east) off the main track heading up above the valley of the river Lakathiya towards Quilambaya (90 minutes' walk). At Quilambaya head left and on up through the cactus avenue. Continue climbing steeply for 15 minutes before the path levels out and you contour round to the left to cross a bridge over the River Lackathiya. Go straight on after the bridge, zigzagging steeply up to reach the village of Lackathiya in 45 minutes. There is a shop here with basic provisions. Walking through the village keep an eye out to the left for the point where two branches of the river meet. You want to follow the left bank of the left branch, crossing the river on a small stone bridge and heading on up the track for an hour until the valley widens out and there are good camping spots. From Sorata it takes four to five hours of steady climbing to reach this camping place, about 2km beyond Lakathiya at 4,000m.

From where the valley widens and the stream you are following swings round to the left (north), 90 minutes' steep walking takes you to the Abra Illampu

(4,741m). As you climb past grazing llamas, there are breathtaking views of the glacier-covered Illampu peak up ahead, and plunging deep, green valleys behind. From the pass follow the track heading down the grassy valley of Quebrada Illampu to the northeast until you reach the valley of the river Chuchu Jahuira and the dirt road from Sorata to Ancohuma and Cocoyo. Follow the road to the right for 3km, or about 45 minutes, and then head right (south), at the small hamlet of Estancia Utana Pampa, just before the road bridge. Cross the river Anco Huma Jahuira on a stone bridge and continue heading up the valley. After ten minutes take the steep path going off to the left (southeast) up and into the hanging valley below Abra Korahuasi (4,479m). This is the second pass, which is reached after two hours' ascent from the valley floor. There are good campsites after leaving Ancohuma in the main valley and at the base of the hanging valley. Once over the pass follow the track down, through luxuriant vegetation, dropping 1,000m to the flat-bottomed, green valley with the small village of Cocoyo ahead. You may be able to buy fresh trout from local children tending llama herds and fishing in the many streams meandering through the valley. Stay on the left side of the rivers along the edge of the valley until you reach Cocoyo where you cross the river over a bridge (two hours from the pass). There is a small shop on the right of the bridge, where very basic supplies can sometimes be purchased. Turn left after crossing the river and head first right up past the school and then along the bank of the thundering waters of the River Sarani. Keep the river on the left and do not cross again, but remain on the right bank ascending the Sarani Valley. There are plenty of campsites on the banks of the river 30 minutes from Cocoyo.

From Cocoyo, 3½ hours of gentle climbing brings you to Paso Sarani (4,600m). The path from Cocoyo initially follows the right side of the river, crossing a huge boulder to the left bank after two hours and then rising steeply to the left as you reach a few thatched stone houses on the valley floor. Water cascades all around into the flat boggy pampa land at the head of the valley, which you leave to your right as you ascend. Just over an hour before the pass and 20 minutes above the stone houses there is a wonderful camping spot next to two abandoned buildings, with dramatic views over the valley below. Look out for condors overhead and viscachas on the boulders on the way up the pass.

Cross the pass and descend steeply towards Chajolpaya. After 15 minutes' descent from the top of the pass, cross a stream to the right and follow the good trail down to the village (one hour from the top). There are several houses in Chajolpaya, but little sign of life other than llamas and sheep in this remote, almost inaccessible place. Aymara is the only language spoken here and the nearest shops are two days' walk away in the town of Achacachi far beyond Abra Calzada. After passing through the village turn immediately right up the valley skirting the boggy ground bordering the River Chajolpaya. From here it is five hours' steady climbing to the highest pass on the trek, Abra Calzada (5,045m). There are abundant camping spots on the way up the pass and even at the top, rubbing shoulders with the glaciers, if the altitude doesn't bother you. The trail here is obvious and there is plenty of water on the way up. The climb, although long, is steady and the reward worthwhile as you reach the top and have spectacular views out to the southwest over Lake Titicaca, and all around of ice-capped rugged peaks. The pass itself is broad and almost barren, with a few hardy plants struggling for survival amid ice-scraped boulders and melt-water lakes.

The initial descent from the pass is steep and tricky for mules, as you make your way through large boulders on a trail heading southwest towards the deep blue-green lakes of Carizal and Khota. After 30 minutes the track levels out and passes close to the lakes, crossing a scree slope of deep red-coloured rock. From

Laguna Khota (one hour from the pass) finding the way becomes more difficult, as the path goes off to the southwest and you want to head northwest towards Laguna San Francisco. It is a 90-minute slog across the grassy pampa of the Quebrada de Kote. You should stay on the right (north) side of the river after Laguna Khota and then on reaching the far end (south) of Laguna Ajoyan head cross-country up and over the boulder-strewn ridge lying to the west above you (a one-hour climb). The views of Lake Titicaca to the west and the high peaks of the Cordillera to the east from the top of the ridge are astonishing and the light over the Altiplano is unsurpassably beautiful. To the northwest lies Laguna San Francisco, your destination.

Head for the right (north) end of the lake about 90 minutes from the top of the ridge. There are several places to camp before reaching the lake, or at the north end of the lake, where there are a few stone houses and possibly grazing Andean geese. It is best not to camp within sight of any houses as you may attract the unwanted attention of local farmers, who are not always friendly and may demand money from you. Finding a way across the numerous silted streams flowing into the Laguna San Francisco isn't easy, unless you have the assistance of local children who may come running. If there is no-one around and you don't want to get wet feet, head north up the valley until you see a suitable place to cross. From Laguna San Francisco head steeply west up the track towards a disused road you see above you. Cross the disused road on the track and continue heading up to the top of the ridge (90 minutes from the lake). Again, finding the way becomes a bit tricky as the path heads down to the left (southwest) and you want to go straight ahead (northwest).

From the top of the ridge where there is a rocky cairn (4,867m), continue northwest down into the next valley and up the other side (30 minutes), over the ridge and down into the next valley too (20 minutes), always heading northwest. In the second valley turn west and follow the valley down until you reach a track crossing your path (40 minutes). It's all downhill from here back to Sorata. Cross over the track and continue westwards across the pampa and the head of the valley of Quebrada Tiquitini to rejoin the same track 50 minutes later. Follow this track down until it joins a dirt road leading to the village of Alto Lojena after 30 minutes. This relatively new road (not marked on the maps) sees very little traffic, but you could catch a truck down to the La Paz to Sorata road from here. Alternatively walk down the road through Millipaya (45 minutes from Lojena), cross the river in the middle of the village and continue down the right bank of the river all the way to Sorata (four hours from Millipaya). There are good camping spots at the old mine on the left of the road, one hour from Millipaya before the village of Cochipata. As you descend to Sorata the landscape changes totally from high mountain puna to cultivated fields of maize, potatoes and beans, human habitation becoming much more apparent as you pass through many small villages of adobe houses. You still catch glimpses of the glaciated massifs of Ancohuma and Illampu up to the right with melt-water cascading down erosion-formed gullies towards the valley bottom. Vegetation becomes prolific, the temperature rises and birds sing all around as you return to sub-tropical Sorata and a welcome rest.

THE TAQUESI (OR TAKESI) TRAIL This is often called an Inca trail, but it was almost certainly constructed well before the Incas conquered the region, probably by the Tiahuanaco culture, who built stone paths following wild tracks in order to expand the empire. Whichever culture was responsible, we can admire the perfection of the work and its underlying engineering principles. The paved section covers half the trail, about 20km, and you'll see all the classic features of pre-Columbian road construction: stone paving, steps, drainage canals and retaining walls.

The walk takes only three days (it's about 40km), but the variety of scenery is astonishing. The going is easy to moderate, but there is an altitude gain of 1,200m at the start and an overall altitude loss (over two days) of 2,550m.

From swirling snow on the 4,650m pass, you drop down to the treeline and through incredibly lush vegetation to the humid rainforest below the Chojlla mine. Above the trees the colours are soft and muted: green-ochre hills, grey stones, brown llamas. In the Yungas it's steamy-hot and bright with butterflies, flowers, green leaves and sparkling blue rivers.

The two main villages along the upper part of the trail, Choquekota and Taquesi, pursue a way of life unchanged for centuries: men herding llamas, making rope or harvesting crops; women trampling chuño and preparing the next meal. Below the treeline, however, *mestizos* mix traditional customs with new innovations. Women still sit weaving outside their homes, but synthetic yarn is in vogue and bright cotton dresses replace the Indian homespun.

At its beginning and end the walk is served by two spectacular and contrasting bus journeys. To reach the trailhead you drive through a lunar landscape of eroded 'badlands' offering a display of brown, red, orange and yellow tones, unrelieved by any green. But the return trip from the Yungas is accompanied by luxuriant vegetation that hangs from cliffs and juts over the road as it winds back up to the bleak Altiplano.

Access to the trailhead is via the town of Ventilla. The easiest way of getting there is by taxi, but make an early start; climbing up to the pass in the midday heat is debilitating and in the early afternoon clouds often start rolling in, blotting out the views. Organising a taxi to Ventilla or San Francisco Mine in La Paz through an agency will cost around US$25, a 4x4 around US$80. Daily buses also pass through Ventilla, see Yunga Cruz trek for details (opposite page).

From Ventilla continue through the village and take a left fork shortly afterwards towards the San Francisco mine. The track climbs steadily, passing through Choquekota after a couple of hours. Keep going up the track, which is the access road for the mine, past a derelict church and a graveyard full of cigar-shaped adobe burial mounds. The snowy flank of Mururata gradually comes into view on the right, with llamas providing a picturesque foreground. Keep to the left of the widening alluvial plateau.

About two hours from Choquekota, after a river crossing, the main track goes to the mine and the 'Inca' trail (rather indistinct at this point) branches off to the right. A large sign with a map (useless for navigation though) marks the turning. The trail soon zigzags steeply upwards to arrive at one of the most perfectly preserved stretches of stone paving in South America. This amazing road winds up the mountainside, easing the traveller's passing with a series of low steps. The top of the pass (4,650m) is reached in about 90 minutes, and if the weather is clear you'll have a fine view of the snowy peaks of the Cordillera Real and the Yungas far below. The first good (but bitterly cold) camping place is just below the pass by a small lake. From here on everything is downhill, dropping down a lot.

The descent from the pass to Taquesi takes about three hours. The path, if anything, is even more perfect; and the hillsides are dotted with grazing alpacas. There is camping by another lake shortly before Taquesi, and lodging can be found in the village if you ask around. Taquesi is very attractive in its isolation and life goes on pretty much unchanged since the villagers' ancestors built the road. Shortly after the village the moist Yungas air asserts itself; boulders are covered in bright green moss and bushes and shrubs provide welcome relief from the stark mountain scene. The trail follows the course of the Río Taquesi, hugging the cliff edge. This is a dry section and you should carry water. About 30 minutes below Taquesi the trail and the river start to make a long curve round Cerro Palli Palli. It

4

will be a good 90 minutes before you'll see the ruins of a chapel and pass several houses surrounded by cultivated flowers. This is Kakapi; you can buy food and drink here, and pure water is available from a well just before the settlement. The trail then drops steeply down to Río Quimsa Chata, which is crossed by a footbridge (just before the river the path splits into three; take the lowest one). Beyond the river you climb up and over a shoulder before crossing the Río Taquesi at 2,100m. There's some lovely swimming in river pools here if you can stand the cold water. Half a kilometre further on, by a small water station at the beginning of an aqueduct, is a good campsite.

Mina Chojlla – the town that you could see from up on the shoulder – is reached in two hours, the path either uses the concrete covering the aqueduct or keeps very close to it. To reach Mina Chojlla scramble up the steep footpath to the left, 100m after crossing the tributary below the town. If you decide to bypass this uninspiring mining village, continue straight on to meet the road in about 1km. Another 5km brings you to Yanacachi. Shortly before Yanacachi there are some large metal gates and a control post (to control access to the mine) where you may be asked to register (no fee). If you are arriving late the gates may be locked, knock to have them opened.

If you are ready for a rest, Yanacachi is a nice place to relax in for a few days. There are several places to stay, although facilities are basic.

If you are in the swing of things and want to keep walking, take one of the trails east from Yanacachi and hike 10km or so to Villa Aspiazu and Puente Villa. The route is confusing since there are many *estancias* and small communities in the area, so there are a profusion of tracks. When you leave Yanacachi simply follow the ridge, crossing the road several times, until you arrive at a football pitch with a view of the Río Unduavi on your left and the Río Taquesi on your right. Turn southeast and follow the often overgrown track which runs parallel to (but above) the Río Taquesi until you reach the old road to Villa Aspiazu which takes you to the road that runs from La Paz to Chulumani. An old road runs from Puente Villa to Coroico via Coripata. There is no regular public transport so it could be a long (but interesting) walk.

If you are leaving direct from Mina Chojlla there is transport at around 05.30 and 13.30, though the buses often fill early, especially at weekends. Otherwise head for Yanacachi where there is a wider choice. Be prepared for the journey – it takes about four hours by minibus to get to La Paz.

THE YUNGA CRUZ TRAIL
James Brunker (www.magicalandes.com)
Arguably the most exciting and remote of the pre-Colombian Trails in the southern part of the Cordillera Real, the Yunga Cruz route starts behind Mount Illimani (as seen from La Paz) and finishes in the South Yungas town of Chulumani. The normal route starts in Chuñavi and takes three days, a harder and even more scenic route, which takes five days, starts in Lambate. Buses for Chuñavi and Lambate (the latter is on the same road 20 minutes further on) leave from the corner of Luis Lara and Riobamba streets (above the Rodriguez market area in San Pedro) at around 08.00 and cost 15–20Bs. Get there early to book a seat as it is not possible to buy tickets in advance. The buses pass through Ventilla so they could also be used to access the Takesi Trail. A group with around US$250 to spend could hire a 4x4. Take spare water bottles as a lot of the route (especially the last part) has little water.

From Chuñavi the route heads roughly northeast on a clear trail from the centre of the village. If you arrive late (not uncommon as the road is poor and buses invariably overloaded) you may well be offered accommodation in the schoolhouse. An hour beyond the village are a couple of small lagoons where you could camp though the water in them is not great. Some 30 minutes further on are a couple of derelict stone buildings where you could also camp, with a small stream nearby. The pre-Hispanic trail then traverses around the flanks of Cerro Khala Ciudad ('Stone City Mountain'); this is the highest part of this section averaging around 4,000m and there are great views behind you to Illimani. A couple of hours further on round the far side of Khala Ciudad you cross a couple of gentle valleys which may have streams running through them and where you could camp, before the trail starts to head upwards to join and then follow a ridge heading northeast. This is where the Lambate route joins.

Lambate is a small village perched on a promontory with impressive views and a couple of basic accommodations shortly beyond Chuñavi; it should be possible to hire a mule and muleteer here if you wish. From here the route drops over 1,000m down to the Kheluluni River (which becomes the Chungu Mayu River) and follows along the right-hand side; ask locals in Lambate for the best route down. Shortly before the Colani River joins it, cross over the main river and head for Quircoma, where you will probably want to camp. This is where the long haul (some 2,000m) up to Cerro Khala Ciudad begins in a beautiful valley. It takes about five to six hours to reach Laguna Khasiri in a superb setting below the rocky flanks of Cerro Khala Ciudad. Keep round to the right of the lake and head over a 4,200m pass, from where the trail descends along the ridge to rejoin the more direct route from Chuñavi.

The trail then pretty much follows the ridge, passing below and to the left of Cerro Cuchilltauca before heading to the right of Cerro Yunga Cruz. This section is generally level and enjoys superb views over hills, valleys and cloud forest, with no sign of habitation. As you pass round Cerro Yunga Cruz (around three hours beyond the junction), cross a low ridge with two notches and head for the left-hand (upper) one. Shortly beyond here is a boggy pampa where you could camp. As you round Cerro Yunga Cruz the trail begins its long drop (around 2,000m) down to the Yungas and Chulumani. After around 30 minutes of descent you cross three streams in quick succession; the third is the largest, has possible camping, and is also the last water supply until you reach Estancia Sikilini shortly before Chulumani. Make sure you fill up. Below here the trail enters the cloud forest, a steep, twisting descent, and at times you are in tunnels of vegetation (a machete may be useful early in the season). When it opens out you find yourself looking over precipices into deep forest-clad valleys. There are a couple of water-less clearings where you could camp, the last of these is some four hours beyond the streams with the low domed form of Cerro Duraznani directly ahead. This is where the path starts to get more overgrown and confusing. It starts heading to the left of the hill before the usual heads right and climbs gently around the right-hand side of the hill (another path keeps heading down and left but gets very overgrown). After a couple of hours the forest gives way to cleared land and you can see the small church of Hacienda Sikilini down below you; look for paths that head down to it (the left-hand route also comes out here eventually). From Sikilini a driveable track winds down to the main road from Chulumani to Ocabaya. Follow it left to Chulumani in a couple of hours (minibuses occasionally pass), or if your knees still have life in them you can short-cut down and up across the valley directly ahead to reach Chulumani.

Chulumani is the capital of South Yungas and has a similar hot climate to Coroico. It is much less visited by tourists though and is a bustling little market town; the area is heavily cultivated with coca a prominent crop. It is also notorious as being where Klaus Barbie and other ex-Nazis lived during the days of military dictatorships. There are plenty of accommodations and basic restaurants if you want to stay for a couple of days. Attractions in the area include the sanctuary of

Chirca perched on a nearby hill, the Afro-Bolivian village of Chicaloma and the Apa Apa Ecological Park; the latter several kilometres along the road to Irupana and protecting one of the last surviving untouched areas of Yungas forest. Trips can be arranged in Chulumani. There is regular transport from Chulumani back to La Paz, a trip that takes around five hours along the spectacular 'Route of the Abysses', not quite as infamous as the one to Coroico but nearly as impressive and possibly more prone to landslides.

THE CORDILLERA APOLOBAMBA Less known and less accessible than the Cordillera Real, the Cordillera Apolobamba lies to the north and west of that range, rising abruptly from the Altiplano and straddling the Peruvian frontier at the northern tip of Lake Titicaca.

This is the place for truly adventurous hikers with lots of time. The beauty of the mountain scenery equals or even exceeds that of the Cordillera Real, and the glimpses of Indian life and wildlife (there is a vicuña reserve in the foothills) are even more interesting than to the south.

The Apolobamba owes its network of good trails to the Spanish lust for gold. This has been a gold-mining area since the conquest, and ruined mines can be visited in remote valleys.

The most popular trek is between Pelechuco and Charazani, takes five to six days, is about 70km in length at an altitude between 3,500m and 5,100m, and difficult going. The days will be cold and nights very cold, and you may encounter rain and snow even in the dry season, although around Pelechuco and Charazani it will be warm enough for T-shirts and shorts. Don't forget your sunglasses and be sure to stock up on supplies in La Paz before setting off.

For those without their own transport, just getting to the Cordillera Apolobamba is challenging enough. There are buses from the cemetery area of La Paz, with some running via Pelechuco and some via Charazani but, either way, it's a very long and very cold journey. For the latest information on departures, check with tour operators in La Paz.

ULLA ULLA NATIONAL PARK

Some people ask for remoteness, others ask for nature in its undefiled state; Ulla Ulla National Park offers both. Located deep within the Apolobamba mountains and approximately 100km north of Lake Titicaca, the park is not only a wonder to see, but a true challenge to get to.

The park has a roughly defined area of just over 200,000ha, and was first established as a vicuña reserve in 1972. At that time, the vicuña count in the area had dropped to a mere 72 animals due to unrestrained poaching. In 1977, UNESCO managed to raise the park's status to biosphere reserve in the hope of protecting not only the native vicuña population, but the entire ecosystem. That same year, the Instituto Nacional de Fomento Lanero (INFOL) was created and put in charge of conducting vicuña research and safeguarding the reserve. Now Ulla Ulla boasts a swelling population of 2,500 vicuñas and healthy numbers of black ibises, Chilean flamingos, Andean geese and viscachas.

The village of Ulla Ulla itself is located in the middle of a sprawling bofedal or ancient lake bed, which extends the length of the Apolobamba range. Most residents are alpaca farmers who share local water and other resources with adjacent villages.

There is much to see and do in the park. If you have your own transport and don't mind the rough ride, the wild vicuña herds can be observed at close range and followed cross-country. During the day, the vicuñas graze with the alpacas, but towards evening, when their domesticated brothers and sisters head home to their stone-wall corrals, the vicuñas wander to more isolated pastures. It is especially beautiful to see these graceful cameloids grazing along the plains at dawn against a backdrop of snow-clad peaks.

In the Apolobamba foothills there are a number of lakes to visit including Katantira and Kanahuma, where you encounter flamingos, ducks, Andean geese, black ibises and other waterfowl. Slightly further north, just east of the road to Pelechuco, are the Putina hot springs, where you can wallow in steaming, sulphur-rich waters while watching isolated rainstorms sweep in over the broad plains.

Travelling by car from La Paz, follow the road to Lake Titicaca, then bear right at Huarina and follow the dirt highway to Achacachi and Escoma. In Escoma, the road turns north, traverses several passes, and then just after the turn-off to Charazani (stay left) descends into the Apolobamba Valley. The total drive takes about ten hours.

Although Ulla Ulla offers no hotel accommodation, lodging may be found with local families. There are also plenty of campsites on the outskirts of the village. In fact, almost anywhere outside the village is a campsite. Supplies in the local store are limited but sufficient. Be sure to bring warm clothing as temperatures often drop below zero at night.

4

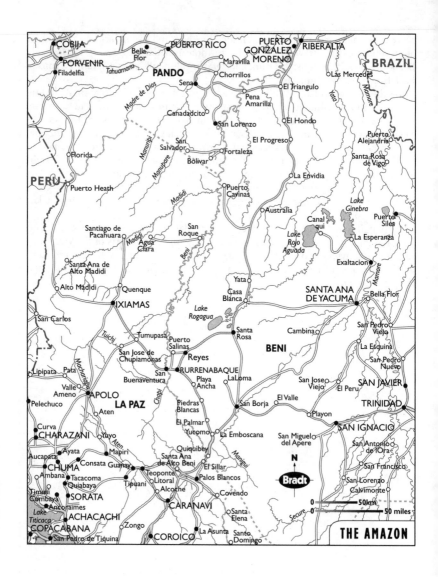

THE AMAZON

5

The Amazon

RURRENABAQUE *Tel code: 03; altitude: 755m; population: 13,668*

Rurrenabaque, better known as 'Rurre' to its fans, is Bolivia's fastest-growing backpacker destination. And deservedly so. It's a great little place with a buzzy vibe and it makes for an ideal escape from the cold nights of the Altiplano with regular flight connections to La Paz. It also boasts an ever-growing infrastructure for travellers and some of the most worthwhile adventure tour options in the country within striking distance. There's actually very little to do in Rurre itself aside from lazing in a hammock and soaking up the jungle nightlife vibe. Except on Sundays, that is, when a frenetic morning market takes over and the whole town puts on its finery to go shopping, although it's clearly more a case of trying to be seen than replenishing supplies. The scenery around Rurre, however, is amongst the best in Bolivia, making it the starting point for jungle and pampas tours (see box, *Jungle versus pampas*, page 136) strung out lazily along the rivers Beni and Tuichi. It's also the centre of Bolivia's fledgling but growing ecotourism industry, with several community-based ecolodges in the region accessible by boat. The biggest attraction of all, however, is the wildlife. Madidi National Park, with 11% of the world's species of flora and fauna, including 10,000 tree and 1,100 animal species, is the gem of Bolivia's natural beauty. As such, the park is currently being touted as the next big eco-tourism destination in the Americas. The reason? A monkey. In February 2005 a team of researchers from the New York-based Wildlife Conservation Society, led by British-born scientist Rob Wallace, discovered a new species of titi monkey in Madidi National Park, a remote enclave of the Amazon region described by NGO Conservation International as the most biologically diverse protected area on the planet (*see Chapter 1, Biodiversity today* section beginning on page 15). The burning question now is: just how fast can Rurre grow – and how can this growth be managed to foster more responsible tourism in the region? Especially as Rurre is expected to receive over 50,000 visitors annually once a new airport opens in 2007. While visits to Madidi are the essential Amazon experience, excursions into Madidi are best undertaken with local, licensed tour

THREE THINGS TO DO AROUND RURRENABAQUE

1 The Amazon regions affords a unique opportunity to spot some of the world's rarest and most colourful wildlife, so head for Madidi National Park – and don't forget your binoculars (page 138).

2 Explore the unique natural environment and try to identify some of the rarest flora on an excursion into the pampas (page 136).

3 Soak up the jungle vibe with some of the liveliest nightlife in the Amazon at the Moskkito Bar in Rurrenabaque (page 141).

RURRENABAQUE

SAN BUENAVENTURA

Beni

FLOW

Madidi National Park
toll gate (10km)

Hotel Jatatal

Hotel Safari
(500m)

Boats to
San Buenaventura

Restaurant Plaza Azul
Restaurant
La Cabaña

Hostal Beni

JUNÍN

Trans Tour
13 de Mayo

Banana's
Pub-disco

Bala Tours

Mapajo EcoLodge office

Amazona
Airlines
office

Turismo Ecologico
Social (TES)

ANICÉTO

ARCE

Bus terminal
(1km),
Residencial Los Andes,
Reyes (40km)

Restaurant
Tacuara

Juice stall

Central Market/
Motor Taxi Rurre stop

Public
swimming pool

SANTA

CRUZ

Jungle Bar Moskkito
& T-shirt shop

Tourist
information
office

Laundry
Number
One

Snack
Palmera
Tropical

Entel

Restaurant
Juliano

Camilla's

Speed Queen
Laundry

La Perla de Rurre

Fluvial Tours

VACA

DIEZ

Enin Tours

Café La Negrita

Chalalan EcoLodge
office

Hostal Santa Ana

CAMPERO

COMERCIO

Plaza
2 de
Febrero

Migrations
office

AVAROA

Police
station

BOLÍVAR

Medical centre

Church

SANTA

BÁRBARA

Conservation
International office

Hotel Oriental

N

Bradt

134

agencies (see page 137). Independent travel to the park is both impractical and insensitive, as only certain regions have been developed for tourism with the necessary facilities, while indigenous tribespeople continue to inhabit other areas of the vast expanse in communities untouched by modernity. Madidi is not the kind of place to go blundering around – go with a good guide to maximise the potential to learn about the wildlife and respect the natural environment in which you are, very much, an invited guest. Note: street numbers are not used in Rurrenabaque, just street names. There is no ATM, post office, bank or medical facilities, so make sure you stock up on cash before leaving La Paz and come prepared. It's also worth knowing that there is very little evidence of malaria to be found around Rurrenabaque, so don't let the mosquitoes put you off a jungle trip – just take lots of repellent.

HISTORY Despite its Amazon location on the banks of the Rio Beni and its sultry, tropical climate, Rurre is part of La Paz Department. The town has a strong indigenous influence and its native people, the Tacana, were one of the few tribes to resist the sweep of Christianity across the continent. Rurrenabaque has long played an important role as a trading post, but these days tourism is the main industry bringing income to Amazon communities.

GETTING THERE AND AWAY

By plane Rurrenabaque's tiny grass airstrip is the domain of Amazonas's growing fleet of small aircraft – a dream for plane spotters, but a little testing for nervous fliers. The Amazonas Airlines office (*Calle Santa Cruz;* \ *892 2466 or* \ *711 33290; www.amaszonas.com*) is located next to the Tacuara restaurant (page 140) with fares for flights to La Paz starting from US$110 one way. Beware: Amazonas flights to Rurrenabaque, while quick and convenient, can be subject to severe delays according to the weather, so be prepared for a very long wait – even overnight. What's more there are no facilities at the airport aside from a smelly toilet and a virtually empty drinks kiosk. Airport taxes of 14Bs are payable on all flights leaving Rurrenabaque. Rurrenabaque has been promised a new airport by the Bolivian Vice Ministry of Tourism to reflect its growing importance as a major traveller hub. The new airport, due for completion by the end of 2007, is expected to boast an asphalt runway and improved connections.

By bus and jeep Bus connections from Rurre can be subject to major delays due to the weather and generally involve long hauls along rough roads. The bus terminal, 2Bs by motorbike taxi or 15 minutes' walk from downtown Rurre, is served by two bus operators: **Trans Totai** (\ *221 0392*) has daily connections at 10.30 to the Yungas and La Paz (18 hours, 50Bs); **Yungueña** (\ *221 2344*) has connections to Trinidad on Mondays and Wednesdays (12 hours, 130Bs) and Cobija on Wednesdays, Fridays and Sundays (22 hours, 180Bs). Opposite the bus terminal there are some very basic snack stalls and located next door is the Residential Los Andes, a basic crash pad with rooms from 20Bs for a shared bathroom and a fan. Frankly, it's well worth the walk into town regardless of how late you arrive. Trans 13 de Mayo have eight places for departures to La Paz by jeep (12 hours, $25); ask in advance about departures as there is no fixed schedule.

GETTING AROUND Amazonas Airlines run hot and busy minibuses along the 2km dirt-track road to/from their office in town (5Bs). Alternatively, a motorbike-taxi ride (5Bs) makes for a breezier ride, but is only really suited to those with very light luggage. Once in Rurre, everything is easily accessible on foot, while boats to San Buenaventura leave daily from 07.00 to midnight for a crossing to the other side of

John Wych

Rurrenabaque is a great place to relax but the main attraction is the choice of tours. The question is, therefore, what kind of trip do you want to take – a pampas or jungle tour? The jungle is probably what you've been expecting and it won't disappoint. The tours start with a morning trip down the river in a long narrow boat powered by an outboard motor. You'll generally arrive at your jungle camp around lunchtime and will be given time to acclimatise while the welcome meal is being prepared. One thing is for sure: it will be hot and humid. Some people find this climate hard to handle at first and the rules state that you need to keep covered up with long-sleeved shirts and long trousers (ideally tucked into your socks for that boy scout look), plus shoes or boots rather than sandals. If you're not covered up properly, the abundance of insect life will eat you for lunch – so take note. It's also a good idea to take an insect repellent for your hands, face and neck. You can buy these cheaply from the market in Rurre, but don't bother with deodorants and perfumes as these will not stop you sweating and can even scare away the wildlife with a keener sense of smell. So, forget your normal hygiene routine and just go a little native. Besides, everyone is in the same boat as you. The exact details of your individual tour will vary depending on which tour agency you choose to go with and the length of time you stay. You can, however, expect lots of guided walks, pointing out medicinal plants, trees you can eat or drink from and any insect or animal life you're lucky enough to encounter. Do make sure your guide only shows these to you and doesn't destroy them. Eco-tourism is gaining ground in Bolivia, so add your weight to the movement while you're there.

The pampas is a less strenuous tour but one that generally features more wildlife. It's still hot and you'll still need to cover up, but you'll be on the river for a lot of the time, so make the most of the nice cooling breeze. This tour will start with a jeep ride over unmade roads. The view out of the window is great, but shut it whenever you pass another vehicle or you'll fill up the jeep with the thick layer of dust that covers the landscape. When you get to the riverside departure point, a waiting boat will make the transfer to the campsite or lodge in time for lunch and a chance to relax in your new surroundings. The next days will then be spent on or around the water, seeing wildlife such as turtles, alligators, freshwater dolphins and capybaras (the biggest of the rodent family, they're about the size of a dog but cuter). Away from the river, with luck, you'll see snakes and monkeys. As in the rainforest, make sure you don't disrupt or harm the natural environment in which they live. If you have time to do both trips, then so much the better. The rainforest is a tougher tour, but really rewarding, especially as you'll come to appreciate a lot more about life in the jungle. The pampas is easier and more relaxing, but you'll still need to be highly prepared for the heat and the insects. As a rule of thumb, try to choose a tour agency with quality camps, an official permit to enter the national parks and a responsible attitude towards bringing tourism to remote indigenous communities. While these trips are all about having a great time, respecting the natural environment should always be uppermost in your mind.

the Rio Beni (1Bs). Motorbike taxis around town charge 2Bs and can be found congregating outside the public market.

TOURIST INFORMATION Good tourist information is hard to come by in Rurrenabaque. The rather threadbare tourist information office, located on Calle Avaroa (no street number or telephone), allegedly opens Mon–Fri 09.00–12.00 and

above left **Cactus flower**
Neoporteria subgibbosa (RC)

above right **Aster** *Asteraceae spp* (RC)

right **Heartleaf arnica**
Arnica cordifolia (RC)

below left **Coca plant**
Erythroxleum coca (JB) page 12

below right **Aloe flower**
Liliaceae aloe umfoloziensis (RC)

top   Pink flamingos, *Phoenicopterus spp,* on the Altiplano (IM)

above left   Blue morpho caterpillar, *Morpho menelaus,* Madidi National Park (JB)

above right   Blue morpho butterfly, *Morpho menelaus,* Madidi National Park (JB)

below   Hawk at Isla de Pescadores, Salar de Uyuni (IM)

top	**Alpacas** *Vicugna pacos* (JB)
above left	**Viscacha,** *Lagidium viscacia,* **Eduardo Avaroa Wildlife Reserve** (JB)
above right	**Llamas,** *Lama glama,* **Cordillera Real** (JB)
below	**Pack horse, Cordillera Real** (RC)

top   **Aymara mother carrying baby, La Paz** (JB)
left   **El Tío effigy in mine, Potosí** (JB) page 182
above   **Yatari (faith healer) making offering to Pachamama, Isla del Sol** (DA) page 102
below   **Shaman blessing Jeep outside Copacabana Cathedral** (JB) page 101

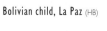

above left Standard bearer at Tinku Festival
near Macha, Potosí (DA)

above right Dried llama foetuses, Witches'
Market, La Paz (RC) page 84

right Bolivian child, La Paz (HB)

top	Musicians playing at Aymara New Year on the Cordillera Real (JB) page 107
left	Priests blessing miniatures with holy water, Alasitas Festival, La Paz (JB) page 37
above	Masked tobas dancer, Chutillos Festival, Potosí (JB)
below	Diablada dancer at Gran Poder Festival, La Paz (JB) page 38

14.30–19.00. In reality, it rarely does so. The far more reliable Ranking Bolivia office had sadly been closed at the time of writing. There are hopes this office may reopen, but for more reliable information, meanwhile, consult the recommended local tour agencies below.

LOCAL TOUR AGENCIES

Bala Tours Calle Santa Cruz; \/f 892 2527; e balatours@yahoo.com; www.balatours.com. The most highly recommended operator in Rurre; trips cost on average US$10 more than other agencies, but that extra US$10 ensures you get a superior quality of service. They are particularly strong on pampas tours (see box, *Jungle versus Pampas*, opposite) & run their own pampas lodge, Caracoles, with simple but satisfying accommodation & food. A 3-day, 2-night package costs from US$125 pp for a small group up to US$190 pp per couple. Prices inc all meals, guide & transfers to Santa Rosa, from where a boat takes you upriver to the lodge. *Open daily 08.00–12.00 & 14.30–19.00.*

Enin Tours Calle Avaroa; \/f 892 2487; e enintours@yahoo.com. Enin Tours is run by Leoncio Janco, a former guide from Madidi's indigenous Tacana community, as the shop front for Mashaquipe, a community association seeking to develop tourism to directly benefit rural Amazonian families. The agency is particularly strong on jungle tours & one of the few local agencies to hold an official licence to lead tours into Madidi National Park. A 3-day, 2-night Madidi discovery package costs from US$110 pp with meals, guide & transfers. The pampas dolphin discovery tour costs from US$50 per day for a couple, US$35 per day for a group of 4. The tours are very authentic but low on frills with basic accommodation & no showers. *Open daily 08.00–12.00 & 14.30–19.00.*

Fluvial Tours Calle Avaroa; \/f 892 2372. The office is part of the backpackers' crash pad, the Hotel Tuichi, & this agency maintains the cheap & sometimes cheerful approach. It's a real no-frills agency, favoured by those on a tight budget, & offering a basic service at a budget price. Standard 3-day jungle & pampas tours cost from US$30 pp, inc meals, guides & transfers. The company recently opened new purpose-built cabañas (huts) for their jungle tours. *Open daily 08.00–12.00 & 14.30–19.00.*

Note: Regardless of which agency you book with, the per-person entrance fees of US$10 for Madidi National Park (jungle) and US$5 for Rio Yacuma National Park (pampas) are payable separately at the point of entry to the park. Make sure you have change – nobody else will.

COMMUNITY PROJECTS AND ECOLODGES

Rurrenabaque is the centre of Bolivia's fledgling but growing eco-tourism industry with plenty of ecolodges. Bookings for many of the projects and lodges can be arranged in La Paz. Otherwise, go direct to their respective offices in Rurrenabaque to discuss their ecotourism credentials.

Conservation International (CI) Plaza 2 de Febrero; \ 892 2495; e jayala@conservation.org; www.conservation.org.bo. Conservation International, the NGO with a local office located on the southwestern corner of the main square, runs the new San Miguel lodge. Located 40 mins from Rurre by boat, this lodge was still under construction at the time of writing & prices were yet to be fixed – ask for more details. *Open Mon–Fri 08.30–12.30 & 14.30–18.30.*

Chalalan Ecolodge Information Office Calle Commercio; \ 892 2419; f 892 2309; www.chalalan.com. The information & booking centre for Bolivia's best-known ecolodge cum community project handles enquiries & arranges trips in collaboration with America Tours in La Paz (page 72) & selected other agencies. A 3-night package costs US$279 pp, based on 2 sharing, with 2 nights in Chalalan on a full-board basis. *Open daily 07.30–12.30 & 14.30–19.30.*

Mapajo Ecolodge Information Office Calle Santa Cruz; \/f 892 2317; e mapajo_eco@yahoo.com; www.mapajo.com. This community-based ecolodge, located 3hrs from Rurre by boat & with a capacity for 15 people, is managed by a Canadian NGO. Prices start from US$60 pp per night, inc meals & transfers, US$65 with a private bathroom. *Open daily 08.00–12.00 & 14.00–18.00.*

Turismo Ecológico Social (TES)/A Day for the Communities Calle Santa Cruz; \ 892 8526, 712 89664; f 892 8526; e turismoecologicosocial@

Chris Lee

During my travels around Rurrenabaque, I became deeply concerned at the number of stories, photos and examples of completely irresponsible and unsustainable approaches taken by tour groups and their guides while visiting Madidi National Park and surrounding areas. The most disturbing example involved tourists who had employed a local guide at the cheapest price, without thoroughly researching the content of their tour package. At US$15 per day there was obviously no room for luxuries, but it was with shock that they found themselves setting up mosquito nets on the forest floor and it was with absolute dismay that they found dinner consisted of rice, a monkey and a squirrel shot in front of them as they were admiring the wildlife. Local game is still a means of sustaining life for many communities but it is not a way of capturing the tourist dollar. What concerned me the most about this story was that they had not researched their trip properly and furthermore they had continued with their trip for the duration, without highlighting to their guides the short-sighted approach to their actions. Another concern was the numerous companies running tours to the Pampas area that took on the 'Crocodile Hunter' approach in capturing wild animals for the viewing pleasure of their guests. A local wildlife expert explained that handling wild animals not only psychologically damages them but, in the case of the anaconda, can cause physical harm when the creature is held in the air without support along its entire body. Destroying the attraction that people have come to see has its own economic problems, but worse, leaving the ecosystem that once supported indigenous communities completely denuded has serious implications. If enough people request responsible tourism, companies will change their approach.

hotmail.com. Working with 4 indigenous Amazon communities, TES runs full-day bus tours to villages within a 42km radius of Rurre. The visit is designed to teach travellers about different aspects of jungle life in each village – from artisan skills to natural medicine. Prices for adults/children are US$25/13, inc guide, transport & lunch in the community. TES promises that 30% of the revenues generated will go back directly into the hands of the communities for social development programmes. *Open daily 08.00–12.00 & 14.00–18.00.*

 WHERE TO STAY Rurrenabaque is still angled towards the backpacker market but a couple of more upmarket properties add a touch of refinement for those seeking home comforts. The following properties are divided by budget category and listed in the order of the author's preference. At the time of writing, work was under way on the Hotel Tacuara (*Plaza 2 de Febrero*), a smart new property promising the most advanced air-conditioning system in Rurre. Soft opening prices were to be pitched around singles/doubles US$18/25 with a buffet breakfast.

Mid-range

⌂ **Jatatal Hotel** (19 rooms) Av Costanera Cipriano Barace #1007, San Buenaventura; ☎ 241 4753, 719 00052; e jatatal@boliviamilenaria.com. The latest opening in the area is also the most upscale property Rurrenabaque has seen in a while, with a museum-style feel & a fine collection of artisan crafts. The rooms have a nice rusticity & welcoming touches, such as free fruit & soft drinks as standard for all arriving guests. A pool, hammocks & AC complete the package. & if you're worried about being on the other side of the water & away from the action, don't be: the hotel has 2 private water taxis at your service 24hrs a day. *Sgls/dbls US$20/40 with buffet b/fast.*

⌂ **Hotel Safari** (10 rooms) Calle Final Comercio; ☎ 892 2210; f 892 0892. This Korean-owned

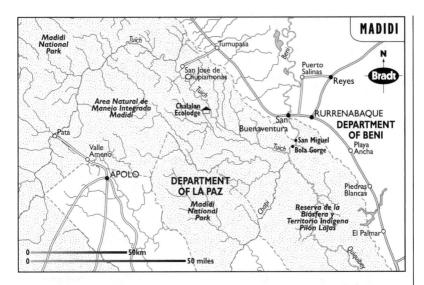

property is definitely at the upper end of the scale both in terms of service & price. There are 7 comfortable, chalet-style rooms for up to 5 people & 3 dbl rooms, all of them set in lush gardens with a pool & a river view that really comes into its own at sunset. The owners also offer airport pickups for 20Bs & meals in the terrace restaurant from 20–40Bs, making this place particularly popular with families. *Sgls/dbls/family room for 5 US$25/34/50 with a buffet b/fast.*

Budget

🏠 **Hostal Beni** (14 rooms) Calle Comercio; ☎ 892 2408; f 892 2273. This reliable, mid-range option has basic but comfortable rooms, many with private bathrooms. This place is due for expansion with a whole new block promised. Meanwhile a laundry service & money exchange are available. *Sgls/dbls with AC 120/150Bs; sgls/dbls with fan 50/70Bs; sgls/dbls with shared bathroom 30/50Bs.*

🏠 **Hotel Oriental** (14 rooms) Plaza 2 de Febrero; ☎ 892 2401. A simple but welcoming mid-range option with a family-run ambience, a shady terrace for essential afternoon hammock-swinging & b/fast served at a communal table. It's a no frills place but very welcoming &, as such, deservedly popular, so book ahead if you can. *Sgls/dbls 70/100Bs; cheaper rooms (shared bathroom, no b/fast & ceiling fan only from 18.00–06.00) cost 25Bs.*

🏠 **Hotel Santa Ana** (20 rooms) Calle Avaroa; ☎ 892 2399. Cheap & cheerful, this rather worn but very welcoming joint is a real favourite with passing backpackers. There's no b/fast & few frills, but the tranquil garden with an array of hammocks spilling out from a shady outhouse is a quintessential Rurre experience. *Sgls/dbls with private bath 50/70Bs; sgls/dbls/tpls/quads 25/50/75/100Bs.*

✖ WHERE TO EAT

✖ **Juliano Calle Comercio** no tel. The best place to eat in Rurre boasts a fusion of French & Italian cuisine, superlative service & a backdrop of cool jazz music to while away hot jungle nights. Mains cost 25–40Bs & house specials 65Bs – try the excellent seafood risotto. For a lighter meal, try the tapas (20Bs) & check out the wine list with samples from Bolivia's excellent La Concepción winery (page 243) from 80Bs. An oasis of quality in the wilds of the jungle, this place is unbeatable. Beware: it has changed address several times in the last year, but this new location is – hopefully – permanent. *Open daily 11.00–15.00 & 18.00–23.00.*

✖ **Camila's** Calle Santa Cruz; ☎ 892 2250. Located right opposite the Amazonas office, this perennial backpacker hangout has the usual gamut of b/fast (10Bs), snacks & meals with fish & meat mains going for 20–25Bs. There's a slightly unreliable internet service (18Bs/hr – ouch!) & the owner, Miguel Reverendo, also runs the kitsch but fun Banana's Pub-Disco (page 141). *Open daily 07.00–23.00.*

There are three ecolodges located close to 'Rurre', strung out along the rivers Beni and Tuichi. The best known of these is Chalalan, which has become Bolivia's most profitable ecotourism project. Located five hours upriver from Rurrenabaque in the heart of Madidi National Park, Chalalan is now managed and staffed entirely by 30-odd employees from the local Quechua-Tacana community of San José de Uchupiamonas. 'We were worried about the exodus of people from a community that had lived in the rainforest for over 300 years. By 1985, over 50% of families had left in search of work,' says Guido Mamami, a village elder turned general manager of Chalalan, sitting behind his desk at Rurrenabaque's Chalalan Information Centre in a starched white shirt. 'So we started a project that would manage tourism to benefit the community,' adds Mamami, who initiated the Chalalan project in 1995 with US$1.5m in funding from the Inter-American Development Bank and NGO Conservation International. In the same year Madidi was officially inaugurated as a national park and the two projects developed hand in hand from then on. Today Chalalan attracts 1,000 tourists annually and turns over a healthy US$25,000 profit, paying a share of its yearly profits to the 74 families from the jungle pueblo of San José de Uchupiamonas now working at the lodge. The profits also contribute towards health and education services for the local community. The cabins are simple and rustic, but not without comforts. Of the 24 available beds, the best cabins are set back into the jungle and are en suite with local stone-built bathrooms and a walk-in shower powered by solar energy; all rooms come with mosquito nets and fresh towels. Meals are served in a central dining hall and range from a traditional supper of catfish cooked in leaves through to rather decent crème caramel. Drinks from the bar are extra and not cheap at 18Bs for a beer, but also include a fruity glass of Bolivian red from the wine-growing Tarija region; tea, coffee and drinking water are available free all day. There are 14 well-marked nature trails of different grades of difficulty around the lodge, ranging from an easy 2km stroll through lowland rainforest to a 9km yomp through differing jungle systems. Most walks set out at first light and return for a shower, relaxed lunch and a lazy afternoon swinging in the hammocks. The pace is slow, with an emphasis on listening for approaching wildlife – tapirs, capybaras, alligators and parrots amongst them – while the guide runs through his repertoire of animal calls, calling out to toucans from the back of his throat and slapping his cheek fervently to produce a mating call when the pigs come into sniffing distance. Remember there is one rule in Chalalan: always remove your shoes before entering a building to avoid damaging the polished mahogany floor. This, in turn, gives rise to another rule, which our guide explains as we lace up our boots to embark on our first nature walk. 'Always check your shoes for insects before you put them on,' he grins.

✕ **Restaurant Tacuara** Corner of Calle Santa Cruz & Calle Avaroa; no tel. A bog-standard, traveller-friendly eatery, it's good for decent pre-trip b/fast (7–12Bs), sandwiches (12Bs) & mains (20—25Bs). No frills but a popular spot for a hearty meal before your tour departs. *Open daily 07.00–23.00.*

✕ **La Perla de Rurre** Corner of Calle Vaca Diez & Calle Bolivar; ✆ 892 2302. A notch above the average traveller eatery, this place is set around an open-air terrace, away from the main drag. The b/fast (8–10Bs) & mains (20Bs) are hearty but, best of all, the fish dishes, prepared to traditional local recipes & cooked in leaves over the grill (25Bs), are delicious. *Open daily 07.00–22.00.*

Overlooking the Rio Beni and spying on arrivals from San Buenaventura, **Restaurant Plaza Azul** and **Restaurant La Cabaña** are located opposite each other on Calle Santa Cruz. Both offer standard traveller fare in rustic surroundings with mains from 20Bs. Of the two, the former (✆ *892 2413*) has the edge for its good-value set lunch (7Bs) to be savoured on the terrace. Both open daily 07.00–22.30. Among the pick of the traveller-friendly, hole-in-the-wall cafés around Rurre, **Snack Palmera Tropical** on Calle Avaroa is good for breakfasts with muesli, yoghurt and nuts (6–10Bs) and fruit shakes (6–8Bs) – try the San Francisco (7Bs). **Café La Negrita** on Calle Avaroa is a shack-like coffee and empañada stop (3Bs) located opposite the tourist office (page 136). For a hit of tropical flavours, try the **Mercado Central** on Calle Avaroa (*open 06.00–21.00*) for juices and shakes (2Bs), while the juice stall on the corner of Calle Avaroa and Santa Cruz charges 2Bs for your vitamin-loaded hit of tropical flavours.Finally, for a uniquely Rurre experience, watch out for US national **Ronnie**, who drives the now-legendary banana bread van. Ronnie, who lives locally and is a deep font of traveller information, can be found every morning around 08.00 and every afternoon around 17.00 at the intersection of Calle Avaroa and Calle Santa Cruz (near Camila's, page 139). He sells homemade banana bread, muffins and muesli bars for around 3.5Bs a pop and claims to 'mash the bananas with my own feet for that extra protein.' Whatever, these snacks are ideal fodder to stock up on before taking your tour and Ronnie is always up for a friendly chat.

ENTERTAINMENT AND NIGHTLIFE

☆ **Jungle Bar Moskkito** Calle Comercio; ✆ 892 2267; e moskkito@terra.com. Rurre's favourite gringo hangout has a tropical vibe, a pool table & a nightly happy hour from 19.00–21.00 (with 50% off cocktails marked with a mosquito, but not beers). What's more, the owners have a mutually beneficial agreement with Pizzeria Italiana (✆ 892 2611) next door to have pizzas (medium/large 27/50Bs) delivered direct to your table. Cocktails range from 20–28Bs, beers (ask for a 'Chopp') 8Bs & mains around 20Bs. It's a great place to meet other travellers & form groups for forthcoming tours, so wade in & soak up the jungle vibe. *Open 18.00–late.*

☆ **Banana's Pub-Disco** Calle Comercio 1/F; ✆ see Camila's restaurant. The latest nightspot to open in Rurre is a far safer place to fraternise with the locals than the shadowy karaoke bars heading away from town down Calle Commercio. A security guard keeps the riff-raff out while the drinks (happy hour 19.00–21.00) keep flowing until the last man falls over (cocktails 15–22Bs, beers 10–15Bs). Watch out for the, ahem, tropical décor – the most kitsch design in the Amazon – &, after one cocktail too many, you can maybe find the courage to enquire about the private karaoke room. *Open 19.00–late.*

SHOPPING The Moskkito T-shirt shop, next to the bar of the same name, changes dollars as well as selling T-shirts (79Bs); open Mon–Sat 11.00–13.00 & 15.00–22.00, Sun 15.00–20.00. Rurrenabaque is also a great place to stock up on gear before setting off on your jungle or pampas trip. There are lots of second-hand clothes available from stalls dotted around Calle Commercio and Calle Santa Cruz, while great hammocks (one–two people 70–90Bs) are to be found opposite the market along Calle Aniceto Arce. They're a great way to take a little piece of the Rurre lifestyle away with you.

OTHER PRACTICALITIES

Entel call centre (*Calle Avaroa; open daily 07.00–23.00*) Internet access, albeit for a hefty 18Bs per hour.

Public swimming pool (*Calle Santa Cruz; open daily 10.00–19.00; entry 20Bs*) A chance to cool off.

Speed Queen laundry and Number One laundry (*Calle Vaca Diez & Calle Avaroa respectively; open daily 07.00–21.00*) Both offer a same-day laundry service for 8Bs per kg.

AMAZON EXCURSIONS IN THE PANDO The Pando is Bolivia's northernmost department and the best place to experience true Amazon rainforest. There are many possible hikes that would make a visit to this department worthwhile. The history of the Bolivian Amazon is generally one of exploitation and extraction – what was needed was taken from the forest with little thought of sustainability. Evidence of this extractive exploitation is still visible throughout the Bolivian Amazon today: old mansions, once belonging to the great rubber barons, now stand empty, slowly being reclaimed by the encroaching jungle. In some places

My first taste of piranha fishing came on a trip through the Bolivia Amazon aboard the floating hotel, Reina de Enin, a journey that followed the tributaries of the Rio Mamore, snaking 1,400km from the Cochabamba basin through the tropical Beni region and on to the Brazilian border. The journey offers a glimpse of the sleepy Amazon lifestyle along waterways little played by tourists. Better still, you will have the chance to spot some of the wildlife of the region, notably the ocelot, the giant otter and the capybara. Most exciting of all, however, is the opportunity to see up close the fabled pink river dolphin, which can grow up to 3m in length. This ancient and endangered species can change its skin colour from pale grey to a bright pink, the latter being more common in older animals. Locals revere the dolphins as mythical beasts – they call them bufeos and killing an animal would bring a terrible blight on a village. On my first day aboard, Thomas, the ship's captain, decided to give us a taste of the Amazon to work up an appetite for lunch. And, to give him credit, he achieved it with quite some aplomb, taking us on the Amazon version of motorboat dodgems in a small-engine, dugout canoe. As we tore off towards the horizon, the Rio Mamore spluttering in our wake, he proceeded to weave through overhanging branches and water-borne creepers, pulling handbrake turns with a wild and deranged look in his eyes. After such heart-in-mouth antics, spending the afternoon languishing in a hammock with a good book and a cold drink would have seemed particularly appealing. But the crew had other ideas. If we wanted dinner, we would have to go out and catch it. The sun was high over the River Mamore as we headed downstream to a mud-hut settlement where we disembarked. After a 15-minute yomp across the jungle to where a rowing boat was waiting and 30 minutes of strenuous oarsmanship, we were floating in a deserted lagoon with only the water lilies for company – that, and of course, some of the biggest and hungriest piranhas in the Amazon.But after struggling manfully for a while I reeled in my first catch of the day. It was a whopper. Just as I'm feeling suitably smug about my fishy face-off, Enrique, my piranha-fishing instructor, casts me a warning look. 'It's not how you catch the piranha but how you reel it in,' he explains sagely. 'Do it wrong and he'll have your finger off with his last breath.' With that he produces the kind of knife that normally only Crocodile Dundee keeps handy and proceeds to shave back the upper lip. There, glimmering in the sunlight, is a set of razor-sharp dentures. Back on board and post shower, we settled down to a supper of fresh piranha, avocado salad and cold beers. I had faced off the fishy nemesis and he'd fallen for it – hook, line and sinker.

Journeys on the Reina de Enin (10 tpl cabins and 2 dbl cabins with air conditioning, 2 dbl cabins with fans) are arranged through Fremen Tours in La Paz (www.andes-amazonia.com/en/flotel.e.asp); prices start from US$349 pp for a 4-day package, inc transfers, all meals & excursions.

overgrown railway tracks hint of some of the more ambitious dreams of frontiersmen hoping to open up the territory. Deeper in the jungle you might come across Brazil-nut (previously rubber) collection sites established in the first decade of the last century. You will also encounter the *siringa* or rubber tree, scarred by many long years of tapping, now left to heal, until, perhaps, the arrival of a new era of exploitation. Most people use Riberalta as their gateway to the Pando. The town sits on the banks of the Río Beni, several kilometres from its confluence with the Madre de Dios. Its location made it a perfect centre for trade during the rubber boom (1890–1914) and some of the old charm from that era still lingers in the architecture. Riberalta has recently become a major stop along the La Paz–Guayaramerin–Cojiba highway. A large percentage of the population works in Brazil-nut processing plants. In fact, so many Brazil nuts are produced here that the husks are commonly used to fill in roads. The smell of dust and nuts fill your nostrils at all times.

This portion of the Amazon is very flat. Trekkers will not find themselves scrambling up muddy ridges or caught in deep ravines, but the heat and humidity punish the spirit at times, and you will find yourself drinking huge quantities of liquid. Bring purification tablets. Even if the numerous streams you encounter look clean, don't drink from them without purifying the water. All kinds of bacteria are found here. Wear shoes at all times, as worms could infest your feet. In some places mosquitoes may also be a problem, while snakes are numerous but rarely seen. Be sure to pack everything in plastic bags to prevent moisture and insects from infiltrating your belongings.

Guided hikes All of the most interesting hikes in the Pando involve venturing into the dense Amazon rainforest. You are advised to hire a guide who knows the jungle well and understands the wildlife of the Pando. The going rate is about US$50 per day, including meals, accommodation and transport. One tiring but unforgettable hike takes you from the port of Loma Alta to the Brazil-nut collection site of Río Negro. To get to the port, a boat can be hired at the docks in Riberalta to make the three-hour trip downstream. From Loma Alta, it's about 35km to Río Negro. The road, which is really a glorified trail, passes through some of the most beautiful jungle I have ever seen. Brazil nut trees tower on all sides, some of them 200ft tall with trunks 8ft thick. Huge palm trees called *motacu* fan out like giant peacocks all along the overgrown track; thinner trees shoot up through openings in the canopy to secure their piece of light. If you're lucky you'll see howler or spider monkeys in the trees. Large lizards often lounge about in patches of sunlight, and in the mornings you might spy agouti or coatimundi feeding alongside the road. En route are small settlements and collection huts where life has remained relatively unchanged for 100 years, with most inhabitants still sheltered from the influence of larger towns like Riberalta. Walking the wild Brazil-nut and rubber-tree circuits around Río Negro is a must in order to get a feel for what the collectors go through on a daily basis. One other hike starts not far from the abandoned boom town of Cachuela Esperanza, 95km north of Riberalta. A boat is required to get across the Beni River. Disembarking several kilometres downstream, jungle paths lead to a small rubber-collection site, comprising five pahuichis or thatched huts. The best way to see the area and its wildlife is to do a day hike from the collection site.

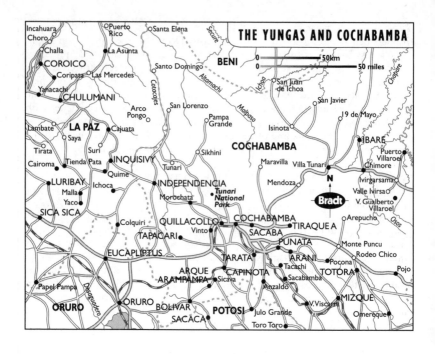

THE YUNGAS AND COCHABAMBA

6

The Yungas and Cochabamba

COROICO *Tel code: 02; altitude: 1,377m; population: 4,500*

From the mountains to the jungle, the Yungas are filled with contrasting scenery: high plains give way to waterfalls and lush green valleys dotted with banana and citrus fruit plantations. As the altitude decreases and the ecosystem turns from scrubland to tropical jungle, the diversity of scenery is immense.

Coroico, the capital of the North Yungas, is the area's hub with a relaxed, tropical feel and a rare chance to spot the country's Afro-Bolivian community at work. Located 119km from La Paz, Coroico makes for a favourite weekend-break destination for *Paceños,* the residents of La Paz, with regular bus services from that city.

Also at weekends, backpackers descend en masse on this rural pueblo, most huffing and puffing after a white-knuckle descent on mountain bikes down what is sometimes known as the world's most dangerous road (see *Biking Bolivia*, page 52). By Sunday afternoon, they're all gone and Coroico effectively closes on Mondays.

Overall Coroico is a gloriously relaxed place, but don't go expecting much nightlife or activity during the week – you'll be sorely disappointed. If, however, you're desperate to burn off some energy, there are some good trekking options to be found around Coroico, most notably the pre-Incan Choro trail (page 121).

Coroico offers some of the best mountain vistas in Bolivia with Uchamachi, the mountain overlooking Coroico, allegedly home to Pachamama, the mother earth.

HISTORY Given its favourable climate and fertile soils, Coroico has long been a centre for the cultivation of fresh produce. During the era of the Spanish conquest, the rivers of the Yungas were found to contain gold and were subsequently pillaged, bringing to the area a short but frenzied period as a prospectors' frontier zone. In small rural communities across the Yungas, the Aymara-speaking descendants of African slaves, imported to work in Bolivia's mines, live on today, bringing a rare multi-ethnic facet to the region's cultural mosaic.

THREE THINGS TO DO IN COROICO

1 Put on your walking shoes and head out for a trek through the nearby subtropical valleys, taking in the unique flora and fauna of the Yungas ecosystem en route (page 151).

2 Use Coroico as your base to explore one of the pre-Incan walking trails that dissect the area (page 148).

3 Settle down with a good book and a great view across the mountains to sample some delicious Yungas coffee on the patio of one of the cafés around the plaza (page 150).

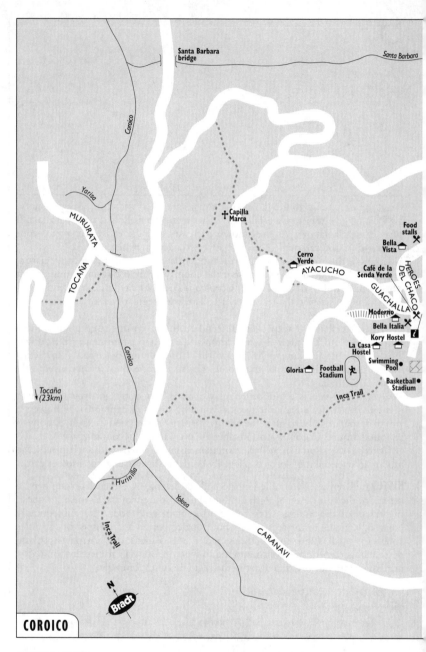

COROICO

GETTING THERE Minibuses to Coroico leave daily from Avenida de las Americas in La Paz's Villa Fatima district and return from Coroico's main square for a standard fare of 15Bs one way. From the plaza in Coroico, **Turbus Totai** (☏ *221 6592*) and **Minibus Yungueña** (☏ *221 3513*) have daily departures to La Paz 06.30–18.00 with a journey time of three hours. **Tours Palmeras** (☏ *221 9442*), located just south of the plaza, runs at similar hours.

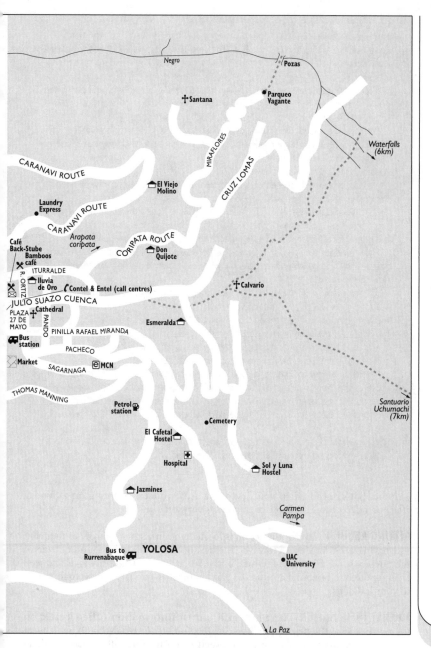

You might be interested to know that, given the rather hazardous nature of the road conditions, the locals suggest that Minibus Yungueña drivers know the road best.

These bus companies can also arrange tickets for buses to Rurrenabaque for around 60Bs. Buses leave daily at 13.00, but it's up to an 18-hour journey according to the road conditions – hence not one for the faint-hearted.

For those in search of the ultimate Bolivian adrenaline high, there is only one option: a trip down what is claimed to be the world's most dangerous road from La Paz to Coroico.

Built by Paraguayan prisoners-of-war in the 1930s, the 64km white-knuckle, downhill route plummets over 3,600m from the snow-strewn peaks of Bolivia's Cordillera Real to the subtropical valleys of the Yungas region.

Much of the rough, dirt road is just one lane wide, with regular intervals cut into the cliff; hence when two vehicles meet, one has to back up so they can squeeze past. It is composed of sharp, blind corners with overhanging, dripping-wet rocks adding to the hazardous conditions.

At least one vehicle allegedly takes the plunge over the edge every week. Hence the crosses that line the roadside – Bolivian traffic signs, the locals say.

In 1995 the Inter-American Development Bank branded the route 'the world's most dangerous road', basing the decision on the large number of vehicles lost over the edge – one accident in 1983 claimed over 100 fatalities in one fell swoop.

The trick to surviving the journey is to select a vehicle that looks halfway roadworthy and a driver that looks halfway sober before starting the three-hour downhill journey.

During the next 90, heart-in-the-mouth minutes, the mists swirl around you and the road gives way to a dirt track. Every hairpin bend, it seems, is lost in the fog until the very moment you're right on top of it with the back wheels already hanging over the edge of a sheer precipice.

Once you do make it, however, the reward is stunning. Coroico is a tropical paradise of palm trees, banana plantations and exotic flowers.

Work on a new toll road that avoids the precipices and takes a longer but safer route to the Yungas still remains in disarray. The whole project has run hopelessly over budget and been plagued by numerous technical problems. Some sections of the road are occasionally in use these days, although many drivers flatly refuse to use it anyway.

The whole project has been due for the final stage of completion for about as long as anyone can remember now – so don't hold your breath.

Note: book ahead when you first arrive as, if you are counting on a Sunday afternoon departure, these buses are always very, very busy.

GETTING AROUND Most of the action is located within a stone's throw of the main square, Plaza 27 de Mayo. However, the best hotels are all to be found outside of the pueblo, some a hefty uphill hike in the Yungas sun. Thankfully taxis and jeep taxis are often to be found around the plaza with a flat-rate fare (10Bs) to ferry you to your lodgings.

TOURIST INFORMATION There is a small **tourist information office** located on the north side of the plaza (*open Tues–Sun 09.00–12.00 & 14.00–19.00*), which can help arrange tours to local beauty spots, such as nearby waterfalls (6kms), a hiking trip to Uchamachi (7kms) or to the Afro-Bolivian community of Tocaña (23kms), for around 100Bs per person, 130–170Bs if taking a jeep. The same building houses the local **hotel association** for help with hotel reservations.

Among the local tour agencies, **Vagantes Eco Aventuras** (✆ *712 54083*) allegedly run a range of local jeep trips (from US$20 upwards) from a kiosk on the plaza, but opening hours seem to be, at best, highly irregular. A more reliable

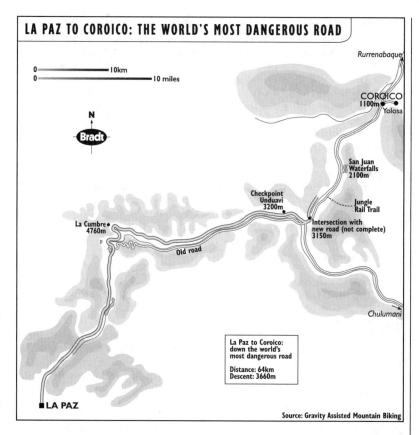

LA PAZ TO COROICO: THE WORLD'S MOST DANGEROUS ROAD

Rurrenabaque

COROICO
1100m●   ●
●Yolosa

San Juan
Waterfalls
2100m

Checkpoint
Unduavi
3200m

Jungle
Rail Trail

La Cumbre●
4760m

Intersection with
new road (not complete)
3150m

Old road

Chulumani

La Paz to Coroico:
down the world's
most dangerous road

Distance: 64km
Descent: 3660m

■LA PAZ

N

Bradt

0 ————— 10km
0 —————— 10 miles

Source: Gravity Assisted Mountain Biking

option is **Cross Country Coroico** (*Calle Pacheco #79;* ↘ *719 73015*), which offers all-day mountain-biking trips around Coroico.

WHERE TO STAY For a small town Coproico has plenty of accommodation options, including a couple of upscale properties down county lanes that are better suited to couples and families. The following properties are divided by budget category and listed in the order of the author's preference.

Mid-range

Jazmines Hotel (12 rooms, reservations via the office in La Paz) Calle Guerrilleros Lanza #1660, Miraflores; ↘ 222 9967; hotel ↘ 715 09001. A rustic, smart hotel located 1km south of the centre, the Jazmines claims 4 stars, but doesn't quite earn them. The rooms have great views (number 7 has the best panorama) & meals are good, though rather pricey at 30Bs for a set lunch. Don't bother with dinner — it's definitely not worth the extra 30Bs. It is a nice setting, however, with family-friendly, self-contained cabins making an ideal base for groups with kids in tow. The road into Coroico has also been newly paved, so the trek into the

centre is now more bearable, while transport is also sometimes available from the hotel. *Sgls/dbls/tpls US$25/40/60 with b/fast; cabins US$130/150 for 6/8 people.*

El Viejo Molino (20 rooms) Camino Santa Barbara; ↘/f 289 5506; e viejomolino@ valmartour.com; www.valmartour.com. Valmar Tours in La Paz specialises in selling all-inclusive packages to this property, Coroico's only 5-star hotel. The facilities are good (non-guests can even buy a pool, sauna & gym day pass for 30Bs), but overall the rooms are rather disappointing given the high prices, with no cable TV & an ageing décor. Worse still, it's a hot & tiring 1km hike from the centre to reach the hotel, although it is, at least, mercifully downhill. *Sgls/dbls/suites US$25/35/60 with b/fast.*

Budget

⌂ **Hotel Bella Vista** (12 rooms) Calle Héroes del Chaco #7; ☎ 213 6059; e coroicohotelbellavista@ hotmail.com. One of the smarter hotels within genuine walking distance of the centre (it's only 200m), the rooms here are nicely decorated with tiled bathrooms & great views (number 207 is particularly striking). Plus there's an in-house restaurant & a sun terrace. *Sgls/dbls/tpls with private bathrooms 90/130/160Bs.*

⌂ **Hostal Kory** (30 rooms) Located just off the plaza; ☎ 715 64050; e info@hostalkory.com. This reliable budget option, located to the west of the plaza, has a pool, hammocks &, best of all, a great sun terrace with panoramic views across the Yungas. Room numbers 1 & 2 have the best views, while kitchen facilities are currently under construction. *Rooms with private/shared bathrooms 100/50Bs with b/fast.*

✕ WHERE TO EAT

✕ **El Café de la Senda Verde** Western corner of Plaza 27 de Mayo; ☎ 715 32703. A nice rustic café with a strong vegetarian influence, this place has good b/fasts (12–18Bs), sandwiches (7–12Bs) & great Yungas coffee (4–8Bs). It's a simple place but a friendly one for drinks & snacks. Recommended. *Open daily 07.00–19.00.*

✕ **Cafe Back-Stube** Western corner of Plaza 27 de Mayo; ☎ 719 54991. This German-owned café has a great panoramic terrace to savour a Yungas coffee (3–7Bs) & German-style cakes or pancakes (6–15Bs), all while taking in a spectacular view. The house b/fast (24Bs) is a huge blow-out, a fry-up with a muesli side serving, while vegetarian mains cost around 20Bs. *Open Wed–Sun 08.30–22.00.*

✕ **Bamboos Cafe** Calle Iturralde, no tel. Cold beers & Mexican food (mains around 20Bs) are the staples at this traveller-friendly haunt, located two blocks east of the plaza. It's supposed to be open daily 18.00–late, with a happy hour until 19.00, but seems to be prone to irregular opening hours.

Of the fairly standard pizzas joints catering to backpackers around the plaza, **Pizzeria Bella Italia** (☎ 719 50154; *open daily 8.00–22.00*), next door to craft shop **Arco Iris**, is worth a look for its English menu, happy hour cocktails (20–25Bs) and pizzas (small/large 23–32/45–65Bs). Otherwise, there's a clutch of **food stalls** for cheap eats along Calle Héroes del Chaco, northwest of the plaza, although they are only suited to those with cast-iron stomachs.

OTHER PRACTICALITIES

Cotel & Entel Call Centres Plaza 27 de Mayo. *Open daily 08.00–20.00.*

Laundry Express Calle Iturralde #4009; ☎ 715 12707. *Offers a laundry service daily 08.00–12.00 & 14.00–17.00.*

MCM Networking Calle Sagarnaga. Has internet access (12Bs/hr) just south of the plaza. *Open daily 08.00–late.*

Post office Plaza 27 de Mayo. *Open Tue–Fri 08.30–12.00 & 14.30–18.00, Sat & Sun 08.30–12.00.*

GETTING OFF THE BEATEN TRACK AROUND COROICO

Outside of Coroico, the Yungas region remains a backwater as far as tourism is concerned. There are lush plantations of tropical fruit and some great day hikes along ancient trading routes, but facilities- wise a basic *alojamiento* (simple lodging) is often the best you can hope for.

Just outside La Paz, close to La Cumbre, the road splits at a traffic checkpoint with two forks signposted North Yungas and South Yungas. The former heads to Coroico and on to Caranavi, the largest town in the Yungas with its market-town feel, before terminating in the gold-mining region of the Alto Beni.

The latter heads for Chulumani, the pretty village that is the capital of the South Yungas, and on to the Afro-Bolivian communities around Irupana. The views are superb en route and a short detour leads to the village of Yanacachi, a base for trekkers to rest up after completing the pre-Inca Takesi trail, which starts just west of La Paz.

Chulumani is situated on the side of a hill with grand vistas across the area and best known for its fresh produce – be sure to sample some of the fragrant local honey. Close by is the Apa Apa Ecological Reserve with camping facilities and abundant wildlife.

Irupana is another sleepy but charming Yungas village and home to several Afro-Bolivian communities, the best-known of which live just outside the village at Chicaloma. The communities stage colourful local festivals in late July and early August with dancing and traditional music in the simple main square. These festivals do not normally attract tourists so cultural sensitivity should always be the primary concern for anyone considering a visit.

Buses do ply these routes, with La Paz and Coroico the hubs for transport, although the roads tend to be washed away during the rainy season.

COCHABAMBA *Tel code: 04; altitude: 2,558m; population: 520,000*

Cochabamba city, the capital of the Cochabamba department, is often known as the 'City of Eternal Spring'. Given its pleasant, year-round warm climate (although do beware of plummeting temperatures in the evening), there's not much arguing with that. Furthermore, Bolivia's fourth city has a cosmopolitan mix with the indigenous population most visible in the street markets of La Cancha. The suited and booted business community, meanwhile, hangs out in the street cafés along El Prado (Av Ballivián) and in the smart outer suburbs of the city.

THREE THINGS TO DO IN COCHABAMBA

1 Take some time to relax and indulge in some people watching in Plaza Colón and soak up the atmosphere of the city surrounded by flowerbeds and fresh air (page 156).

2 Sample the local specialities, such as the strong but excellent local tipple, *chicha cochabambina*, a fermented maize drink, and *pique macho*, a traditional dish of sausage, eggs and chillis (page 155).

3 Strike out into the lush countryside of the Chapare and explore one of Bolivia's lesser-known regions with ample wildlife-spotting opportunities (page 157).

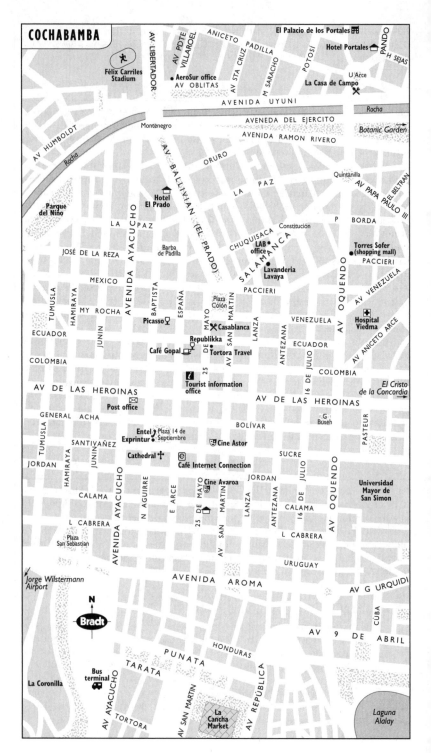

COCHABAMBA

Félix Carriles Stadium

AV PDTE VILLAROEL
AV· LIBERTADOR

ANICETO PADILLA
AV STA CRUZ
M SARACHO

El Palacio de los Portales
Hotel Portales
PANDO
H SEJAS
POTOSÍ

AeroSur office
AV OBLITAS

U'Arce
La Casa de Campo

AVENIDA UYUNI

Rocha

Montenegro

AV HUMBOLDT

Rocha

AVENEDA DEL EJERCITO
AVENIDA RAMON RIVERO

Botanic Garden

Parque
del Niño

AV BALLIVIAN (EL PRADO)

ORURO

LA PAZ

Quintanilla

AV PAPA PAULO III
EL BELTRAN

Hotel
El Prado

LA PAZ
AVENIDA AYACUCHO

Barba
de Padilla

CHUQUISACA
SALAMANCA
Constitución

LAB
office

P
BORDA

Torres Sofer
(shopping mall)
PACCIERI

JOSÉ DE LA REZA

MEXICO

TUMUSLA
HAMIRAYA
MY ROCHA

BAPTISTA

ESPAÑA

Lavanderia
Lavaya

PACCIERI

AV VENEZUELA
O OQUENDO

Picasso

Plaza
Colón

DE MAYO
SAN MARTIN
LANZA

Casablanca

VENEZUELA

Hospital
Viedma

AV ANICETO ARCE

ECUADOR

JUNIN

Republikka
Café Gopal
Tortora Travel

ANTEZANA

ECUADOR

COLOMBIA

25

Tourist information
office

16 DE JULIO

COLOMBIA

El Cristo
de la Concordia

AV DE LAS HEROINAS

Post office

AV DE LAS HEROINAS

GENERAL ACHA

BOLÍVAR

G
Buseh

PASTEUR

TUMUSLA
SANTIVAÑEZ
HAMIRAYA
JUNIN

JORDAN

Entel
Exprintur

Plaza 14 de
Septiembre

Cine Astor

SUCRE

DE JULIO

CALAMA

AVENIDA AYACUCHO

N AGUIRRE

E ARCE

Cathedral
Café Internet Connection

Cine Avaroa

25 DE MAYO

SAN MARTIN

JORDAN

LANZA

ANTEZANA

16 DE

CALAMA

AV OQUENDO

Universidad
Mayor de
San Simon

L CABRERA

Plaza
San Sebastian

L CABRERA

SAN

URUGUAY

Jorge Wilstermann
Airport

N

Bradt

AVENIDA AROMA

AV G URQUIDI

CÚBA

AV 9 DE ABRIL

HONDURAS

La Coronilla

Bus
terminal

PUNATA
TARATA

TORTORA

AV AYACUCHO

AV SAN MARTIN

La
Cancha
Market

AV REPÚBLICA

Laguna
Alalay

152

Cochabamba is one city that many tour itineraries through Bolivia tend to miss off. As such, it has fewer tourists than, say, Sucre, and tends to offer better-than-average value for money. In particular, the range of foodstuffs in Cochabamba is cheap, plentiful and very, very tasty, making it a good place to eat out both well and economically (see box, *A true taste of Cochabamba*, page 155). The city is not without its cultural attractions, however, and it acts as a useful gateway to the wider region, one littered with natural marvels, such as the wonderfully remote Torotoro National Park.

Probably best known in the area are the tropical lowlands of the Chapare region, situated to the northeast of the city of Cochabamba and with Villa Tunari as their regional capital. This is the political heartland of indigenous leader turned Bolivian president, Evo Morales, and the place where much of the coca leaf used to produce Bolivia's contribution to the global cocaine market is grown. As such, this is one place where travellers are advised not to wander too far from the well-worn tourist path.

There are ongoing reports of robberies against tourists around San Sebastian Hill, southwest of the bus terminal, and in the area south of Avenida Aroma, around the old train station. Take care in these areas at all hours, but especially at night. Similarly, the Inca ruins of Inca-Rakay, located about 30km from Cochabamba near Sipe-Sipe, should only be visited during daylight hours. Travellers are strongly advised to avoid camping in rural areas around Cochabamba as a whole.

HISTORY While Potosí flourished as a mining and mineral extraction centre, Cochabamba's favourable climate helped the region to flourish as an agricultural centre to feed the burgeoning population. This led to the Cochabamba Valley becoming known as the 'breadbasket of Bolivia'; a name that remains relevant today as the region still produces a huge amount of fresh produce – from citrus fruits to maize and wheat.

Founded 1 January 1574, with the name Villa de Oropeza, it was the fifth city to be founded in Bolivia. Today the 16 provinces celebrate their departmental anniversary on 14 September in remembrance of the 1810 revolution.

GETTING THERE Cochabamba's **Jorge Wilstermann Airport** (✎ *459 1820/1821*) is just a short taxi journey from the centre of town and serviced by local buses. Although primarily used for domestic flights with local carriers Lloyd Aero Boliviano (LAB), AeroSur and TAM, it also hosts some international connections to Buenos Aires, Santiago, Bogotá, Caracas, Mexico City and São Paulo. There's a 25BS/US$25 airport tax payable on domestic/international flights.

On the ground floor, airport facilities include an ATM, Entel call centre, a money exchange, news stand, Fedex office, a hotdog stand and the Brazilian Coffee Shop (coffee 6–9Bs, sandwich 8—20Bs and mains 29Bs). Upstairs there's a less popular restaurant (sandwich 20Bs, mains 35Bs) and Internet Airport Net (8Bs per hour) for internet access.

From outside the terminal building, minibuses to the city charge 1.50Bs, while airport taxis (✎ *428 2001*) charge 25Bs for a private taxi and 15Bs for a shared taxi.

The **bus terminal** (*Av Ayacucho;* ✎ *422 0550*) is a 15-minute walk from the city centre, or a taxi downtown will cost about 3.5Bs. Due to its fairly central location, pretty much any city in Bolivia can be reached from Cochabamba, including La Paz (7 hours, 25Bs), Santa Cruz (10 hours, 30Bs), Sucre (11 hours, 30Bs) and Potosí (11 hours, 40Bs). Buses to Torotoro National Park leave from the corner of Avenida 6 de Agosto and Avenida Republica twice a week: Thursdays and Sundays at 06.00. There are also international departures to Buenos Aires, although with a journey time of 48 hours it's not for the easily bored.

There's a 2.5Bs tax payable on all departures from the bus terminal.

GETTING AROUND Much of Cochabamba is easily accessible on foot, although there is a good network of buses linking the centre with the suburbs, augmented by private taxis and *truffis*. For a taxi to the bus terminal or airport, call **Taxis Aranjuez** (📞 *424 1212/428 1718*). A taxi journey within the centre costs 3–6Bs and a downtown bus journey 1.5Bs.

TOURIST INFORMATION The tourist information office (*Calle Colombia #340;* 📞 *422 1793;* f *411 6755; open Mon–Fri 08.30–16.30*) provides information on what to do in Cochabamba and its environs, as well as maps and listings of restaurants and hotels.

Otherwise, there are a number of tour agencies in Cochabamba that will help to organise excursions and activities throughout the region, including regional sister offices to Fremen and Turismo Balsa offices in La Paz (page 71).

Recommended local agencies are shown below.

AGENCIES

Exprintur Plaza 14 de Septiembre #252; 📞 425 7790; f 425 0710; e exp-cbb@pino.ccb.entelnet.bo. Located on the west side of Cochabamba's main square, this agency can book international flights & bus journeys, as well as tours of the region. Day trips available include excursions to El Chapare National Park, Incallajta, Valle Alton & Incachaca in the Amazon. Open Mon–Fri 08.30–12.00 & 14.30–18.00, Sat 09.00–12.00.

Totora Travel Calle 25 de Mayo #268; 📞 452 4924; e totora_travel@hotmail.com. This agency also specialises in local trips, inc a 4-day adventure trips taking in the flora & fauna of Villa Tunari (US$42 pp) & a 3-day visit to the caves & dinosaur footprints of Torotoro National Park (250Bs pp). Open Mon–Fri 09.30–12.30 & 14.30–18.30 & Sat 09.30–12.30.

🏠 WHERE TO STAY
As a city, Cochabamba tends to cater more for the local business trade than mass tourism, but cheap places to overnight can be found if you're passing through. The following are divided by budget category.

Top of the range
🏠 **Hotel Portales** (106 rooms) Av Pando #1271; 📞 448 5151; f 428 5446; e reservas@portaleshotel.com. This hotel is one of just a few 5-star properties in Cochabamba. Located in Recoleta, one of the smarter suburbs of the city, it has a rather austere entrance hall, giving way to an open area with a swimming pool & outdoor seating. The restaurants & bedrooms are set around this area & there are a variety of standard rooms & suites, some inter-connecting, hence ideal for families. The bedrooms are slickly if unimaginatively decorated & hotel facilities include a sauna, fitness centre & tennis courts. *Sgls/dbls US$77/95, inc an American b/fast.*

Mid-range
🏠 **El Puerte Jungle Lodge**, operated by Fremen Tours (www.andes-amazonia.com/en/cocha.e.asp#ElPuente) & booked from their offices in La Paz & Cochabamba, is set in 20ha of preserved rainforest & located 4km from the Inti Wara Yassi wildlife sanctuary. *Sgls/dbls/tpls $19/27/38, inc b/fast.* Ask Fremen Tours about package deals.
🏠 **Hotel El Prado** (25 rooms) Av Ballivián #709; 📞 452 8333; f 452 9788; e elpradohotel@supernet.com.bo. The service at this 3-star hotel is very friendly, lending to the family atmosphere. The hotel bar overlooks the hustle, bustle & bright lights of Cochabamba's main boulevard from which the hotel takes its name, so this place is ideally located for the bars & restaurants along this stretch. The rooms are clean & comfortable, with cable TV in all bedrooms, while internet access is available free of charge for guests & an outdoor swimming pool is a welcome addition. The in-house restaurant serves basic meals all day. *Sgls/dbls/tpls US$30/35/45, inc buffet b/fast.*

Budget
🏠 **Hostal Florida** (30 rooms) Calle 25 de Mayo #583; 📞 425 7911 or 426 5617. A sunny, open-air courtyard is the focal point of this cheap but cheerful hostel, making up for the fact that many of

Caroline Calvert of the Llama Express (www.theexpress.org)
Cochabamba is home to *pique macho*, one of Bolivia's heartiest traditional meals, so there really is nowhere better to try it. Along El Prado (Avenida Ballivián) there's a range of pavement restaurants and cafés that are a hive of activity in the evening. A plate is best shared between two at least because it's a filling mix of meat, sausage, chips, tomatoes and eggs. Beware of the spicy *locoto* (chilli pepper) hiding amongst the juices as the hot tang can take you by surprise. The dish is best enjoyed with a glass of Taquiña, Cochabamba's favourite local brew, and don't forget to soak up the juices at the bottom of the plate with the fresh bread provided.

the clean but basic rooms are a little on the gloomy side. All the bathrooms are shared &, beware, not all have hot water. However, all staff are very friendly & it is a good place to meet other travellers. A variety of b/fasts (9–13Bs) is available, while the location is excellent: midway between the bus station, Plaza 14 de Septiembre & the La Cancha market. *Rooms 30Bs pp, without b/fast.*

✖ WHERE TO EAT

✖ **Café Gopal** Calle España #250; ☎ 423 4082. This is the best option when budgets are tight as, tucked away from the street in a sunny courtyard, Gopal is a vegetarian Indian restaurant offering a very reasonable self-service buffet for just 10Bs pp, inc tea. The selection includes 12 kinds of salads, soups, beans, brown bread & vegetables, plus desserts. There are also biscuits & pastries on sale. Get there early for the best choice of food. *Open Mon–Fri 11.00–21.00, Sat & Sun 11.00–15.00.*

✖ **Casablanca** Calle 25 de Mayo; ☎ 452 9328. Popular with gringos & hip, young locals alike, Casablanca is a chilled-out jazz café, great for eating during the day & drinking in the evening. The menu is extensive, inc Spanish tapas, pizzas & b/fast with mains around 20–30Bs. The portions are very generous, especially the Casablanca b/fast, which consists of toasted bread, a huge fruit salad & a glass of muesli drenched in yoghurt & honey. After dark, cocktails or a glass of the local Taquiña beer are de rigueur while playing one of the board games or perusing the newspapers. *Open daily 08.00–late.*

✖ **La Casa de Campo** Paseo Boulevard #618; ☎ 424 3937. Though touted as a *restaurant turístico*, this eatery is a sunny afternoon favourite for local business people, families & couples alike. The service is smooth & rapid while the menu offers hearty & well-prepared Bolivian cuisine (mains around 35Bs), although vegetarians will struggle. A bottle of local wine is particularly good value at around 26Bs. *Open daily 12.00–late.*

SHOPPING **Torres Sofer Shopping Mall** (*Av Oquendo #654; no tel; open daily 08.00–22.00*), is the nearest thing you'll find to a Bolivian shopping mall. Part of a towerblock-style development with a whole range of shops and offices, it's the best place for a major shopping trip, though less authentic and more expensive than the markets.

La Cancha, the covered market located south of the city centre, is Cochabamba's most authentic shopping experience. The best place to find everything and anything – fruit and vegetables, CDs, household supplies, artisan goods, traditional musical instruments, electrical items on the black market and more – it is also one of the most fascinating places to watch local life at its most vibrant and colourful. Just make sure to keep a careful eye on your possessions while browsing. Open daily 08.00–late, although best on Wednesdays and Saturdays.

ENTERTAINMENT AND NIGHTLIFE The best areas to enjoy Cochabamba's nightlife are either in the open-air bars, restaurants and clubs along El Prado, or in the smaller, dustier streets between Plaza Colón and Plaza 14 de Septiembre, where there is a range of more beatnik bars and cosy eateries.

The Yungas and Cochabamba **COCHABAMBA**

6

☆ **Picasso** Calle España #327; no tel;. The place to go for Western music and DJ requests, though there's not much room to dance. Behind the main bar area there are a few snug rooms, so people looking for a quite chat can escape the more raucous revellers. Table service is available but can be quite slow on busy nights, so sitting at the bar is often a better option if you're thirsty — and more sociable anyway. *Open daily 20.00–late.*

☆ **Republika** Calle Ecuador #342; no tel. A low-key, arty drinking haunt, offers basic but tasty bar meals, snacks and drinks. The front bar area gives way to an open-air courtyard that often plays host to live bands. The whole place is geared towards travellers, being one of few spots in the city to include an international book exchange, and hence is a good place to hook up with other travellers.

Cochabamba has two **cinemas**: Cine Avaroa (*Calle 25 de Mayo;* ↘ *422 1285*), and Cine Astor (*corner of Calles Sucre & 25 de Mayo;* ↘ *422 4045*).

OTHER PRACTICALITIES

AeroSur office Calle Oblitas #1107; ↘ 440 0909. *Open Mon–Fri 08.30–12.45 & 14.30–18.40, Sat 09.00–12.30.*

Cafe Internet Connection Calle Arze #245; no tel. One of numerous centrally located internet centres with internet access for 3Bs/hr. *Open Mon–Fri 08.30–20.30, Sat & Sun 08.30–14.00.*

Entel call centres are also widely available; the most central is located on the west side of Plaza 14 de Septiembre & opens daily 07.00–23.00.

Laundry Lavaya Calle Salamanca #602; ↘ 422 5106. Has a laundry service for 6Bs per kg, or washed & pressed for 7Bs per kg. *Open Mon–Fri 08.30–12.30 & 14.30–19.30, Sat 08.30–13.00.*

Lloyd Aereo Boliviano (LAB) office Calle Salamanca #675; ↘ 423 0325. *Open Mon–Fri 08.30–12.30 & 14.30–18.30, Sat 08.30–12.00.*

Post office Av Ayacucho #1131; ↘ 423 0979. *Open Mon–Fri 08.00–20.00, Sat 08.00–1800, Sun 09.00–12.00.*

WHAT TO SEE AND DO

El Cristo de la Concordia Located at the far end of Avenida de las Héroinas, next to Plaza San Pedro. El Cristo de la Concordia may not be as famous or as iconic as its Rio de Janeiro counterpart, but he can at least lay claim to being the bigger of the two at 33.3m. The huge statue of Jesus stands watch over Cochabamba and is well worth a visit for its stunning views over the city, surrounding hills and out towards the Chapare region. A short cable-car ride goes to the summit of the Cerro de San Pedro, though the journey on foot can be tackled without too much exertion. At the weekend you can climb up inside El Cristo for an even more elevated view of the city. But beware of pickpockets at the top, on the walk up and on the way back down. Cable car open Tue–Sat 10.00–18.00, Sun 09.00–18.00; entrance 3Bs per person each way.

Plaza Colón is a more pleasant spot than the main square, Plaza 14 de Septiembre, to hang out and relax. Plaza Colón is where the wider boulevards of Avenida Ballivián and Salamanca meet the narrower dustier streets of central Cochabamba. There's plenty of space here to sit down on the freshly cut grass, surrounded by colourful flowerbeds and soothing water fountains, and indulge in some serious people-watching. From the right angle you can spot El Cristo de la Concordia on the hilltop, while on special occasions, there are even small market stalls selling traditional artisan handicrafts.

El Palacio de los Portales (*Av Potosí #1450;* ↘ *424 3137;* **e** *centropatino@ fundacionpatino.org*) Tucked away in Queru Queru, one of the smart suburbs in the north of the city and surrounded by pristine gardens, El Palacio de los Portales is the former home of Simon Patiño, a local entrepreneur and tin baron. Though on a much smaller scale, it is vaguely reminiscent of the Palace of Versailles outside Paris, as many of the furnishings, wall decorations and floor tiles were imported from

Jacqui Ning of the Llama Express (www.theexpress.org)

For three weeks we volunteered at this surreal animal sanctuary (*Parque Machia, Villa Tunari, Chapare;* ℡ *413 6572; www.intiwarayassi.org*), perched on the shoulder of a fast river with a rainforest and misty mountain views. Founded in 1992, the refuge houses over 200 monkeys, dozens of birds, tortoises, coatis and wild cats. All have been illegally poached and kept in private homes, hotels and circuses.

For international volunteers, there's a mandatory 15-day commitment. To be precise, it's a 15-day commitment if you are working with the birds, monkeys, snakes or anything else that has just arrived for rehabilitation. But it's a minimum three- or four-week commitment if you are with the cats (pumas, jaguars and ocelots) on account of the more intense need to bond with the individual.

And intense it can be. The not-for-profit organisation, Inti Wara Yassi, located 1km outside Villa Tunari, is about as grassroots Bolivia as things get, with limited resources and the history of each animal kept in files for volunteers to read and update. A lot of them have been rescued from terrible conditions and some still bear the scars of trauma.

The park is a sanctuary for all the animals, some of which are endangered species. For example, the spider monkeys here make up a small but significant percentage of their total world population. The running of the place is a huge responsibility for its four Bolivian founders, with the number of cats alone more than tripling in the last two years to 16. To complicate matters social problems often deter tourism and therefore volunteers not only provide their time and effort, but also a crucial US$80 donation that includes their accommodation fee.

Fortunately, with the help of funding from Quest, an English volunteer organisation, land has been acquired for expansion. And with luck, more long-term volunteers will come along shortly, as volunteer numbers can fluctuate between 20 and 70 at any one point. When they get below the 35 mark, certain animals simply can't come out of their cages.

Overall, this place is unique as most people turn up with no previous experience. They then learn how to care for a wild animal by feeding, walking and playing to earn respect and bond with the creature.

Europe and influenced by European trends. The huge doors, which give the palace its name, open out onto a terrace with views over the gardens and an open-air theatre, which stages traditional folk music and dance performances. There is also an art gallery with exhibitions in the basement. Gardens and exhibitions open Mon–Fri 14.30–18.30, Sat 10.30–12.30. The house can only be visited by twice-daily guided tours: Spanish commentary 17.00 weekdays and 11.00 Saturdays; English commentary 17.30 weekdays and 11.30 Saturdays. Entrance: tourists/locals 10/5Bs with a guided tour; 4Bs for just the gardens.

GETTING OFF THE BEATEN TRACK AROUND COCHABAMBA

The area around Cochabamba is not best known for its tourism potential, especially the deepest, darkest recesses of the Chapare region, where the proliferation of coca plantations makes it the kind of place where foreigners would be well advised to keep to the main routes. However, for a more adventurous spirit there are a few notable diversions from the main highway leading to Santa Cruz that merit exploration – just don't go bumbling around a coca plantation. The lush tropical vegetation of the Chapare starts about 90 minutes outside of Cochabamba, where a turning east off the main highway leads to the pre-Inca site of Incachaca. The settlement of Quillacollo, meanwhile, is a traditional community located 13km from Cochabamba, where a major folkloric festival is staged in mid-August each year.

The main settlement on the Cochabamba to Santa Cruz highway is, however, Villa Tunari. Located deep in the Chapare and 153km from Cochabamba, it's a lush and tropical place with natural springs. The settlement is also the staging point for the Carrasco National Park (see page 7) with its slew of ecological zones and ample birdwatching opportunities. On the northeastern fringe of the park, the Cavernas del Repechon is a wildlife sanctuary composed of a series of caves and famous as a breeding ground for the rare guacharo, or oil bird, which comes out at night to feed on fruits and nuts.

Access to the park is best handled by jeep as regular bus routes through the Chapare are often highly erratic with climatic extremes, notably heavy rainfall, leading to services being cancelled at short notice.

7

Oruro and Uyuni

The local tourism authorities are earning their money in Oruro. It's not an obvious place to stay, nor exactly a hotbed of attractions for tourists, but they are, however, trying very hard to encourage travellers to spend a night as opposed to just having lunch then taking the train further south. It's a noble effort overall, but Oruro remains something of a one-trick pony with its folklore carnival seeing the city packed to bursting point (and prices hiked sky high) each February, only to then fall back into its slumbers for the rest of the year.

The cold, windswept climate and rather aloof locals ensure the city has little to distract tourists outside of the heaving carnival season (page 165). Indeed, so few tourists tend to spend time here that this is one city in Bolivia when you can actually expect to be actively stared at on the street. For the more adventurous, however, Oruro does make a good staging point to strike out into the Altiplano in search of the real spirit of Andean Bolivia.

HISTORY Oruro has been a mining capital and a cornerstone of Bolivian industry since the 17th century, with its abundance of silver, copper and tin once making it one of the richest cities in South America. The industry also gave rise to a massive rail network, which even today retains Oruro as its primary rail hub. The industry, however, has since died off and Oruro's manufacturing base is now a shadow of its former self.

Founded in 1606 by Manuel Castro de Padilla with the name Real Villa de San Felipe de Austria, the department's 16 districts celebrate their anniversary on 10 February to mark the 1871 revolution.

GETTING THERE AND AWAY
By train See box, *Ticket to ride*, page 163.

THREE THINGS TO DO IN ORURO

1 Oruro is home to the biggest, most colourful and traditionally folkloric carnival in Bolivia, so get your dancing shoes on and join in the street party (page 165).

2 The city has traditionally been the industrial hub of the Altiplano and you can learn more about Oruro's mining heritage with a visit to the worthwhile Museo Etnográfico Minero (page 166).

3 Even if you're just passing through in transit, Oruro is a good spot for a hearty lunch with some of the best lamb and vegetarian restaurants in Bolivia, so indulge your tastebuds (page 164).

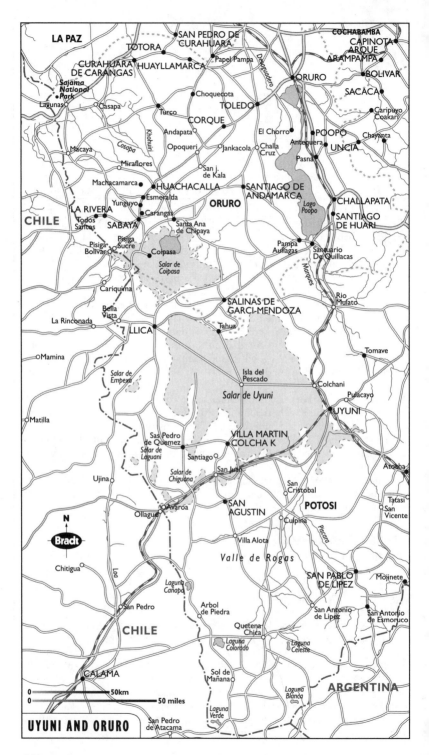

UYUNI AND ORURO

Dr James Allen

In order to be considered the original site of Atlantis, the site must at least conform to some of the aspects of Plato's story. Thus we can rule out Cyprus, Crete, Malta, the south of Spain and the Azores. None of these correspond in any details to the long geographic description that Plato offered.

To find Atlantis then is relatively simple. All you have to do is follow Plato's directions: first of all he said Atlantis was a continent the size of Libya and Asia combined, and that it lay in the Atlantic Ocean opposite the Pillars of Hercules (aka the Straits of Gibraltar).

Plato also said that Atlantis sank in a single day and night of earthquakes and floods. Modern geology tells us that a continent cannot sink in the space of a single day and no sunken continent exists between America and Gibraltar. The conclusion, therefore, is that the lost continent of Atlantis is actually still here: it is located in the Atlantic Ocean opposite the Strait of Gibraltar and today it carries the name of South America.

But if the continent of Atlantis is still there, where is the sunken Atlantis of Plato? The answer is simple. Plato also described the capital of Atlantis as a small round volcano. He indicated that the entire continent of Atlantis did not sink, simply its island capital, which sank into a large inland sea in the centre of the continent.

I believe the sea is Lake Poopo in Bolivia and the island is called Cerro Santo Pedros Villca at a village called Pampa Aullagas to the south of the lake.

Plato tells us that a large plain sits in the centre of the continent and next to the sea. This plain is in the centre of the longest side of the continent, is enclosed by mountains, is high above the level of the sea, is perfectly level and has the shape of a quadrangle, rectilinear and elongated.

This is a perfect description of the Bolivian Altiplano and the centre of this plain is where we find the ruined volcanic island of Pampa Aullagas, which has been sunk by earthquakes and covered by fossilised sediments from the time it was submerged beneath the sea.

In the Bolivian Legend of the Desaguadero, the chief of the gods decides to punish a city for its greed and for forsaking the teachings of the gods. He subsequently destroys the city and submerges it beneath the sea. Could this be the true origin of the Atlantis story?

The chief characteristic of Plato's island was a central island surrounded by two rings of land and three of water. The remains of these rings of water and former channels can still be seen at Pampa Aullagas today. Pampa Aullagas is located about 160km, three hours by jeep, south of Oruro. Unlike other proposed sites for Atlantis, this is a site that tourists can actually visit. If they do so, they will see for themselves the level rectangular plain, cross the rings of land and former channels, climb the central mountain and see the sea in the distance at a distance of five miles – all exactly as Plato described it.

Dr James Allen is the author of Atlantis: The Andes Solution (Macmillan, 1999) and runs the website www.geocities.com/webatlantis.

Oruro and Uyuni ORURO

By bus The **bus terminal** (*Calle Bakovic;* ☎ *527 9535*) is a 15-minute walk northeast of the centre, or 3Bs by taxi. There are sparse services with a small Entel call centre, a clutch of shops and a small information office located at the eastern end of the terminal, which only keeps some very basic maps.

There are frequent connections to Potosí, Cochabamba and La Paz; a 1.50Bs tax is payable on departures from the bus terminal.

ORURO

CAP BARRIGA
🐾 Zoo

🏛 Eduardo López Rivas
Anthropological Museum

N Bradt

Santuario del Socavón
✝ 🏛 Museos Sacro Folklorico
& Etnografico Minero

Sagrado Corazón de Jésus
☀ viewpoint

LEON

LA PLATA

Plaza de
Rancheria
Pub
La Alpaca
La Paz

S GALVARRO
LA PAZ
LA PAZ

I DE NOVIEMBRE

Avaroa
Park

HERRERA

CARO

LINARES

MONTECINOS

POTOSI

PAGADOR

AV 6 DE OCTUBRE

● Faro de Conchupata

PETOT

AYACUCHO

CAMACHO

JUNIN

Fermin
López
Market

PDTE MONTES

Post office

COCHABAMBA

CARO

AV VELASCO GALVARRO

Buses to
Obrajes hot springs

ADOLFO MIER

LA PLATA

✝ Cathedral
S GALVARRO
X Restaurant La Cabaña

AYACUCHO

Las Delicias
X

Potosí

LINARES

WASHINGTON

BOLIVAR

Plaza 10 de
Febrero
(ATMs)

● Police

Plaza-Castro
Padilla
🖥 Mundo
Internet

X Artesanias Oruro

● Govinda
X

JUNIN

PETOT

SUCRE

CAMACHO

Entel call centre 📞

Palais Concert Cinema 🎬

Los Andes Laundry

S GALVARRO Tourist
information kiosk

ADOLFO MIER

PAGADOR

Campero
Market

PRESIDENTE MONTES

Gran Hotel Sucre

BOLIVAR

SUCRE

POTOSI

AV VELASCO GALVARRO

MERGUIA

Restaurant
Nayjama X

● Alojamiento
Copacabana

ALDANA

LA PLATA

AV 6 DE OCTUBRE

BALLIVIAN

Railway station

PAGADOR

SAN FELIPE

General 🏥
Hospital

ARCE

ARCE

ARCE

AV VELASCO GALVARRO

SANTA BARBARA

Museo Antropológico
Eduardo López Rivas

JAEN

JAEN

RENGEL

PAGADOR

General
Cemetery

T FRIAS

PDTE MONTES

SORIA

GALVARRO

AVENIDA LA PLATA

ESPAÑA

AV GALVARRO

Bus terminal,
International
Park Hotel

Oruro is the rail hub of Bolivia with the Chilean-run Empresa Ferroviaria Andina (FCA) (*Av Velasco Galvarro corner with Calle Aldana;* ☎ *527 4605; www.fca.com.bo*) now bringing calm and order to the once chaotic rail system.

There's a luggage store at the station (2Bs per piece of luggage), which opens Tuesdays & Fridays 10.00–11.30 & 14.00–15.00, Wednesdays & Sundays 10.00–11.30 & 16.00–18.00.

There are two trains heading south to Uyuni (page 168), Tupiza (page 231) and onto the Argentinean border via Villazon: the more comfortable Expresso del Sur (Tuesdays and Fridays at 15.30) and the cheaper but rougher Wara Wara del Sur (Sundays and Wednesdays at 19.00).

The former offers first-class cabins, which include drinks, blankets and pillows and are located next to the restaurant car (the only place you can smoke on the train, hence a fuggy haze) with mains (21–28Bs), beers (10Bs) and a set dinner (13Bs).

The ticket office opens according to a rather complex itinerary as follows:

Mon 08.15–11.30 and 14.00–18.00
Tue 08.15–18.00, with no lunch break
Wed 08.15–12.00 and 14.30–18.30
Thu 08.15–11.30 and 14.30–18.00
Fri 08.15–18.00, with no lunch break
Sat Closed
Sun 08.15–11.00 and 15.00–18.30

Tickets are sold the day before and on the day of travel only. You need to take your passport to make a purchase.

PRICES (BS) ARE AS FOLLOWS:
Expresso del Sur

Destination/class	First	Normal	Economic
Oruro to Uyuni	81	45	31
To Tupiza	170	84	55
To Villazon	191	95	67

Wara Wara del Sur

Destination/class	First	Normal	Economic
Oruro to Uyuni	69	35	29
To Tupiza	124	60	50
To Villazon	150	75	61

For more details of train schedules and prices, check the website www.fca.com.bo/fca1/itinerarios_tarifas_1.htm.

GETTING AROUND Everything in Oruro is easily accessible on foot with most places of interest within a few blocks of the main square. To save your feet, a bus/taxi journey within the centre costs 1–3Bs.

To call a taxi, try **Radio Taxi Oruro** (☎ *527 3399*).

TOURIST INFORMATION The tourist information kiosk (*Corner of Calle Bolivar & Calle Soria Galvarro;* ☎ *525 7881*) actually turns out to be one of the friendliest and most helpful information offices in Bolivia with decent maps and useful advice on attractions. During Carnival it's packed and offers extended opening hours, but normally it opens Monday–Friday 08.00–12.00 & 14.00–18.00.

WHERE TO STAY As a main transport interchange, Oruro has plenty of crashpads close to the train station but few places you'll actually want to stay more than a night. The following are safe options and divided by budget category.

Mid-range

Gran Hotel Sucre (56 rooms) Calle Sucre #510; ℘ 527 6800; **f** 525 4110; **e** hotelsucreoruro@ hotmail.com. This reliable, mid-range option with comfy rooms, equipped with phone & cable TV, makes for the best bet in town, especially given its very central location. Particularly good are room numbers 25 to 30, set apart along a glass-fronted corridor that faces out onto a sunny roof terrace & hence retains more heat. The in-house restaurant, Pucara, serves b/fast & does a good set lunch (15Bs). *Sgls/dbls with private bathrooms US$22/30 with b/fast.*

International Park Hotel (159 rooms) Calle Rajka Bakovic (above the Terminal de Buses); ℘ 527 6227; **f** 527 5187; **e** iparkhot@coteor.net.bo. Very handy for the bus terminal (page 161) – the entrance to reception is located opposite Snack Terminal on the upper floor – this place is ideal for anyone simply passing through & not too interested in seeing the centre of Oruro. The rooms are a bit dark but all come with private bathrooms. *Sgls/dbls US$20/35 with b/fast.*

Budget

Alojamiento Copacabana (19 rooms) Calle Velasco Galvarro #1856; ℘ 525 4184. If you need a cheap crashpad near the train station, this is the best of the bunch. It's basic but friendly & they will store

luggage. All rooms are shared, however, so it's only really suitable for groups of 2 or 3 travelling together. They don't accept single travellers. *Shared rooms 20Bs pp.*

WHERE TO EAT

Restaurant Nayjama Calle Pagador #1880; ℘ 527 7699. Now looking smarter after a major refit, this is, for many, the only place to eat in Oruro &, rather handily, located just one block from the train station. The house special is lamb with the huge Mecheado lamb platter (38Bs), essentially half a lamb served with a side salad, enough to feed a whole family. Thankfully half portions are available & à la carte mains (no set menus) are well prepared. Also worth a try are the fish (38Bs), steaks (35Bs) & the vegetarian platter (28Bs). It's pricier than average but offers far superior quality. *Open Tue–Sun 11.30–15.00 & 18.30–22.00.*

Restaurant La Cabaña Calle Santa Junin #609; ℘ 525 8023; **e** restlacabana@coteor.net.bo. A rustic, upmarket eatery with a decent menu, the dining room is rather dominated by a giant TV often screening football matches. Popular with passing tour groups, the service is friendly & helpful overall. *Mains around 30Bs; open Tue–Sat*

12.00–15.30 & 18.30–midnight, Sun & Mon lunch only.

Govinda Calle 6 de Octubre #6071; ℘ 525 5205. A great little place staffed by Hare Krishna devotees with murals on the wall & the kind of fresh food that most vegetarians can only dream of while on the road in Bolivia. The set lunch comes in large & small portions (14/8Bs), plus there's a vegetarian dish of the day (12Bs) & fruit shakes with soya milk/yoghurt (4/5Bs). It's a good spot, but a shame about the rather frosty service. *Open Mon–Sat 09.00–21.30.*

Las Delicias Calle 6 de Octubre; ℘ 525 7256. This barbecue restaurant has moved a couple of times recently leaving regular devotees confused. At the time of writing it was due to move back close to its original location on Calle 6 de Octubre. Despite all this confusion the service is as good as ever & the Argentinian steaks top notch with mains 20–35Bs. *Open Mon–Sat 12.00–15.00 & 18.00–22.30.*

ENTERTAINMENT AND NIGHTLIFE The main drinking den in town for gringos has traditionally been **Pub La Alpaca** (*Calle La Paz #690; beware: there's no sign, just a wooden stencil Alpaca outside, so it's very easy to miss*). The problem is that the owners no longer serve food and open increasingly irregular hours (theoretically Thu–Sat

The Bolivian mining town of Oruro is home to one of the least-known but most vibrant and traditional carnival fiestas in the Americas. Over 5,000 musicians alone descend on the town every February, bringing a splash of colour to its normally drab streets. Indeed, the Oruro Carnival has been recognised by UNESCO since 2001 as a World Heritage event. It is held traditionally on the first Saturday before Ash Wednesday.

The Bolivian carnival as we know it today can trace its roots back to the late 18th century. The event is a colourful and imaginative blend of differing influences, reflecting the clash between the indigenous beliefs and those of the Catholic Church.

The festivities get under way with the Entrada, the 20-hour entry procession, with numerous dance troupes and marching bands from all over the country. The dancers, dressed in elaborate, sequinned costumes representing a mixture of Christian and indigenous folkloric legends from the era of the conquistadors, parade around town, dancing, drinking and generally partying like there's no tomorrow.

Next along the route is La Diablada (the Dance of the Devils) with throngs of masked dancers led by characters representing the devil. In their wake a stream of popular characters from history bring up the rear, all of them sporting grotesque masks and highly elaborate costumes.

One of the most important groups to participate are known as Los Morenos, who perform a traditional dance, the Morenada, led by the black king. This group represents the black slaves brought to South America to work in the mines of Potosí. Their protruding eyes and tongues symbolise their fatigue and the hard treatment they received.

It's a colourful affair, but simply finding a spot to watch the parade is not for the faint-hearted. Touts sell tickets but most people just clamber up on the makeshift viewing platforms that line the streets, buy a crate of beers from a passing vendor and, inevitably, join in the nearest water fight breaking out around them. To make the most of it, get there early, bring snacks and waterproof clothes, and be prepared to laugh it off when someone bounces a large water bomb clean off your forehead.

The parade continues until the early hours of Sunday morning when the dancers arrive at the Sanctuary of the Virgin of Socavon to seek her blessing. From there the crowds disperse to indulge in several days of outright hedonism at private parties.

More information about the Oruro Carnival from the website: www.boliviacontact.com/en/sugerencia/carnaval/carnaval.php

22.30–late). Come here only if you really adore dogs. The owners have quite a menagerie and the animals don't leave you alone.

You might get a quieter drink at some of the other nearby bars, such as **Morrison Rock Bar** (named after Jim of The Doors fame) and **Eclipse**, but these do tend to be very much places for the locals.

Otherwise, **Palais Concert Cinema** on Plaza 10 de Febrero has several screenings daily for 10–12Bs.

SHOPPING **Artesanias Oruro** (*Calle Soria Galvarro corner with Calle Adolfo Mier;* ✎ *525 0331;* e *arao@coteor.net.bo; open Mon–Sat 09.00–12.30 & 14.30–18.30*) is a quality souvenir and gift shop selling artisan goods produced by the Asociación Rural de Artesanias Oruro (ARAO). Sweaters costs 190–220Bs.

OTHER PRACTICALITIES Banks with ATMs line Plaza 10 de Febrero. Try Banco de Credito (on the southwest corner of the plaza). Open Mon–Fri 09.00–12.30 and 14.30–18.00, Sat 09.00–12.00.

Entel call centre Calle Bolivar, next to the tourist information kiosk (page 163). *Open daily 08.00–20.00.*
Laundry los Andes Calle President Montes #1711. Has a laundry service for 7Bs per kg. *Open Mon–Fri 09.00–12.30 & 14.30–18.00.*

Mundo Internet Calle Bolivar #573. Offers internet access for 3Bs/hr. *Open daily 09.00–midnight.*
Post office Calle President Montes #1456. *Open Mon–Fri 08.00–20.00, Sat 08.00–16.00 & Sun 09.00–12.00.*

WHAT TO SEE AND DO
Museos Sacro Folklórico y Etnográfico Minero (*Located next to the Santuario de la Virgen del Socavon; open Mon–Fri 09.00–11.15 then 15.15–17.30; entrance foreigners/Bolivians 15/5Bs; camera usage 3Bs extra*) Built in an old mine tunnel, both museum circuits last about 30 minutes with the latter, examining Bolivia's mining tradition and worship of El Tio, the more rewarding of the two.

Museo Antropológico Eduardo Lopez Rivas (*Located at the southern tip of town by the zoo; open Mon–Fri 09.00–12.00 & 15.00–18.00; entrance 3Bs*) Despite remodelling and investment by the German government, this museum still has little

---

VISITING SAJAMA NATIONAL PARK

Sajama National Park, Bolivia's oldest, feels like the end of the world. With its vast expanse of 81,000ha, it's one of the largest and most desolate open spaces in the country. The park is also home to Nevado Sajama, Bolivia's highest volcano at 6,542m.

The park entrance lies on the paved road from La Paz to Arica (Chile). From La Paz's bus terminal, buses run by Trans Litoral and Chile Bus will both take you near the park's entrance for about US$12; hop off at Lagunas and then you're on your own. Otherwise follow my example and hire a jeep and driver in La Paz from around US$50 a day.

Before we can enter the wilds of the park proper, we first needed to stop for supplies. And the only outpost of near-civilisation around these remote parts is Tambo Quemado, a dusty one-strip drag 280km from La Paz, which squats at around 5,000m on the Bolivian–Chilean border. Border towns the world over are traditionally the domain of whores, hustlers and hoodlums. Tambo Quemado doesn't disappoint in this respect. Think stocky border guards manning a rough, stone gate and an assortment of shady characters infesting the local snakepits with the kind of thousand-yard stare that only a cocktail of high altitude and copious amounts of hard liquor can induce.

Around the border gate wizened old crones with toothless grins and grubby aprons squat, selling bags of llama meat and roasted corn. The thoroughfare to the Chilean beach resort of Arica lies beyond but they're not going anywhere. Tambo Quemado feels like the kind of place that is all too easy to find but hard to leave.

From here, bumping along dirt track roads, we travel two hours cross-country into the heart of the national park. The twin volcanoes of Parinacota and Pomerape, each straddling the rough border region, loom over us as we make our late afternoon ascent to our new home, the tiny pueblo of Río Blanco.

A border community of around 100 Aymara-speaking mountain dwellers, it also forms a community centre for Alma de Los Andes, a La Paz-co-ordinated NGO, which markets jumpers expertly knitted by the local women to an international market (www.spiritoftheandes.com).

The next morning I'm awoken by a strange sound: the unmistakable cacophony of a full brass band tuning up. Deporte, the local tuba-thumpers, it transpires, have been together nearly 20 years and, apart from regular stints in Oruro, are the local lungs for hire when it comes to providing a rousing musical accompaniment to a sporting event at 08.00 in the middle of nowhere.

explanation (and the little there is is all in Spanish). There's a collection of ghoulish skeletons and a display of masks from Oruro's foklore carnival (page 165), but it's only really one for the school parties. To get there, take an orange minibus (marked 'Sud') from the main plaza or opposite the train station. A green minibus (#1) will then take you back to the plaza (1Bs each way).

If the cold is getting to you, there are **hot springs** 25km from downtown Oruro at Obrajes (entrance 10Bs). Buses leave from the corner of Avenida 6 de Agosto and Calle Caro (30 minutes, 4Bs) and run daily from 08.00–17.00.

GETTING OFF THE BEATEN TRACK AROUND ORURO

Oruro department is primarily given over to the area's industrial heritage with the scenery reflecting the heavy industry that was its trademark. Of the mining centres, the best known is Llallagua, a three-hour journey from Oruro by car. The area is now increasingly looking like a ghost town with the industry having fallen into terminal decline.

'I love to play to see people dancing and having fun when we play,' says drummer Victor Apaz, in between bashing the skins of his strap-on kit for all he's worth. That's as maybe. But how do they work up the puff to play at over 5,000m of altitude?

'We've got big lungs,' says trumpeter Pablo Apaz. 'Besides, we've also got a big supply of beer. That'll keep us going.'

The reason why the guys from Deporte have been lured out into the middle of nowhere in particular is this: every year, in late January, Río Blanco plays host to the Encuentro Anual de Futbol, a 14-team round-robin competition whereby local men's and women's football teams compete against each other in order to win the pride of their pueblo. The rivalry is so intense it makes the World Cup final look like a kickaround at the local youth club.

And, hotly tipped for glory this season is Alma de los Andes, the all-female team of cholitas (indigenous womenfolk) who normally spend their time knitting sweaters for the eponymous NGO.

'We're not a macho team like the boys,' insists team captain and goalkeeper, Norbeta Pillco de Cabellero, pulling a pair of tracksuit trousers under her flowing layered skirt. 'We play for fun and exercise but, when we beat the boys, they're always pretty surprised.'

By mid-afternoon the band is already half-cut and Andean temperatures are plummeting across the mountains. Meanwhile, back on the pitch, it's been a game of two halves, both of them, frankly, scrappy.

A combination of on-pitch histrionics, flying shoes and complete ignorance of the offside rule has made for a disappointing display of footballing prowess. Indeed, the only highlight comes when Puente Quino's star striker, Rebecca – Alma's bitter nemesis – develops a nosebleed during a gruesome bitch-fight of a tackle. She plays the second half with a Kleenex stuffed up each nostril. If it's a beautiful game, then this match is turning pretty ugly.

Alma de los Andes finally pull back an equaliser late in the second half, thanks to a lucky off-post rebound, slotted home by striker Marlene Caballero Manani, Alma's answer to Maradona. But, clearly, neither side is satisfied with the draw.

'We played like girls,' says defender Idema Verna, desolate after the match. 'Not like women.'

For wildlife fans, more rewarding is the Lake of Uru Uru Miracle, located 8km from Oruro and best reached by taxi. A popular fishing spot, the birdlife inhabiting the lake includes flamingos, ducks and gulls.

From an anthropological perspective, the most interesting community is Chipayas, where an ancient Andean tribe continue to maintain their own unique music, textiles and beliefs. The tribe originally lived by lakes similar to the Uros people on Lake Titicaca but were forced inland to the remote enclave of the Altiplano where they live today by hunting, fishing and working in the nearby Chilean copper mines. The Chipayas are deeply religious with beliefs based around *chullpas* (tombs) and the worship of numerous deities drawn from the natural world around them. They speak Aymara and their own native tongue, Puquina.

Access to the community requires a taxi ride from Oruro to the village of Sabaya. From here it's a 30km hike across to the community itself – make sure you go with a guide and keep cultural sensitivity uppermost in your mind during any visit. The area can only be reached during the dry season, however, as the roads and trails are washed away during heavy rain.

UYUNI Tel code: 02; altitude: 3,665m; population: 18,705

Most people tend to get out of Uyuni as soon as possible. You can see why, with its harsh climate and freezing-cold nights. But, to be fair, Uyuni is highly developed as a traveller hub given its status as the gateway for tours to the Salar de Uyuni and onward travel to Chile. As such, it's really not a bad spot to hole up for a couple of days while planning your next journey – just make sure you've stocked up on warm clothes beforehand.

Frankly there's little in the tiny centre for tourists to see and do but, as a place to get organised and rest up a while, you could do a lot worse. The tourist information centre is excellent, there are a couple of decent places to stay and, if you like pizza, you'll love Uyuni's (rather limited) dining scene. Practically every restaurant in town serves pizza but none of them can match the excellent Minuteman Pizzeria (page 173). Just don't go expecting much nightlife – most things close up at 22.00 so everyone can keep warm under the covers.

HISTORY Nestled into the Potosí department, Uyuni's history is based around the mining industry and railways in much the same vein as Oruro. Also in a similar vein, its industrial base has long since been eroded with tourism now the main money-spinner. Uyuni celebrates its claim to fame as the place where football first found a home in Bolivia thanks to an introduction from British railway engineers. Indeed, the British connection to Uyuni is very strong as the following extract explains.

THREE THINGS TO DO IN UYUNI

1 The Salar de Uyuini is one of Bolivia's greatest natural wonders and makes for a fascinating three-day excursion, combining soft adventure with a chance to spot some of the rare indigenous wildlife (page 175).

2 Uyuni is a lively hub for travellers, so make friends over a hot toddy at one of Uyuni's friendly cafés or swap travellers' tales browsing at the excellent Ranking Bolivia office (page 171).

3 Soak up the eerie sense of history at the Train Cemetery just outside Uyuni, where the town's rich rail heritage now decays in splendid isolation (page 173).

GETTING THERE

By plane Air connections operated by AeroSur from Cochabamba to Uyuni have been suspended and, despite the rumour mill going into overdrive, look unlikely to be reinstated in the short term. Meanwhile, Aerolinea Canedero do offer seats on their private planes from Cochabamba if you're desperate for a flight into Uyuni – but there's only space for six people and the going rate is US$120 per person. However, at the time of writing, there was much speculation that a new airport will open in Uyuni in 2007/2008 with international connections mooted to boost tourism from major European hubs. Watch this space for more.

By bus Buses leave from **Avenida Cabrera**, located three blocks north of the train station, just above the market area. There's no actual terminal as such, just a grouping of buses and vendors with 12 companies offering onward connections from Uyuni.

There are departures for Oruro, Tupiza, La Paz, Sucre and Potosí plus connections to other destinations. Check with the Ranking Bolivia office (page 171) for up-to-date details of prices and journey schedules. There's a 1.50Bs tax payable on all bus departures.

Top tip: The bus journey from La Paz to Uyuni makes not only for one of the coldest journeys in Bolivia, but many buses arrive in Uyuni around 04.00. Rather than pay for a hotel for a few hours sleep, what most travellers don't realise is that they can ask the driver to let them stay on the bus and try to keep warm for a few hours until the market opens around 06.30, when they can get a hot drink. Tour

Michael Jacobs

Everyone in Uyuni seems to have a story to tell about the British railway engineers who once worked there. They started arriving at the end of the 19th century, and formed a sizeable community at the time when Uyuni was conceived as a South American Crewe. The last engineer remained right up to the decline of Bolivian Railways, and was apparently responsible for the incongruous rows of trees that greet you as you come out of Uyuni's stone-washed station.

It was the British-founded Antofagasta and Bolivia Railway Company, now the FCAB, which first brought the British to Uyuni. The railway line they built from the Pacific to La Paz was initiated in 1888 and had reached Oruro by 1892. Its construction was greatly encouraged by the then Bolivian president Aniceto Arce, who believed that all that was needed was a good transport system to make his country the 'land of the future'. Unfortunately, his vision of progress was not shared by the local Aymara indigenous Indians, who considerably delayed the completion of the line by constantly sabotaging it.

Among the many engineers employed by the FCAB in Bolivia was one Bethel Jacobs, a Yorkshire Jew whose uncle Charles Jacobs had achieved international fame and a vast fortune for his work on the Port of New York. Bethel himself would have gone through history largely unrecorded had it not been for the detailed letters he wrote from Bolivia between 1911 and 1914. Addressed to the young Irish woman whom he would later marry, these give a unique insight into the daily lives of those British engineers forced to work in remote and frequently inhospitable parts of the world. These letters now form the backbone of my book.

Quite apart from anything else, Bethel's letters exemplify the remarkable physical hardships and dangers suffered by those engineers who worked in the Andes. The extreme fluctuations of temperature, the constant winds and the blinding glare of the sun severely reduced the daily amount of surveying work that could be carried out; and, on top of this, were such regular hazards as landslides, impossibly steep slopes, and attacks on the line by armed and ruthless bandits.

Worse still, however, the human tensions among the engineers and those who worked under them were rising. Though Bethel and his colleagues were often complaining about their Indian labourers (whom they accused of drunkenness and laziness), the latter were wonderfully behaved in comparison with the European beachcombers, who formed a most unruly group of adventurers and social misfits. The engineers themselves often proved no better. The most boorish of all, in Bethel's opinion, were the Americans, who always carried with them a loaded gun, and were generally suspected of having dubious pasts. At least one of the Americans was a proven murderer on the run from the law.

The legacy of the British railway engineers in Bolivia was considerable, from the invention of the *chufflay* (a cocktail based on the local spirit, singani) to the introduction of football and freemasonry (nearly all the engineers were masons). The Carnival association, to which many of the engineers belonged, remains in Uyuni even today. Ironically, however, given the former rivalry between the British and the American engineers, this is now known as the 'Yankee Boys'.

Michael Jacobs is the author of Ghost Train through the Andes: On My Grandfather's Trail in Chile and Bolivia (John Murray, 2006).

agencies and the ranking Uyuni office open at 08.30, so you can get some breakfast and get booked straight onto your Salar tour departing around 10.30 – saving a night's hotel bill in the process.

There's also a new upmarket bus service connecting Uyuni to La Paz via Oruro. It's run by **Todo Turismo** (*Av Camacho #203;* ☎ *693 3337;* e *info@touringbolivia.com; www.touringbolivia.com*). Services, with an on-board bilingual guide, leave La Paz daily at 08.00 and Uyuni daily at 20.00 with a journey time of 12 hours (US$25 per person).

Uyuni also serves as a hub for travellers seeking to travel onwards into Chile via the Salar de Uyuni (page 175). From the Chilean border posts at San Pedro de Atacama and Calama there are regular bus connections onwards to Chile and to Argentina. Due to the inefficiency of the Bolivian border post when exiting for Chile, all travellers are now encouraged to secure their exit stamps for Chile in Uyuni before starting their Salar tour. You should apply at the immigration office in Uyuni (page 173) and will get an exit stamp according to the day you plan to leave Bolivia as part of your tour.

Bradt reader Carolyn Datta writes: 'Crossing into Chile, we got dropped off at Laguna Blanca, where all the jeeps drop the people off who are going into Chile and you go over in a Colque Tours bus. You probably should organise this through your own agency prior to setting off on the Salar trip as the bus was full and there is only the one each day.

'There is again a very, very basic lodging, where you can get a bed and some food. You drive to San Pedro de Atacama and the immigration post is actually on the outskirts of the town itself. They do bag searches and you have to wipe your 'dirty' feet on some kind of mat with disinfectant if you have come from Bolivia. The whole trip, including waiting at the border checks, took about two hours.'

For more details of onward bus services in Chile, check with the Ranking Bolivia office in Uyuni (see below) before leaving Uyuni.

By train The train station is located at the southern edge of town and receives four weekly connections from Oruro, plus handles onward connections to Tupiza and Villazon for the Argentinian border. The ticket office opens only around the times that trains are passing through and tickets can be purchased only the day before and on the day of travel itself. You need your passport to make a purchase.

Schedules and prices are posted next to the ticket office. Alternatively, check the website www.fca.com.bo/fca1/itinerarios-tarifas-1.htm.

The Ranking Bolivia office (see below) also has the latest details of train times and fares.

GETTING AROUND Uyuni is a small place with everything easily accessible on foot. Should you need a taxi, call **Taxis 11 de Julio** (☎ *693 3137*).

TOURIST INFORMATION Uyuni has the good fortune to be home to the most efficient and cosy tourist information office in Bolivia: **Ranking Bolivia** (*Av Potosí #9;* ☎ *693 2616;* e *rankingbolivia@hotmail.com*). Built in a salt hotel design, it has a wealth of information about Uyuni and the Salar, plus other destinations around Bolivia, and the latest transport details. They rate and rank local tour operators according to travellers' feedback and provide a bridge to lodge complaints when things go wrong. They also recently opened a new area for travellers with a small snack bar and a video room, where you can keep warm while waiting for train departures to Oruro that leave in the early hours. Open daily 08.30–20.00; lounge open until midnight.

Uyuni is packed with tour agencies – 48 official agencies at the last count – and all of them are vying for the lucrative market in Salar de Uyuni tours. To be honest, most of them are much the same with standards of accommodation and catering, at best, variable. Once on the Salar, agencies rush to the night stopping point as accommodation seems to be dished out on first-jeep-first-served basis. As such, the second night of the typical three-day Salar trip is notoriously rough. The typical price for a real no-frills trip starts from US$60 per person per day.

Remember that if things do go wrong, you have the right to complain. If you do, you could even get some of your money back. Stories abound on the travellers' grapevine about drunk drivers and drivers falling asleep at the wheel, not to mention agencies leaving folks behind once the car is full – even though they have a reservation. The crucial point is that when you book your tour, you must request a written contract that sets out in detail what services are included for the price you are paying.

LOCAL TOUR AGENCIES Agencies that receive consistently good reports are:

Toñito Tours Av Ferroviaria #152; \f 693 2094; e tonitotours@yahoo.com; www.boliviaexpeditions.com. ;This agency's tours are more expensive (up to US$90 pp per day) but generally are of higher quality & based on smaller groups. *Open daily 08.30–12.00 & 14.00–20.30.*
Esmeralda Tours Av Ferroviaria corner with Av Arce; \ 693 2130; e esmeraldaivan@hotmail.com. A

popular backpacker choice for more budget-end trips, but do expect a few cut corners. *Open daily 09.00–12.00 & 14.00–20.00.*
Andes Salt Expeditions Calle Potosí #71; \f 693 3137; e turismo_uyuni@hotmail.com; www.andes-salt-uyuni.com.bo. The sister agency to the Potosí office (page 184) with years of experience in Salar tours. *Open daily 08.30–12.00 & 14.00–20.00.*

WHERE TO STAY As a travellers' hub, Uyuni has plenty of options but many are grubby, stark and prone to taking on the feel of a large deep-freeze at night when the mercury heads south at an alarming rate. The following are divided by budget category.

Mid-range

Los Girosoles Hotel (20 rooms) Calle Santa Cruz #155; \ 693 3323; e girasoleshotel@hotmail.com; www.girasoleshotel.com. The newest hotel in town is a smarter, albeit slightly pricer, addition to Uyuni's range of places to stay. Rooms are en suite with all-day hot water & heaters to fend off the bitter cold. There's even a, ahem, 'presidential suite' if you have US$250 to splash. The in-house restaurant does a decent buffet b/fast, but the dinner is a bit steep for what you get at US$7 per head. *Sgls/dbls/tpls US$35/60/75 with b/fast.*

Toñito Hotel (18 rooms) Av Ferroviaria #48; \f 693 2094; e tonitotours@yahoo.com; www.bolivianexpeditions.com. The travellers' favourite (with Minuteman Pizza, see opposite, located on the premises) is a comfortable spot to prepare for any Salar tour. Rooms are not flash but the beds are comfy & come with private bathrooms. Plus, crucially, there's a decent supply of hot water all day round – a rarity in Uyuni. *Sgls/dbls/tpls $20/30/40 with b/fast.*

Budget

Hotel Avenida (16 rooms) Av Ferroviaria #11; \f 693 2078. At the budget end of the market, this simple but convenient place is the best of the bunch of properties located directly opposite the train station. Beware: hot showers 07.00–09.00 only. *Sgls/dbls with private bathroom 40/80Bs; sgls/dbls/tpls with shared bathrooms 20/40/60Bs.*

Hostelling International (10 rooms) Corner of Calle Potosí & Calle Sucre; \f 693 2228; e hostelling_international_bolivia@yahoo.com; www.hostellingbolivia.org. Uyuni's youth hostel is simple but useful for those carrying HI membership cards. Beware the strict 22.00 curfew after which the doors are locked. *Rooms 35Bs pp.*

WHERE TO EAT

Pub Pizzeria Arco Iris Av Arce #27; \ 693 2517. A reliable pizza joint, this place is handy for the station with an atmospheric feel & decent meals.

Small/medium/large pizzas 20/40/45Bs & pastas 20–25Bs. *Open daily 12.00–14.30 & 18.00–20.00.*
Café Central Walk Parque Arce; no tel. A hole-in-

the-wall café located under the central bandstand in a small park just a stone's throw from the train station. It's a great spot for b/fast before your Salar tour starts, with set b/fast (7–15Bs), pancakes (8.50Bs) & muesli, fruit & yoghurt (9Bs). *Open Mon–Sat 08.00–20.00.*

ENTERTAINMENT AND NIGHTLIFE

🍷 **La Loco** Av Potosí; ☏ 693 3105. A French-owned bar with a nice open fire, a locomotive motif & a dartboard for Brits missing their local boozer back home. It's a popular spot for a hot toddy with a shot of singani (10Bs) to beat the cold, as well as snacks, such as sandwiches (12Bs) & croque monsieurs (10Bs). *Open Tue–Sun 15.00–02.00.*

🍷 **Wipala** Av Potosí; no tel. This place has a spit-&-sawdust feel & live music at weekends with a friendly bunch of resident drunks always happy to make new friends. The owners serve up – you guessed it – pizzas (small/medium/large 25/48/50Bs) & a decent llama curry (25Bs), while hot toddies (10Bs) are a perennial fave. *Open Mon–Sat 19.00–late.*

SHOPPING

Comart Tukuypaj Fair Trade Handicrafts Av Arce #2 corner with Av Ferroviaria; no tel; e comart@comart-tukuypaj.com. A quality souvenir & gift shop selling goods produced by local artisans with prices for 100% alpaca sweaters ranging from 60–140Bs & hats from 40–80Bs. *Open Mon–Sat 09.00–12.30 & 14.30–18.30.*

Bookshop Popular Av Potosí #356; ☏ 693 2501. A handy little stationery/bookshop which, notably, stocks a range of hard-to-find maps of Bolivia, the Salar & other areas. Plus they offer money exchange & camera film. *Open daily 08.00–12.00 & 14.30–19.30.*

OTHER PRACTICALITIES

Banco de Crédito Av Potosí #34. Changes US dollars & opens Mon–Fri 08.30–12.30 & 14.30–17.00.
Entel call centre Av Arce. Has phone & fax connections but no internet access. *Open daily 08.00–20.00.*
Immigration Office Av Potosí #35; no tel. This is the place to arrange your exit stamp before leaving Uyuni for a Salar tour; there's a 15Bs fee for the service. *Open Mon–Sat 08.30–12.00 & 14.00–19.00, Sun 08.30–12.00 & 18.00–19.00.*
Money exchangers line Av Potosí. Charges a 3%

commission on travellers' cheques but none on cash exchanges of US$, euro, Argentinian & Chilean pesos. Open 08.00–12.00 & 14.00–19.00
Post office Av Arce; ☏ 693 146. Located by the bus stops; open Mon–Fri 08.30–20.00.
Pharmacy Santa Isabel Av Potosí #386; ☏ 693 2097. Also takes a turn as the town's emergency 24hr chemist. *Open daily 08.00–22.00.*
Servi Net Av Arce. Has internet access for 6Bs/hr & a photocopying service. *Open daily 09.00–20.00.*

WHAT TO SEE AND DO

Museo Arqueólogico y Antropólogico (*Av Arce; no tel; open Mon–Fri 09.00–12.00 & 14.00–18.00; entrance 2.50Bs*) Uyuni's solitary cultural attraction has a small and not hugely compelling collection of skulls with a limited amount of information available all in Spanish.

The Train Cemetery, located 3km outside of Uyuni following the train lines, is Bolivia's most famous attraction for rail buffs. This eerie place, woefully neglected, is the place where old iron horses come to push up daisies. The cemetery dates from the 1940s, when the minerals that had once made the region rich started to run out and the mining industry began to falter.

Today, the handiwork of the British engineers that came to Bolivia to build its fledgling railway network (see *The Brits and Bolivia's first railways*, page 170) stands rusting in a wasteland. Talk of building a railway museum remains, so far, just that – talk.

Most of the Salar tours include a stop at the cemetery, otherwise head west along the train tracks following Avenida Ferroviaria for 3km out of town.

THE SALAR DE UYUNI with James Brunker (www.magicalandes.com)

The Salar de Uyuni is Bolivia's greatest natural wonder. It's flatter than Holland and whiter than Mont Blanc. By day the temperature is a skin-bleaching 30°, while by night the cold is so intense it would freeze a llama in its tracks. It may be the back of beyond, but it is truly spectacular.

These huge salt flats, covering an area of approximately 10,000km^2 at an altitude of 3,653m in Bolivia's remote southwest, nudge the Chilean border and stretch across an expanse of land with an area greater than that of Switzerland. Its surface is composed of pure crystalised salt, but dig just 5cm in some places and you'll hit a vast expanse of subterranean lakes, water that rises to the surface during the rainy season (December to March) and floods the entire area like a giant floating ice rink.

The Salar is often closed to tourists in the rainy season due to flooding problems. There are two charges levied for entrance to certain protected areas of the Salar, namely 10Bs for the Isla Incahuasi and 30Bs at Laguna Colorada, where you enter the Reserva Nacional de Fauna Andina Eduardo Avaroa. Some agencies include these charges in their tour price, but most will expect you to pay separately.

SALAR DE UYUNI

James Brunker (www.magicalandes.com)

The bleak southern regions of the altiplano offer landscapes unparalleled anywhere on the planet. Among the most distinctive formations are the 'Salares' or salt pans, often referred to as 'salt lakes'. These include the Salares of Coipasa, Uyuni, Empexa, Chiguana and Chalviri in Bolivia; Surire, Huasco, Coposa, Cacote, Ascotan and Atacama in Chile and a few in northern Argentina. For sheer scale, beauty and purity, however, none match the shimmering white expanse of the Salar de Uyuni, making it deservedly the best known and most visited. And no other Salar contains rocky islands covered with giant cacti, its most distinctive feature.

Geologically the altiplano was covered by various huge lakes in the Quaternary Period; several of these later disappeared to leave two, of which Lake Minchín covered the region which is now southern Bolivia. The Quaternary Period was also a time of intense volcanic and glacial activity, resulting in the unusually intense mineral concentrations in the region today. Lake Minchín (along with the other lakes) gradually began a process of evaporation as the climate became drier around 40,000 years ago, terminating around 10,000 years ago to leave the Salares in their present condition. Former lake shore terraces in the area (at 3,760m and 3,720m) suggest this drying occurred in two stages.

Legend as always has a far more colourful explanation: a giant love struggle involving the surrounding peaks of Tunupa, Kusku and Kusuña. Tunupa was a beautiful woman with many admirers continually disputing her affections. She married Kusku and they lived happily for a long time until Kusuña arrived on the scene. She was also a beautiful woman who had taken a fancy to Kusku and after many advances Kusku began to take notice. Eventually she managed to convince Kusku to leave Tunupa and flee with her, leaving

Most of the three-day Salar trips start from Uyuni (page 168) but it's also possible from Tupiza (page 231). On this latter route you can make a stop at Colchani, the Salar's frontier town and a major centre for salt extraction and processing, to browse salt-made souvenirs. They then head to Hotel de Sal Playa Blanca (✆ 693 2772), which has the most expensive toilet stop in Bolivia (5Bs) and forces all visitors to buy a coffee (7Bs) or something from the shop at reception. Officially tourists are not supposed to overnight here – and given the basic facilities, you'd be mad to do so anyway – but the owners do tout rooms (without a licence) for US$20 per person on a full-board basis.

From the salt hotel it's 80km across the flats to Isla Incahuasi, also known as Isla de Pescadores, located 200km from the Chilean border's immigration post. There's an 8Bs park entrance fee payable, a shop that changes Chilean pesos and plans at the time of writing to install both an Entel call centre and a small museum. Most tour groups use this lovely spot, with 1000-year-old cacti set against a backdrop of pure, bleached-white salt flats, for a picnic lunch. Go off season and you could be enjoying the views without the hordes.

If you find yourself without supplies, there is a small restaurant by the park office with burgers (19–24Bs), a decent llama curry (30Bs) and drinks (5Bs). At the time of writing this was run by Mongo's as an offshoot of the café bar in La Paz (page 82), but the licence was up for renewal and its future was uncertain. It is illegal to overnight on the island. After the Salar the multi-day tours usually continue to the small village of San Juan for the first night (though more villages in the area are now offering lodgings). Close to San Juan is a small pre-Columbian cemetery and there is a new museum in the village (5Bs entrance, not normally included in tour price) with artefacts and a brief history about the 'Lords of Lipez', who used to live in the area. The southwestern leg of the circuit then ventures into

Tunupa alone. Tunupa began to cry while breast feeding her son, until her tears began to mingle with her milk, thus forming the Salar de Uyuni. Today the Tunupa Volcano dominates the northern shore of the Salar; many locals consider the peak an important deity and say the Salar should be known as the Salar de Tunupa rather than the Salar de Uyuni.

The Salar de Uyuni consists of a solid salt cap whose thickness varies from a few tens of centimetres to several metres; beneath it is a lake of saturated salt and mineral solutions that varies between 2m and 20m in depth. It is estimated that some 64,000 million tonnes of salt exist in the Salar. It is also an important source of minerals; potassium, lithium, borax and magnesium exist in significant quantities, as well as sodium.

The Salar itself is virtually devoid of flora and fauna, although many interesting high-altitude desert species can be found in the region (see section on the Reserva Nacional de Fauna Andina Eduardo Avaroa, page 7). In the immediate vicinity of the Salar vicuñas, lesser rheas or suris and in shallow lakes flamingoes can be seen, while a colony of viscachas lives isolated on Incahuasi Island (sometimes called Isla del Pescadores). The islands in the Salar themselves are of particular interest, the remains of ancient volcanoes that were totally or partially submerged during the era of Lake Minchín. This can be seen in the unusual and fragile coral-like formations and deposits that often consist of fossils of algae known as stromatolites that cover the rocks. The stars of the flora are the giant cacti, a species known as 'k'eru celumbral'; over 6,000 grow on Incahuasi alone. These grow very slowly at an estimated 1cm per year, though the highest is over 12m high. Other shrub species include the Pilaya, used to cure catarrh, and Thola, common over the whole region and used as fuel by local inhabitants.

the Reserva Nacional de Fauna Andina Eduardo Avaroa to take in excursions to the Laguna Colorada and Laguna Verde with their respective terracotta and jade hues derived from their rich mineral properties. Laguna Colorada is a breeding ground for local flora and fauna and encapsulates the serene natural beauty of the Salar area. The most famous of these inhabitants is the rare James flamingo with the largest such population of this graceful species on the planet. Chilean and Andean flamingos are also common, all of them taking on a delicate pink glow due to the pink algae that is their main source of foodstuffs. Aside from the flamingo population, there are a further 80 species of birds to be found in the area, including the horned coot, the Andean goose and the Andean hillstar. The animal population is equally diverse with Andean foxes and rabbit-like viscacha, while the flora includes quinoa plants and the queñua bush. Tours usually spend their second night here.

Laguna Verde, with the conical Licancabur volcano on the Chilean border forming a superb backdrop, marks the southernmost point of the tours. From here you retrace your steps to Uyuni with the occasional detour. An increasingly popular alternative is to cross into Chile and onto San Pedro de Atacama via the

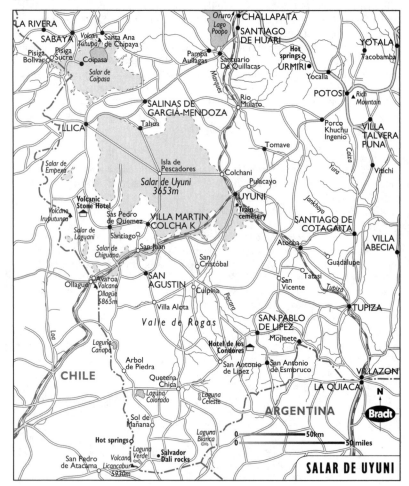

SALAR DE UYUNI

During 2006 a major new community project was initiated in the Salar de Uyuni region with twin aims: to foster the benefits of tourism for local communities and to improve the overall standard of accommodation in the region.

A 15-year project, the funding was derived from a mix of private enterprise and local authorities with a share contributed by the La Paz-based tour agency Fremen (page 71). Fremen have a managing hand in the project and now sell exclusive packages for Salar tours based around the new properties.

There are four properties in the project:

1 Tahua Salt Hotel (14 rooms), located 90 minutes from Uyuni in the northern Salar

2 San Pedro de Quemez Volcanic Stone Hotel (14 rooms), located 2½ hours from Tahua and about 90 minutes from the Chilean border

3 Hotel del Desierto Volcanic Stone Hotel (14 rooms), located at Hito 72 close to the Chilean border

4 Hotel de los Condores (10 rooms), located at San Pedro de Lipez, six hours from Tupiza

All the rooms across the network are finished with salt/stone aesthetics and furnished with cactus-wood fittings, thatched roofs plus rugs and curtains made from local textiles. Hot water and light are powered by solar energy with backup generators. All come with private bathrooms and rooms comprise two twin beds with a separate convertible sofa bed.

A tourist information centre is now planned at a location along the route with the aim of raising awareness about the topography of the Salar and the culture of its indigenous pueblos.

Prices for all tours include a standard US$1 per person tourist tax that goes directly into local community development projects.

Prices across the network are as follows:
Sgls/dbls/tpls/quads US$75/75/80/85
Breakfast/lunch/dinner/full board US$3,75/6,25/6,25/16,25
Packages start from US$301 per person for a two-day package, based on two sharing.

For more information and full price details contact Fremen Tours Andes & Amazonia (tel in Uyuni: 693 2987; www.andes-amazonia.com).

border crossing at Hito Cajón. Agencies will make all the necessary arrangements for Chilean transport to meet you at the border, and at the time of writing you need to obtain an exit stamp at immigration in Uyuni before you leave. Again agencies will be able to advise you of the latest situation.

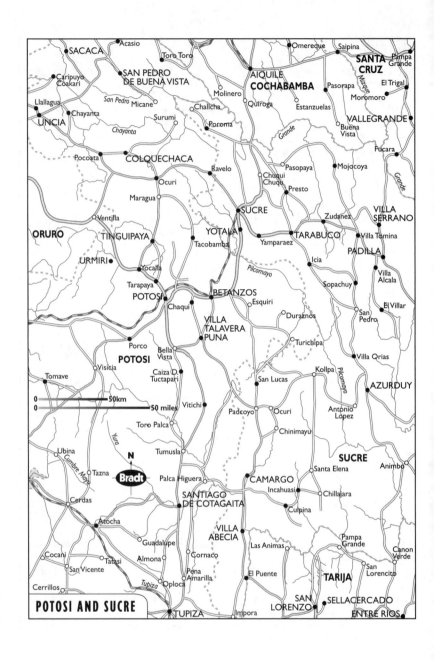

POTOSI AND SUCRE

8

Potosí and Sucre

POTOSÍ *Tel code: 02; altitude: 3,976m; population: 145,047*

Potosí is all about living history. Once considered the economic powerhouse of the Americas, it boasted a population greater than that of Paris and its silver reserves, mined from the mountain, Cerro Rico, which looms over the city, funded the Spanish conquest of Latin America. Today the mines have all but closed and the Casa de la Moneda, the erstwhile national mint, is now a museum exploring Potosí's glorious heritage. Potosí has found a new role, however: a colonial city that speaks volumes about Bolivia's colourful history.

Potosí is not, however, the most immediately attractive travel prospect with its high altitude and tendency towards extreme weather, notably the biting cold. But wrap up warm and you'll find a couple of worthwhile distractions to occupy you for a few days. Better still, for a small town with not too much going on, Potosí has surprisingly large numbers of both vegetarian eateries and tour operators, making it an established favourite on the gringo trail.

From its former position as a world silver-mining capital to its current status as a historical curiosity, Potosí is a classic riches-to-rags story and, as such, the city today retains a rather elegiac feel. The city was declared a UNESCO site on 11 December 1987, and today lives off tourism as its main source of income with only its baroque churches hinting at its former glory.

HISTORY The second city to be founded in Bolivia, Potosí was established with the original name of Villa Imperial de Carlos V in 1545.

Potosí once rivalled Paris, London and Venice as one of the world's most important urban centres and was renowned for its superlative colonial architecture and strong European influence. Its population had swelled to a massive 160,000 inhabitants, according to the 1611 census, as it grew into the largest and wealthiest city in the Americas.

This rapid expansion was due to the mountain of silver found in its backyard,

---

THREE THINGS TO DO IN POTOSÍ

1 Soak up the sense of elegiac history on a tour of the Casa de Moneda, the Royal Mint, to explore Potosí's erstwhile heritage as the centre of the Spanish colonial empire (page 186).

2 Take your life in your hands and venture down the mines of Cerro Rico to witness first-hand working conditions that are straight out of a bygone era (page 182).

3 Strike out into the remote and little-explored countryside to the north of Potosí Department to see the wildlife and landscape of Toro Toro National Park (page 187).

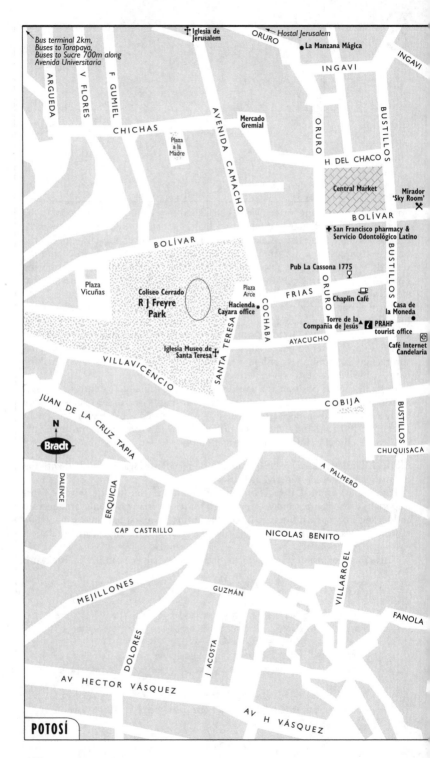

Iglesia de Jerusalem

ORURO — Hostal Jerusalem

● La Manzana Mágica

INGAVI

INGAVI

Bus terminal 2km,
Buses to Tarapaya,
Buses to Sucre 700m along
Avenida Universitaria

ARGUEDA

V FLORES

F GUMIEL

CHICHAS

AVENIDA CAMACHO

Plaza a la Madre

Mercado Gremial

ORURO

BUSTILLOS

H DEL CHACO

Central Market

Mirador 'Sky Room'

BOLÍVAR

San Francisco pharmacy & Servicio Odontológico Latino

BOLÍVAR

Plaza Vicuñas

Coliseo Cerrado
R J Freyre Park

Plaza Arce

SANTA TERESA

COCHABA

FRIAS

Pub La Cassona 1775

ORURO

Chaplin Café

BUSTILLOS

Casa de la Moneda

Hacienda Cayara office

Torre de la Compañía de Jesús

PRAHP tourist office

AYACUCHO

Café Internet Candelaria

Iglesia Museo de Santa Teresa

VILLAVICENCIO

COBIJA

JUAN DE LA CRUZ TAPIA

BUSTILLOS

CHUQUISACA

N

Bradt

DALENCE

ERQUICIA

A PALMERO

CAP CASTRILLO

NICOLAS BENITO

VILLARROEL

MEJILLONES

GUZMÁN

FANOLA

DOLORES

J ACOSTA

AV HECTOR VÁSQUEZ

AV H VÁSQUEZ

POTOSÍ

180

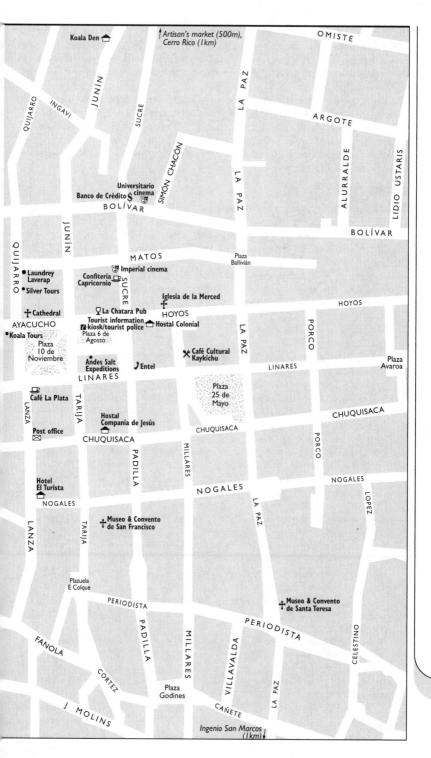

Koala Den

Artisan's market (500m),
Cerro Rico (1km)

OMISTE

QUIJARRO

INGAVI

JUNÍN

SUCRE

LA PAZ

ARGOTE

ALURRALDE

LIDIO USTARIS

SIMÓN CHACÓN

LA PAZ

Universitario
cinema

Banco de Crédito $

BOLÍVAR

JUNÍN

BOLÍVAR

MATOS

Plaza
Ballivián

QUIJARRO

Laundrey
Laverap

Silver Tours

Imperial cinema

Confitería
Capricornio

SUCRE

Iglesia de la Merced

HOYOS

Cathedral

La Chatara Pub

AYACUCHO

Koala Tours

Tourist information
kiosk/tourist police

Plaza 6 de
Agosto

Hostal Colonial

LA PAZ

PORCO

HOYOS

Plaza
10 de
Noviembre

Andes Salt
Expeditions

Entel

Café Cultural
Kaykichu

LINARES

Plaza
Avaroa

LINARES

Café La Plata

LANZA

TARIJA

Plaza
25 de
Mayo

CHUQUISACA

Post office

Hostal
Compañía de Jesús

CHUQUISACA

CHUQUISACA

PORCO

PADILLA

MILLARES

Hotel
El Turista

NOGALES

NOGALES

LA PAZ

NOGALES

LOPEZ

LANZA

TARIJA

Museo & Convento
de San Francisco

Plazuela
E Colque

PERIODISTA

PADILLA

Museo & Convento
de Santa Teresa

PERIODISTA

CELESTINO

FANOLA

CORTEZ

MILLARES

VILLAVALDA

LA PAZ

J MOLINS

Plaza
Godines

CAÑETE

Ingenio San Marcos
(1km)

Potosí and Sucre POTOSÍ

8

181

the giant Cerro Rico that towers 4,824m over the city. Indeed, its silver veins underwrote the entire Spanish economy, and its monarchs' extravagance, for over two centuries. The city's centrepiece, the Casa de la Moneda, was a cornerstone of the Spanish conquest, serving as the national mint, fortress and prison since its 1572 construction.

Behind this wealth, however, lies the story of millions of African and indigenous Indian slaves, who died on the hill to line the pockets of the conquistadors. And this is not to mention the city's subsequent fall from grace whereby, when Bolivian independence came in 1825, the mines were already in terminal decline.

Today the department's 16 districts celebrate their anniversary on 10 November to mark the 1810 revolution.

GETTING THERE

By bus Potosí is primarily a bus destination, with regular overnight connections to and from La Paz. At the bus terminal (*Av Universitaria;* ☏ *624 3361*), you'll find some basic snack bars and a luggage storage office (3Bs per hour) just outside the back of the terminal building. There's a 2Bs tax payable on all bus departures.

Regular bus services for Sucre leave from Plaza Uyuni, or you can arrange to share a taxi through your hotel. Regular minibuses leave the Mercado

---

POTOSI'S CHILD MINERS

Jo Wright

Eight-year-old Javier works a seven-hour day in a mine in Cerro Rico outside Potosí. 'I go to school for two hours in the afternoon. I don't like the mine. But the job is good to get money,' he says, as he crams the food we had brought with us into his mouth.

His father died in the mine before he was eligible for compensation or a pension, hence the then eight-year-old eldest son simply took his place. Today Javier looks ancient beyond his years.

It is illegal for under-18s to work in Bolivia's mines but desperate poverty in the central highlands and a rise in world mineral prices are driving more and more Bolivian children into the mines. Former miners estimate 9,000 people now work in Cerro Rico's mines in conditions that have barely changed since colonial times. About 1,000 of these workers are children, with their number doubling during school holidays.

Child miners have a life expectancy of between 28 and 33 years. Silicosis, a non-reversible lung disease caused by exposure to dust from silica crystals, is the major killer, although cave-ins in the poorly maintained tunnels also exact a high toll. Those suffering from silicosis often have to sleep sitting up because of the pain in their lungs, and have a high risk of contracting tuberculosis.

Living conditions outside the mines, where human waste and garbage mix with the toxic dust, also contribute to high instances of respiratory diseases. The altitude of Cerro Rico, which at 4,798m towers to within 10m of the summit of western Europe's highest peak, Mont Blanc, adds to the miners' difficulties as temperatures can plummet to minus 20°C on its exposed slopes.

Women traditionally do not work in Cerro Rico because it is believed Pachamama (the earth mother) would be jealous of their presence, although many work through scraps of rocks outside. Sometimes, however, if a husband dies having not worked long enough for his family to receive compensation, his wife takes his place in the mine in order to support the family.

A further indicator of the appalling working environment is that many miners believe Cerro Rico is inhabited by a devil, known as El Tío (the Uncle). Every mine has at least

Chuquimia for Tarapaya (page 188) daily during daylight hours and for Uyuni from the corner of Calle Benedetto Vinchentti and Avenida Universitaria each morning.

By train Train services have recently returned to Potosí with a new service to Sucre run by the Empresa Ferroviaria Andina (FCA), which also runs the trains out of Orruro (page 159). The so-called **Ferrobus** service, albeit rather slow with a total journey time of six hours, runs three services per week, leaving Potosí at 08.00 and arriving at El Tejar at 14.00; first/second class 35/25Bs.

GETTING AROUND The city centre is easily covered on foot while a taxi out to the bus terminal should cost no more than 5Bs. To call a **taxi**, try Radio Movil Centauro (↘ *622 4444*).

TOURIST INFORMATION The **tourist Information kiosk and tourist police** are housed in a tiny kiosk on Plaza 6 de Agosto, but it opens irregular hours at best. Thankfully more reliable is a new **information centre**, run by local heritage organisation, PRAHP, which opened in November 2004 in the Edificio de la Nave de la Compañía de Jesús; open Mon–Fri 8.30–noon and 14.00–18.00. It's a bit sparse so far, but a better bet for quality information.

one shrine of a horned, red El Tío where miners leave offerings of coca leaves, alcohol and often a llama foetus. 'More llama blood means less miner blood,' say the workers in the hope of appeasing the devil for taking 'its' minerals so that they do not pay with their lives.

Child miners say that, despite the health risks, their main concern was the need to earn money. Juan, a 14-year-old who has worked in the mines since he was 11, said: 'There is no money for me to go to school. I have five brothers and two sisters. I do a 24-hour shift sometimes because the prices are good at the moment.'

Some children attend evening classes after finishing gruelling shifts underground, although many drop out of school before learning Spanish and speak only Quechua, hence hindering their chances of employment in anything but manual labour. CARE Bolivia, in collaboration with a local NGO, El Centro de Promoción Minera (Cepromin), has set up an educational programme to improve schooling standards in to help prepare children for non-mining occupations. The programme also tries to increase understanding among mining families about the effects of child labour and the value of education.

Today Potosí has become another stop on Bolivia's backpacker trail with an estimated 500 visitors a month donning waterproofs and hard hats, buying gifts for the workers of coca leaves, alcohol and dynamite from the miners' market, and heading for Cerro Rico for a trip underground with an ex-miner. Most visits are to larger operations, such as La Candelaria, which do not routinely take on child labour, or at least keep their 'young helpers' well hidden.

To descend between levels involves sliding on your back, feet planted in the dust and hands gripping the ceiling. Asbestos shards spike through the low tunnels and where arsenic is exposed the temperature and humidity soar. For travellers it makes for a frisson of adventure but, for Potosí's child miners, such hardship is simply part of everyday life.

Potosí has numerous travel agencies offering mine tours. Koala Tours (page 184) provides overclothes, hard hats and a headlight; the company claims to donate 10% of its US$10 charge to help the miners.

The alternative is to go straight to the various tour operators around town, all of whom jostle for the lucrative market in mine tours (see box, *Potosí's child miners*, page 182). The standard rate is US$10 per person for a mine visit. You can find cheaper prices but, before you book, always ask about what safety arrangements will be made for your visit.

LOCAL TOUR OPERATORS

Koala Tours Calle Ayacucho #5; ✆ 622 4708; f 622 2092; e k_tours_potosi@hotmail.com; www.koalatoursbolivia.com. It may not be the cheapest operator in town, but their tours do tend to be of higher quality & more considerate to local communities. As well as the standard mine tour, Koala Tours also offer *tinku* tours (see box, the *Bolivian fight club*, page 186) & itineraries to more offbeat locations. The owners also run the Koala Den hostel (see below). *Open 09.00–22.00.*

Andes Salt Expeditions Plaza Alonso de Ibañez #3; ✆/f 622 5175; e turismo_potosi@hotmail.com; www.andes-salt-uyuni.com.bo. A good general all-round operator for trips, tours & tickets, plus they are specialists in tours to the Salar de Uyuni with a sister office in Uyuni (page 172). *Open 09.00–22.00.*
Silver Tours Calle Quijarro #12; ✆/f 622 3600; e silvertoursreservas@hotmail.com; www.silvertours.net. A smaller agency offering mine & Salar tours, plus excursions to the hot springs at Tarapaya for 40Bs, inc transport. *Open 09.00–22.00.*

 WHERE TO STAY Potosí is not overly blessed with good-quality accommodation options. Beware plummeting night temperatures and always ask for extra blankets. The following properties are divided by budget category and listed in the order of the author's preference.

Top of the range

🏠 **Hostal Colonial** (20 rooms) Calle Hoyos #8; ✆ 622 4265; f 622 7146; e hcolonial_potosi@hotmail.com. The sister property to the popular Sucre hotel (page 193) remains the best address in town &, as such, it has the prices to match.

Built around a central courtyard, all rooms are en suite & offer cable TV, a fridge &, crucially for Potosí's infamously cold nights, radiators. *Sgls/dbls/tpls US$33/43/48 without b/fast (US$1.50 extra).*

Mid-range

🏠 **Hostal Jerusalem** (32 rooms) Calle Oruro #143; ✆ 622 4633; f 262 2600; e hoteljer@entelnet.bo; www.hoteljerusalem.net. Although a little way from the centre – it's located just past the central market – the Jerusalem is the best budget option in town, although better rooms are to be found in

the new block. A decent b/fast buffet is also included in the price. *Sgls/dbls/tpls US$12/15/20.* The owners also run the youth hostel-style **Residential Sumaj**, Calle Gumiel #12; ✆ 622 3336, but it is situated rather out of town; *sgls/dbls/tpls for US$5/8/12.*

Budget

🏠 **Hostal Compañía de Jesús** (22 rooms) Calle Chuquisaca #445; ✆ 622 3173. Converted from an old monastery, this hostel is welcoming &, unlike some places, offers constant hot water in the showers to make up for the cold & creaking wooden floors. The b/fast is inc but disappointing. *Sgls/dbls with private bathroom 70/100Bs, with shared bathroom 40/70Bs.*
🏠 **Koala Den** Calle Junin #56; ✆ 622 6467; www.koalatoursbolivia.com. The latest opening in town is also the dedicated party hostel. As such, it's the backpackers' favourite for its book exchange, TV room with cable channels & communal kitchen, the

last complete with a giant Pink Floyd mural. Just don't expect much sleep if you're shoehorned into one of the cramped, tpl-bunk dorms. *Dbl rooms 70Bs pp, 10-person dorms 20Bs.*
🏠 **Hotel El Turista** (22 rooms) Calle Lanza #19; ✆ 622 2492; e osmedtur@hotmail.com. A reliable central option run by the people behind tour operator South American Tours. The rooms are clean with private bathrooms but the best ones are definitely on the top floor, notably room numbers 31 & 34, which offer great panoramic views across the city. *Sgls/dbls/tpls 60/100/130Bs, b/fast 10Bs extra.*

Outside Potosí For something a bit special, try **Hacienda Cayara** (20 rooms) (*www.cayara.com.bo*). It is located 25km out of Potosí and remains one of the few working haciendas in Bolivia today. Dating from 1557 and with a living-museum feel, the 100ha grounds also include a hydro-electric power plant and a working dairy farm. The latter produces the 350l of milk each day that are used in the making of branded Cayara ice creams, milk and yoghurt products available around Potosí. The rooms, though en suite, are not overly luxurious and can feel a bit cold at night. Nevertheless the place is full of character and it feels like you are taking a real step back in history. Don't miss a siesta after lunch in the suntrap plant room, or a night sitting by the roaring fire with a wee dram. Rooms US$25 with breakfast, lunch US$5, dinner US$4, afternoon tea US$3. Reservations can be made at the **Hacienda Cayara office** in Potosí (*Calle Cochabamba #532;* ⟍ *622 6380;* e *cayara@cotapnet.com; www.cayara.place.cc*).

✗ WHERE TO EAT

✗ **Café Internet Candelaria** Calle Ayacucho #5; ⟍ 622 8050. Located upstairs from Koala Tours (see opposite), this twin-level restaurant has a vegetarian-friendly café with a comprehensive menu on the first floor, while internet terminals are located upstairs (3Bs/hr). The 4-course set lunch/dinner (22Bs) & vegetarian set menus (17Bs) offer particularly good value. *Open daily 07.30–21.00.*

✗ **Chaplin Café** Calle Matos #10, no tel. Best for dinner (try the excellent set burger meal at 12Bs) & vegetarian friendly, this little eatery, located one block from the main square, has an English menu. There's Mexican food at weekends (6Bs), set b/fast (8–10Bs) & good fruit shakes (4Bs). *Open daily 07.30–13.00 & 16.00–22.00.*

✗ **Ingenio San Marcos** Calle La Paz corner with Calle Betanzos; ⟍ 623 0260. Potosí's primary upmarket eatery is styled out of an old mineral plant & has an industrial theme. The food is of very high quality with llama steaks (30Bs) & set mains (30Bs), plus salads & omelettes (15Bs). There's also a textile shop & a viewing point as part of the complex. *Open daily 09.00–23.00.*

✗ **Café Cultural Kaypichu** Calle Millares #16; ⟍ 622 6129. This vegetarian-friendly spot is best for its range of healthy b/fast (10–18Bs), inc the blow-out Kaypichu special, which will set you up for the day – when it finally arrives that is. Otherwise mains are around 20Bs & llama steaks 30Bs. A good bet for vegetarians but the painfully slow service means some people just give up & move on. *Open Tue–Sun 07.30–14.00 & 17.00–21.00.*

✗ **Restaurant Mirador Sky Room** Edificio Matilde 3/F, Calle Bolivar #701; ⟍ 622 0138. The views are better than the food at this standard Bolivian eatery, but it's a useful spot for a filling set menu (4-course lunch 10Bs; set dinner 9Bs). *Open daily 08.00–21.00.*

✗ **Confiteria Capricornio** Calle Padilla #11, no tel. A simple but popular student hang-out for sandwiches (5Bs) & spaghetti (10Bs). *Open daily 09.00–22.00.*

✗ **Café La Plata** Edificio Club Internacional, Plaza 10 de Noviembre; ⟍ 622 6085. Serves the best coffee in town with liqueur coffees (12Bs) & set b/fast (12–18Bs). *Open daily 08.00–22.00.*

ENTERTAINMENT AND NIGHTLIFE Potosí has two **cinemas**, the Imperial at Calle Padilla #31 and the Universitario at Calle Bolivar #893. Otherwise try to keep warm with a hot toddy at the city's two bars: **La Chatarra Pub** (*Plaza 6 de Agosto, no tel; open daily 21.00–02.00*) which has a divey feel with graffiti-covered walls, liqueur coffees (10Bs) and cocktails (12/14Bs); smarter and very gringo-oriented is

---

THE AUTHOR'S FAVOURITE EATERY

La Manzana Mágica Calle Oruro #239; ⟍ 718 36312. Potosí's best little restaurant has moved so many times in recent years that baffled vegetarian food fans have been left in despair. But it now, finally, has a new permanent home & continues to serve an excellent set lunch/dinner (12Bs), salads (5Bs) & soups (7Bs) with friendly service. It's all healthy, organic produce – even non-vegetarians will love it. *Open Mon–Sat 08.00–22.00.*

Pub La Cassona 1775 (*Calle Frias #41; tel 622 2954; open daily 18.30–02.00*) with a cellar bar location and beers-a-plenty (6Bs).

SHOPPING The **central market** (entrance on Calle Oruro) and **Mercado Artesenal** (Plaza Savaadra) have silver and tin goods that make for good souvenirs.

OTHER PRACTICALITIES

Banco de Crédito Calle Bolivar corner with Calle Sucre. Has an ATM service & offers credit card cash advances; *open Mon–Fri 09.00–18.00, Sat 09.00–13.00.*

Entel call centre Southeast corner of Plaza 6 de Agosto; *open daily 08.00–22.00.*

Laundry Laverap Calle Quijarro corner with Calle Matos; offers same-day laundry for 8Bs/kg; *open*

Mon–Sat 09.00–20.30.

Post office Calle Lanza #3. Also has a friendly postcard shop; *open Mon–Fri 08.00–20.00, Sat 09.00–12.00.*

Pharmacy San Francisco Calle Bolivar #702 & **Servicio Odontologico Latino** Calle Bolivar #702, 2/F, offer medical treatment.

WHAT TO SEE AND DO

La Casa de la Moneda (*Calle Ayacucho;* ✆ *622 2777;* e *moneda@cedro.pts.entelnet.bo; entrance 20Bs; open Tue–Sat 09.00–12.00 & 14.30–18.30, Sun 09.00–12.00*) This classic Potosí site, dating from 1572, remains the biggest draw, although the compulsory two-hour guided tour is rather dry. Nevertheless, for an appreciation of

---

THE BOLIVIAN FIGHT CLUB

The first rule of the Bolivian Fight Club is there are no rules. The second rule of the Bolivian Fight Club is there are *no rules*. The festival is *tinku*, a series of highly ritualised folk ceremonies held in Bolivia's rural Potosí region during the harsh Andean winter, which tourists seeking off-the-beaten-track destinations are now starting to discover.

Bolivia's *tinku* season, essentially a harvest festival celebrating the end of the agricultural year, is a colourful clash of Catholic and pagan beliefs, which draws on the rituals of Potosí's indigenous communities.

Five major festivals are held around Potosí annually, with smaller fiestas taking place in remote highland communities. In an agreement with the local community leaders, selected Potosí-based tour operators can now bring groups into the villages in return for a cut of every traveller's payment.

After two days of festivities in the villages, rival villagers come together on the third and final day to dance, drink and settle their differences from the past year with a good, old-fashioned, alcohol-fuelled punch-up.

The mother of all *tinkus* is held in Macha, a community of 4,000 people, sitting astride the Andes at 3,500m and a six-hour drive north of Potosí by bus. In Macha's central town square there is dancing, drinking and indigenous women in traditional garb patrolling the crowd with whips to administer a lash of community justice to anyone fighting dirty.

Dancing groups of villagers collide and end up brawling, while out in the fields villagers are sacrificing llamas in an offering to Pacahamama, the earth goddess.

'These are country people still living in the Old Testament,' says Hernan Tarqui, the Catholic priest of Macha. 'About 90% are Catholics, but the traditions of the ancient civilisations are still very strong in this region.

'The Church opposes *tinku*,' he adds. 'We want to see a coming-together of communities to share their blessings, but we can't change indigenous culture overnight.'

Potosí's halcyon days as centre of the silver trade, this remains the must-see tourist attraction in town. Hence expect large, slow-moving groups at times. The huge, grinning face of Bacchus looms over the courtyard and symbolises the greed that fuelled the mint in its heyday.

Museo y Convento de Santa Teresa (*Calle Santa Teresa #15;* ☎ *622 3847; entrance 21Bs; open daily 09.00–12.00 & 15.00–18.00*) Founded by Carmelite nuns, the compulsory two-hour guided tour offers an insight into the brutality of medieval life with a disturbing array of flagellation tools.

Museo y Convento de San Francisco (*Calle Tarija corner with Nogales;* ☎ *622 2539; open Mon–Fri 09.00–11.00 & 14.30–17.00, Sat 09.00–12.00*) Bolivia's oldest church has a fine collection of religious artworks. A 45-minute guided tour costs 15Bs.

Torre de la Compañía de Jesús (*Calle Ayacucho corner with Calle Bustillos;* ☎ *622 7408; entrance 10Bs; open Mon–Fri 08.30–12.00 & 14.00–18.00, Sat 09.00– 17.30, Sun 10.00–12.00*) There are great views to be had across the city from the viewing tower of this former Jesuit church. That is, of course, if you can face climbing the steps.

Iglesia de la Merced (Calle Hoyos corner with Calle Millares) and **Iglesia de Jerusalem** (Calle Camacho corner with Calle Oruro) are two churches covered by the same ticket, which is available to buy from either. Entrance 20Bs; open 10.00–12.00 & 15.00–18.00.

EXCURSIONS FROM POTOSÍ For a half-day trip out of Potosí, the hot springs of **Tarapaya** are a 30-minute drive towards Oruro with minibuses leaving from the Mercado Chuquimia (3Bs each way). The springs have traditionally been a popular bathing site since Inca times and a new 5Bs entrance fee ensures that facilities are, mercifully, far cleaner now than they ever used to be. Tour agencies in Potosí also arrange trips out to the springs, but beware bathing at the nearby Ojo del Inca, a deep-blue crater lake with high thermal temperatures, where the whirlpools and currents can be seriously treacherous.

SUCRE *Tel code: 04; altitude: 2,790m; population: 215,778*

Sucre, the 'White City', is so called because all the façades are painted white and offset by terracotta roof tiles. A colonial gem, the city has been listed by UNESCO as a World Heritage Site and today features some of the most striking and well-preserved architecture in Latin America. Indeed, many of the city's hotels are converted from old, colonial mansions while faded haciendas litter the surrounding countryside. Sucre is also of major historical significance, with the founding seat of the Bolivian independence movement's first post-independence parliament located off the main plaza.

As such, Sucre is one of Bolivia's most attractive cities with a large student population adding a lively edge to a place already very well equipped for tourism. Increasingly the city is also becoming popular as a destination for foreign students to take their Spanish classes before continuing journeys onward through Latin America. Indeed, it provides an attractive and good-value alternative to the likes of Cusco or Quito as a study centre.

THREE THINGS TO DO IN SUCRE

1 Explore the world of Bolivian textiles with a visit to the excellent Museo del Arte Indígena 'ASUR', or take an excursion out to the textile villages near Sucre to see the craftsmen working at first hand (page 196).

2 Go hiking or biking with guides from the Joy Ride Café, or just catch a film and enjoy a decent dinner at Sucre's favourite place to meet other travellers (page 194).

3 Treat your tastebuds to some excellent *salteñas* at El Paso de los Abuelos and delicious chocolates from Chocolates Para Ti, both of them the best in their respective trade in Bolivia (page 194).

Given the lower altitude, pleasant climate (best avoid the rainy season) and the fact that everything around town is easily accessible on foot, Sucre makes for an ideal base to start any journey through Bolivia. If you're visiting at a weekend, the traditional market of Tarabuco, a culturally rich and traditional trading post, is just a short drive away from the centre and held each Sunday.

Recently there has been a lot of talk about building a Jurassic Park-style theme park outside of Sucre to maximise potential from the cave paintings and dinosaur tracks found in the countryside out of town, and visited by the Dino Truck (page 197). Despite a lot of talk, however, plans have so far stalled and no decision has yet been taken on just how kitsch any final result could turn out to be.

HISTORY Sucre was the first city to be founded in Bolivia, the original site established on 29 September 1538, with the name La Plata. The name was changed to Sucre in 1825 out of respect for the first president of the new republic. Today it remains the official capital of Bolivia and the Supreme Court continues to sit here, bubt otherwise the majority of the legislative work has since been reloacted to La Paz.

Today the city remains the number one destination in Bolivia for fans of colonial and religious architecture. Its ten provinces celebrate their anniversary on 25 May to commemorate the 1809 revolution that led to the War of Independence.

GETTING THERE

By plane AeroSur have regular direct flight connections between Sucre and La Paz, while Lloyd Areo Boliviano usually flies via Cochabamba. For updated flight information and weather conditions, call Sucre's **Juana Azurduy de Padilla Airport** (↘ 645 1445), which is located 5km northwest of the centre. To get into town from the airport, bus #1 connects to the Mercado Central (1.20Bs), while a taxi costs 15Bs.

Correo del Sur (↘ 703 22050) also offer a limited number of places on their small mail service planes for flights to Potosí (US$75 for two people) leaving daily at 07.15. Tour agency **Sur Andes** (page 192) can also help arrange places on Correo del Sur flights to Uyuni (US$110 per person, space for up to four people). Flights leave daily at noon and the journey lasts one hour.

Sucre is notorious for its changeable weather and, as such, flights can often be cancelled or delayed due to freak climatic conditions, notably fog. Always be prepared for a long wait at the airport.

By bus Bus connections leave from the **bus terminal**, located 2km northeast of the centre on Calle Alfredo Ostria Gutierrez (↘ 644 1292). To get there, take bus #3 or #4 from the Mercado Central (1.20Bs), or a taxi (3.5Bs).

By train In 2004, Sucre's long-forgotten **train station** (↘ 646 1531) sparked back into life with a Ferrobus service on Mondays, Wednesdays and Fridays to Potosí via Yotala. The journey takes six hours (it's only three hours by bus), trains leave at 08.00 and the journey costs first/second class 35/25Bs each way, with return trains on Tuesdays, Thursdays and Saturdays (see Potosí, page 183).

GETTING AROUND Sucre, laid out according to a simple-to-navigate grid system, is easily explored on foot with only the cemetery (page 196) and Parque Bolívar (page 196) actually worthy of a bus or taxi ride. Within the city centre all buses cost 1.20Bs and taxis cost 3Bs. For a radio taxi, call **Taxi Sucre** (↘ 645 1333).

You can arrange **walking tours** of Sucre with a range of different circuits, including a colonial tour and a 1900s tour (US$10–12 per person for a guide with

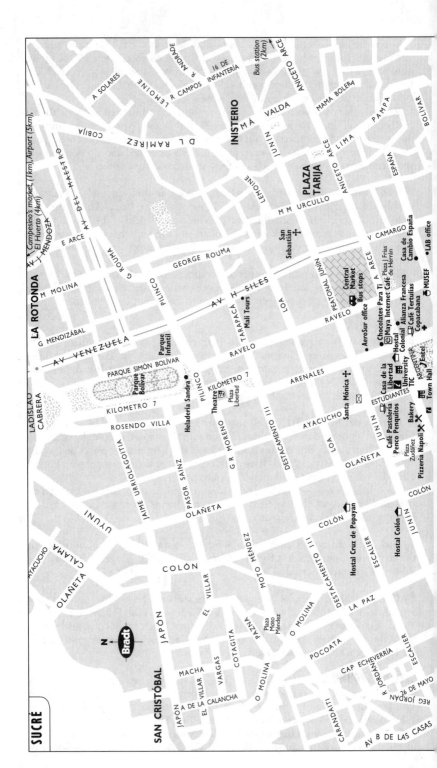

SUCRÉ

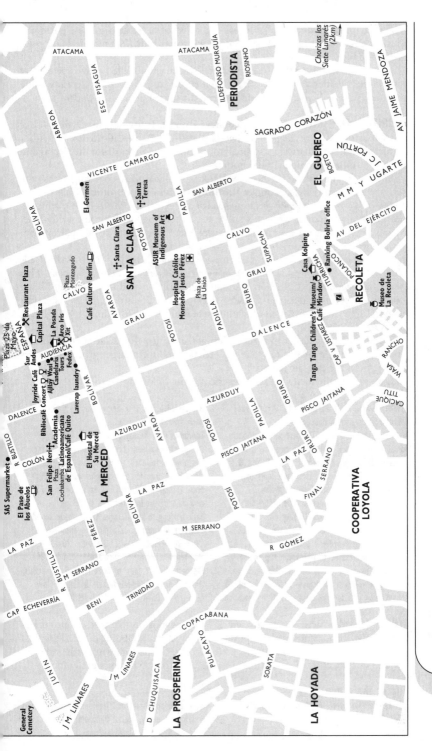

transport, plus entrance fees). To ask for a list of accredited guides, go to the tourism department on the first floor of the **town hall** (*Plaza 25 de Mayo #17;* ℑ *645 5983*).

Sucre is generally a safe place but watch your bag on Calle Junin, especially at lunchtime and after dusk. There have been reports of pickpockets operating along this busy stretch. If you have problems, call the tourist police (ℑ *648 0467*).

TOURIST INFORMATION The **University Tourist Information Office** (*Calle Estudiantes #35;* ℑ *644 7644; open Mon–Fri 08.30–12.00 & 14.30–18.30*), is a rather hit and miss affair. There are also small tourist information kiosks at the airport and the bus terminal, opening similar hours.

Sucre is home to one of the new Ranking Bolivia offices opening across the country. For better advice, contact **Ranking Bolivia**'s Sucre office (*Calle Ituricha #300;* ℑ *716 56346;* e *rankingbolivia@hotmail.com; open daily 08.30–19.30*), which is professionally run and, while it's still a new operation, staff are knowledgeable, enthusiastic and provide a far more sparky alternative to the traditional tourism authorities.

Alternatively, the travellers'·grapevine is centred on the **Joy Ride Café** (*Calle Nicolás Ortíz #14;* ℑ *642 5544;* e *info@joyridebol.com; www.joyridebol.com*) This gringo-run agency specialises in hikes and bike trips, including a one-day hiking jaunt in the countryside around Sucre ('A Day in the Country', US$19 based on a group of four) and a dirt-road, downhill bike tour ('95% Downhill', US$22 based on a group of three).

Top tip: solo travellers can meet each night at the Joy Ride Café at 18.30 for the 'meeting point'– a chance to make new friends and form larger groups for tours leaving from the café the next day.

Other recommended tour agencies include the following.

Candelaria Tours Calle Audiencia #1; ℑ 646 1661; e catur@mara.scr.entelnet.bo; www.candelariatours.com. The best agency in Sucre for community-based tourism, the company is run by Elizabeth Rojas Toro, the former head of ASUR & an expert on Bolivian textiles. Candelaria Tours focuses on working with the local Quechua Indian community & textile producers. *Open Mon–Sat 08.30–12.30 & 14.30–18.30.* They own the **Hacienda Candelaria**, located 22km from Tarabuco (page 199), where weekend packages cost from US$99 pp, based on 2 sharing, inc a trip to the market at Tarabuco. Visitors have the option to go trekking or volunteer to help with the work tasks & should bring gifts for the community. Accommodation is provided but is very simple with electricity, but no hot water, & basic meals.

Sur Andes Calle Nicolas Ortíz #6; ℑ 645 3212; e surandeses@hotmail.com; www.surandes.8m.com. This a well-established agency with a good reputation for trekking trips for all experience ranges. Typical prices include US$32 pp for a day's trekking to the cave paintings at Incamachay & US$50 pp for a day's trekking to the Maragua Crater. Prices include transport, bilingual guide, a picnic & entry fees. *Open Mon–Sat 09.00–12.30 & 14.3–20.00.*

Mali Tours Av Hernando Siles #813; ℑ 646 1843. The best place in town to book flight & bus tickets; the staff are very knowledgeable & helpful. *Open Mon–Fri 08.00–12.00 & 14.30–18.30.*

⌂ **WHERE TO STAY** Sucre is not only one of Bolivia's most livable cities, it also offers a great range of accommodation options for all budgets, including one real colonial gem (see box, *The author's favourite hotel*, page 193). The following properties are divided by budget category and listed in the order of the author's preference.

Top of the range

⌂ **Capital Plaza Hotel** (24 rooms) Plaza 25 de Mayo #29; ℑ 642 2999; f 645 3588; e cphotel@cotes.net.bo; www.capitalplazahotel.com. Traditionally Sucre's most luxurious property, Capital Plaza Hotel, comes with a sauna & well-appointed, spacious rooms but, despite its grandeur, this place is starting to feel a bit old-fashioned. The rooms are rather on the dark side, while the much-vaunted pool is a bit of a letdown when it actually comes to taking a dip. *Sgls/dbls US$45/55 with buffet b/fast; credit cards accepted.*

Mid-range

🏠 **Casa Kolping** (27 rooms) Pasaje Iturricha #265; ✆ 642 3812; f 643 5249; e sucre.bo@ casakolping.net; www.casaskolping.net/sucre/ sucre_eng.html. Opened in March 2005, Sucre's newest hotel is owned by a German Catholic organisation that aims to train local staff in the hospitality trade. The result is smart & modern, making it especially popular for business groups (they specialise in conferences). All rooms are comfortably appointed with cable TV & private bathrooms, plus there's a decent b/fast in the morning & free internet access in the computer room. *Sgls/dbls US$22/30 with b/fast; apts with a kitchenette US$40.*

🏠 **La Posada** (12 rooms) Calle Audiencia #92; ✆ 646 0101; f 691 3427; e laposadahostal@ entelnet.bo; www.laposadahostal.com. This 4-star

hotel, home to the best set lunch in Sucre (see page 194), also has some charming rooms set above its central colonial courtyard. The standard furnishings are tasteful while the 2-room attic suite (US$70) is ideal for families. *Sgls/dbls/tpls US$22/40/50 with b/fast.*

🏠 **Hostal Colonial** (17 rooms) Plaza 25 de Mayo #3; ✆ 645 4709; f 644 0311; e hoscol@ mara.scr.entelnet.bo. The sister property to Potosí's slighter grander Hostal Colonial (page 184), the colonial has similar facilities to the Capital Plaza (above), which it faces across Plaza 25 de Mayo, but at a lower rate. The rooms have less ambience but still offer cable TV & private bathrooms – all at a lower price. *Sgls/dbls/family rooms US$27/38/50 with b/fast.*

Budget

🏠 **Hostal Colon** (7 rooms) Calle Colon #220; ✆ 645 5823; e colon220@bolivia.com. At the budget end of the spectrum, the family-run Colon is set in an attractive, colonial house with simple but comfortable rooms & b/fast served in a living room. The owners speak English & German & are very welcoming. *Rooms with shared bathroom/dbl with cable TV & private bathroom 35/70Bs with b/fast.*

🏠 **Hostal Cruz de Popayan** (11 rooms) Calle Loa #881; ✆/f 644 0889; e popayan@ boliviahostels.com; www.boliviahostels.com. Another friendly budget option with simple rooms (a little dark, maybe, but all ensuite) set around a colonial courtyard. The owner, Abad Rios, also runs the website www.boliviahostels.com, an association of hoteliers with a network of rooms for budget travellers across Bolivia. *Sgls/dbls/tpls $16/21/27 with b/fast.*

Outside Sucre For a weekend break, **Hacienda Las Siete Cascadas** (8 rooms) is located 8km outside of Sucre in the pueblo of Katalla. This colonial hacienda, dating from 1860, has been completely refurbished into a weekend country retreat with a swimming pool, rustic rooms and an in-house restaurant. The terrace is a great suntrap and popular with families. Reservations are made directly through the owner, Carmen Rosa, in Sucre (*Calle Ecuador #349, Bario Petrolero;* ✆ *646 0603;* e *las7cascadas@andeanjewels.com*). A two-day, one-night package costs US$36 per

Potosí and Sucre SUCRE

8

193

person on a full-board basis, including transport (children under 12 pay 50%). Camping is also available (12Bs per person) in the grounds, including use of a toilet block with hot showers.

✕ WHERE TO EAT

✕ **La Posada** Calle Audiencia #92; ☎ 646 0101. The best set lunch in Sucre (20Bs) is served in a garden courtyard setting with a tranquil ambience & a fresh salad bar. Service is attentive & the choice of mains (25Bs) is comprehensive but, best of all, it's all washed down with some delicious homemade lemonade. *Open Mon–Sat 07.00–22.30, Sun 07.00–15.00.*

✕ **Restaurant Plaza** Plaza 25 de Mayo #34; ☎ 645 5843. Aim for a table on the balcony overlooking the plaza to make the most of your 5-course set lunch (18Bs) with a view. It's a nice spot overall & the menu also takes in pasta (20Bs) & fish (30Bs) mains, but it's a shame about the terminally slow service. *Open daily 11.30–14.30 & 18.00–22.00.*

✕ **El Germen** Calle San Alberto #231; no tel. A German-owned restaurant, it has a strong vegetarian influence but also offers dishes for carnivores as well as German-style pastries. There's a 12Bs set lunch with a daily changing menu while vegetarian mains range 15/20Bs. *Open Mon–Sat 08.00–22.00.*

✕ **Napoli Pizzeria** Calle Argentina #85; ☎ 645 2707. Sucre's best pizza joint has a wood-fired oven & a good range of flavours with prices from large/small 14/25Bs. *Open Mon–Sat 11.00–22.00.*

✕ **Arco Iris** Calle Bolivar #567; ☎ 642 3985. An upmarket Swiss eatery with good-quality food (mains around 30Bs), this place has occasional live music. *Open Wed–Mon 18.00–22.00; credit cards accepted.*

✕ **El Huerto** Calle Ladislao Cabrera #86; ☎ 645 1538. Sucre's best-known upmarket eatery is located out of town on the airport road with above-average prices but quality to match. It's a great spot on a sunny day for lunch. *Open Thu–Sun 11.00–15.00 & 18.30–22.00.*

Cafés and snacks For more of a snack, Sucre's most famous old café is **Café Tertulias** (*Plaza 25 de Mayo #58;* ☎ *645 1735; open Thu–Tue 10.00–midnight*), where thinkers and artists have traditionally gathered to chew the fat over coffee (5Bs) or the choice of three set lunches (20Bs). **Café Pastelería Penco Penquitos** (*Calle Arenales #108;* ☎ *644 3946; open daily 07.30–23.00*), is a useful place to know for a coffee stop (5Bs) and a piece of lemon pie (3Bs). They also offer a range of delicious cakes to eat in or take away, plus ice creams (10–16Bs). Look out for the slightly psychedelic, magic mushroom-inspired interior design. For a snack on the run, there's a fantastic **bakery** at Calle Argentina #53 – no name, no telephone but great cakes, *empañadas* and pastries. **Café Mirador at** Museo de Niños Tanga Tanga (☎ *643 3038; open Tue–Sun 10.00–dusk*) is very laid-back – caffeine addicts can pull up a deckchair for the most scenic coffee (5Bs) in Sucre. Another little gem is **El Paso de los Abuelos** (*Calle Bustillos #216;* ☎ *645 5173*), which has been serving the best *salteñas* in Sucre for over 20 years. In meat or chicken varieties (3Bs each), they come stuffed with an olive and a tiny egg, and are reputed to be amongst the finest Bolivia has to offer for *salteña* purists. Another hidden gem is **Chorizos Los Siete Lunares** (*Av Manco Kapac#247;* ☎ *646 1297*), which is famous throughout Bolivia for serving the best *chorizo* (sausages) in the country.

Finally, if you're self-catering (and you can be if staying at Hostal Colon, page 193), the **SAS Supermarket** (*Calle Bustillos #131,* ☎ *645 5899*) opens Mon–Sat 08.00–20.00. The **central market**, located on Calle Ravelo, next to San Francisco church, has a huge range of fresh produce and a great section towards the back devoted to fresh fruit juices and salads. Those with a sweet tooth should head to the left-hand corner of the hall, where you can find homemade jams, huge gateaux and more of Sucre's famous local chocolate.

ENTERTAINMENT AND NIGHTLIFE

Joy Ride Café Calle Nicolás Ortíz #14; ☎ 642 5544; e info@joyridebol.com; www.joyridebol.com.

Does breakfasts (14–20Bs, until 11.00) and lunches (mains 18–25Bs, panini 10–12Bs, 11.00–17.00), but it really comes into its own after dark when just about every traveller in town, plus a decent smattering of locals, head for this buzzy, Dutch-run bar. Beers by the glass/tankard 8/15Bs, house cocktails (10–12Bs) and international beers (25–30Bs) flow in abundance. Films are screened most nights in the upstairs lounge, complete with leather sofas and a separate bar. *Open 07.30–late, weekends 09.00 opening.*

Xit Calle Audiencia #98; ☎ 703 26076. The latest bar opening in town, has an emphasis on cool sounds and live music, plus beers and snacks.

Bibliocafé Concert and Bibliocafe Calle Nicolás Ortíz #42 & #50; ☎ 644 7574. Both popular student bars under the same management. The former is a live music venue with meals (Bolivian mains 15Bs, pastas 20Bs), while the latter is more of a café cum bar for drinks, coffees and

lunches (15–20Bs, vegetarian mains 15Bs). *Open daily 11.30–late.*

Café Kultur Berlín Calle Avaroa #326; ☎ 645 2091. Part of the Instituto Cultural Boliviano Alemán cultural centre, this café bar offers German beers (20Bs), sandwiches (5–10Bs) and mains (10Bs). Every Thu night they screen films with a changing programme of world cinema. *Open Mon–Fri 09.30–12.30 & 15.00–21.00, Sat 10.00–12.00.*

Alianza Francesa Calle Aniceto Arce #35; ☎/f 645 3599; e dirsucre@afbolivia.org. Sucre's French cultural centre has a programme of events for local Francophiles based around its library, the Mediatheque. Its French-style restaurant, La Taverne (☎ 728 81863), opens Mon–Fri 18.00–23.30 for a cultured taste of France. *Open Mon–Fri 09.30–12.30 & 15.00–19.30, Sat 10.00–12.00.*

SHOPPING

Chocolates Para Ti Calle Arenales #7; ☎ 645 4260; www.chocolates-para-ti.com. The shopfront for the best chocolate in Sucre, probably in all of Bolivia, serves to confirm that Sucre is Bolivia's chocolate capital. Gift packs and individual selections with prices from 5Bs for a small, loose pack, or 60Bs per kilo. *Open Mon–Sat 08.30–20.30.*

Ajllay Wasi Calle Audiencia #17; ☎ 646 1661. Attached to Candelaria Tours (page 192) next door, this craft shop showcases the traditional Bolivian textiles from the Macha, Pocoata, Jalq'a, Tarabuco and Candelaria regions. Better still, your purchase ensures funds go directly into the hands of local artisans. *Open Mon–Sat 09.00–12.30 & 15.00–19.30.*

OTHER PRACTICALITIES

Academia Latinoamericana de Español (*Calle Dalence #109;* ☎ *646 0537;* e *latinosucre@cotes.net.bo; www.latinoschools.com*) A popular language school for international students to start their Spanish tuition, this language academy helps to arrange homestays with local families and volunteer work with local charity projects in addition to the actual classes (Mon–Fri 08.15–12.15 and 14.30–18.30). Downstairs, they also run **Café Quito**, a café bar for students and travellers, which offers sandwiches (5–10Bs) and mains (20Bs), but suffers from rather erratic opening hours.

You can arrange classes over the internet from overseas for convenience but, once you're in Sucre, you may find the school's management are more willing to negotiate on rates for classes, while homestays can be arranged direct to cut out the middle man.

AeroSur Office Calle Arenales #31; ☎ 646 0737. *Open Mon–Fri 08.30–12.30 & 14.30–18.30, Sat 09.00–12.00.*

Casa de Cambio España Calle España #134; ☎ 643 2368. Changes currency. *Open Mon–Fri 08.30–12.30 & 14.30–18.30, Sat 08.30–12.30.*

Entel call centre Plaza 25 de Mayo. *Open daily 07.30–22.30.*

Fedex Calle Audiencia #89; ☎ 644 6479; www.fedex.com.bo. *Open Mon–Fri 09.00–20.00.*

Hospital Monseñor Jesus Perez Calle Calvo #381;

☎ 642 2524 for emergencies.

Laundry Laverap Calle Bolivar #671; ☎ 642 4501. A service wash & dry costs 20Bs. *Open Mon–Sat 08.00–20.00.*

Lloyd Aéreo Boliviano (LAB) office Calle España #105; ☎ 691 3182. *Open Mon–Fri 08.30–12.30 & 14.30–18.30, Sat 08.30–12.30.*

Maya Internet Café Calle Arenales has internet access from 2.50Bs/hr. *Open daily 08.00–23.00.*

Pharmacy Copacabana Plaza 25 de Mayo #42; ☎ 646 1141. *Open 24hr.*

Post office Calle Ayacucho corner with Calle Junín; ☎ 645 4960. Once you've posted your parcel, you can pay 2Bs for a panoramic view over Sucre from the roof terrace. Open Mon–Fri 08.30–20.00, Sat 08.30–16.00, Sun 09.00–12.00.

WHAT TO SEE AND DO

Museo del Arte Indigena 'ASUR' (*Calle San Alberto #413;* ☎ *645 3841;* e *asur@ entelnet.bo; www.bolivianet.com/asur/; open Mon–Fri 08.30–12.00 & 14.30–18.00, Sat 09.30–12.00 & 14.30–18.00; entrance 16Bs*) Run by the non-profit Indigenous Art Renaissance Programme, Sucre's most rewarding museum features a series of rooms examining the area's Jalq'a and Tarabuco textile heritage. Upstairs local craftspeople showcase their weaving skills, while downstairs the museum shop has articles for sale, including 450Bs for a hand-woven shawl and 170Bs for a woven wallet. ASUR pays a fixed fee to local communities to sell their textiles in the shop.

Museo de Niños Tanga Tanga (*Pasaje Iturricha #281;* ☎ *644 0299; enquiries via Fundación Cultural Quipus in La Paz* ☎ *02 244 4196; www.quipusbolivia.org; open Tue–Sun 09.00–12.00 & 14.30–18.00; entrance adult/child 8/5Bs*) An educational museum and play garden, this place is for children aged six to 12 years to help foster understanding of the world around them. The museum badly needs more funding to maintain its valuable programme of events for local school groups. The grounds include the superbly chilled-out Café Mirador (see *Where to eat*, page 194).

Museo Nacional de Etnografía y Folklore (MUSEF) (*Calle España, no tel; open Mon–Sat 09.30–12.30 & 15.00–19.00, Sun 09.30–12.30; free entrance*) Opened in February 2004 as part of a cultural association with the Casa de la Libertad (see below), Sucre's newest museum is housed in the former colonial bank building. It hosts a rotating series of temporary exhibitions based around indigenous culture, including a display of masks from the Oruro carnival (page 165).

La Casa de la Libertad (*Plaza 25 de Mayo #1;* ☎ *645 4200; open Mon–Sat 09.15–11.45 & 14.45–17.45, Sun 09.15–11.45; free entrance but guided tours in English cost 10Bs*) The most important historical building in Bolivia, the old Legislative Palace, today known as the Casa de la Libertad, is the seat of the founding of the modern Bolivian nation. The building includes the former Jesuit private chapel and the great hall of the university, where the assembly that deliberated and proclaimed the independence of Bolivia met on 6 August 1825. Today there's a room dedicated to Mariscal Sucre, founder of the modern nation, while the president's room includes a portrait of Lidia Gueiler Tejada, Bolivia's only (so far) female president (1979–80).

Located slightly away from the centre, both the **General Cemetery** and **Simón Bolívar Park** are popular escapes for some fresh air, green space and a chance for contemplation. The former (☎ *645 1075, open daily 08.00–11.30 & 14.00–17.30*), is at the end of Calle Linares and, while entrance is free, a guide for 10Bs will explain the history behind one of Bolivia's oldest and best-kept cemeteries. The latter, dating from the 18th century, is popular with families, houses a replica of the Eiffel Tower and, best of all, is home to **Heladería Sandra**, Sucre's favourite ice-cream parlour, located in the park's northwest corner opposite the Supreme Court. Try the *tumbo* flavour ice cream (3Bs).

EXCURSIONS FROM SUCRE

Castillo de la Glorieta (☎ *645 4138*) Located 5km south of Sucre on the Potosí road, this 19th-century estate was closed for refurbishment at the time of writing.

Plans are afoot to restore the property, which mixes European and Moorish styles of architecture, and to build a tourist train circuit around the estate. When it finally reopens, visits are scheduled daily 08.30–12.00 and 13.30–17.30. To get there, take bus #4 or #12 from the Mercado Central (1.20Bs), 10Bs by taxi.

The Cal Orcko Dinosaur Tracks are visited by the unmistakable, bright red Dino-Truck (*operated by Abbey Path, ☎ 645 1863; www.abbeypath.com*). The truck picks up visitors outside the cathedral three times a day from Monday to Saturday at 09.30, 12.00 and 14.30 for the two-and-a-half hour round-trip (25Bs) with English commentary.

Discovered in 1994 at the Fancesa limestone quarry on Sucre's northern outskirts, the dinosaur tracks are reputed to be the world's largest palaeontological site with around 5,000 footprints from 320 types of dinosaur. The prints measure up to 80cm and have been tilted to 65°. One set is thought to belong to a young iguanodon about 10m long and 5m tall. Another has the characteristics of a tyrannosaurus. Due to the erosion of the soft limestone, new tracks are being revealed every day.

THE DINOSAUR TRAIL

John Pilkington

Sixty-eight million years ago, when tyrannosauri and their cousins were at large in the Andes, a certain type of mudstone in what is now Bolivia's Chuquisaca province had the consistency of wet cement. The creatures left deep footprints in these strata, which then hardened and were uplifted, tilted and sometimes overlain by limestone. Amazingly, a few of these impressions have survived. Some remarkable tracks of tyrannosauri and iguanodon were exposed a few years ago during quarrying at the Fancesa cement works on the outskirts of Sucre. The walk described here gives you the opportunity to see similar tracks in a natural setting, the highlight of a four- or five-day circuit at an altitude of between 2,500m and 3,700m, which also takes in the best scenery of the Cordillera de los Frailes.

It may be cool and breezy on the Chataquila ridge and the crater rim, but the rest of the hike will be warm to hot. Take shorts and sneakers for wading the Pilcomayo. Snacks and soft drinks are available at Talula thermal baths, but otherwise you'll have to carry your own supplies. Fill water bottles in Sucre for exploring the Chataquila ridge.

After the dusty journey from Sucre, the 3,700m Chataquila ridge will come as a relief, and your first inclination may be to explore it, starting with the dramatic outcrops visible to the north. There's no water on the ridge, but with a good supply in your rucksack it offers wonderful walking and scrambling. Water is available 20 minutes down the Ravelo Valley path.

To get a taste of the ridge, start from the Capilla de la Virgen and walk northwest along the road for 500m. Just before it starts to descend head off right over bare rock. This soon turns into a rocky path, which after five minutes joins a broader track coming up from the left. Follow this up and then along the ridge, passing to the left of some outcrops, to the imposing boulders which form the summit of Cerro Torrecilla (3,842m). Beyond here requires serious commitment and ideally a guide, who, amongst other things, will be able to take you to the rock paintings at Incamachay, three to four hours north of the road.

When you're ready to descend, return to the chapel and with your back to Sucre pace out 75m along the road. Here on the left you'll find a roadside notch, marking the beginning of a fabulous Inca road into the Ravelo Valley beyond.

The path drops steeply, and after 20 minutes crosses a stream of good drinking water before commencing an airy traverse of the valley side. The next kilometre is breathtaking: a finely engineered Inca road offering views of the Ravelo Valley and, to the southwest, the Pilcomayo Gorge. On this section you'll also begin to appreciate the striking bowl of the Cráter de Maragua, a swirling pattern of rock strata rising to 3,400m.

Unfortunately in two places the Inca road has been obliterated by landslides, the result of serious soil erosion further down the valley. To avoid the first, 40 minutes after crossing the stream, turn right up a red rocky path. Ten minutes later do the same again. Shortly after the second landslide you'll come to a saddle, and here take the right-hand path, which in half an hour will bring you to a concrete water channel – one of two serving Sucre. Turn right along a track to the main road, then follow this left for 20 minutes to the village of Chaunaca, where a left fork will take you in five minutes to a second left turning which leads to the Río Ravelo and good riverside camping.

If the water is low, stepping stones make for an easy crossing; otherwise wade the river and follow the jeep track which climbs steadily up the opposite valley side. After 90 minutes you'll come to a stream called Quebrada Charco Khea; here a path to the left offers a small short cut. In a further 90 minutes the jeep track will bring you to the centre of the crater and the village of the same name. Maragua sees few visitors and its people are shy rather than unfriendly; but you may find the church square mysteriously empties at your approach.

A further 30m past the church, turn right and in five minutes you'll come to the village school. This has been considerably expanded with international aid. Your next goal is Sapal Khochi, a 3,275m notch on the southwestern crater rim, distinguished by a couple of eucalyptus trees (the right-hand of two such notches). This is a stiff 90-minute climb away. To begin, descend left of the school to a stream, and follow this for ten minutes until, 100m before a windpump, the clear path to Sapal Khochi takes off to the right. Halfway up the hill, the narrow valley forks. Take the right-hand branch, and at the top of this valley keep left of the trees and follow the curving path left until it levels out into a wheat field. Now hop over the rocks to your right for a panoramic view to the Pilcomayo Gorge and beyond. To find the route down, cast about on the escarpment for a notch. The clear path first descends to the right, then doubles back past a muddy spring to a prominent stone corral, reached in ten minutes. Turn right here to a second corral, marked by two eucalyptus trees, then follow the clear but steep path which accompanies a buried water supply pipe. An hour or so from the top, you'll find yourself descending very steeply to Quebrada Niñumayu, a tributary of the Pilcomayo and once the home of at least six dinosaurs.

We know this because a short distance upstream from the water pipe crossing, at the far end of a smooth mudstone slab, they have left behind six clear sets of tracks. The 30cm prints have been identified by Bolivia's National Museum of Natural History as belonging to a group of saurornithoids, one of the smaller members of the dinosaur family, which like most creatures of that era, mysteriously died out some 65 million years ago. Although not as large or numerous as those in the Fancesa quarry near Sucre, these tracks are nevertheless impressive, and only their isolation has prevented them from becoming more widely known. From underneath the pipe crossing, climb a small rock band across the riverbed and you'll find them 200m upstream on the left.

From upstream and just downstream of the pipe crossing two paths lead up the hillside, joining and then levelling out before continuing in broad sweeps through wheat fields, across a small valley and past farms. After something over an hour the path begins its descent into the Pilcomayo Gorge, passing to the right of a red mud compound and then dropping steeply among red and white hillocks to the abandoned settlement of Humaca. From the dinosaur tracks to Humaca is two hours. At Humaca you can explore the ghostly red-mud ruins, seek out the remains of the Candelaría chapel, or simply bask in the shade of one of the half-dozen palm trees which grace this once prosperous hacienda.

At first sight it may seem as if you have to cross the Pilcomayo to progress downstream; but if you wade through the shallows on the near bank you'll find footholds which carry you safely across the foot of the cliff, just on the waterline. From here it's a simple walk across sand and pebbles until, 400m before the clearly visible thermal baths of Talula, the river once again makes progress impossible. On your left here a steep path offers an alternative over the 40m cliff (don't be tempted to take the route across the cliff face). From joining the Río Pilcomayo to the thermal baths takes an hour.

After your exertions these baths will be pure delight. There are three pools, ranging from hot to very hot (45°C), and for the sum of 15Bs you can lounge in them all day. At weekends the baths are popular with day trippers from Sucre; but from Monday to Thursday you'll have the place virtually to yourself. A vendor sells soft drinks and basic supplies. To the right of the bathhouse is a rough room which, for a small payment, can be rented overnight.

From Talula a road winds back to Sucre, 28km distant, first climbing steeply to the straggling village of Purunkila (4km), then passing through fertile farmland to Quila Quila, where on the right-hand side a shop sells basic supplies. Although now almost a ghost village, Quila Quila has an imposing church suggesting a more distinguished past; and indeed efforts are being made to revive the settlement as a centre for the surrounding valleys, with a health post and a fine new school. It's 9km, or three hours' walking, from Talula. Traffic on this section is seen only at weekends.

Another 90 minutes will bring you to the 3,100m Paso Obispo, from where two routes descend to the Río Cachi Mayu. The southern path leaves the road at a left-hand bend five minutes beyond the pass, and crosses a small saddle before dropping steadily through fertile farmland to the river, reached in 90 minutes. From here a road winds over a low sierra to the colonial village of Yotala. You may well be offered a lift; otherwise it's just an hour on foot. Yotala is 16km south of Sucre on the road to Potosí. Micros are plentiful.

If you prefer to try your chances on the more northerly route taken by the road from Talula, continue along it to the flower-growing village of Chullchuta (45 minutes). From here the road descends steeply to the river where, on the opposite bank, a stall serves refreshments to travellers drying out their shoes (there's no bridge). From the river it's just 11km to Sucre. The first 4km are steeply uphill, but there's more traffic on this stretch and you'll have every chance of a lift.

TARABUCO

Located two hours or 65km from Sucre, Tarabuco comes alive for its weekly Sunday morning market and for its colourful, annual *Pujllay* festival (held on the third Sunday of March), both of which are now well established on the tourist circuit. The festival attracts 3,500 people annually and celebrates the battle of Jumbate, when locals defeated the Spanish on 12 March 1816.

Founded in 1578, Tarabuco is now a favourite excursion from Sucre for travellers seeking to stock up on textiles and artisan crafts at the vibrant market. Hence, in recent years, the prices have risen sharply and vendors have become wise to the ways of greenback-carrying tourists. It's worth knowing, however, that many artisans sell their wares during the week in Sucre anyway, but the market certainly makes for a highly colourful experience.

For a break from the shopping spree, visit the **Inca Pallay** artisan centre and café (☎ 646 1936; e incapallay@alamo.entelnet.bo; open Sun 09.00–12.00), to the

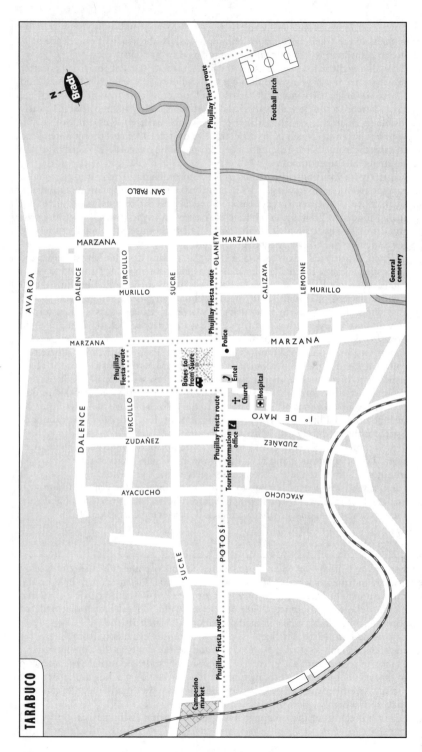

TARABUCO

- Campesino market
- Phujillay Fiesta route
- SUCRE
- POTOSÍ
- AYACUCHO
- ZUDAÑEZ
- Tourist information office
- Phujillay Fiesta route
- DALENCE
- URCULLO
- MARZANA
- AVAROA
- MURILLO
- DALENCE
- MURILLO
- SUCRE
- MARZANA
- SAN PABLO
- Phujillay Fiesta route
- OLANETA
- Buses to/from Sucre
- Police
- Entel
- Church
- Hospital
- 1º DE MAYO
- ZUDAÑEZ
- AYACUCHO
- MARZANA
- CALIZAYA
- LEMOINE
- MURILLO
- Phujillay Fiesta route
- Football pitch
- General cemetery
- N
- Bradt

northeast of the central square, where all purchases put money directly in the hands of the local community artisans.

To get there, take any bus from Avenida de las Americas in Sucre's Bario Petrolero district early on Sunday morning (7Bs), or flag down a taxi (15Bs).

GETTING OFF THE BEATEN TRACK AROUND SUCRE

The area around Sucre is home to several rustic but charming villages, famous for their production of textiles, notably Candelaría, Macha, Pocata and Ravelo. They are connected by slow-running buses and you can buy wares direct from the villagers, many of whom regularly come to Sucre to ply their goods.

On the road to Padilla, a turn-off heading north runs 20km to Villa Serrano, a remote village best known as the home of the famous Bolivian musician Mauro Nuñez. His birthday is marked by a low-key but compelling festival, which brings music to the village each year from 28–30 December.

Viscacha

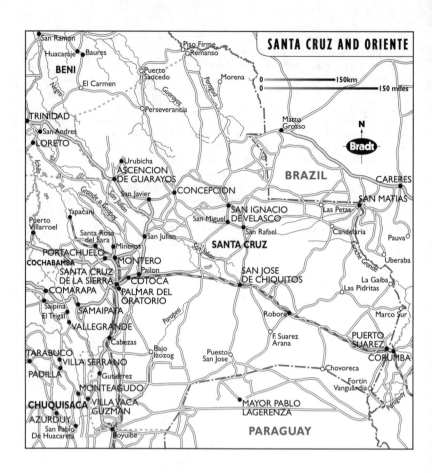

SANTA CRUZ AND ORIENTE

9

Santa Cruz and the Oriente

SANTA CRUZ *Tel code: 03; altitude: 417m; population: 1,1356,00*

Santa Cruz de la Sierra, capital of Santa Cruz Department, is the economic powerhouse of contemporary Bolivia, and the de facto arch-rival to its administrative capital, La Paz. Currently it is also Bolivia's largest city, representing 34% of the country's territory – and growing fast.

The city is a curious mix of the flash, the superficial and the uniquely Latino. It holds more than 400 beauty pageants per year, generates 38% of Bolivia's taxes and is home to the biggest domestic companies and headquarters for the transnational gas and oil corporations.

In recent years Santa Cruz has become the crucible for the country's autonomy movement, with locals, or *cambas* as they are called, seeking to distance themselves from the strikes and conflicts of the Altiplano. Indeed, given that Brazil borders Santa Cruz Department to the east, some residents prefer to align themselves politically with their cross-border neighbours. The Brazilian influence is also strongly reflected in the nightlife, with the city's sultry, tropical nights ideal for cool cocktails and hot discos. By day it's also sweltering with an average annual temperature of 24.7°C and an average relative humidity of 66%.

During carnival season in February, the whole of Santa Cruz grinds to a shuddering halt with street parades, parties and hedonism de rigueur. The *cambas* are as renowned for their love of fiestas as they are for failing to turn up to work after a hard night on the sauce.

Santa Cruz has expanded massively in recent years with money pouring into the city. Indeed, the city now accounts for 90% of Bolivia's industry, 60% of its

SIX THINGS TO DO IN SANTA CRUZ

1 Enjoy a taste of big-city living Bolivian style along Avenida San Martín and Avenida Monseñor Rivero (page 210).

2 Pull up a chair in a cafe, order a coffee and indulge in the city's favourite sport of people-watching from your pavement vantage point in the El Cristo district (page 209).

3 Explore the urban culture with a visit to one of the city's museums or catch an exhibition at the Casa de la Cultura Raúl Otero Reich (page 212).

4 Enjoy a slap-up meal at one of the city's upmarket eateries then head for cocktails and late-night revelry in the cool Equipetrol district (page 210).

5 Go shopping for bargains at one of the fashionable boutiques dotted around the city (page 211).

6 Escape the bustle of the city with a visit to the excellent wildlife centre Biocentro Guembe or a walk in the gardens at the tranquil Parque Ecológico Yvaga Guaza (page 212), both a short excursion from the downtown area.

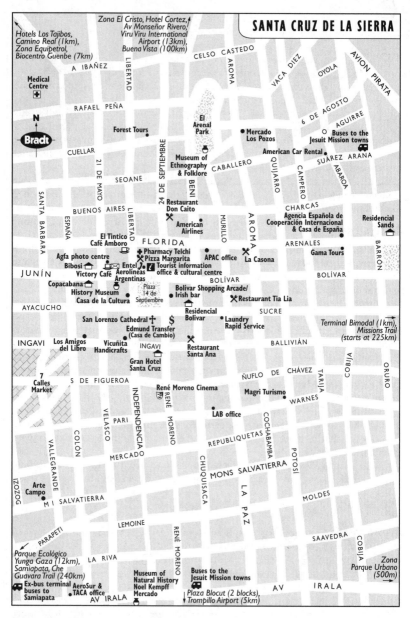

SANTA CRUZ DE LA SIERRA

Zona El Cristo, Hotel Cortez,
Av Monseñor Rivero,
Viru Viru International
Airport (13km),
Buena Vista (100km)

Hotels Los Tajibos,
Camino Real (1km),
Zona Equipetrol,
Biocentro Guembe (7km)

CELSO CASTEDO

A IBAÑEZ
LIBERTAD
AROMA
VACA DIEZ
OYOLA
AVION PIRATA

Medical
Centre

RAFAEL PEÑA
6 DE AGOSTO
AGUIRRE

N

Bradt

Forest Tours

El
Arenal
Park

Mercado
Los Pozos

O Buses to the
Jesuit Mission towns

CUELLAR
21 DE MAYO
24 DE SEPTIEMBRE
American Car Rental

SUÁREZ ARANA
SEOANE
Museum of
Ethnography
& Folklore
CABALLERO
QUIJARRO
CAMPERO
ABAROA

BENI
SANTA BARBARA
BUENOS AIRES
LIBERTAD
Restaurant
Don Caito
MURILLO
AROMA
CHARCAS

ESPAÑA
American
Airlines
Agencia Española de
Cooperación Internacional
& Casa de España
Residencial
Sands

El Tintico
Café Amboro
FLORIDA
ARENALES
Gama Tours
BARRÓN

Agfa photo centre
Pharmacy Telchi
Pizza Margarita
APAC office
La Casona

Bibosi
Entel
Tourist information
office & cultural centre

JUNÍN
Victory Café
Aerolíneas
Argentinas
BOLÍVAR
BOLÍVAR

Copacabana
History Museum
Casa de la Cultura
Plaza
14 de
Septiembre
Bolívar Shopping Arcade/
Irish bar
Restaurant Tia Lia

AYACUCHO
Residencial
Bolívar
SUCRE

San Lorenzo Cathedral
$
Laundry
Rapid Service
Terminal Bimodal (1km),
Missions Trail
(starts at 225km)

Edmund Transfer
(Casa de Cambio)

INGAVI
Los Amigos
del Libro
Vicuñita
Handicrafts
INGAVI
Restaurant
Santa Ana
BALLIVIÁN

Gran Hotel
Santa Cruz

7
Calles
Market
S DE FIGUEROA
René Moreno Cinema
ÑUFLO DE CHÁVEZ
TARIJA
COBIJA
ORURO

INDEPENDENCIA
RENÉ
Magri Turismo
WARNES

VELASCO
PARI
MORENO
LAB office
COCHABAMBA

COLÓN
MERCADO
REPUBLIQUETAS
POTOSÍ

VALLEGRANDE
CHUQUISACA
MONS SALVATIERRA

IZOZOG
Arte
Campo
M I SALVATIERRA
LA PAZ
MOLDES

LEMOINE
RENÉ MORENO
SAAVEDRA
COBIJA
Zona
Parque Urbano
(500m)

PARAPETI
Parque Ecológico
Yunga Gaza (12km),
Samaipata, Che
Guavara Trail (240km)
LA RIVA

Ex-bus terminal
buses to
Samaipata
AeroSur &
TACA office
Museum of
Natural History
Noel Kempff
Mercado
Buses to the
Jesuit Mission towns
AV IRALA

AV IRALA
Plaza Blocut (2 blocks),
Trompillo Airport (5km)

oil wells and more than 50% of its GDP, fuelling calls for autonomy. While the infrastructure and the breadth of facilities for tourists have boomed, crime rates have also hiked sharply. Little of the crime is directed towards tourists per se but, nonetheless, you should try to be a bit more aware of your belongings and which district you're walking around than in certain other Bolivian cities. After dark it's best to stay in the main downtown area and some of the more popular inner suburbs.

While the city itself has attractions worthy of a day or two's visit, the main attraction is striking out into the rural Oriente region to visit Samaipata (page 213), Amboro National Park (page 220) and the Jesuit Missions (page 224).

HISTORY Santa Cruz has undergone an enormous transformation in recent years – from tropical backwater to the engine of the Bolivian economy. Just 40 years ago, only the main square was paved and industry almost exclusively devoted to the area's long tradition of soya farming and cattle rearing.

That all changed when, in the 1950s, new road and rail links to Brazil and across Bolivia revived Santa Cruz's fortunes and ended its rural isolation. In recent years foreign investment in the oil and gas industries has brought a new prosperity to the city, but venture beyond the outer suburbs and the countryside soon returns to its former agricultural bias.

Founded in 1561 by Capitan Ñuflo de Chavez, the sixth city to be founded in Bolivia, the department's 15 provinces celebrate their anniversary on 24 September to mark the 1810 revolution.

GETTING THERE
By plane **Viru Viru International Airport** (✆ *385 2400*), located 18km from downtown Santa Cruz, is served by international carriers American Airlines, Aerolineas Argentinas and Varig, plus the local airlines Lloyd Aero Boliviano, AeroSur and TACA. There's a 15/25Bs airport tax payable on domestic/international flights.

Airport facilities include an ATM, Entel call centre, newsstand, gift shops and an information desk, located by arrivals, for hotel reservations. A baggage-storage office charges 40Bs for keeping luggage. There's a Subway café and a Café Brasil coffee shop, the latter better value and serving sandwiches, breakfasts and coffee for around 20/15/8Bs respectively. Internet access (a hefty 15Bs per hour) is available from the L'Alianxa tour agency office by arrivals, but free wi-fi internet has now been installed throughout the airport for laptop-toting travellers.

El Tropillo Airport (*Av Capitan Horacio Vazquez;* ✆ *352 6600*) is located on the second ring (see *Getting around*, page 206) and served by a complex series of smaller, mainly domestic, flights, notably those handled by Amazonas (page 212), whose office is located within the airport. Santa Cruz's second airport has few terminal-based facilities.

Santa Cruz now has connections to Brazil with Latin America's first ever 'low-cost' airline carrier, GOL Linhas Aereas Inteligentes. Flights to and from CampeGrande, in the Brazilian State of Mato Grosso do Sul started in November 2005. For more information see the website (*www.voegol.com.br*).

Airport transfers From Viru Viru International Airport, minibus #135 departs every 20 minutes from outside the terminal and heads for El Trompillo airport via the statue of Christ the Redeemer. Minibuses run 05.30–21.30 and cost 5Bs, after which a taxi downtown costs 40Bs. From El Tropillo, a taxi downtown costs 15Bs.

By train Trains depart from the **Terminal Bimodal** (*Av Brasil corner with Av Tres Pasos, between the third & fourth rings;* ✆ *348 8482*), where the major bus departures also leave from.

The rail company, **Ferroviara Oriental** (✆ *338 7300*), runs four major departures in descending order of comfort for travellers as follows:

🚆 **FerroBus** departs for Quijarro via San Jose de Chiquitos on Tue, Thu & Sun at 19.30. A bed/reclining seat costs 234/202Bs.

🚆 **Express Oriental** departs for Quijarro via San José de Chiquitos on Mon, Wed & Fri at 17.00. Super Pullman/first class costs 115/52Bs.

🚆 **Tren del Este** has slow trains to Quijarro via San José de Chiquitos Mon–Sat at 13.30. Seats cost

52Bs. This service is rather unfortunately referred to by travellers as 'the death train' – think about that before buying your ticket.

Tren del Sur has slow trains to Yacuiba for crossing the Argentinian border on Mon, Wed & Fri at 17.00. Pullman/first/second class costs 101/47/37Bs.

To get a tongue-in-cheek taste of the journey, check Colin Churcher's Railway Pages (*www.railways.incanada.net/bolivia/oriental1.htm*).

By bus **Terminal Bimodal** (*aka Nueva Terminal, Av Brasil corner with Av Tres Pasos, is located between the third & fourth rings;* ✆ *348 8482*) About 1km from downtown (10Bs by taxi), this sprawling terminal building is the hub for most travel out of the city. At the main entrance there's a handy **tourist information kiosk** (✆ *332 6003*), with signs to the numerous operators running services between sectors A and B.

Sector B has a luggage store (take a right from the tourist information kiosk), which opens 06.00–22.00 and stores luggage for up to 25 hours (3Bs per piece of luggage). There's also an Entel call centre (open 06.00–21.00) with internet access (3Bs per hour), while sector A has ATMs and a pharmacy (open 07.00–21.00).

Note: the terminal is renowned as a hangout for pickpockets, so guard your baggage well. And beware ticket hawkers, who approach you in the terminal building sometimes selling false tickets at inflated prices. The most reputable companies have signs with the prices clearly marked, although it's best to double check on departure times at the counter.

The Ex-Terminal aka Terminal Viejo is now pretty much closed to bus departures. Nearby, however, buses still leave from Avenida Omar Chavez for Samaipata (page 213) with the bus company Expresso Picaflor (✆ *333 5067*).

This area is also the unofficial dumping point for most long-distance bus services arriving in Santa Cruz in the early hours. It's not at all a good place to be after dark, so take a taxi straight to your hotel and be prepared to pay over the going rate to get out quickly. Avoid the nearby hostels – they're not safe for travellers.

Note that some buses for the **Jesuit Mission towns** of San Javier and Concepción (page 224) leave at lunchtime from the **Mercado Los Pozos** on the corner of Calle Suárez Arana and Calle Barron, but other morning and evening departures leave from the Terminal Bimodal.

GETTING AROUND The main streets of the city are structurally organised in circles of concentric rings, which are crossed by the main avenues. The downtown area, fanning out from **Plaza 14 de Septiembre** where the main facilities for tourists are located, is easily covered on foot, but you will need to take taxis to reach attractions within the first few rings. Tourists rarely venture out beyond the third ring, especially at night when the outer districts are best avoided.

Buses around the centre charge a flat rate of 2.50Bs per journey, while taxi fares start at 6Bs (daytime) and 8Bs (at night) within the downtown area, adding 1Bs per ring covered. For example, a daytime taxi to the second ring costs 7Bs, to the second 8Bs etc. To call a **taxi**, try Radio Movil Chiriguano (✆ *344 4949*). You can also hire a taxi with a driver for 20Bs per hour to save on shoe leather outside of the main downtown area.

For car rental, try **American Rent a Car** (*Av Suárez Arana #230;* ✆ *334 1235;* 24-hour ✆ *708 31326;* 🖷 *333 7376*). You will need to provide your driving licence, passport and a credit card. Prices start from US$39 per day for a sedan and US$55 per day for a jeep, based on covering up to 100km a day.

TOURIST INFORMATION
Tourist information office and Tourism and Cultural Interpretation Centre
(*Plaza 24 de Septiembre;* \ *336 9595*) Located on the north side of the plaza, this cultural complex has two floors of exhibits examining local ethnicity and a rotating series of exhibits exploring Santa Cruz's past. The information office is located downstairs in the left-hand corner and opens Mon–Fri 08.00–20.00.

LOCAL TOUR AGENCIES Recommended tour agencies in the city include:

Magri Turismo Calle Warnes #238, corner with Calle Potosí; \ 334 5663; f 334 3591; e magri-srz@cotas.com.bo; www.magri-amexpress.com. The local branch of this large, nationwide agency offers a diverse programme of cultural & nature tours at the upper end of the price range. Options include a 2-day trip to Samaipata (US$198), a 2-day trip to Buena Vista (US$251) & a 5-day trip along the Jesuit Missions trail (US$675). Prices quoted are per person & based on a group of 2 with discounts available for larger groups. They also act as the local agents for American Express. *Open Mon–Fri 08.30–12.00 & 14.30–18.30, Sat 08.30–12.00.*

Nativo Tours Edificio Arte Urbano, Calle Jaime Freire, Zone Equipetrol; \ 339 4019; f 337 6667; e info@nativotour.com; www.nativotour.com. A new tour operator specialising in adventure tourism & complete packages that offers something a bit different from the traditional agencies. The options include a 2-day biking trip (from US$40 pp per day), a 3-day quad-biking trip (from US$400 pp per day) & 3-day trips along the Jesuit Missions Trail from US$868 pp with accommodation in upscale properties, nearly all meals & use of a private minibus. *Open Mon–Fri 08.30–12.30 & 14.30–18.30, Sat 09.00–12.00.*

Forest Calle Cuéllar 22; \ 337 2042; f 336 0037; e info@forestbolivia.com; www.forestbolivia.com. A smaller operator offering trips along the Jesuit Missions trail with prices starting from US$250 pp for 2 days & US$690 pp for 5 days, based on a group of 2. Prices include guide, transport, accommodation & most meals. They also offer 2-day trips along the Che Guevara trail with prices from US$260 pp, based on a group of 2 & camping rather than hotels. *Open Mon–Sat 08.00–12.00 & 14.30–18.00.*

Gama Tours Calle Arenales #566; \ 334 0921; f 336 3828; e gamatur@roble.scz.entelnet.bo. A good bet for booking tickets & flights, this place is handily located right opposite the Spanish embassy. *Open Mon–Fri 08.30–12.00 & 14.30–18.30, Sat 08.30–12.00.*

WHERE TO STAY Santa Cruz has a good mix of properties for all budgets and caters equally well for both the tourism and business markets, although many of the better properties are located out of the downtown area. As such, taxi rides around the city are a necessary part of getting around. The following properties are divided by budget category and listed in the order of the author's preference.

Top of the range

Los Tajibos Hotel & Convention Centre (192 rooms) Av San Martin #455, Equipetrol district; \ 342 1000; f 342 6994; e ventas@lostajiboshotel.com; www.lostajiboshotel.com. Seriously upmarket & frequented by high-flying executives, this luxurious property has all the services you'd expect at these prices – & more. The rooms are large with balconies & nice fittings, while the poolside restaurant, where executive lunches & a generous b/fast buffet are served, is the place to spot local diplomats & politicians having a quiet drink with their, ahem, 'personal assistants'. They recently installed wi-fi for laptop carriers, otherwise you can order in-room broadband access for US$5 for up to 5 days. *Standard sgls/dbls US$159/179; executive sgls/dbls US$169/189 with b/fast & free use of the business centre.*

Hotel Camino Real (110 rooms) North Equipetrol district, 4th ring; \ 342 3535; f 343 1515; e hotel@caminoreal.com.bo; www.caminoreal.com.bo. The city's other main international-standard property has a good range of high-class facilities, inc pool, sauna & a business centre. It's also particularly handy for Viru Viru International Airport (page 205). The rooms are generously sized with marble bathrooms & large, comfy beds, plus all the usual mod cons. There's wi-fi for laptop users in public areas & broadband internet available in your room for US$5 per day. *Sgls/dbls/suites US$138/158/88 with b/fast & free use of the business centre.*

Mid-range

🏠 **Hotel Copacabana** (60 rooms) Calle Junin #217; ☎ 336 2770; f 333 0757; e hotelcopacabana@ hotmail.com. A 3-star property very handy for the main square, this place is a good, solid mid-range option. The rooms come equipped with fridges & cable TV, while there's also an in-house restaurant serving meals all day, inc a decent lunch (10Bs). Recommended. *Sgls/dbls/tpls with fan 100/150/180Bs; sgls/dbls/tpls with AC 140/180/220Bs, all with b/fast.*

🏠 **Hotel Cortez** (100 rooms) Av Cristobal de Mendoza #280; ☎ 333 1234; f 335 1186; e hotelcortez@ hotelcortez.com; www.hotelcortez.com. A 4-star property with a good range of services, although the rooms do look a little tired now. There's a poolside bar & restaurant (try the set business lunch 35Bs, or Saturday vegetarian buffet 30Bs), a business centre & sauna; but it's the excellent location — just behind the café

strip of Calle Monseñor Rivero — that is the main selling point. *Sgls/dbls/tpls US$65/75/85 with b/fast. Ask about family & weekend promotions with special deals for groups of 2 adults & 2 children.*

🏠 **Gran Hotel Santa Cruz** (110 rooms) Calle Rene Moreno #269; ☎ 334 8811; f 332 4194; e hotelsantacruz@ cotas.com.bo; www.granhotelsantacruz.com. A 4-star property with a real sense of history about it, this place still retains its stately old feel. The rooms are well equipped but do feel a little stuffy these days, although a pool & business centre help to compensate for the slightly scuffed fittings. The main selling point, however, is that it's located just a few blocks south of the main square. Watch out for the lurid murals on the walls, though. It's enough to put you off your b/fast. Non-residents can use the swimming pool for 30Bs per day. *Sgls/dbls US$87/97 with buffet b/fast. Ask about special rates & promotions.*

Budget

🏠 **Hotel Bibosi** (30 rooms) Calle Junin #218; ☎/f 334 8887; e htlbibosi@ hotmail.com. This is a cheaper, 2-star option but features a reasonable range of facilities for the price. The rooms are simple but airy with cable TV & private bathrooms, while there's also a roof terrace for lounging. The restaurant offers a set lunch (10Bs) & the location, close to the main square, is very convenient for all the attractions. *Sgls/dbls/tpls with fan 90/140/160Bs with a simple b/fast.*

🏠 **Residential Sands** (8 rooms) Calle Arenales #749; ☎ 337 7776. Homely & airy, this place is a bit of a gem at the price, albeit a fair old hike from the main square right at the far western edge

of the downtown area. The rooms are nicely furnished & come with cable TV & private bathrooms, plus there's a small pool. This guesthouse tends to be popular with Bolivian families. *Sgls/dbls/tpls 70/80/120Bs with b/fast.*

🏠 **Residencial Bolivar** (10 rooms) Calle Sucre #131; ☎ 334 2500; e residencial_bolivar@ hotmail.com. A simple backpacker joint, better known for the 3 friendly toucans that hang out amongst the hammocks in the communal garden than its range of facilities. This is a real budget option but it is worth paying that bit extra for the privacy that a single room will bring you. *Dorms/sgls 50/70Bs with continental b/fast.*

✖ WHERE TO EAT

✖ **Candelabro** Calle 7 Oeste #9, Barrio Equipetrol; ☎ 337 7271; f 332 1085; e candelabro@ cotas.net. The smartest eatery in Santa Cruz has a classy, international feel & is divided between a dining room & a more informal bar area with live music from Wed to Sat. The restaurant has an excellent sushi menu (11/25 pieces 55/150Bs) & international-standard mains (45–85Bs) — try the paella. *Restaurant open Mon–Sat 12.00–15.00 & 19.00–midnight; bar open Mon–Sat 19.00–03.00.*

✖ **La Casa del Camba** Av Cristóbal de Mendoza #1365, 2nd ring; ☎ 342 7864; f 342 7449; www.casadelcamba.com. A very tourist-friendly spot, this restaurant has a nice garden setting & a huge

barbecue area churning out an all-day service of Argentinian steaks & typical local fare. There's live music nightly at 20.00, a decent wine list (bottles 40–150Bs) & a huge menu, inc a mini-buffet for 4 people (100Bs), a barbecue for 4 people with Argentinian steaks (130Bs) & a range of meaty mains (20–55Bs), all served with rice, yucca & salad. Yum. *Open daily 12.00–01.00.*

✖ **Los Lomitos** Av Uruguay #758, 1st ring; ☎ 332 8696. A large barbecue-speciality restaurant, it has a huge range of meals, all-day service & an English menu for the passing tour groups. Steaks range in price from 40–60Bs pp & the main dishes, priced 20–40Bs, are excellent value; there's also a kids' menu. Drinks include beers (9–14Bs) & wines by the

La Casona Calle Arenales #222; ☎ 337 8495; e bistrolacasona@yahoo.com. A superbly rustic little restaurant with a deli attached, La Casona sells a range of expat-friendly goods, such as cheeses & liqueurs. The setting is very attractive &, by night, the garden restaurant is particularly appealing. The German owner keeps a regular menu of German-style favourite dishes (29–43Bs), while a daily-changing menu offers mains (22–38Bs) & vegetarian options (21–27Bs). There's also a good-value set lunch (19Bs) & occasional live music (with cover charge). *Open Mon 19.00–late, Tue–Sat 11.30–late, closed Sun.*

bottle (35–65Bs). Friendly & hearty, it's a winner. *Open daily 09.00–midnight.*

✗ **Pizza Margarita** Calle Junin #116, corner with Calle Libertad; ☎ 337 0285. A Finnish-owned pizza restaurant that is popular with travellers & tour groups, pizzas are 24–40Bs & mains 25–45Bs. It's set in an arcade just off the northwest corner of the main square – look out for the sign on the wall. *Open Mon–Fri 09.00–midnight, weekends 18.00–midnight.*

✗ **Restaurant Don Caito** Calle 24 de Septiembre #166; ☎ 336 6101. Close to the main square, this airy eatery offers a good range of menus without having to break the bank. There's a lunch buffet

Mon–Thu (12Bs), a Creole barbecue lunch on Fri (17Bs) & a family buffet on Sun (25Bs). A la carte mains in the evening cost 25–35Bs. *Open daily 09.00–23.00.*

✗ **Restaurant Tia Lia** Calle Murillo #40; ☎ 333 8183. A popular lunch spot, the huge Brazilian buffet makes for the best all-you-can-eat experience in town. From Mon to Sat the buffet costs 12Bs, on Sun 15Bs. Make sure you go hungry. *Open daily 11.30–15.00.*

✗ **Santa Ana** Calle Ingavi #164; no tel. Another good spot for lunch, this backpacker favourite has an all-you-can-eat buffet for 12Bs. *Open Mon–Sat 11.30–14.30.*

Cafés and snacks

▢ **Alexander Coffee** Av Monseñor Rivero #400, El Cristo district; ☎ 337 8653; e alexander@caoba.entelnet.bo. *Open for coffee (8Bs) & snacks 08.00–late.*

▢ **Mr Café** Av Monseñor Rivero, El Cristo district; ☎ 335 5270. *Open for coffees (6Bs) & pastries 08.00–late.*

▢ **El Tintico Café Amboro** Calle Libertad corner with Calle Florida; ☎ 330 1618. Centrally located, this place offers an alternative to the coffee shop chains for a quick hit of Amazonian blend coffee (3–5Bs) plus pastries (2–4Bs). *Open daily 08.00–21.00.*

▢ **Victory Café** Galeria Casco Viejo 2/F, Calle Junin corner with Calle 21 de Mayo; ☎ 332 2935. A smarter than average café set in an old, colonial building with an open-air terrace overlooking the street. It's a good spot for coffees (5–10Bs) & light snacks, such as sandwiches & burgers (12–15Bs) & omelettes (11–15Bs). *Open daily 08.00–late.*

▢ **Wrap & Roll** Calle Libertad, El Cristo district; ☎ 339 3339. A great little sandwich bar tucked away behind the Hotel Cortez (page 208), for a light bite. It's simple but friendly with wraps (15–20Bs) & juices (6Bs). *Open Tue–Sun 08.00–22.00 & 18.00–midnight.*

Supermarkets

Supermercado El Cristo Located at the southern end of Av Monseñor Rivero, El Cristo district. A handy spot for stocking up on essentials. *Open 08.00–22.00.*

Supermercado Sur Fidalga Plaza Blacut, Av René Moreno; ☎ 332 2294. It has a large range of goods, plus a small food court for take-away meals. *Open Mon–Sat 07.00–23.00.*

Also around the **Plaza Blacut** are a host of small stalls for drinks and snacks at bargain prices, which are popular with locals at night. **Super Lomo** and **Helados Finos Cabrera** are particularly good for steak sandwiches and fresh juices respectively. Otherwise, the **Los Pozos** and **Seven Calles** markets are good places to find cheap eats and stock up on supplies – just make sure you're strong of stomach before indulging.

ENTERTAINMENT AND NIGHTLIFE There are two main areas after dark: the strip of bars, clubs and karaoke joints along **Avenida San Martín** in the Equipetrol district, where the younger crowd hang out; and the strip of cafés and smarter eateries along **Avenida Monseñor Rivero** in the El Cristo district, where a more mature crowd tend to congregate. At weekends, the strip of restaurants known as **Cabañas del Rio Pirai**, located next to the river of the same name, is popular with al fresco diners, who keep the cold beers and cool cocktails flowing long after sundown.

Casino

☆ **Bingo Bahiti** Av Cristobal de Mendoza #635; ☏ 348 7000; f 314 1380; e restaurantbahiti@cotex.com.bo. If you're craving a taste of Las Vegas kitsch, this restaurant/dinner show is the nearest Bolivia has to a proper casino (gambling on cards and dice is illegal under Bolivian law). It's not cheap, and more a place to be seen than capture that Viva Las Vegas feeling, but the slot machines at least keep rolling until late if you're that way inclined. Restaurant mains 27–79Bs. *Open daily 12.00–04.00; over 18s only.*

Bars

🗗 **Irish Bar** Shopping Arcade Bolivar 2/F, Plaza 24 de Septiembre; ☏ 333 8118; e shamrock@mail.cotas.com.bo. The most popular gringo hangout in town attracts a young, good-looking local crowd mixing in with the expats and backpackers. Light bar meals range from mains (25–40Bs) to sandwiches (10–15Bs), and there's a good set lunch served daily (18Bs). For hangovers there's even an Irish breakfast (20Bs) but, sadly, no Guinness. Beers cost 9–14Bs. *Open daily 09.00–midnight.* Another branch opens the same hours at the 3rd ring (Anillo Interno #1216; ☏ 343 0671) near the zoo, and has live music on Wed and Fri nights.

Cinemas

Cine Center Av El Trompillo, 2nd ring between Calle René Moreno y Monseñor Santiesteban; ☏ 337 5456. Bolivia's only multiplex cinema, with ten – count 'em – screens, is set inside an arcade with a slew of fast-food-style places to snack in before the screening. *Open daily 11.30–late.*
René Moreno Cinema Calle René Moreno #448; ☏ 334 7448. Nightly showings; screenings 16Bs.

Cultural centres

Asociación Pro Arte y Cultura (APAC) Calle Beni #228; ☏ 333 2287; e info@festivalesapac.com; www.festivalesapac.com. A local arts co-operative, this volunteer body organises the biannual International Renaissance and American Baroque Music Festival along the Jesuit Missions Trail (page 224) and strives to promote other cultural events concerning the cultural tradition of the Chiquitos region. *Office open Mon–Fri 09.00–13.00 & 15.00–19.00, Sat 10.00–13.00.*

Agencia Española de Cooperación Internacional and Casa de España Calle Arenales #583; ☏ 335 1311. Part of the Spanish embassy complex (page 211), this centre hosts events and conferences. Spanish films are screened every Tue at 19.00; free entry. *Open 09.00–12.00 & 15.00–20.00.*
Centro Cultural Franco Aleman Av Velarde #200 at Plaza Blacutt; ☏ 332 9906. As well as a library, they host language classes and cultural events. *Open 09.00–12.00 & 15.00–20.00.*

SHOPPING Santa Cruz is particularly strong on fashion, shoes and artisan crafts with more than its fair share of upmarket boutiques. For souvenirs, try the following.

Arte Campo Calle Monseñor Salvatierra #407; ☏ 334 1843; e cidac@unete.com. The not-for-profit CIDAC works to preserve the native arts and crafts of Santa Cruz and the surrounding indigenous communities, including those of the Jesuit Missions trail (page 224). This shop serves as a showroom for local artisans' products. Given the NGO nature of the business, this is one place where prices are not for negotiation. *Open Mon–Fri 09.00–12.30 & 15.30–19.00; Sat 09.00–12.30.*

Anahi Joyerias Calle Guemes #5, Equipetrol district; ℡ 335 4054; e joyerias_anahi@ametrine.com; www.anahi.com. In a city where it's all about show, this upscale jewellery emporium is the face of moneyed Santa Cruz – and a favourite stop-off for tour groups. If you want to splash out on ametrine stones, the necklaces cost around US$135. A cheaper option is to take a guided tour of the nearby factory, which explains the history of the Anahi mine. *Open Mon–Sat 10.00–20.00, Sun 11.00–19.00.*
Vicuñita Handicrafts Calle Ingavi corner with Calle Independencia; ℡ 334 0591. A good all-rounder for

gifts and souvenirs located close to the main square, it has a range of craft items. They will ship goods to anywhere in the world and accept all major credit cards. *Open Mon–Sat 09.00–12.30 & 14.30–19.00.*
Los Amigos del Libro Calle Ingavi #14; ℡ 332 7937. This book and stationery shop still carries some English-language copies of *Newsweek* and the odd copy of *The Economist*, but a now increasingly depleted stock of English-language books. *Open Mon–Fri 09.00–19.00, Sat 09.00–12.00.*

OTHER PRACTICALITIES

Agfa photo centre Calle Junin corner with Calle 23 de Mayo. Develops slide film for 20Bs per roll. *Open Mon–Sat 08.00–20.00.*
Clinic Angel Foianini Av Irala #468; ℡ 343 6221. *Opens 24hrs for emergency medical treatment.*
Edmund Transfer Casa de Cambio Calle Rene Moreno #20; ℡ 337 2505; e info@edmundtransfer.biz. Changes a range of currencies with no commission on US dollars in cash & a 2.5% commission on travellers' cheques. *Open Mon–Sat 09.00–11.45 & 14.15–18.15.*
Entel call centre Plaza 24 de Septiembre, corner with Calle Libertad #166; ℡ 336 5555. Offers internet access (4Bs/hr). *Open daily 07.00–22.00.*
Immigration office Located on the 3rd ring internal at Av Ovidio Barbery, opposite the zoo; ℡ 343 8559.

For visa extensions. *Open Mon–Fri 08.30–16.00..*
Laundrette Rapid Service Calle Sucre corner with Calle La Paz. Offers a laundry service for 15Bs/kg. *Open Mon–Sat 07.30–19.30.*
Pharmacy Telchi Calle Libertad #164; ℡ 336 5555. *Open Mon–Fri 08.00–12.30 & 14.30–20.00, Sat 08.30–12.00.*
Post office Calle Junin #150; ℡ 334 7445. *Open Mon–Fri 08.00–20.00, Sat 09.00–18.00 & Sun 09.00–12.00.*
Volunteer Challenge Av Capitan Arrien #41, Parque Urbano district; ℡ 700 99190; e info@volunteerchallenge.com; www.volunteerchallenge.com. This small, local group will arrange homestays & work experience placements on a voluntary basis for foreigners coming to visit Santa Cruz.

Consulates For a full list of embassies, see the La Paz chapter (page 86).

E **Argentina** Calle Junín #22, 3/F; ℡ 332 4153; *open 08.00–13:00.*
E **Brazil** Av German Busch #330; ℡ 334 4400; *open 09.00–15.00.*
E **Chile** Calle 5 Oeste #224, Equipetrol district; ℡ 343 4272; *open 08.00–12.45.*
E **France** Av Marcelo Terceros Banza #310; ℡ 341 0030; *open 16:30 to 18:00.*
E **Germany** Calle Ñuflo de Chavez #242; ℡ 336 7585; *open 08.30–12.00.*
E **Holland** Calle Ayacucho #284; ℡ 335 4498; *open 09.00–12.30.*
E **Italy** Edificio Honnen, Av El Trompillo; ℡ 353 1796; *open 08.30–12.30.*

E **Israel** Av Bailon Mercado #171; ℡ 342 4777; *open 10.00–12.00 & 16.00–18.30.*
E **Japan** Calle Cochabamba #314; ℡ 333 1329; *open 08.15–11.30 & 15.00–17.30.*
E **Paraguay** Calle Manuel Ignacio Salvatierra #99; ℡ 336 6113; *open 07.30–12.30.*
E **Spain** Calle Monseñor Santistevan #237; ℡ 332 8921; *open 09.00–12.00.*
E **Switzerland** Calle Los Gomeros #98; ℡ 343 5540; *open 08.30–12.00 & 14.30–18.00.*
E **United States** Calle Guemes Este #6, Equipetrol district; ℡ 333 0725; *open 09.30–11.30.*

Note: You will need a yellow fever certificate for travel into Brazil and some nationalities need a visa for onward travel within Latin America. Make sure to check with the respective embassy before departing Santa Cruz.

Airlines For a full list of airlines, see the La Paz chapter (page 86).

9

✈ **American Airlines** Calle Beni #167; ☎ 334 1314; www.aa.com; *open Mon–Fri 09.00–18.30, Sat 09.00–12.00.*

✈ **Lloyd Aéreo Boliviano (LAB)** Calle Warnes corner with Calle Chuquisaca; ☎ 334 4509; www.labairlines.com.bo; *open Mon–Fri 08.00–12.30 & 14.30–19.00, Sat 08.30–12.30.*

✈ **AeroSur & TACA** (shared offices) Av Irala #616; ☎ 336 4446; www.aerosur.com & www.taca.com;

open Mon–Fri 08.00–12.30 & 14.30–19.00, Sat 08.30–12.30.

✈ **Amazonas** Aeropuerto El Trompillo; ☎ 357 8988; www.amaszonas.com; *open Mon–Fri 08.00–12.30 & 14.30–19.00, Sat 08.30–12.30.*

✈ **Aerolineas Argentinas** Plaza 24 de Septiembre, Edificio Banco de la Nación Argentina 2/F; ☎ 333 9776 77; www.aerolineas.com.ar; *open Mon–Fri 08.00–12.30 & 14.30–19.00, Sat 08.30–12.30.*

WHAT TO SEE AND DO

Museo de Historia y Archivo Historical Calle (*Junín #151;* ☎ *336 5533; open Mon–Fri 08.30–12.00 & 15.00–18.30; free entry*) This university-owned museum explores the history and traditions of the local indigenous cultures. As part of the museum there's an artisan gift shop run by the Mancomunidad de Municipios de la Gran Chiquitania – your purchase supports their community artisans.

Museo Etnofolklórico (*Corner of Calles Beni & Caballero, Parque Arenal;* ☎ *335 2078; open Mon–Fri; 08.00–12.00 & 14.30–18.30; entry 5Bs*) A brief trawl through some of the traditions and costumes employed during festivals makes this a worthwhile museum for a short visit before heading out into the villages for a festival event.

Museum of Natural History Noel Kempff Mercado (*Av Irala #565;* ☎ *336 6574; Open 08.30–12.00 & 15.00–18.30; entrance 1Bs*) A worthwhile visit for anyone considering a visit to the nearby national park of the same name, although the displays of flora and fauna are rather poorly maintained by seriously uninterested staff.

Catedral de San Lorenzo (*Plaza 24 de Septiembre; open Tue & Thu 10.00–12.00 & 16.00–18.00, Sun 10.00–12.00 & 18.00–20.00; entrance 10Bs*) The main cathedral houses the small Museo de Arte Sacro.

Casa de la Cultura Raúl Otero Reich (*Plaza 24 de Septiembre, Calle Libertad #65;* ☎ *334 2377; open Mon–Fri 08.00–12.00 & 15.00–21.00, Sat–Sun 10.00–12.00 & 16.00–21.00; entrance according to the event*) Santa Cruz's main cultural centre hosts art shows, concerts and other cultural activities.

EXCURSIONS FROM SANTA CRUZ

Biocentro Guembe (*Road to Porongo, Zona Los Batos;* ☎/f *370 0542;* e *info@biocentroguembe.com; www.biocentroguembe.com; open daily 08.00–18.00; entrance 50Bs*) Run by people behind tour agency Nativo Tours, this huge, new nature centre, 7km from downtown Santa Cruz, is a great spot for families and offers an educational but fun experience for kids. The 2,500km^2 site includes nature trails plus fully functional butterfly and orchid research centres with 104 species of butterflies and 260 species of orchids respectively. There's a good on-site restaurant, which is packed on Sundays with visitors from Santa Cruz. Barbecue mains cost 35–45Bs, dinner 40–70Bs and pastas 35Bs.

Parque Ecológico Yvaga Guaza (*Doble Via La Guardia;* ☎ *352 7971;* f *357 3767;* e *parqueyvagaguazu@infonet.com.bo: www.parqueyvagaguazu.org; open daily 08.00–17.00*) These botanic gardens are a 20-minute drive out of town, taking a minibus marked for El Torno and La Guardia, which leaves from the Terminal Bimodal (page 205; 2Bs). The vast collection of orchids, indigenous plants and native animals make this a tranquil spot to pass the afternoon, although it's only one for real flora fans and families seeking some green space. There's a rustic restaurant waiting for you at the end of the trail with mains (20–40Bs), vegetarian mains (22Bs) and jugs of fresh juice from the garden (15Bs). Half-day packages, including lunch, a guided two-hour walk and transport, cost adults/children US$22/12. Bolivians pay B125/90 for the same deal. Guided visits without lunch and transport cost adults/children 120/90Bs with a free soft drink.

SAMAIPATA *Tel code: 03; altitude: 1,639m; population: 9,739*

Located 120km or two hours from Santa Cruz, Samaipata is becoming increasingly popular as a place for a few days' rest before continuing onward journeys. This reflects the town's crossroads-like position with Sucre (page 179) to the west and, towards the east, the Oriente stretching out along the Jesuit Missions trail (page 224) and the Pontanal.

Most of all, Samaipata is a really nice little spot with a superbly well-organised structure for tourism and an easy-going, tranquil ambience. No wonder that people from Santa Cruz love to descend upon the pueblo at weekends and for public holidays, so make sure you book your accommodation well in advance at these times.

Samaipata is also the hub for visits to the archaeological ruins at El Fuerte (page 216) and trips to the south side of the Amboro National Park (page 220), both of which are within easy striking distance. Given the excellent local facilities, it makes for an ideal base from which to explore these attractions.

Note: bring a torch for walking around at night and watch out for the wild dogs on roads leading out of town. And Samaipata tends to be pretty quiet on Mondays, with a lot of places closing up after a busy weekend.

GETTING THERE Buses to Samaipata with Expresso Picaflor (`\ 336 2312`) leave daily at 17.00 from Santa Cruz at Avenida Omar Chavez (17Bs), located near the old bus terminal in Santa Cruz. The journey takes two to three hours. Return buses to Santa Cruz leave Samaipata daily at 06.00 from Plaza 15 de Deciembre (`\ 716 67242 for details`).

Most buses from Santa Cruz stop just outside the village on the main road to Vallegrande (page 230), where there's a small, makeshift bus terminal.

Alternatively, an express **taxi** from the corner of Avienda Omar Chavez in Santa Cruz costs 100Bs one way (try to make up a group of five to share the cost). To book a return taxi from Samaipata call Taxis Samaipata (`\ 944 6133`).

GETTING AROUND Everything in Samaipata is easily accessible on foot, except for the ruins of El Fuerte; see page 216 for transport details.

TOURIST INFORMATION There is a small **tourist information office** within the museum complex (page 216), but it seems to be subject to very irregular opening

---

THREE THINGS TO DO IN SAMAIPATA

1 Hang out in the main square with a delicious ice-cream sundae from Heladería La Vaca Loca (page 216).

2 Visit the ruins at El Fuerte to learn about the legacy of the ancient civilisations in the region (page 216).

3 Take an excursion to the southern side of Amboro National Park to marvel at the variety of wildlife and indigenous plant species (page 220).

SAMAIPATA

El Fuerte (9km),
Santa Cruz
(120km)

Hospital

Cochabamba - Santa Cruz Highway

Bus stops

Vallegrande (120km),
Sucre (240km),
Cochabamba (300km)

Landhaus

Viewpoint

Café Latina

Residencial Don Jorge

Roadrunner
Tours

Amboro
Tours

Pharmacy
Red Cross

Centre de Invetigaciones
Arqueológicas de Samaipata (CIAS)/
Tourist information office/museum

Michael Blendiger
Nature Tours

BOLIVAR

CAMPERO

Police

Buses to Santa Cruz

SUCRE

Casa de la Moneda

Plaza 15 de
Diciembre

Heladería
La Vaca Loca Market

La Chakana

Entel call centre

La Posada

Mosquito Bar

El Descanso en Las Alturas

Football pitch

Football pitch

Finca La Víspera,
Cabañas de Traudi

AV ROQUE AGUILERA

Quinta Piray

N

Bradt

hours. Far more useful, therefore, are the handful of highly knowledgeable tour agencies in town. Recommended tour agencies in Samaipata include the following:

Michael Blendiger Nature Tours Calle Bolivar; ╲/f 944 6227; e info@discoveringbolivia.com; www.discoveringbolivia.com. The most knowledgeable guide in town, Blendinger is a specialist in nature tourism. The tours are more expensive than average but they're also of higher quality, particularly good for birdwatching & animal-spotting trips to more remote locations. The prices range from US$73.50 pp for an all-inc, 1-day trekking trip around the ruins at El Fuerte (based on a group of 2) to US$250 pp for an all-inc, 3-day nature interpretation trip to Amboro National Park (based on a group of 2). Also available are longer 4x4 trips, such as a 3-day trip along the Che Guevara trail (page 227) & the Jesuit Missions trail (page 224) — ask for details. English, German & Spanish spoken. There's also a range of local artisan products available for sale from their shop —cum office. *Open daily 08.30–12.30 & 14.30–19.30.*

Amboro Tours Calle Bolivar; ╲ 944 6293; e erickamboro@yahoo.com. Run by Erick Prado, a former manager of Amboro National Park, this agency offers a range of trips with multi-lingual guides to Amboro (page 220) with prices from US$12 pp per day, US$28 for 2 days. There's also a laundry service & a book exchange, plus they will arrange bus tickets for onward travel to Vallegrande, Sucre & nationwide. *Open daily 08.00–12.30 & 15.00–19.00.*

Roadrunner Tours Calle Bolivar; ╲/f 944 6193; e roadrunners@hotmail.com. This is a reliable backpacker agency with a comprehensive service, inc a book exchange & cashing of travellers' cheques (albeit with a 4% commission). Amongst their products, a 2-day Amboro tour costs US$50 pp, exc food, based on a group of 2. A 2-day camping trip with full board costs US$60 pp based on a group of 2. *Open daily 08.00–12.30 & 15.00–19.00.*

⌂ **WHERE TO STAY** For a small place, Samaipata has some good accommodation options, reflecting its status as a favoured weekend-break destination. The following properties are divided by budget category and listed in the order of the author's preference.

Mid-range

⌂ **La Posada** (5 rooms) Calle Ruben Terrazas; ╲ 944 6218; e bolivianromance@yahoo.com. The newest opening in town is an intimate spot run by an American–Bolivian couple. Tastefully decorated & welcoming, the rooms are comfortable & there's a comfy communal lounge with internet access & DVDs to watch. Best of all, it's just one block from the main square, making this the best spot in town to overnight — book ahead as there's only a few rooms. As an additional service, the owners also offer language classes (3hrs of survival Spanish per day, plus an hour's visit to a local site or market) from US$20 per day. *Sgls/dbls with private bathroom $5.50/10 with a good b/fast & free internet. Sgls/dbls with shared bathroom, no b/fast or internet use US$4/5.*

⌂ **Quinta Piray** (20 rooms) Located at the southwestern tip of town; ╲ 944 6136; f 944 6136; e quinta-piray@cotas.com.bo. Chalet-style apartments set in gardens 1km southwest of the plaza: it's a bit of a hike if you're carrying luggage, but only 5Bs by taxi. It's an attractive & peaceful setting to overnight, but hot water in the hand basins would be a welcome addition. The chalets are best suited to families or groups, but they offer no food — so make sure you come prepared. *Chalets range from US$20–55 for 2 & 6 people respectively; a sgl room costs US$10 while a small dorm for 2 costs US$15 (week-day prices). Add around US$10 on average for a weekend stay & around US$20 for a public holiday.*

Budget

⌂ **Residential Don Jorge** (20 rooms) Calle Bolivar; ╲ 944 6086. At the eastern entrance to town, located opposite Café Latina (see below), these simple rooms represent the best of the budget end of the market. It's no frills & the showers look a bit

lacking on safety regulations, but it's a reliable budget choice overall. *Sgls/dbls with private bathroom 30/40Bs; with shared bathroom 25Bs; buffet b/fast 7Bs.*

✕ **WHERE TO EAT**

✕ **Café Latina** Calle Bolivar; ╲ 944 6153; e latinacafe@latinmail.com. Hugely popular &

deservedly so, the former Café Hamburg has been refurbished & reopened with a homely, lounge-style feel. Excellent mains range from 20–27Bs (try the chicken curry), plus pasta (16–25Bs) & vegetarian options (12–20Bs). Don't miss the homemade lemonade (from 5Bs). An all-round great option – shame it closes Mon. *Open Tue–Sun 12.00–14.00 & 18.30–22.00.*

✕ **Landhaus** Calle Murillo; ☎ 944 6257; e landhaus@cotas.com.bo. This German-run eatery is always busy for its excellent, upmarket cuisine. The German specialities cost 28–36Bs, there's a great range of mains served with a salad bar (22–44Bs) & the afternoon German-style coffee & cakes (from 15Bs) are always a big favourite with visiting European tour groups. The owners also manage 4 centrally located chalets & 7 self-contained rooms in the town with prices starting from US$10 pp (☎ 949 6033). *Open Thu–Sat 09.00–22.00, Sun 09.00–21.00.*

✕ **La Chakana** Plaza 15 de Deciembre; ☎ 944 6146; e chakanabol@yahoo.com; www.geocities.com/chakanabol/cafeteria.htm. An excellent spot for meals, this place is located right on the main square with a rustic interior & friendly service. Mains range from 25–30Bs, plus b/fast (9–18Bs) & sandwiches (10–18Bs), & there's a daily set 2-course lunch (18Bs). Better still, this is one of the few places that does not close on Mon. *Open daily 11.00–22.00.*

✕ **El Descanso en las Alturas** Located at the western edge of town; ☎ 944 6072. This popular pizza restaurant has a rustic interior & an outdoor terrace for al fresco meals. There are 45 types of pizza available (prices range 20–50Bs) with flavours ranging from German sausage to octopus to vegetarian options. Don't miss the homemade lemonade (from 5Bs). *Open daily 12.00–14.30 & 18.30–22.00.*

✕ **Heladería La Vaca Loca** Plaza 15 de Deciembre; no tel. Next to Entel on the south side of the plaza, this excellent little coffee shop cum ice-cream parlour has real espresso coffee (5Bs) & delicious ice creams (1Bs per scoop), plus ice-cream sundaes (6–19Bs). *Open Mon–Fri 12.00–20.00, Sat–Sun 08.00–20.00.*

ENTERTAINMENT AND NIGHTLIFE

Mosquito Bar ☎ 944 6232, A late-night hangout for beers and cocktails, it's located next to the restaurant El Descanso en las Alturas (see above) at the western tip of town. Look out for the wall-mounted yellow taxi outside – it's pretty unmistakable. *Open Mon–Sat 20.00–late.*

OTHER PRACTICALITIES

Entel call centre Plaza 15 de Deciembre. Opens daily 08.00–20.00 & has internet access for 10Bs/hr.

WHAT TO SEE AND DO

Centro de Investigaciones Arqueológicas de Samaipata (CIAS) (*Calle Bolivar corner with Av Ponce Sanginez;* ☎ *944 6065; open Mon–Sat 08.00–12.00 & 14.00–18.00, Sun 08.00–16.00 without a lunch break; entrance to both museum & ruins: Bolivians/foreigners 16/32Bs*) The centre for local archaeological research team CIAS, this is home to a small museum showcasing finds from the ruins of El Fuerte (see below). There's also a video room with a documentary about the history of the site.

El Fuerte The ruins of **El Fuerte** are located 9km from the museum (see above). You can take a taxi, which costs 50Bs, regardless of how many people, for a return ride. To arrange this, call Taxis Samaipata (☎ *944 6133*).

Alternatively, to stretch your legs, the easternmost Inca ruins in the empire can be reached on foot. Follow the road back towards Santa Cruz and, after about 2km, you'll see a kiosk on the left-hand side and a small road leading off on the right. Follow this for 5km; cross a stream (upstream is a beautiful bathing spot so be sure to take your swimming things); then climb for the final 2km to the ruins on top of a hill.

El Fuerte has represented a key ceremonial and administrative site for several different peoples throughout history, namely the Chane, the Incas and later the Spanish. The site's most striking feature is the largest carved rock in the world (that's 220m x 60m, since you ask), which is recognised by UNESCO as a World Heritage Site.

EL FUERTE

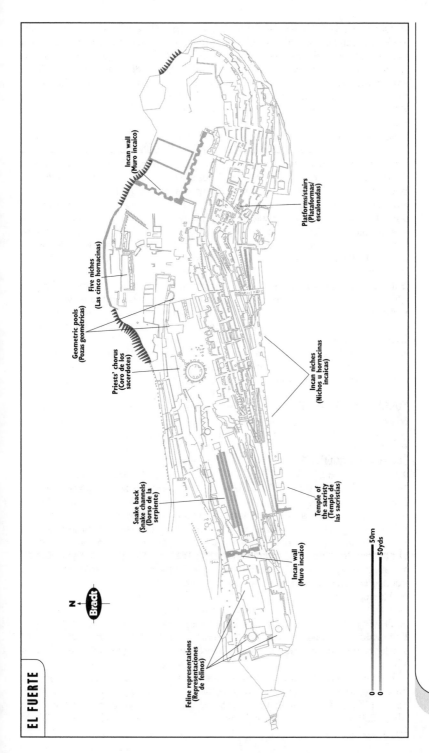

N Bradt

Incan wall
(Muro incaico)

Platforms/stairs
(Plataformas/
escalonadas)

Five niches
(Las cinco hornacinas)

Geometric pools
(Pozas geométricas)

Priests' chorus
(Coro de los
sacerdotes)

Incan niches
(Nichos u hornacinas
incaicas)

Snake back
(Snake channels)
(Dorso de la
serpiente)

Temple of
the sacristy
(Templo de
las sacristías)

Incan wall
(Muro incaico)

Feline representations
(Representaciones
de félinos)

0 — 50m
0 — 50yds

At the site, there's a ticket office and a small drinks kiosk, from where four trails lead off around the site along well-signposted, fixed routes, ranging from a short 20-minute hop to the full 90-minute circuit.

The latter takes in both the main site and a short ecological hike through the ruins via a series of watchtowers. There's a free map available at the ticket office, which marks out the four trails for visitors to follow, or you can arrange for a guide to escort you. The site opens daily 09.00–17.00.

BUENA VISTA *Tel code: 03; altitude: 289m; population: 13,273*

Located 100km or 90 minutes from Santa Cruz, Buena Vista is still relatively unknown compared with the traveller hub of Samaipata, but it's a nice little spot with an easy-going feel and a fledgling but growing infrastructure for tourists. The main selling point is the trips that head out to the north side of Amboro National Park, which can be easily arranged using Buena Vista as your base from which to explore the area.

Street addresses are not generally used in Buena Vista, so locations are in this section as described in relation to the main square.

GETTING THERE Buses to Buena Vista leave from Santa Cruz at Avenida Grigota on the third ring (external) in Santa Cruz and run via Montero, where you sometimes need to change buses; the journey takes two to three hours and costs 12Bs. Return buses to Santa Cruz pass the east side of Plaza 26 de Noviembre in Buena Vista at regular intervals during the day.

Alternatively, a **taxi** from in front of the old bus terminal at the corner or Avenida Irala in Santa Cruz costs 80Bs one way and takes one hour; return taxis can be booked via Taxis 10 de Febrero (✆ *932 2036*).

TOURIST INFORMATION There is no official **tourist information office** in Buena Vista and only a couple of tour operators. Ask in the Hotel Amboro (page 219) for more tourist information, or try the following tour agencies.

LOCAL TOUR AGENCIES

Amboro Tours Southwest corner of Plaza 26 de Noviembre; ✆ 710 85528; Santa Cruz office ✆ 339 0600; e amborotours@yahoo.com; www.amborotours.com. The local branch of this Santa Cruz-based tour agency specialises in trips to Amboro National Park (page 220). The prices for 1-/2-/3-day trips are US$59/89/139 respectively, based on a group of 2 people travelling from Santa Cruz. They also run trips along the Jesuit Missions Trail (page 224) – ask for details. *Open daily 08.00–12.30 & 15.00–19.00.*

Amboro Travel & Adventure Calle Celso Sandobal; ✆ 710 08444; e amborotravel@hotmail.com. A friendly agency running camping trips to Amboro National Park, although there have been a few grumbles about the quality of their service on the traveller grapevine. An overnight trip costs US$135 pp, based on a group of 2, inc transport, guides & camping equipment. *Open daily 08.00–12.30 & 15.00–19.00.*

THREE THINGS TO DO IN BUENA VISTA

1 Take a trekking excursion to the northern fringe of Amboro National Park to explore the diversity of flora and fauna (page 220).

2 Get close to nature and try to spot a new species from the birdwatching platform at the edge of town (page 220).

3 Relax with a cold beer and a chance to watch the world go by in the main square at the Bar Irlandais (page 219).

WHERE TO STAY

WHERE TO STAY Options to overnight in Bella Vista are limited but a couple of interesting options make it a place where lingering is time well spent. The following properties are divided by budget category and listed in the order of the author's preference.

Mid-range

Hotel Amboro (14 rooms & 6 cabins for up to 8 people each) Located 500m west of the plaza; ✆ 932 2104; e hotelamboro@cotas.com.bo. The best place to stay in town is especially popular at weekends for families visiting from Santa Cruz – so make sure you book ahead. Rooms are comfortable with private bathrooms & fridges, while the cabins come with a small kitchenette. There's also a pool, a nature trail & horses (40Bs/hr) & bikes (10Bs/hr) available to hire, plus ongoing work to expand the gardens. The genial expat Irish owner will arrange visits to the park; ask for details. *Rooms/cabins work out on average at US$10–15 pp per night.*

El Cafetal (8 cabins for up to 8 people each) Located 3.5km west of the plaza; ✆ 932 2067; e elcafetal@antitradecoffee.com. Set on a coffee plantation, these rustic cabins make for a comfortable escape, but are quite a long haul from the plaza without your own transport. The furnishings are tastefully rustic, while there's a barbecue area (they only offer b/fast, so bring your own supplies) & a pool, plus a birdwatching tower. The rooms have fans but no AC, which could put some people off. The owners can help to arrange a free visit to the adjoining 340ha coffee plantation to learn about the coffee-making process & sample the different styles of coffee produced. *Cabins work out at US$10 pp per night, with b/fast.*

Flora y Fauna (4 cabins) Southeast of the plaza; ✆ 710 43706; e hotelfandf@hotmail.com. A small grouping of simple cabins, this place is definitely one for birdwatchers & nature lovers. The owner is a real expert on local flora & fauna – ask to see the beetle collection. This is not a mainstream place to stay, but targeted specifically at visitors with a strong interest in nature & science, hence the rather tucked-away location & the excellent birdwatching tower in the grounds. It's a couple of kilometres out of town, so take a taxi from the plaza (20Bs). *Cabins work out at US$50 pp per night, inc meals & drinks.*

Budget

Residential Nadia (6 rooms) Calle Mariano Saucedo Sevilla #186; ✆ 932 2049. If you're looking for a basic crashpad close to the plaza, this place will do the job. It's a bit dark & very no-frills with no food available, but at least it's cheap & cheerful. *Rooms with shared/private bathroom 25/50Bs.*

WHERE TO EAT

La Casona Plaza 26 de Noviembre; ✆ 932 2083. This simple but friendly eatery sometimes serves main dishes (15Bs), albeit at rather irregular hours. More definite is a daily supply of coffees & snacks, served all day (around 3Bs). They also offer basic lodging rooms for 25Bs pp. *Open daily 09.00–21.00.*

La Tranquera Plaza 26 de Noviembre; no tel. A very basic eatery on the west side of the plaza, it serves simple mains for around 20Bs. One for emergencies only. *Open daily 08.00–20.00.*

ENTERTAINMENT AND NIGHTLIFE

Bar Irlandais Plaza 26 de Noviembre; no tel. A kiosk-style bar, located right in the middle of the plaza, this sister bar to Santa Cruz's famous Irish bar (page 210) is run by the same people that own & run the Hotel Amboro (see above). It's the main drinking & people-watching spot in the centre after dark & a good place to meet the locals over a cold one. *Open Tue–Sun 16.00–late.*

SHOPPING

Artecampo Calle Mariano Saucedo Sevilla; ✆ 710 84036. The sister shop to the well-known Santa Cruz branch (page 210), this branch also sells a range of local artisan goods from 4 local communities. The majority of the items are based around palm products. Open Mon–Sat 08.30–12.00 & 14.00–18.00.

Patuja West side of Plaza 26 de Noviembre; ✆ 932 2073. This is a small shop selling a range of local artisan goods & local produce. There's also a small café serving coffees (2Bs) & *empañadas* (2Bs). *Open Mon–Sat 08.00–12.00 & 15.00–20.00.*

OTHER PRACTICALITIES

Internet and international phone calls on the east side of the plaza, has internet access for 4Bs/hr; open 09.00–21.00.

Pharmacy Sara Calle Celso Sandobal; no tel; opens

Mon–Fri 08.00–12.00 & 15.00–19.00, Sat 08.00–12.00.

Punto Viva call centre Plaza 26 de Noviembre, opens daily 07.00–20.00.

WHAT TO SEE AND DO

Amboro Interpretation Centre *(Located two blocks east of the plaza; ⤫ 932 2055; open Mon–Sat 08.00–12.00 & 14.00–18.00, Sun 08.00–12.00 & 15.00–18.00)* For anyone planning a visit to Amboro National Park (see below), make this your first port of call for some background information. There's a documentary room and a nature trail previewing the kind of flora and fauna you will encounter in the park as part of the exhibits.

Curichi Cuajo Heron Pool *(Located 1km from the plaza; ⤫ 716 07356; open Mar–Oct 06.00–08.30 & 16.00–18.00, Oct–Mar 05.00–08.00 & 16.00–19.00)* A wildlife reserve with a viewing platform for birdwatching. Ask in the Amboro Interpretation Centre (above) for more details; visits 30Bs per person.

VISITING AMBORO NATIONAL PARK

Amboro National Park, covering an area of over 630,000ha, lies within three distinct ecosystems: the foothills of the Andes, the northern Chaco and the Amazon Basin. The park was originally established as the Reserva de Vida Silvestre German Busch in 1984, but, with the help of native biologist Noel Kempff, British zoologist Robin Clarke, and others, the park was expanded to its present size. Because the park straddles different ecosystems, it is a haven for wildlife. The diverse animal population includes jaguars, peccaries, several species of monkeys, agouti, river otters, tapirs, capybara, raccoons and deer. There are over 830 bird species recorded – the highest confirmed bird count for any protected area in the world.

The conditions for trekking are uniformly tropical. Perhaps the single greatest problem facing trekkers is, therefore, how best to prevent moisture from ruining everything you own. The best defence is to pack everything in plastic bags – and I mean everything. And remember, whatever is waterproof will also be bugproof. The best way to deal with the various dips in the river is to simply have a set of clothes (and trainers) that will stay wet, then bag them when you get to the campsite. Unless you have a good fire, it is difficult to dry clothes in the high humidity of the forest. A rain poncho is also useful, but more as an open covering – a rain-jacket is too hot. Anti-malaria pills should be taken, despite the negligible threat of the parasite. Snakes are fairly common, so watch where you place your feet.

There are two options when organising an excursion to the park. Firstly, you can book a trip with one of the tour companies in Samaipata (for entry via the southern fringe) or in Buena Vista (for the north side). Secondly, you can hire a guide from one of the park ranger stations. Keep in mind that, if you elect the latter option, you may have to cross rivers to enter the park, hence you also need to hire a jeep.

THE MACUÑUCÚ TRAIL This is the best known of the jungle trails through the park, following the Macuñucú riverbed. It's an easy to moderate, four- to seven-day trek, although the full trek is only for the fit and adventurous, requiring some jungle-bashing and a machete.

At Las Cruces, about one hour's drive from Buena Vista, a sign indicates the unofficial boundary of the park. A rough road winds through fields and patches of jungle for 8km until it runs into the Surutú River. In the dry season the waters are low and the crossing easy. It is a good idea to keep clothes on as there are a myriad of tiny *marigui*, which love to feast on human blood. It is often easier to stick to the river's course (and resign yourself to wet feet) rather than the bordering jungle trail.

Not far beyond the river is Villa Amboró, a seasonal town, and your last chance for provisions. Beyond this point you have to pass through a number of gates, designed to contain errant cattle. From here the trail tends to stick more to the forest. You will come to the confluence of a freshwater stream and the Río Macuñucú, a good place to rest. Beyond this point there is another small village of several thatched huts and a football field and then the forest closes in. An hour or so further along a good trail is the Campamento Macuñucú, a park station comprising several thatched huts, a toilet and some crude showers fed by a pump at the river below. The camp also boasts numerous fruit trees. Although you can camp here it is preferable to continue along the trail for 15 minutes and camp by the river.

Beyond Camp Macuñucú there is only jungle and the going gradually becomes more difficult. Sometimes the trail will seem to disappear, especially as it meanders in and out of the Macuñucú, but by following the course of the river you will not get lost. The jungle along this portion of the route is awe-inspiring. Great liana vines hang from branches as large as trees themselves. There's a good chance you might see spider or howler monkeys, agouti, squirrels and toucans. Early morning is the best time for spotting wildlife. Eventually the trail narrows and, after a few more dips in the river, you should keep a careful lookout on the left side for an overhang of red rock, partially hidden by vegetation. This is an interesting place to spend the first or second night, and has some interesting graffiti dating back to 1933. The overhang will shelter two two-people tents quite comfortably. There's lots of dead wood to be found for a fire, and just downstream is the mouth of a freshwater stream. There is also a more attractive campsite near the river about half an hour further on.

Another half-hour's trudge up the river will take you between steep canyon walls. If the waters are not too high you should be able to wade through the canyon without much trouble, but take time to feel around for the safest passage. Sometimes the waters of the Macuñucú are silty, especially if there has been a landslide farther upstream (which is common), and deeper pools are not easily anticipated. Remember, never have backpack chest or waist straps fastened when wading through deeper waters, particularly when there is a current of any kind. The weight of your pack could easily pull you under. Just beyond this narrow point, the canyon walls draw back. On the left side is another overhang/cave large enough to shelter six tents, and a sandy beach. While river otters seemed by far the most prolific mammals in the area, tapir, peccary, capybara, coatimundi and river otter can also be spotted.

The farther upstream you go from here the more spectacular the scenery becomes. On either side of the river tower the red cliffs, freshwater streams tumbling down their sheer faces in crystal cascades. In places, huge chunks of rock have fallen to leave great gaping holes. *Tojos*, or weaver birds, suspend their meticulously made nests from frail trees clinging to narrow ledges. A few twists in the river will bring you to a place where slides have intermittently blocked the river. In some places it is necessary to climb up through the jungle in order to circumvent the slides. From here the going is much tougher, especially if there have been recent rains. The trail sometimes disappears, and a machete may be helpful. You might want to try fishing in the larger pools – there are reportedly plenty of fish.

The stream continues to narrow, and you will find yourself scrambling over beautiful red and grey sandstone formations caused by the eroding effects of water spilling down from the Andes. It is a good idea to bring one or two heavy-duty

9

plastic bags or an air mattress so that, if you get tired of always climbing the banks of the river, you could swim, trailing your floating pack behind you.

After a couple of hours of hard going you will stumble upon a larger waterfall. This is a good place to try to make camp, as sandy areas are few and far between after this point. Just below the falls you might find a good site, and there is always driftwood for a fire. Beware: in heavy rain flash floods are common; when you set up camp, make sure you have an escape route planned just in case the waters start to rise. Stingless sweat bees are common here; irritating but harmless.

For the truly adventurous, a climb higher up the riverbed will take you to the headwaters, which have rarely been explored. A guide might also be able to take you up over the back of Mount Amboro and down along the Isama River back to the Surutu, but this is extremely hard going and you would have to be very well equipped.

VISITING NOEL KEMPFF MERCADO NATIONAL PARK

The huge expanse of Noel Kempff Mercado National Park is situated on Bolivia's northeastern border with Brazil. The park was renamed to commemorate one of Bolivia's most distinguished naturalists who was gunned down by drug traffickers in 1985. It is characterised by near-vertical cliffs that rise to meet a broad plateau, where dense forests, rolling hills and countless freshwater streams broken intermittently by sparkling cascades dominate the scene. In this geographically isolated area, flora and fauna have evolved separately, and many species are unique.

In 1908 British explorer Colonel P H Fawcett ventured into this unknown territory – supposedly inhabited by ferocious cannibalistic tribes and dangerous beasts. Fawcett's enthusiasm was one of the inspirations for Arthur Conan Doyle's novel *The Lost World* published four years later.

The Nature Conservancy has included Noel Kempff Mercado National Park in its 'Park in Peril' programme, initiated to protect vulnerable ecological sites throughout Latin America. The park has also been classified by organisations such as the United Nations Development Programme and UNESCO as a vital area for the conservation of Amazon wildlife.

The impressive birdlife includes the giant rhea, jabiru stork, harpy eagle and hyacinth macaw (one of the rarest and most beautiful of parrots). The giant armadillo and giant otter, jaguar, maned wolf, bush dog, prehensile-tailed porcupine and dusky titi monkey are some of the rare members of this astonishing ecosystem.

CAMPS AND TRANSPORT Getting to the park depends on how much time and money you have to spare – because it is such a remote area it can get relatively expensive. There are two ways to reach Flor de Oro (the main station in the park): by hiring a small plane (a Cessna 206 carrying four or five passengers), or by driving in a private 4x4 for 21 hours to Piso Firme (just outside the extreme northwestern corner of the park), and then by private speadboat nine hours upstream, and six hours downstream to Flor de Oro. The only way to visit the Serrania escarpments is by small plane, although you can walk up to Mirador de los Monos from Bahia Caiman in a few hours.

To reach Los Fierros from Flor de Oro you must also fly (roughly 30 minutes one way). The Ahlfeld Waterfall is accessible from Flor de Oro, taking roughly five hours by boat in the rainy season. Los Fierros, the second station that is more accessible by land and, hence, more frequently visited, can be reached from Santa Cruz with a 15-hour 4x4 drive. These roads need a powerful 4x4 with good mud-terrain tyres during the rainy season (December–April), but should be fine during

Simon Carnegie

Visits to Noel Kempff Mercado National Park can be organised directly through the Fundación Amigos de la Naturaleza (FAN), which is broadly responsible for running the park, including providing visit permits and booking accommodation at one of the two main camps.

One of the biggest challenges of visiting Noel Kempff is actually getting there. One camp, La Flor de Oro, located on the Brazilian border, can be accessed only by air. Another camp, Los Fierros, is at least seven hours' drive north of Concepción, sometimes much more if using the unreliable local public transport network. FAN can provide details of transport options and also book return buses.

Los Fierros is acknowledged to be the better of the two camps for seeing mammals, with jaguars, pumas and tapirs spotted here reasonably regularly. The really lucky may even see the very shy and rare maned wolf, seemingly a cross between a wolf and a fox, which lives in the long grass of the savannah. If possible, visitors should take a very powerful torch for night excursions: the reflection of animals' eyes can be the best way to find them in the dark.

Day trips from Los Fierros, which will require transport within the park, include the spectacular El Encanto Waterfall and a climb up to the Caparú plateau, from where the views of the jungle and the savannah stretch for mile and miles. More details from FAN (*www.fan-bo.org*).

the dry season, albeit making for a very dusty journey. The overland route is tiring but worth the discomfort. An alternative to help break up the journey is to overnight along the Jesuit Missions trail (page 224) en route.

From here, you have to head for Flor de Oro by plane and visit the attractions by speedboat as there no roads. Those on a tighter budget can take a 4x4 to Los Fierros from the Missions region, as you will need transport to visit the attractions and those around Los Fierros are some 40–60km apart from each other. Finally, if you hire a medium-sized, 19-seater plane for a bigger group, then the costs are reduced.

Visitors can stay at the camps located within the park, but to visit Flor de Oro you should first contact Fundación Amigos de la Naturaleza (FAN) to check availability. Los Fierros and the waterfalls are under the administration of FAN and form an ecotourism research site and the main protection and management camp for the northeastern section of the park. For anyone wishing to visit the other camps, or any other location within the park, FAN must first check and co-ordinate facilities. Reservations are necessary if you plan to stay at the camp itself, where basic accommodation is available. Anyone wishing to visit the park must be accompanied by a local guide from the nearest community, to ensure the safety of visitors as well as to check that they don't harm the flora and fauna.

Although this may all sound complicated, such regulations help maintain the pristine nature of the area. The people at FAN are friendly and helpful, and they will do what they can to ensure your trip into the park is unforgettable.

HIKING This region can be suffocatingly hot, even during the winter months and when the occasional *surazo* (south wind) is blowing, so it's best to be prepared for tropical and rainy conditions – summer storms bring intense short showers, but then it's sunny again for the rest of the day. Ticks can be a problem, especially the little ones (seedticks or *garapatillas*), which caused extreme discomfort to Colonel Fawcett and many subsequent visitors. Guard again these mischievous members of nature by sprinkling repellant or sulphur powder on your socks and around your ankles and make sure your trousers are stuffed firmly into your boots. Ticks are best removed with masking tape before they become lodged in your skin. Introduced bees are around all the time in Los Fierros; just be careful and pack antihistamines if you are allergic. Non-stinging bees bite on the plateau for the one-and-a-half day visit from Los Fierros, so take moisturising lotion, which repels them. Finally, avoid wearing shorts, except when in camp, and wear boots not trainers. Many types of grass are razor sharp and can cause cuts.

Backpacking possibilities into the interior of the park are many and varied. However, you need to plan what to do before you go, because of the problem of co-ordinating cars, planes and speedboats for transport.

You can view the most picturesque areas in the park in three to seven days but, to really do it justice, you need two weeks. In such a biologically diverse place lots of animals and plants that you've never spotted before come out over a two-week stay, marking a major difference from the pampas tours in Rurrenabaque, where you tend to see all the wildlife in three or four days. Visits can also be arranged on an independent basis, but it's not easy (see box on previous page).

TOURISM CIRCUITS AROUND SANTA CRUZ

Santa Cruz may be the international hub for transport, but many travellers simply use the city as a staging point for visits to two of Bolivia's most interesting tourist trails – the Jesuit Missions and Che Guevara trails.

THE JESUIT MISSIONS TRAIL The jungles of southeast Bolivia are alive with the sound of music. The Jesuit Mission settlements have changed little since the Jesuits first arrived towards the end of the 17th century and colonised the indigenous Indians with religion and music. Today, thanks to their designation as World Heritage Sites by UNESCO and world-class music and theatre festivals held in alternating years, these remote outposts are once again alive with the culture of the Missions. The churches are supremely well preserved while the strains of music fill the jungle night for a unique taste of jungle baroque. For more details, see www.santacruz.gov.bo/chiquitos.

San Javier San Javier has a less-developed infrastructure than the other Mission settlements with a group of shops strung out along the main drag, Avenida Santa Cruz, and a couple of telephone call centres, but no ATM or internet.

🏠 Where to stay
🏠 **Hotel Momoqui** (9 rooms) Av Santa Cruz; ☎ 963 5095; e hotelmomoqui@hotmail.com. These cabin-style rooms, set in gardens with a swimming pool, are the best option in town. They're great for groups as most rooms fit up to 4 people to split costs; all have private bathrooms. Sgls/dbls/tpls US$20/30/40 with b/fast.

✖ Where to eat
✖ **Restaurant Luigi** Calle 24 de Septiembre; ☎ 963 5121. Tucked behind the plaza, this rustic, Italian-influenced eatery serves up a good range of dishes from pastas (30Bs) to pizzas (30–40Bs), plus meaty mains (15–30Bs). Check out the gaudy murals on the wall – 1970s kitsch is alive & kicking here. Open daily 11.30–15.00 & 18.30–21.00.

Concepción Concepción is the main hub of the Missions trail with a developed infrastructure and a growing choice of places to stay and eat – but still nowhere to

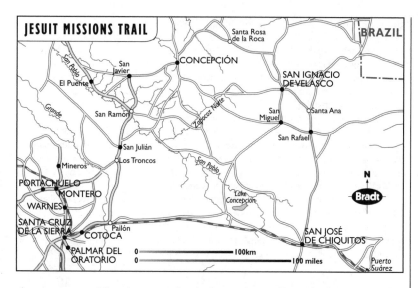

JESUIT MISSIONS TRAIL

change money. There's a **tourist information office** (℡ *964 3057; open 08.00–12.00 & 14.00–18.00*) on the east side of the plaza, which offers guided tours from 25Bs/hour (based on a group of two). There's also an **Entel** call centre (*open 08.00–22.00*) on the western corner of the plaza and very slow **internet access** (10Bs per hour) on the south side of the plaza.

Where to stay

🛏 **Hotel Chiquitos** (19 rooms) Av Killian Final; ☏/f 964 3153; e hotel_chiquitos@hotmail.com; www.hotelchiquitos.place.cc. The smartest option in town is a bit of a walk from the plaza, but very attractive with a garden, pool & a collection of orchids. The rooms are comfortable with private bathrooms, fridge & local TV channels, plus there are hammocks for that essential post-prandial snooze. *Sgls/dbls/tpls US$25/35/45 with b/fast.*

🛏 **Gran Hotel Concepción** (20 rooms) Plaza Principal; ☏ 964 3031; f 964 3032; e granhotelconcepcion@hotmail.com. Located at the west side of the plaza, this smart & tasteful property has a colonial feel & a garden filled with hammocks & rustic chairs. The suite (US$70) is particularly fancy with AC, but watch out for the dubious leopard-skin throws on the bed – they might bite. *Sgls/dbls/tpls US$25/40/45 with b/fast.*

Where to eat

✗ **Club Social 8 de Deciembre** Plaza Principal; ☏ 964 3210. The traditional social club, located in the western corner of the plaza, is a reliable option for à la carte mains (20Bs) & an evening barbecue served out on the terrace overlooking the church (20Bs). *Open daily 11.00–15.00 & 18.30–21.00.*

✗ **Restaurant El Buen Gusto** Plaza Principal; ☏ 964 3117. Set in a garden just off the main square, this

relaxed eatery has a good range of soups (10Bs) & mains (20–44Bs), served with rice, fried yucca & salad. *Open daily 11.00–15.00 & 18.30–21.00.*

✗ **Helados Alpina** Plaza Principal; ☏ 964 3137. In the same building as the town's internet service (see above), this offers cold drinks, seats overlooking the plaza & 1/2/3 scoops of ice cream for 3/5/7Bs.

What to see and do

Museo Misional (*Plaza Principal; open Mon–Fri 07.30–12.00 & 13.30–17.45, Sat 08.00–12.00 & Sun 10.00–12.00; entrance 5Bs*) On the south side of the plaza, this museum looks at the history of the Mission and celebrates the work of Hans Roth. There's an artisan studio attached showcasing the work of local craftsmen in wood-carving and mask-making.

Santa Cruz and the Oriente **TOURISM CIRCUITS AROUND SANTA CRUZ**

9

Geoff Groesbeck

Far from the madding crowd – in fact, far from any crowd – lie the Jesuit Mission towns, slumbering in the torpor of eastern Bolivia's *la gran Chiquitania*, a vast, remote area that has changed little since the Jesuits first arrived towards the end of the 17th century.

These charming little settlements were founded as mini theocracies called *reducciones*: autonomous, self-sufficient communities of 1,000 to 4,000 inhabitants, usually with two priests at their head, assisted by a council of eight native leaders. Amazingly, apart from the missionaries, colonists were not allowed to live in the settlements and could not even remain in them for more than a few days' time. Only the natives and their Jesuit patrons were legal inhabitants. At the time of the Jesuits' expulsion in 1767, there were about 37,000 people throughout the ten settlements of the Chiquitania under their guidance.

These settlements – nine of which have survived more or less intact – are barely decipherable dots on the map for most travellers. However, all of that is about to change. Thanks to their designation as World Heritage Sites by UNESCO in 1990, world-class music and theatre festivals held in alternating years, and a concerted push by the Bolivian government to promote the Jesuit missions in 2006 as its first 'National and Global Tourist Destination', these tiny outposts now represent the crown jewels of Bolivia's tourism crown.

The irony of it is that these pueblos – and their famous churches (the likes of which are found nowhere else on earth) – even exist. Nowadays, one would never guess that a few decades ago every one of them was in a state of near ruin. In 1957, a Jesuit missionary visiting Bolivia, Fr Felix Plattner, travelled to the Chiquitania in an attempt to retrace the route of missionaries who preceded him centuries before. He was amazed at what he saw: seven massive *templos* seemingly frozen in time, but decaying by the minute.

Plattner made a vow that he would save at least one of these spiritual masterpieces before they all sank into oblivion. Years later, he sent to the tiny hamlet of San Rafael – home to one of the finest churches – a Swiss architect, Hans Roth. Fr Plattner gave Roth six months to finish the restoration, along with round-trip air fare. Roth never went back home.

Working with a few European colleagues but otherwise with entirely native talent, Roth almost single-handedly saved these unique monuments from ruin. He spent almost three decades at this labour of love, and had a role in every aspect of each church's restoration. By the time he died in 1999, he had successfully or largely restored the churches and other colonial buildings of San Javier, San Rafael, San José de Chiquitos, Concepción, San Miguel and Santa Ana – all now World Heritage Sites – and the reconstruction of the church of San Ignacio.

The churches are now beginning to play a role as magnets for tourists from the world over. They house rare musical instruments, musical scores and priceless works of art. They also train the next generation of local artists and artisans, who remain faithful to the music and carvings their ancestors produced centuries ago.

And they play host every other year to the International Festival of American Baroque Music, *Misiones de Chiquitos*, with the Santa Cruz-based Asociación Pro Arte y Cultura (*www.festivalesapac.com*), a not-for-profit organisation primarily responsible for organising cultural activities throughout the region.

Geoff Groesbeck runs www.chiquitania.com, a specialist website dedicated to the culture of the Jesuit Missions in the Americas.

San Ignacio de Velasco The other principal hub of the Missions trail, San Ignacio has a decent infrastructure for tourists with places to change money, make phone calls and access email. It has a more commercial feel than other Mission pueblos and a large public market, which is a useful spot to stock up on supplies along the trail.

Where to stay and eat

⌂ **Hotel La Misión** (32 rooms) Plaza Principal corner with Calle Libertad; ☏ 962 2333; f 962 2460; www.hotel-lamision.com. This grand, colonial-style, 5-star property is the most luxurious place to stay along the trail. In addition to all mod cons & a swimming pool, the hotel has a good but expensive restaurant. *Standard sgls/dbls US$45/55; suites sgls/dbls US$85/95 with buffet b/fast.*

What to see and do
The Casa de la Cultura (*Plaza Principal*) is home to a small museum, which houses rare instruments and artefacts from the original Mission church.

THE CHE GUEVARA TRAIL One of the most interesting new routes to develop in recent years follows in the footsteps of Latin American hero Che Guevara, whose revolutionary zeal met an untimely end in a remote Bolivian pueblo in 1969. The project, supported by international NGOs, now represents one of the most rewarding excursions in the Oriente. For more details, see www.rutadelche.com.

Visiting the Che Guevara trail
Lagunillas This rustic pueblo, close to the location that was Che's former base camp, has little infrastructure to overnight, but its Che Museum makes it a worthwhile stop along the trail for a short visit.

Where to stay

⌂ **Residential SN** (12 rooms) Calle Ayacucho; no tel. A simple but very clean hostel with a small shop on-site, plus b/fast & meals available at extra cost (lunch 5Bs). *Rooms with private/shared bathrooms 30/20Bs.*

Where to eat

✕ **Pensión Lagunillas** Plaza 24 de Septiembre; no tel. Next to the church on the plaza, this very basic eatery offers a simple but filling set lunch (6Bs). *Open daily 11.30–15.00.*

What to see and do
Centro de Información Turística (*Calle Bolívar corner with Calle Padilla; no tel; open daily 09.00–12.00 & 14.00–18.00; entrance 5Bs*) This local tourist information centre combines an artisan shop with local crafts, a scattering of tourist information brochures and, most rewarding of all, the Che Guevara Museum, Carcel de Piedra, where photos and memorabilia trace Che's 1967 Bolivia campaign.

Camiri The hub town for the southern leg of the Che Guevara trail is a fairly sleepy place today, but it was a hotbed of history and intrigue during the Che era.

Where to stay

⌂ **Residential Premier** (14 rooms) Av Busch #60; ☏ 952 2204. The best place to stay in Camiri is a simple but clean place offering a mix of more equipped rooms with AC & private bathrooms, plus simple rooms with just a fan. *Sgls/dbls 50/100Bs; with shared bathroom 25Bs; b/fast 5Bs.*

Where to eat

✕ **Club Social Camiri** Calle Santra Cruz#55; no tel. A simple place serving a reasonable set lunch (7Bs), plus coffees & snacks throughout the day. *Open daily 11.30–15.00 & 18.30–21.00.*

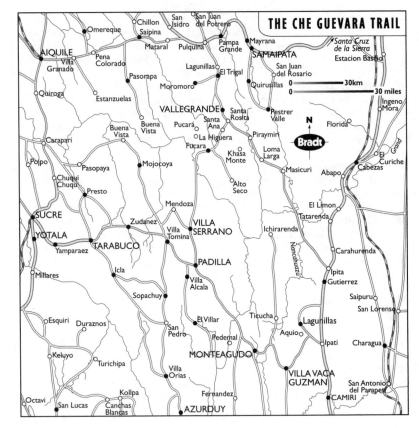

What to see Casino Militar, located in the northwest corner of the main square, is where the French activist, Debray, was imprisoned by the Bolivian army after he joined Che's campaign. Today you'll need to clear a visit with local army officials but, once inside, the building remains little changed since his days spent languishing in jail.

La Higuera The remote, dusty pueblo of La Higuera is the holy grail for Che pilgrims, its tiny main square dominated by a huge bust of Che, which was constructed to commemorate the anniversary of his death. Since the first tourists started following the trail, this is one place that really has seen the effects of increased tourism bringing greater prosperity to the community.

🏠 Where to stay

🏠 **Auberge communal** (dorm beds for 8 people). A converted former school, located just off the main square, it now looks more like a scout hut with dorm beds & a shared outside bathroom/shower block. *Very basic but cheap beds 10Bs per night; ask for the key in the village.*

🏠 **La Posada del Telegrafista** (4 rooms) Located on the road leading back to Vallegrande, no tel but call the village's public phone on 313 7114. This guesthouse & camp site, run by French couple Juan

& Oda, is one of the new private enterprises along the trail. The 4 bedrooms (a dbl, a twin & a 4-person dorm) are simple but homely with a shared bathroom & feature the only hot showers to be found in town. There is no electricity but the candlelight & the communal kitchen lend a hippy vibe to the proceedings – as do the hammocks. The owners are looking to develop adventure sports in the area – ask for details. *Rooms 40Bs pp; b/fast 8Bs; camping 5Bs.*

Life as a guerrilla combatant is not all Marxist ideology and hand-to-hand combat. Che Guevara's *Bolivian Diary* describes the daily misery of the guerrillas' final advance: ticks, malaria, diarrhoea and lancing pustules from marching-sore feet, not to mention betrayal by then general secretary of the Bolivian Communist Party, Mario Monje Molina.

Indeed, towards the end of the 1967 Bolivian campaign combatants Miguel, Dario and Chino had taken to drinking their own urine to quench their thirst, while Che himself had acquired a new nickname for his DIY dentistry skills extracting rotten teeth: Fernando the Tooth Extractor.

Some 38 years after Che penned his final entries in *The Bolivian Diary*, the story of his last struggle provides the inspiration for a revolutionary tourism project, which traces the rebel's tracks through tropical southeastern Bolivia. Che would meet a wretched end, his dream of catalysing a pan-American social movement lying in a pool of blood in a remote Bolivian pueblo. Ironically, this new Che trail aims to bring prosperity to the very people Che's revolution was intended to emancipate.

After several years in development, the Che trail has been handed back to the Guarani community to manage under the auspices of FUNDECHE, a collective of interested groups and private enterprises working to promote the trail.

According to Nelly Romero, president of the Assemblia del Pueblo Guarani (APG), an indigenous political movement based in Camiri: 'As Che fought for the poor and disadvantaged, I'm sure he wouldn't feel his name was being exploited by us, the Guarani community, to improve our lives.'

The trail comprises two main sections, north and south, covering an area of 300km². The northern route is better known, leading from Santa Cruz, via colonial Vallegrande and, depending on road conditions, terminating in the tiny pueblo of La Higuera. The southern leg of the trail leads directly along a new, asphalt road to the city of Camiri, where the French intellectual and author of *Revolution dans la Revolution?*, Jules Régis Debray, was imprisoned in the Casino Militar for his role in the uprising.

Since the official opening in October 2005, the trail has started to take on a life of its own. Branded signposts now mark the trail along rough, country roads, tourist facilities have blossomed and hand-painted ceramic tiles, designed by Santa Cruz-based Taller de Lorgio, Bolivia's leading ceramic design house, now mark the 25 main historic sites of interest.

Last year, Argentinian painter, Rodolfo Saavadra, completed a series of Che murals along the trail. Both designers gave their services free of charge in support of the project. One of Saavedra's most striking murals can be seen today at the Señor de Malta Hospital, where Che's body was laid out in the hospital's laundry outhouse to be paraded before the world's press.

The Che Guevara trail is one initiative that aims to prove that tourism can be both managed responsibly and serve to directly benefit local communities. But tour operators in Santa Cruz now offer regular Che tours as part of their itineraries and backpackers are starting to roll up in the plaza in search of the cult of Che.

Wounded, weak and wheezing from the chronic asthma that plagued him all his life, Che was captured in a shoot-out after fearful local people informed the Bolivian army of his movements. He was held captive in the local school building, the final – and most poignant – site on the Che trail.

'I remember the day in 1967 when they brought Che to the schoolhouse. He was with two other guerrillas and wounded in the leg,' says Don Manuel, a former animal herder turned local Che guide.'Local people were afraid of Che,' he adds. 'He came to help them, but they betrayed him.'

Vallegrande The main hub of the Che trail is an old, colonial town with a leafy main square and a real sense of history. For travellers it's the best place to overnight and stock up on supplies before following the trail.

Where to stay

Hostal Juanita (16 rooms) Calle Manuel María Cabellero #123; ☏ 942 2231. Located 2 blocks from the main square, this family-run place is friendly & clean. There's a large selection of rooms for every budget, ranging from US$5 for a dorm with shared bathroom, through to US$15 for a private room for 3 with private bathroom & a hot shower. The b/fast costs 7Bs extra.

Where to eat

El Mirador Located on the hill overlooking the town (hence the name); ☏ 9422341. This German-Bolivian-run restaurant is a cut above anywhere else in town, with a homely feel & excellent set mains (13–18Bs) plus fish dishes (20Bs). *Open daily* 11.30–14.30 & 18.30–21.00.

Café Galeria de Arte Santa Clara Calle Florida & Plaza 26 de Enero; no tel. This small & arty café is ideal for a coffee or snack after a day following the trail. *Open daily 18.00–22.00.*

What to see and do

Casa de la Cultura (*Plaza 26 de Enero; open daily 08.00–12.00 & 14.00–18.00; entrance free*) This colonial building houses a Che Guevara room, located upstairs from the less rewarding archaeological museum. The room has a fine collection of photos, documents and memorabilia from Che's 1967 campaign, including black and white images of Che after his body was laid out at the Señor de Malta Hospital. The hospital contains murals by the Argentine artist, Rodolfo Saavedra, as a testimonial to Che's legacy.

10

Tupiza and Tarija

TUPIZA Tel code: 02; altitude: 2,956m; population: 38,337

Located 189km south of Uyuni and 600km from the rail hub of Oruro, Tupiza, part of Potosí Department, is slowly growing as a tourist destination. This is thanks primarily to the mythology surrounding the two Wild West outlaws who (allegedly) met their end in the region (see box, *The Legend of Butch Cassidy and the Sundance Kid*, page 234).

It soon becomes apparent to visitors that Tupiza's fledgling tourism scene is very much tied up in the hands of two local agents: Tupiza Tours and Valle Hermoso Tours (page 232). Between these companies you can easily arrange your whole stay in Tupiza and any accompanying tours. Indeed, given that Tupiza, while pleasant, has few sights per se, the main attraction for travellers is striking out into the Wild West-style countryside around town on a jeep, horse or bicycle tour.

There are two things to beware of in Tupiza, however. Firstly, everything, but everything, closes on a Sunday, so try not to coincide your tour with this day. Secondly, there are very limited facilities to get cash in Tupiza, so best come prepared. If you are carrying travellers' cheques or a credit card, then expect to pay a hefty commission on all transactions undertaken.

HISTORY Officially Tupiza was founded at the same time as Tarija but, given its tumultuous and bloody past, no official records are to be found. What we do know is that the region saw some of the bloodiest battles of the war of independence. As its mineral wealth and favourable agricultural conditions became apparent to the Spanish settlers, it also grew as a frontier town for those making a new start. Even today Tupiza has a growing population, although much of its mineral wealth has long since been exhausted and tourism is replacing tin and silver as the main source of economic development.

GETTING THERE
By train The **train station** located on the western edge of town along Avenida Serrano (✆ *694 2527*) has regular connections to Uyuni (page 168) and Oruro

THREE THINGS TO DO IN TUPIZA

1 Take a seat in the sunshine and soak up the Wild West atmosphere of Tupiza's workaday main square (page 235).

2 Retrace the (alleged) final footsteps of Butch Cassidy and the Sundance Kid with an excursion to the cemetery of San Vicente, where the outlaws are said to have made their dramatic last stand (page 234).

3 Strike out into the badlands around Tupiza on a horseback or jeep tour and marvel at the wild landscape with its collection of cacti and birdlife (page 237).

TUPIZA AND TARIJA

(page 159). For more details of train schedules and prices, check the website www.fca.com.bo/fca1/itinerarios-taritas-1.htm).

The ticket office opens according to a rather complex itinerary as follows:

Monday	08.00–11.00 and 15.30–18.00
Tuesday	00.30–04.00, 08.00–11.00 and 15.30–17.30
Wednesday	08.00–11.00 and 15.30–17.30
Thursday	08.00–11.00 and 15.30–18.00
Friday	08.00–11.00 and 15.30–17.30
Saturday	00.30–04.00, 08.00–11.00 and 15.30–17.30
Sunday	Closed

Tickets are sold the day before and on the day of travel only.

By bus The **bus terminal**, five minutes' walk southeast of the centre, has long and tiring connections to Potosí (8 hours, 30Bs), Uyuni (12 hours, 40Bs), Villazon (3 hours, 12Bs) and La Paz (16 hours, 70Bs). For Tarija, the recommended connection is with **Trans Tour Juarez** (✆ 694 4514), leaving daily at 20.00 (8 hours, 50Bs).

There's a 1.5Bs tax payable on departures from the bus terminal.

GETTING AROUND Everything in Tupiza is easily accessible on foot, with most places of interest within a few blocks of the main square.

TOURIST INFORMATION There's no tourist information office in Tupiza, so for reliable information, consult Tupiza's two recommended agencies.

LOCAL TOUR AGENCIES

Tupiza Tours Av Chicas #187; ✆ 694 3003; e tpztours@entelnet.bo; www.tupizatours.com. This long-established agency specialises in Butch Cassidy tours & has worked with several documentary crews. A half-day tour to Huaca Huañusca (Dead Cow Hill) costs US$30 pp, based on a group of 2, while a full-day trip to San Vicente costs US$75 each; prices inc picnic lunch, guide & transport. The owners also recently introduced their 'Triathlon' trip, a full-day trip by bike, horse & jeep, taking in the 10 most impressive sites around Tupiza from 230Bs pp, based on a group of 2.

A group of 4 pays 180Bs each – hence it's worth trying to join up with other travellers to keep the cost down. Open Mon–Sat 08.00–20.00.
Valle Hermoso Tours Av Pedro Arraya #478; ✆ 694 2370; f 694 2592; e hostalvh@hotmail.com; www.bolivia.freehosting.net. The main rival to Tupiza Tours offers horseback tours of the countryside around Tupiza from 20Bs pp, plus motorbike tours from US$23 pp (based on a 3hr ride). They will also arrange trips to Uyuni; prices inc meals, guide & transport. Open Mon–Sat 08.00–20.00.

TUPIZA

They were born Robert LeRoy Parker and Harry Alonzo Longabaugh respectively. They picked up their nicknames after stints working as a butcher and serving an 18-month stint for robbery in Sundance, Wyoming. And their tale went on to be adapted for the 1969 box-office smash, *Butch Cassidy and the Sundance Kid*, starring Paul Newman and Robert Redford, which turned the tale of the Wild Bunch outlaws who fled to South America with US$1,000 rewards on their heads into the stuff of Hollywood legend.

The truth behind the legend of Butch and Sundance is, however, harder to find. We know that they fled to South America in 1901 to evade pursuit from the Pinkerton Detective Agency, following a string of bank raids on the Union Pacific railroad. They spent several years working as law-abiding cattle ranchers in Patagonia before returning to a life of crime in Bolivia.

Letters written by Butch from the time suggest the pair were looking for one last job before retiring and buying a cattle range near the frontier town of Santa Cruz in tropical southeastern Bolivia.

Today, with a fledgling backpacker trail carving out a trail in their footsteps, interest in the legend of Butch and Sundance is fuelling a new boom for Butch Cassidy tours.

The trail starts in Tupiza, where the colonial town square, overshadowed by the bleached-white façade of the cathedral, looks unchanged since the days in 1908 that Butch and Sundance spent casing the local bank. It was while laying low in Tupiza that Butch learned of a payroll to be transported by mule for workers of the Aramayo mine near Huaca Huañusca (Dead Cow Hill), 50km northeast of Tupiza.

The robbery took place just after 09.30 on 3 November 1908 after which the pair set off at a canter, reportedly heading for 'Uyuni and the north'. They made it as far as San Vicente.

Today San Vicente is a jarring three- to four-hour jeep ride from Tupiza along a rough road. A less hospitable place is hard to conceive of. At 4,500m above sea level and swept by fierce winds, the 700-person strong mining settlement feels like the end of the road. San Pedro de Atacama, across the frontier with Chile, is 350km south across rough terrain.

WHERE TO STAY Options to overnight are limited in Tupiza but the two main hotels cum tour agencies in town both have the market sewn up and serve it well. The following properties are divided by budget category and listed in the order of the author's preference.

Mid-range

Hotel Mitru (43 rooms) Av Chicas #187; ✆ 694 3001; e tpztours@entelnet.bo; www.tupizatours.com. The stalwart of the Tupiza accommodation scene, the Mitru remains the traveller's favourite & has recently had a whole new wing added with smarter rooms & new fittings. Regular features include a self-service continental b/fast & a swimming pool, plus cable TV in the bedrooms. Massages are also available, & there's a laundry service (8Bs/kg) & a book exchange. *Sgl/dbl with private bathroom 65/120Bs; sgl/dbl with shared bathroom 25/50Bs; suites sgl/dbl 200/320Bs.*

Hotel Mitru Annex (19 rooms) Calle Avaroa; ✆ 694 3002. This remodelled hotel across town has a mix of dbls & tpls with private & shared bathrooms if the main hotel if full. Cabañas at El Recreo, 2km from Tupiza, were under construction at the time of writing. It's worth knowing, however, that if you arrive by train in the early hours, you have to pay for the extra night. *Rooms in the new section are priced as follows: sgls/dbls with private bathrooms 120/160Bs; sgls/dbls with shared bathrooms 65/120Bs. Rooms in the old section: sgls/dbls with private bathrooms 65/120Bs; sgls/dbls with shared bathrooms 25/50Bs; suites: sgls/dbls 200/320Bs.*

Hostal Valle Hermoso (43 rooms) Av Pedro Arraya #478; ✆ 694 2370; f 694 2592; e hostalvh@hotmail.com; www.bolivia.freehosting.net. The Mitru's main rival, offering a similarly broad range of services, is

The village, home today to the Pan American silver mine, remains isolated from civilisation, lost and forgotten amid the Cordillera Occidental mountain range. The only nod to the legacy of San Vicente's most famous stiffs is a weather-beaten sign at the entrance to town. It reads: 'Here death's Butch Kassidy [sic] and Sundance Kid'.

At sundown on 6 November 1908, Butch and Sundance rode into town on a couple of mules and asked for shelter. Cleto Bellot, the local administrative officer, advised them there was no lodging, but locals could put them up in an outhouse and sell them provisions. Fortified by a last meal of beer and sardines, they tended to their animals and bedded down for the night, unaware that Bellot had taken his leave to make contact with a four-man posse from Uyuni, led by Captain Justo P Concha.

By daylight on 7 November, Butch and Sundance lay dead. But did they really go out in a blaze of bullets and glory as the film suggests, or did they take their own lives rather than face capture?

The trail runs cold at San Vicente's windswept cemetery. The outhouse where they stayed is now a deserted abode shack filled with llama dung. There's no Jim Morrison-style tomb with homage-rendering graffiti. In fact, there's no tomb at all.

In 1991 a team of forensic scientists from the United States exhumed the grave where the fallen bandits were supposed to have been buried. DNA tests eventually found the body was that of Gustave Zimmer, a German engineer, who worked at local mines at a similar time to Wild Butch's robbing spree. It's likely that their bodies are buried somewhere in the cemetery but the precise locations remain unknown. 'The fact that there are no definite conclusions is probably what fascinates people,' says local guide, Alejandro Quispe Alfaro. 'Tourists come here expecting to find the holy grail, but all they find is a huge question mark.'

There's more about Butch and Sundance from the excellent website http://ourworld.compuserve.com/homepages/danne.

Tupiza Tours and Valle Hermoso Tours in Tupiza (see page 232) both run dedicated Butch and Sundance tours.

Tupiza's only member of the Hostelling International (HI) network — &, as such, offers a 10% discount to HI card holders. The rooms are looking a bit faded these days. The owners also run a small shop for essential supplies next door. *Rooms with private/shared bathroom 35/20Bs; b/fast 6–12Bs.*

⌂ **Hostal Valle Hermoso 2** (13 rooms) Av Pedro Arraya #505. A smarter, brand-new option. The rooms, designed for up to 4 people, are comfortable & bright with brand-new beds. Amongst the raft of services, they will change travellers' cheques (albeit with an 8% commission) & advance money on Visa cards (with 20% — ouch! — commission), plus there's a laundry service (8Bs/kg) & a book exchange. *Rooms with private/shared bathrooms 35/20Bs; b/fast costs an extra 6–12Bs.*

Budget
⌂ **Residencial Centro** (13 rooms) Av Santa Cruz #287; ☏ 694 2705. Simple but handy for the main square, this is the real budget option in town. Rooms are basic but comfortable, albeit a bit on the cold side. Meals are sometimes available. *Rooms with private/shared bathrooms cost 30/20Bs with/without b/fast.*

⌂ **Residencial Terminal** (10 rooms) Calle Suipacha #8; ☏ 694 2743. If you're stranded in the early hours by the bus station, try this place. It's simple in a port-in-a-storm kind of way. *Sgls/dbls/tpls 20/30/40Bs without b/fast.*

WHERE TO EAT
✗ **California** Plaza Independencia; no tel. The most traveller-friendly eatery in town has a Wild West cactus décor & offers a menu of hearty staples, such as pasta & steaks. It's best for dinner but they also serve b/fast 8–12Bs, burgers 5–12Bs & beers 7Bs. Best of all, this is one place that is

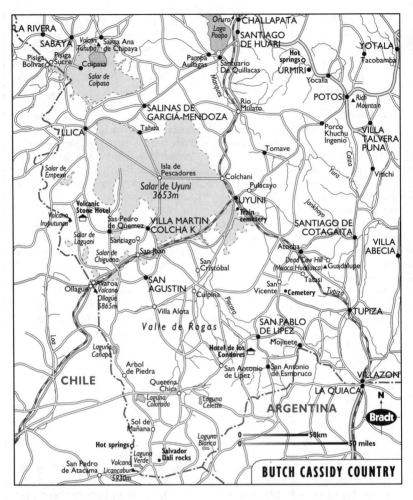

BUTCH CASSIDY COUNTRY

actually open on a Sun night. *Open daily 09.00–22.00.*

✗ **Café El Garage** Av Chicas; ☎ 694 3147. A great hole-in-the-wall snack joint, located bang opposite the Hotel Mitru (page 234), with a range of burgers (around 8Bs) & sandwiches (6Bs). A cactus motif & friendly welcome make this a useful place for a snack. *Open Mon–Sat 07.00–22.00.*

✗ **Bolivia 2950** Calle Florida; no tel. A hidden gem & miraculously open on Sun, this steak restaurant has pictures of John Lennon on the walls & a half-built look that only lends to its slightly

chaotic charm. A huge steak, plus the run of the self-service salad bar, costs 26Bs. *Open daily 18.00–22.00.*

✗ **Il Bambino** Calle Florida #396; no tel. A good spot for a hearty, 3-course set lunch (8Bs); it's no frills but a reliable lunchtime option. *Open Mon–Sat 11.00–15.00.*

✗ **Heladería Cramer** Plaza Independencia #396; ☎ 694 2340. A pit-stop coffee & ice-cream parlour at the north end of the main square, it's simple but satisfying. Try the beer-flavour ice cream (1.5Bs) to liven up your elevenses. *Open daily 08.00–18.30.*

Mercado Antonio Gil Duran has a small range of fresh produce for stocking up on snacks, while there are a few small **supermarkets** grouped on Calle Florida behind Hotel Mitru (page 234) so you can stock up on supplies before starting your tour.

ENTERTAINMENT AND NIGHTLIFE Karaoke is king in Tupiza after dark. If you're desperate to exercise your vocal chords, try **Diver Gente** (*Calle Florida;* ☏ *718 34052*) for beers and bad tunes; open Wed–Sat 19.00–late. A better bet is to hang out at the **Hotel Mitru** (page 234), where they screen the film *Butch Cassidy and the Sundance Kid* most evenings at 20.00, plus a range of documentaries about the famous outlaws.

OTHER PRACTICALITIES

Banco de Crédito Plaza Independencia. Charges a flat-rate US$5 commission on all transactions & offers cash advances only on Visa, but not American Express. *Open Mon–Fri 08.30–12.30 & 14.00–17.00.*

Cyber Mihagni Calle Cochabamba #2. Has internet access for 3.50Bs/hr; *open daily 07.00–23.00.* Also offers money exchange.

Entel call centre Plaza Independencia. *Open daily 07.00–23.00.*

Hospital Eduardo Eguia ☏ 694 3272. Located opposite the bus station for emergencies.

Latin America money exchange Calle Avaroa #154. Charges 4–6% commission on travellers' cheques. *Open daily 08.00–12.00 & 14.00–20.00 (if they're shut, just ring the bell on the wall next to the door).*

Lourdes pharmacy Plaza Independencia #415. *Open daily 09.00–12.30 & 15.00–20.00.*

Post office Av Villarroel #409. *Open Mon–Fri 09.00–18.30, Sat 09.00–12.00 & 14.00–17.00, Sun 09.00–12.00.*

RocaNet Calle Florida. Has internet access for 3Bs/hr in a non-smoking environment. *Open daily 09.00–22.00.*

WHAT TO SEE AND DO The **Municipal Museum** (*Calle Sucre; open Mon–Fri 12.00–18.00 but suffers from highly irregular opening hours; entrance free*) is the only sight in town as such and, frankly, the musty collection of old photos, relics and artefacts will not detain you for too long.

TREKKING AROUND TUPIZA

John Pilkington and James Brunker (www.magicalandes.com)

The choice of hikes in the area is almost endless. You may find 1:50,000 scale maps for sale at the IGM office on the second floor of the government building on the main square, otherwise the people at the Hotel Mitru may be willing to give directions.

The altitude is 2,900m to 3,700m and the climate is equable, with mild winters and warm summers. But remember that this is desert country: unless you're sure of finding water en route you should carry at least two to three litres per person per day. While on the subject of water, if you plan to hike in the summer months (November to March), remember that the *quebradas* can be subject to potentially dangerous flash floods. Keep an eye on the weather and camp well away from them.

Your footwear should be strong enough to withstand the sharp desert stones and even sharper prickles of the saguaro cactus. Be sure to carry a compass on longer hikes.

QUEBRADA DE PALALA AND EL SILLAR To experience the quebradas and get a taste of the high country, take one of the regular trufis marked 'Palala' from Avenida Regimiento Chichas to its terminus 2km north of Tupiza. From this village a track leads north and then, joining the quebrada opposite an industrial plant, turns west under power lines past towering 'shark's fin' formations of red sandstone. There's virtually no traffic, but the track is frequented by villagers collecting firewood. In winter you may meet packs of llamas or donkeys carrying salt and other Altiplano staples for exchange in the lowlands. These annual pilgrimages – often covering 600km and taking two months or more – have been going on for at least 400 years, their participants seemingly untouched by the modern world.

The quebrada floor provides good walking and a welcome relief from the track. You could easily spend a day exploring its 10km of main and side valleys. Most of these, however, end in sheer cliff faces; to gain access to the uplands you have to return to the track. About 3km from Palala this turns southwest up a side valley called Quebrada Chiriyoj Waykho, then climbs via a series of switchbacks to arrive at the vertiginous 3,700m balcony known as El Sillar (the Saddle).

From here you can enjoy breathtaking views east across the Tupiza Valley, south towards Argentina and north to the 5,600m cone of the volcano El Chorolque. But it is the cactus-studded landscape beneath you that makes El Sillar special. Flash floods have created a Disneyworld of cliffs, spires, fins and canyons in colours that range from red and orange to ochre and even blue. This is also the start of the four-day route from Tupiza via Lagunas Verde and Colorada to the Salar de Uyuni.

QUEBRADA DE PALMIRA AND THE VALLE DE LOS MACHOS Only 4km from the centre of Tupiza, these canyons offer an outstanding day or half-day hike, with some dramatic shark's fin formations and, in the Valle de los Machos, rock pillars sufficiently phallic to bring tears to the eyes. (Not for nothing is it also called Valle de los Penes, Valley of the Penises.)

To get there from Tupiza, walk three to four blocks south from the main square Plaza de Independencia until you reach Avenida 26 de Agosto. Turn right and head towards the outskirts of town; you will soon see to your left a gap in the slate grey ridge. Turn left when you reach the road that passes through this gap and out into open, if rubbish-strewn, countryside.

After crossing another small saddle 20 minutes from the main square, turn right up a wide riverbed, which is dry for most of the year. The bright orange / red flanks of Quebrada de Palmira now beckon you directly ahead. After 20 minutes of gentle ascent, you pass some strange vertical rock walls known as 'The Devil's Door'; some 15 minutes further up the river bed just beyond the first bend, the Valle de los Machos comes into view on your right, an area with some notable gravity-defying phalluses.

Continue up the main valley, admiring the contrast of orange cliffs and green acacia trees, for a further ten to 15 minutes to a point where it narrows to a slit. You can follow the stream bed into this section, though on several occasions you will have to scramble up ledges (small waterfalls in rainy season) and red sandstone boulder chokes. For the adventurous it is possible to continue up the canyon in this fashion for a considerable distance; reaching the far end will take a few hours. Drinking water can be found in a few places among the boulders for most of the year (though it is often very salty and murky), and a short distance back down the valley are several good camping spots.

You can return to Tupiza the way you came, or continue south along the road through further badlands to the Río San Juan del Oro, 8km south of Tupiza. During the dry season you can turn left before the bridge here and follow the riverbank downstream to a railway crossing, returning to Tupiza along the railway track. The river crossing is known as 'Entre Ríos' and is the point where the yellow/brown waters of the Río San Juan de Oro meet the blue/green waters of the Río Salo that flows through Tupiza. This 20km circuit can be completed in a long day. Shortly before the railway crossing on the far side of the river is a 40m-high rock pinnacle known as 'La Torre' (the tower). To walk from the railway crossing to Tupiza takes around 2½ hours.

HUACA HUAÑUSCA You can visit Huaca Huañusca on a day trip with Tupiza Tours, based at the Hotel Mitru (see page 234). To get there independently, you will have to either hitchhike or organise a taxi.

An increasingly popular route for exploring the Salar de Uyuni and wild scenery of the southwest, especially for those travelling up from northern Argentina, is to start from Tupiza, where various agencies offer the trip. The route normally takes four days. At the time of writing very few if any agencies in Uyuni were offering the trip in reverse.

Tours leave Tupiza via the Quebrada de Palala and El Sillar (described earlier) then climb across bleak rugged terrain punctuated by a few remote llama-herding communities to arrive at San Antonio de Lipez (4,200m), gateway to the spectacular scenery of South Lipez province, for the first night. The second day parallels the Cordillera Lipez range, which includes the highest peak in southern Bolivia at 6,010m, Uturuncu volcano. The route then takes in turquoise Laguna Morijón and villages of Quetana Grande and Chico before crossing the predominantly borax Salar de Chalviri to rejoin the usual Uyuni–San Pedro route. After a detour to Laguna Verde, tours continue to spend the second night at Laguna Colorada. For those with time, some tours spend an extra night in Quetana Chico (confusingly bigger than Quetana Grande). This gives an extra day to explore a series of beautiful lakes to the south of Uturuncu towards the Argentine border, including lagunas Celeste and Amarillo. The third day traces the Uyuni route in reverse to overnight in one of the options close to the southern shore of the Salar de Uyuni, before leaving before dawn on the final day and driving onto the Salar in time for sunrise. Watching the dawn colours break the horizon and the vast expanse of white slowly reveal itself before your eyes is an unforgettable, if an anatomically chilling experience! After breakfast on Incahuasi Island tours continue to Uyuni where most people leave, though if you wish you can continue back to Tupiza with your driver.

The site of Butch and Sundance's final hold-up is about 15km northwest of Salo, on a trail that was superseded by the present road in the 1960s. You can trace the trail all the way to the summit, but it's a stiff 1km climb and still leaves you with several kilometres of road-walking on the crest of the ridge. If you attempt it, allow about four hours in total.

The road from Salo climbs the ridge in a series of sweeps, then, after converging on the old trail, keeps close to the crest for its entire length. Some 12km from Salo it passes a small corral away to the left, then makes a double bend at a broad saddle. Shortly beyond here you should catch a fleeting glimpse into the valley of the Quebrada Flores Palca to your left; and 0.5km from this point you'll come to a notch on the left where the old trail leaves the road and drops down into this valley.

Follow this trail to the stream, which as Butch and Sundance would have noted, offers good drinking water throughout the year. The cave where they lay in wait is slightly behind you to the left. They took the payroll on the small gravel plain where the trail emerges at the foot of the hill. The robbery was obviously well planned; the valley is far from any village, and since the building of the road it has been known only to llama herders, who occasionally make campfires in the cave. Looking around, you may well reflect that far from being romantic, the life of an outlaw is likely to have been a desperately lonely one.

When you're ready to return to the road, head up the small gorge to your right, keeping left of the stream. In 0.5km the valley opens up and you'll see the road directly ahead on the stream's opposite bank. Hitchhiking back to Tupiza is best in the afternoon. If you want to explore further you could continue north on a good trail up the valley of the Río Yana Khasa. This leaves the road at a place called Abra Guadalupe, on the outside of a right-hand bend about 300m after it begins the climb to Huaca Huañusca. It leads, in 17km, to the village of Guadalupe.

Tupiza and Tarija **TREKKING AROUND TUPIZA**

10

Tarija is the hub of Bolivia's fledgling wine industry (see box, *A fruity little number*, page 243) and, as such, makes for a very pleasant diversion from the typical Bolivian tour itinerary. Indeed, its Mediterranean climate (best experienced in summer as, during winter, Tarija appears to be locked into hibernation) and fondness for a drop of the local vino lend the city a very different feel from Bolivia's other urban centres. The local residents are known for their bonhomie, a sense of humour and a very strong accent, heavily influenced by the proximity of bordering Argentina.

Despite this, Tarija is not yet a major tourist destination and suffers from above-average prices for generally good-value Bolivia. The concept of wine tourism is Tarija's unique selling point but the local tourism authorities seem slow to recognise its potential. The local wineries are, however, pushing ahead with plans to boost Tarija's profile as more than just a place to break your journey before crossing the border into Argentina (the border crossing at Villazon is just 194km away) and develop its wine tourism potential.

Beware: Tarija is pretty much a ghost town from 12.30 to 15.30 each day, while everyone takes a long lunch and a siesta. You can't fight it, so get your business done in the morning and simply learn to go with the slow-paced flow.

HISTORY Tarija has always been rather removed from the usual cut and thrust of Bolivian politics, with a strong alignment with Argentina both politically and culturally. The city declared independence from Spain in 1807, the first region of South America to found its own republic. But Tarija's independence was short-lived after being absorbed into the newly declared Republic of Bolivia in 1825.

Founded in 1574 with the name Villa de San Bernardo de la Frontera, the department's six districts celebrate their anniversary on 15 April to commemorate the 1817 revolution.

GETTING THERE

By plane Tarija's small but modern airport (✆ *664 3135*) is located 4km from downtown, or a 10Bs taxi ride. Currently there are domestic connections only with daily flights to La Paz with AeroSur (direct) and Lloyd Aéreo Boliviano (via Cochabamba). Facilities include a newsstand, a café, Entel call centre and a Danny Tours office to arrange hotel reservations. There is no ATM or internet access. There's a 10Bs tax payable on all departures.

By bus The **bus terminal** on Avenida Las Americas (✆ *663 6508*), is located 20 minutes east of the centre, or a 5Bs taxi ride into town. It has long and tiring connections to Potosí (8 hours, 30Bs), Uyuni (12 hours, 40Bs), Villazon (3 hours, 30Bs) and La Paz (16 hours, 70Bs), plus a host of connections for cities in

---

THREE THINGS TO DO IN TARIJA

1 Tarija is all about sampling the excellent local wines, so book a bodega visit, stock up on quality Bolivian vino and strike out for a walk in the vineyards (page 245).

2 Soak up the sun at a pavement table while sipping a glass of local wine on the main square (page 244).

3 Explore the countryside around Tarija with its gentle walking, vine-scented countryside and colourful local festivals (page 246).

EL CARMEN

Oscar Alfaro
Zoo

Corazón
de Jesús

SAN JUAN

AVENIDA LOS MEMBRILLOS

Obrero Hospital

AV ESPAÑA

CARLOS LAZCANO

AV ESPAÑA

BOLIVAR

AV BELGRANO

CLARET

FEDERICO AVILA

EULOGIO

DELFIN PINO

RUIZ

AV DEL CARPIO

AVENIDA LAS AMERICAS

Airport
(4km)

University
Campus

AVENIDA ESPAÑA

GUSTAVO RUIZ

BERNARDO NAVAJAS

CALABI

ICHAZO

ANGEL

HUMBERTO

CELIDONIO AVILA

EL TEJAR

NAPOLEÓN RAÑA

AV LA PAZ

Bus terminal

PUENTE BOLIVAR

AVENIDA LA PAZ

ORURO

AV POTOSI

BOLIVAR

IV Centenario
Stadium

Bolívar Park

V DE FATIMA

AVENIDA PADILLA

AVAROA

San Juan de
Dios Hospital

AV PAMPA POTOSI

INGAVI

EJERCITO

O'CONNOR

Garcia Agreda
Park

LA PAMPA

JUNIN

BOLIVAR

SANTA CRUZ

LA MADRID

15 DE ABRIL

JUNIN

ISSAC ATTA

DELGADILLO

Puente del Peregrino

MENDEZ

AV DOMINGO PAZ

SUIPACHA

Tarija Supermarket

Rujero winery office

Café Mokka/Internet
centre/Mr Pizza Viva Tours

VIRGINIO LEMA

Banco Unión

SAN ROQUE

COLÓN

La Concepción/
La Esmeralda Laundry

Chingo's

Plaza
Sucre

AV DEL CARPIO

LAS PANOSAS

AVAROA

DANIEL CAMPOS

Grand Hotel Tarija

Victoria Plaza Hotel

Artisanía

15 de Abril

AeroSur
office

Cinema
Universal

CORRADO

Central
market

Municipal
tourist information office

Café Campero

La Casa
Dorada

La Viñateca

Taberna
Tarijeña

Buffalo

Gattopardo

Plaza
L de
Fuentes

El Tropero

Kohlberg winery office

DHL/
Western Union

SUCRE

GRAL TRIGO

Los Parrales

JM SARACHO

AV DOMINGO PAZ

Full Internet

INGAVI

CAMPERO

San Bernardo
de Tarija
Cathedral

Departmental
tourist information office

Piscis bookshop

Museum of Archaeology
& Palaeontology

LAB office

La Costanera

Guadalquivir

EL MOLINO

Hostal Carmen/
VB Tours

LA MADRID

15 DE ABRIL

BOLIVAR

RAMON ROJAS

BALLIVIAN

AV VICTOR PAZ ESTENSSORO
(PASEO LA COSTANERA)

San Martín
Bridge

SEVILLA

SAN JUAN

AV VICTOR PAZ ESTENSSORO

N

Bradt

(SKETCH MAP)
Not to scale

TARIJA

10

241

Argentina. For Tarija, the recommended connections are with **Trans Tour Juarez** (↘ *694 4514*), leaving daily at 20.00 (8 hours, 50Bs).

There's a 1.5Bs tax payable on departures from the bus terminal.

GETTING AROUND Most of Tarija is easily accessible on foot. For a taxi to the bus terminal or airport (for both, see page 240), call **Taxis 4 de Julio** (*Plaza Luis de Fuentes y Vargas;* ↘ *664 7676*). A minibus ride around town costs 1.50Bs and a taxi journey within the centre costs 3Bs.

TOURIST INFORMATION

🄸 **Departmental Tourist Information Office** Plaza Luis de Fuentes y Vargas; ↘ 664 2060; f 466 3100. The government tourist office has a rather small collection of maps & brochures, but they are happy to help with tourists' enquiries. *Open 08.00–12.00 & 14.30–18.30, Sat & Sun 09.30–12.00.*

🄸 **Municipal Tourist Information Office** Calle Sucre corner with Calle Bolivar; ↘ 663 8081. This friendly alternative to the government tourist office has a decent selection of maps & brochures, but watch out for the slightly irregular opening hours. *Open Mon–Fri 08.00–12.00 & 14.30–18.30.*

TOUR OPERATORS

VTB Tours Calle Ingavi #784; ↘ 664 4341; f 611 3571; e vtb@entelnet.bo. Housed within the Hostal Carmen (page 244), this agency specialises in wine tours (US$13 pp based on a group of 2, inc a tasting, but not lunch) & a fossil tours to paleontological sites located 50km from Tarija (US$22 pp based on a group of 2). *Open*

Mon–Sat 09.00–12.00 & 14.00–19.00.
Viva Tours Calle 15 de Abril #509; ↘ 663 8325; e vivatour@cosett.com.bo. This agency arranges travel tickets, plus offers a city tour & winery visits with prices from US$15 pp. *Open in theory Mon–Sat 09.00–12.00 & 14.00–19.00, but suffers from irregular hours in practice.*

🏠 **WHERE TO STAY** Tarija has some average properties in the downtown area with a bias towards the business-traveller trade. More rewarding is the city's sole upscale property (Hotel Los Parrales), which is one of Bolivia's best five-star hotels. The following properties are divided by budget category and listed in the order of the author's preference.

Top of the range

🏠 **Hotel Los Parrales** (36 rooms) Urbanisation Carmen de Aranjuez; ↘ 664 8444; f 664 8448; e info@losparraleshotel.com; www.losparraleshotel.com. Tarija's, & indeed one of Bolivia's most luxurious hotels, this place is a clear cut above most properties, although the service can be a little on the frosty side at times. It's hugely popular with convention & conference groups, so can also be extremely busy – despite

being 4km from downtown Tarija. On the plus side, lush gardens, large, airy rooms with great views & a spa centre, El Lagar, with its panoramic hot tub, make for a thoroughly pampered experience all round. *Sgls/dbls/suite with buffet b/fast & complimentary newspaper US$95/115/120. Ask about special package deals for families with airport transfers & use of spa facilities from US$70 pp.*

Mid-range

🏠 **Plaza Hotel Victoria** (30 rooms) Calle La Madrid corner with Calle Sucre; ↘ 664 2600; f 664 2700; e hot_vit@olivo.tja.entelnet.bo. A smarter than average property, this is the favoured spot in town for business travellers. The rooms come fully equipped with fridges, cable TV & private bathrooms, & boast nice views across the main square. The place does feel a bit old fashioned overall but the location is hard to beat at the price. *Sgls/dbls/tpls*

US$25/35/45 with b/fast.
🏠 **Grand Hotel Tarija** (30 rooms) Calle Sucre #770; ↘ 664 2684; f 664 4777; e reserves@ hoteltarija.com. Make sure to ask for a room on the front to avoid being stuck in the rabbit-hutch-like rooms down the dark corridors that surround the central atrium. It's more expensive but well worth it for the sake of having some daylight. Otherwise, this centrally located property does offer a reasonable

With a micro-climate similar to that of Andalusia and scenery to match any European bodega, the Tarija Valley is the gateway to Bolivia's fledgling but growing wine-making industry.

'People say wine-making in Bolivia started 40 years ago with the introduction of modern technology, but I say it started 400 years ago when the Spanish and Jesuits missionaries first brought grapes to Tarija,' says Sergio Prudencio, owner of Bolivia's leading winery, La Concepción.

The road through the Tarija Valley, 25km from downtown Tarija, passes CENAVIT, the National Centre of Viticulture, charged with policing the quality of Bolivian wines. The resident wine-maker, Candido Tolaba, dreams of one day bringing local wines to the international market place.

'There's still a long way to go with only seven commercial bodegas in Tarija and 60 in all Bolivia,' he says. 'In the last ten years Bolivia has made huge strides, but we still lack the production capacity.'

There are 8,000 cultivable hectares of vines in Bolivia, compared with 200,000ha in Chile and 300,000 in Argentina. Bolivia currently produces around five million litres of wine and wine-based spirit per year, 60% of that coming from the sweet, white Muscatel de Alejandria grape, reflecting the country's artisan tradition of producing singani, Bolivia's answer to Peruvian and Chilean pisco.

In the main square of the 12,000-strong village of La Concepción, a clutch of colonial houses group around the bleached-white façade of the local church. The Concepción winery lies along a dirt track, where an old *finca*, preserved since the era of the Jesuits in 1606, stands guard over the wines.

While other wineries are content to cater to the domestic market, Sergio Prudencio believes he has identified the key to the future success of Bolivian wine-making: the concept of wines at altitude.

'Few of the world's leading wine-making areas lie above 500m above sea level, but La Concepción has 70ha spread across three altitudes between 1,750 and 2,100m, producing 200 million litres annually,' he says, as we inspect the orderly rows of vines, including Cabernet Sauvignon, Chardonnay, Merlot, Shiraz and Muscatel.

In essence, the high altitude of the Andes region makes for a unique selling point. The higher the vineyards, the greater is the level of solar radiation, hence a higher level of oxidants is produced and a more intense concentration of aromas achieved. La Concepción is now using this marketing tool to liberally promote their wines as 'the highest wines in the world' in a bid to boost international sales.

Currently only 5% of stock is sold outside Bolivia with wine merchants in the US and Switzerland the first to carry the La Concepción brand. A bottle of Cepas de Altura quaffing wine retails for US$11 in Bolivia, while a simple Merlot can be picked up in supermarkets for US$5.

'The problem is not the wine – we are confident of the quality and integrity of our wines. It's the image of Bolivia as a wine-producing country,' says Sergio, over lunch.

He smiles and offers a toast to the future of Bolivian wines: 'But I believe,' he says, draining his glass, 'our wine industry has the potential to finally put Bolivia on the map.'

range of home comforts, such as cable TV & minibar. *Sgls/dbls US$20/40 with views; sgls/dbls US$15/30 without views; all come with continental b/fast.*

🏠 **Hostal La Costanera** (20 rooms) Av Las Americas #594; ☎ 664 2851; f 663 2640;

e costanera@olivo.tja.entelnet.bo; www.cosett.com.bo/hcostanera. The excellent vegetarian set lunch (page 244) is the biggest attraction here, especially compared with the rather mediocre rooms. This place can be a useful mid-range option if other properties are full, but don't expect great service. Private bathrooms, refrigerators & cable TVs come as standard at least, but the

place is in desperate need of a good lick of paint. *Sgls/dbls/tpls US$20/25/35 with buffet b/fast.*

Budget

🏠 **Hostal Carmen** (28 rooms) Calle Ingavi #784; ↘ 664 3372; f 611 3571; e vtb@entelnet.bo. This 3-star property could do with freshening up & some of the mustier rooms need a major airing, but rates do include a continental b/fast & in-room cable TV.

It's the bottom end of the scale but very handy for travellers looking to arrange tours with the in-house tour agency, VTB Tours (page 242). *Sgls/dbls/tpls 80/120/150Bs.*

✖ WHERE TO EAT

✖ **Bufalo** Calle Madrid; ↘ 665 0000. Located next door to Gattopardo (above), Bufalo has a similarly relaxed feel with a wide menu & gringo-friendly fodder. Mains range from fresh pasta with a choice of sauces (18–22Bs) & steaks (30Bs) to Mexican dishes (15–20Bs) & burgers (9–15Bs). The service is highly attentive & the wine list extensive. Recommended. *Open daily 07.00–23.00.*

✖ **Café Mokka** Plaza Sucre; ↘ 665 0505. Quality food, a homely feel & tables with a coffee-bean motif make this an excellent place for everything from snacks (sandwiches 15Bs) to full meals (mains 30Bs). A good wine list offers wines by the glass (6Bs) & bottle (from 25Bs), while speciality liqueur coffees (15Bs) make for an excellent *digestif. Open daily 07.00–23.00.* Upstairs there's **internet access** available (entrance to the left of the café) for 3Bs/hr; open 09.00–13.00 & 15.00–23.00. Next door, **Mr Pizza** offers whole pizzas to take away (25–33Bs) & by the portion (4Bs).

✖ **Hostal La Costanera** Av Las Americas #594; ↘ 664 2851; f 663 2640; e costanera@ olivo.tja.entelnet.bo; www.cosett.com.bo/hcostanera. In a steak-obsessed city, this is an oasis for vegetarians

with a set vegetarian lunch (15Bs) complemented by a self-service salad bar & a tranquil ambience. The food is great, which is more than can be said for the hotel rooms upstairs (page 243). *Open daily 11.00–14.30.*

✖ **Chingo's** Plaza Sucre; ↘ 664 4864. This is a cheap & cheerful place for a snack meal with tables overlooking the square — best for sunny days. The menu takes in sandwiches (4Bs) & burgers (6–11Bs) — try the super macho burger for your meat fix. Especially good value, however, are the brochettes (15–20Bs), which come served with chips & salad. *Open daily 11.00–23.00.*

✖ **El Tropero** Calle Lima #226; no tel. A popular lunch spot with a self-service salad bar & a good-value set lunch (10Bs), but get there early as the food goes fast in this place. The locals see to that. Otherwise BBQ meaty mains range 25–30Bs. *Open daily 11.00–14.30 & 18.00–22.00.*

✖ **Café Campero** Calle Campero #765; ↘ 663 0496. This bakery cum café is a useful spot for a coffee break (3Bs) & to stock up on pastries, but it's a shame about the face-liked-a-slapped-arse service. *Open daily 08.00–18.00.*

Supermercado Tarija (*Calle 15 de Abril #373;* ↘ *664 4045; open Mon–Sat 08.00–12.30 & 15.00–21.30*) is well stocked for emergency supplies. Finally, the **central market** on Calle Sucre is a good spot for snacks, fruit and basic bus-journey supplies.

ENTERTAINMENT AND NIGHTLIFE Apart from a few highly avoidable karaoke joints, Tarija's nightlife is based around the café culture with **Café Mokka** and **Taberna**

Gattopardo the main draws. Plaza Sucre attracts the teenage crowd while the main square is the domain of the older and slightly more discerning demographic. Otherwise **Cine Universal**, located on Calle Lema next to the Kohlberg winery office, shows up-to-date films.

SHOPPING

Artesanía 15 de Abril Calle 15 de Abril #423; ☏ 666 4006. This artisan shop has a range of hand-made goods by indigenous families around Tarija with an emphasis on textiles and leather goods. *Open Mon–Sat 09.00–21.30.*
La Vinoteca Tarijeña Calle Sucre corner with Madrid;

☏ 666 1863. This wine and singani outlet, located just off the main square, has samples from all the major wineries in Tarija. Better still, it operates a policy of selling at factory prices with bottles of quality plonk starting from as little as 25Bs. *Open Mon–Sat 09.00–12.30 & 14.30–19.00.*

OTHER PRACTICALITIES

Banco Union Plaza Sucre; ☏ 664 0980, has an ATM compatible with Visa & Mastercard. Banks also line the main square.
DHL/Western Union Calle Sucre corner with Calle Lima; ☏ 664 6474. *Open daily 09.00–12.30 & 14.30–18.00.*
Entel call centres have two locations at Plaza Luis de Fuentes y Vargas & Plaza Sucre. *Open daily 07.00–23.00*
Full Internet Calle Campero #751 has internet access for 3Bs/hr. *Open daily 09.00–22.00.*

La Esmeralda laundry Calle Madrid #157 has laundry service for 8Bs/kg. *Open Mon–Fri 08.00–12.30 & 15.00–19.30, Sat 08.00–13.00.*
Post office Calle Sucre corner with Calle Virginio Lema; ☏ 664 2586. *Open Mon–Fri 08.30–20.00, Sat 08.30–18.00, Sun 09.00–12.00.*
Stationery and book shop Librería Piscis Plaza Luis de Fuentes y Vargas. Carries some English-language publications. *Open Mon–Sat 08.30–12.15 & 15.00–20.00.*

Wineries There are seven commercial wineries in Tarija, 60 in all of Bolivia. Most of the wineries are a short taxi ride from the centre, but La Concepción – located in the Concepción valley, 25km from downtown Tarija – is best tackled by bus, with regular departures leaving from Calle General Trigo. Visits are also easily arranged with via the winery offices listed below, or with local tour operators (page 242).

The two most important wineries are:

Kohlberg winery office Calle Lema; ☏ 664 3784. *Open Mon–Fri 09.00–12.30 & 15.00–19.00, Sat 09.00–12.30*

La Concepción/Rujero winery office Calle 15 de Abril #176; ☏ 664 0933. *Open Mon–Fri 09.00–12.30 & 15.00–19.00, Sat 09.00–12.30.*

Airlines

Lloyd Aéreo Boliviano (LAB) office Calle General Trigo #329; ☏ 664 2195. *Open Mon–Fri 08.30–12.30 & 14.30–18.30, Sat 09.00–12.00.*

AeroSur office Calle 15 de Abril #143; tel: 663 0893. *Open Mon–Fri 08.30–12.30 & 14.30–18.30; Sat 08.30–12.00.*

WHAT TO SEE AND DO

Archaeological and Paleontological Museum (*Calle General Trigo #402; ☏ 663 6680; f 664 3403; open Mon–Fri 08.00–12.00 & 15.00–18:00, Sat 09.00–12.00 & 15.00–18:00; free entry*) Before taking one of the local dinosaur tours (see VTB Tours on page 242), it's worth a quick look around this small museum for its collection of prehistoric remains. Less compelling is the upstairs room with its array of more anthropological artefacts.

La Casa Dorada (*Calle Ingavi #370; ☏ 664 4606; open Mon–Fri 09.00–12.00 & 15.00–18.00; Sat 09.00–12.00*) The former Casa de le Cultura was closed at the time of writing because it was being completely refurbished as a brand-new theatre. Some of the more elaborate – some would say gaudy – fittings, dating from the 1930s, are to be preserved to showcase its lavish history as the property of a rich local landowner. Guided tours are expected to continue after the long-overdue refurbishment is completed.

GETTING OFF THE BEATEN TRACK AROUND TARIJA

While most visitors make a beeline for Concepción Valley, there are several other worthwhile excursions to soak up the ambience of the region. Better still, many of the hamlets are easily accessible by bus from downtown Tarija or by taxi, followed by a gentle half-day hike.

A one-hour bus ride from Tarija, Padcaya is a pleasant little village and a good base for day hikes. In mid-August it's a haven for pilgrims attending the Festival of the Virgin of Chaguaya in the nearby village of Chaguaya.

Just outside of Tarija the road to San Lorenzo passes through 5km of monoliths known as Tomatas, an eroded landscape popular with city dwellers as a picnic spot. There's also a small footbridge over the River Guadalquivir where you can take an impromptu dip. After Tomatas, the road continues onto Erquis, the access point to climb Cerro Morro Alto, the broad mountain that dominates the valley and is home to the mountain spirit known as Coquena, a cheeky imp who protects climbers in return for gifts of cigarettes and coca leaves.

The end of the line is San Lorenzo, which hosts a colourful local fiesta in the second week of August to celebrate the town's patron saint. This is a great opportunity to catch some traditional Tarijan folk music, as is the festival of the grape harvest in mid-March when the countryside around Tarija dances to a tune of thanks for the harvest and the valley resonates to the sound of well-oiled locals playing their favourite folk tunes.

Appendix I

LANGUAGE

Bolivia is a great place to learn Spanish as the language schools often charge a fraction of the fees of schools in Peru and Ecuador (see the *La Paz and Sucre chapters* for more information). Better still, you'll get plenty of opportunity to practise as little English is spoken outside of the main cities and tour operators. A few phrases really will serve you well, so use the following to get you started, then try to brush up those language skills while on the road.

SURVIVAL SPANISH, QUECHUA AND AYMARA
Basic phrases

English	Spanish	Quechua	Aymara
Hello	*Hola*	*Imaynalla*	*Kamisaki*
Good morning	*Buenos días*	*Allin p'unchay/qansina*	*Aski willjtakipan*
Good afternoon	*Buenas tardes*	*Allin p'unchay/qansina*	*Jayp'u urukipan*
Good evening/night	*Buenas noches*	*Allin p'unchay/qansina*	*Aski Jayp'ukipan/ Aski arumakipan*
Goodbye	*Adiós*	*Qansina*	*Waliki-jikisñkama*
See you soon	*Hasta pronto/ Hasta luego*	*Askamalla*	*Qhipurkama*
See you tomorrow	*Hasta mañana*	*Tinkunakama*	
Thank you	*Gracias*	*Pachi*	*Juspara*
Please	*Por favor*	*Ma, ama jina kay*	*Amp suma*
Yes	*Sí*	*Ari*	*Jisa*
No	*No*	*Mana*	*Janiwa*
How are you?	*¿Cómo está?*	*Imaynalla*	*Kamisaki*
I'm fine/not good	*Estoy bien/mal*	*Allillan/mana waliq*	*Waliki-jan/Waliki*
My name is …	*Mi nombre es …*	*Sutiyqa*	*Sutijaxa*
What is your name?	*¿Cuál es su nombre?*	*Imataq sutiyi?*	*Kunas suitmaxa?*
Where are you from?	*¿De dónde es?*	*Maimanta canqui?*	*Kawkhankiritasa?*
I am from …	*Soy de …*	*Manta kani*	*Nayaxa …*
Pleased to meet you	*Mucho gusto*	*Kusikunu, imaynalla*	*Ancha waliki*
I don't understand	*No entiendo*	*Mana unanchanichu*	*Janiw yakiti*
Please speak slower	*Más despacio, por favor*	*Pisipismanta ma/ allillamanta*	*K'achhatak amp suma*
Go away	*Váyase*	*Ripuya*	*Saram!*
Excuse me	*Permiso/Perdón*	*Qhisphiway*	*Pampachita*
Where is?	*¿Dónde esta?*	*Maypitaq … kasha*	*Kawkhankisa?*
How much does it cost?	*¿Cuánto cuesta?*	*Qhaw qhas chamipaxa?*	*Mayklapitaq*
What time is it?	*¿Qué hora es?*	*Maypiña inti?*	*Kuna pachaxisa*

English	Spanish	Quechua	Aymara
Numbers			
1	*un, uno/una*	*Uq*	*Maya*
2	*dos*	*Iskay*	*Paya*
3	*tres*	*Kinsa*	*Kimsa*
4	*cuatro*	*Tawa*	*Pusi*
5	*cinco*	*Phisqa*	*Phiska*
6	*seis*	*Suqta*	*Suxta*
7	*siete*	*Qanchis*	*Paqallqu*
8	*ocho*	*Pusaq*	*Kimsaqallqu*
9	*nueve*	*Isqun*	*Llatunka*
10	*diez*	*Chunka*	*Tunka*

Days

Sunday	*domingo*	*Intichaw*	*Wanturu*
Monday	*lunes*	*Kinachau*	*Q'illuru*
Tuesday	*martes*	*Atichaw*	*Ch'uxñuru*
Wednesday	*miércoles*	*Quyllurchaw*	*Laqpuru*
Thursday	*jueves*	*Illapachaw*	*marmuru*
Friday	*viernes*	*Ch'askaxhau*	*Kulluru*
Saturday	*sábado*	*K'uychichaw*	*Cahuru*

Months

January	*enero*	*Musuq intiraymi killa*	*Chinula*
February	*febrero*	*Kamaq killa*	*Qhulliwi*
March	*marzo*	*Pacha puquy killa*	*Achuqa*
April	*abril*	*Jatun puquy killa*	*Llamay*
May	*mayo*	*Jawkay kuski killa*	*Q'asiwi*
June	*junio*	*Kuski aymuray killa*	*T'aqaya*
July	*julio*	*Jawkay kuski killa*	*Phawawi*
August	*agosto*	*Situwalki killa*	*Thalari*
September	*septiembre*	*Chaqraypuy killa*	*Awtila*
October	*octubre*	*Qhuya raymi killa*	*Satawi*
November	*noviembre*	*Aya marq'ay killa*	*Lapaka*
December	*diciembre*	*Raymi killa*	*Kutili*

More information on Spanish from www.spanicity.com and www.bbc.co.uk/languages/spanish/
More information on Quechua from www.quechua.org.uk
More information on Aymara from www.aymara.org and www.infoarica.cl/renatoaguirre/02aymaras2.htm.

For a comparison vocabulary of words in Spanish, Quechua and Aymara, see www.perou.org/es/dico/frases.html.

Appendix 2

FURTHER INFORMATION
BOOKS
History
Buck, Daniel and Meadows, Anne, *Digging Up Butch and Sundance*, Bison Books, 3rd edn 2003. The definitive history of the lives of the famous outlaws, who are currently pushing up daisies in Bolivia.

Guevara, Ernesto Che, *Bolivian Diary*, Pimlico, 2004. An unique insight into the daily misery of the final advance of Che's ill-fated guerilla force.

Jacobs, Michael, *Ghost Train through the Andes: On My Grandfather's Trail in Chile and Bolivia*, John Murray, 2006. A vivid and personal account of the importance of the British to developing Bolivia's industrial infrastructure, as seen through the eyes of the author's grandfather.

Mountaineering
Biggar, John, *The Andes – A Guide for Climbers*, Andes, 2001. A good general guide for the entire Andes mountain range, supplemented with a few photos of the routes.

Brain, Yossi, *Bolivia – A Climbing Guide,* The Mountaineers, 1999. Excellent pictures, vital route information and helpful logistics compiled by the leading, but now deceased, mountaineer and guide.

Mesili, Alain, *Les Andes de Bolivie*, CIMA, 2004. The latest book by the Bolivia-based French alpinist available in both French- and Spanish-language versions.

Natural history
Ministerio de desarrollo Sostenible y Planificación, *National Biodiversity Strategy,* Fundación Amigos de la Naturaleza (FAN), Bolivia, 2001. This academic study combines a synthesis on the condition of conservation and sustainable use of the biodiversity in Bolivia with advice on strategy for sustainable management.

Politics
Good, Peter, *Bolivia: Between a Rock and a Hard Place*, Plural Editores, 2006. An excellent background to the political situation, leading right up to the election of Morales, written by long-term expat Sorata resident Peter Good.

Crabtree, John, *Patterns of Protest: Politics and Social Movements in Bolivia,* Latin America Bureau. Essential guide to the vagaries and turmoil of Bolivian politics.

Shultz, Jim, The Democracy Owners' Manual: A Practical Guide to Changing the World, Rutgers University Press, 2002. A unique, hands-on guide for people who want to change public policy, from the man behind the Democracy Center in Cochabamba, Bolivia.

Society
Elliott, Tim, *The Bolivian Times,* Random House Australia, 2001. A humorous account of working for an English-language newspaper in La Paz.

Young, Rusty, *Marching Powder*, Macmillan, 2002. The backpacker's must read in Bolivia. This fascinating true-life story recounts the full horror of life in San Pedro prison in La Paz.

Travelogues

Duguid, J, *Green Hell: A Chronicle of Travel in the Forests of Eastern Bolivia*, Jonathan Cape, 1931. Boy's own adventure exploration through the Chaco region.

Fawcett, Colonel Percy, *Exploration Fawcett*, Century, 1988. Legendary British explorer Colonel Percy Harrison Fawcett disappears in the unknown in 1925 to explore Bolivia's Amazon region.

Ghinsberg, Yossi, *Back From Tuichi*, Random House, New York, 1993. A tale of survival in the Amazon jungle by the legendary Israeli backpacker turned writer.

Mann, Mark, *The Gringo Trail*, Green Candy Press, 2002. A page-turningly entertaining rite of passage tale set across South America.

Parris, Mathew, *Inca Kola*, Phoenix Press, 1993. An entertaining romp through Peru and Bolivia penned by a journalist for *The Times*.

Shukman, H, *Sons of the Moon*, Fontana, 1991. An insight into the culture of the Aymara people.

Wildlife

Dunning, John S and Ridgely, Robert S, *South American Birds: A Photographic Aid to Identification*, Harrowood Books, 1989. An excellent illustrated guide for amateur enthusiasts.

Fjeldsa, Jon, *Birds of the High Andes*, Apollo Books, 1990. The experts' preferred guide for the serious birdwatcher.

Hennessey, A B, Herzog, S K and Sagot, F *Lista Anotada de las Aves de Bolivia*, 5th edn. Asociación Armonía/BirdLife International, Santa Cruz de la Sierra, Bolivia, 2003. Essential reference for twitchers and wildlife fans alike.

WEBSITES
Background information

www.boliviaweb.com A Bolivian community website with a huge resource of contextual information.

http://countrystudies.us/bolivia An academic resource with exhaustive links to background information and context.

www.redbolivia.com A community website with a focus on political and social issues.

www.solobolivia.com A general website with a strong focus on contextual information.

Mountaineering

www.andes-mesili.com Excellent resource from the French alpinist.

Natural history

www.sernap.gov.bo The home page of the Bolivian national parks authority.

www.wcs.org The home page of the Wildlife Conservation Society, which is very active in Madidi National Park.

www.geocities.com/webatlantis The site, compiled by Dr James Allen, author of *Atlantis: The Andes Solution*, explores the mythology behind the country's natural features.

Politics

http://democracyctr.org Excellent insight into the complex web of Bolivian political life; see also **www.democracyctr.org/blog/** for the latest dispatch from the front line.

www.greenleft.org.au The home page of Australia's radical weekly newspaper, which campaigns for human and civil rights, global peace and environmental sustainability, democracy and equality.

www.lab.org.uk Home page for the London-based Latin America Bureau (LAB), an independent research and publishing organisation, working to broaden public understanding of issues of human rights and social and economic justice in Latin America and the Caribbean.

http://narcosphere.narconews.com Home page for the Narcosphere, a participatory, online forum, where readers and journalists come together to discuss, add new information and relevant links, and debate the work of the journalists who publish at www.narconews.com.

www.plenglish.com A Latin American news agency based in Havana, Cuba, with an alternative take on local events.

Society
www.mujerescreando.com Feminist website run by a La Paz-based pressure group of women campaigning for female rights, lesbian rights and organising street protests to draw attention to inequalities.

Tourism
www.boliviaguide.com Growing tourism resource with a travellers' community motif.

www.chiquitania.com Comprehensive and well-executed online resource dedicated to one of Bolivia's most interesting regions for tourists.

www.lata.org The home page of the UK-based Latin America Travel Association (LATA).

www.saeexplorers.org The South American Explorers Club is an excellent resource for travellers, with clubhouses in Cusco, Lima, Quito and Buenos Aires. They publish very useful trip notes for countries and activities.

Bradt Travel Guides

www.bradtguides.com

Africa

Africa Overland	£15.99
Benin	£14.99
Botswana: Okavango, Chobe, Northern Kalahari	£15.99
Burkina Faso	£14.99
Cape Verde Islands	£13.99
Canary Islands	£13.95
Cameroon	£13.95
Eritrea	£12.95
Ethiopia	£15.99
Gabon, São Tomé, Príncipe	£13.95
Gambia, The	£13.99
Ghana	£13.95
Johannesburg	£6.99
Kenya	£14.95
Madagascar	£14.95
Malawi	£13.99
Mali	£13.95
Mauritius, Rodrigues & Réunion	£13.99
Mozambique	£13.99
Namibia	£14.95
Niger	£14.99
Nigeria	£15.99
Rwanda	£14.99
Seychelles	£14.99
Sudan	£13.95
Tanzania, Northern	£13.99
Tanzania	£16.99
Uganda	£15.99
Zambia	£15.95
Zanzibar	£12.99

Britain and Europe

Albania	£13.99
Armenia, Nagorno Karabagh	£14.99
Azores	£12.99
Baltic Capitals: Tallinn, Riga, Vilnius, Kaliningrad	£12.99
Belgrade	£6.99
Bosnia & Herzegovina	£13.99
Bratislava	£6.99
Budapest	£7.95
Cork	£6.95
Croatia	£12.95
Cyprus see North Cyprus	
Czech Republic	£13.99
Dubrovnik	£6.95
Eccentric Britain	£13.99
Eccentric Cambridge	£6.99
Eccentric Edinburgh	£5.95
Eccentric France	£12.95
Eccentric London	£12.95
Eccentric Oxford	£5.95
Estonia	£13.99
Faroe Islands	£13.95
Helsinki	£7.99
Hungary	£14.99
Kiev	£7.95
Latvia	£13.99
Lille	£6.99
Lithuania	£13.99

Ljubljana	£6.99
Macedonia	£13.95
Montenegro	£13.99
North Cyprus	£12.99
Paris, Lille & Brussels	£11.95
Riga	£6.95
River Thames, In the Footsteps of the Famous	£10.95
Serbia	£13.99
Slovenia	£12.99
Spitsbergen	£14.99
Switzerland: Rail, Road, Lake	£13.99
Tallinn	£6.99
Ukraine	£14.99
Vilnius	£6.99

Middle East, Asia and Australasia

China: Yunnan Province	£13.99
Georgia	£13.95
Great Wall of China	£13.99
Iran	£14.99
Iraq	£14.95
Kabul	£9.95
Maldives	£13.99
Mongolia	£14.95
North Korea	£13.95
Oman	£13.99
Palestine, Jerusalem	£12.95
Sri Lanka	£13.99
Syria	£14.99
Tasmania	£12.95
Tibet	£13.99
Turkmenistan	£14.99

The Americas and the Caribbean

Amazon, The	£14.95
Argentina	£15.99
Bolivia	£14.99
Cayman Islands	£12.95
Costa Rica	£13.99
Chile	£16.95
Chile & Argentina: Trekking	£12.95
Eccentric America	£13.95
Eccentric California	£13.99
Falkland Islands	£13.95
Panama	£13.95
Peru & Bolivia: Backpacking and Trekking	£12.95
St Helena, Ascension, Tristan da Cunha	£14.95
USA by Rail	£13.99

Wildlife

Antarctica: Guide to the Wildlife	£14.95
Arctic: Guide to the Wildlife	£15.99
British Isles: Wildlife of Coastal Waters	£14.95
Galápagos Wildlife	£15.99
Madagascar Wildlife	£14.95
Peruvian Wildlife	£15.99
Southern African Wildlife	£18.95
SriLankan Wildlife	£15.99

Health

Your Child Abroad: A Travel Health Guide	£10.95

WIN £100 CASH!

READER QUESTIONNAIRE

Send in your completed questionnaire for the chance to win £100 cash in our regular draw

All respondents may order a Bradt guide at half the UK retail price – please complete the order form overleaf.

(Entries may be posted or faxed to us, or scanned and emailed.)

We are interested in getting feedback from our readers to help us plan future Bradt guides. Please answer ALL the questions below and return the form to us in order to qualify for an entry in our regular draw.

Have you used any other Bradt guides? If so, which titles? ....
....

What other publishers' travel guides do you use regularly? ....
....

Where did you buy this guidebook? ....

What was the main purpose of your trip to Bolivia (or for what other reason did you read our guide)? eg: holiday/business/charity etc.........................
....

What other destinations would you like to see covered by a Bradt guide?
....

Would you like to receive our catalogue/newsletters?

YES / NO (If yes, please complete details on reverse)

If yes – by post or email? ....

Age (circle relevant category) 16–25   26–45   46–60   60+

Male/Female (delete as appropriate)

Home country ....

Please send us any comments about our guide to Bolivia or other Bradt Travel Guides. ....
....
....
....

Bradt Travel Guides

23 High Street, Chalfont St Peter, Bucks SL9 9QE, UK
☎ +44 (0)1753 893444 **f** +44 (0)1753 892333
e info@bradtguides.com
www.bradtguides.com

CLAIM YOUR HALF-PRICE BRADT GUIDE!

Order Form

To order your half-price copy of a Bradt guide, and to enter our prize draw to win £100 (see overleaf), please fill in the order form below, complete the questionnaire overleaf, and send it to Bradt Travel Guides by post, fax or email.

Please send me one copy of the following guide at half the UK retail price

Title	Retail price	Half price
. . . .	. . . .	. . . .

Please send the following additional guides at full UK retail price

No	Title	Retail price	Total
. . .	. . . .	. . . .	. . . .
. . .	. . . .	. . . .	. . . .
. . .	. . . .	. . . .	. . . .

Sub total . . . .
Post & packing . . . .
(£1 per book UK; £2 per book Europe; £3 per book rest of world)
Total . . . .

Name . . . .

Address . . . .

Tel . . . .   Email . . . .

☐ I enclose a cheque for £ . . . . made payable to Bradt Travel Guides Ltd

☐ I would like to pay by credit card. Number: . . . .

  Expiry date: . . . / . . .   3-digit security code (on reverse of card) . . . . .

☐ Please add my name to your catalogue mailing list.

☐ I would be happy for you to use my name and comments in Bradt marketing material.

Send your order on this form, with the completed questionnaire, to:

Bradt Travel Guides BOL/1
23 High Street, Chalfont St Peter, Bucks SL9 9QE
☏ +44 (0)1753 893444   f +44 (0)1753 892333
e info@bradtguides.com   www.bradtguides.com

Index